"Caselawe," Baptized "Israel."

Ripe Fruit of the Moravian Mission Among the Cherokees.

HISTORY

OF THE

MORAVIAN MISSIONS AMONG SOUTHERN INDIAN TRIBES

OF THE

UNITED STATES

BY

THE REV. EDMUND SCHWARZE, Ph.D.,
Pastor Calvary Moravian Church, Winston-Salem, N. C.

TRANSACTIONS OF THE MORAVIAN HISTORICAL SOCIETY.
SPECIAL SERIES. VOL. I.

BETHLEHEM, PENN'A.
Times Publishing Company, Printers
1923

TO THE SOUTHERN PROVINCE OF THE MORAVIAN CHURCH
IN AMERICA

where, through the last decade, the remarkable growth
of the interest in Moravian missions seems the bright
beginning of the renewal of our days as of old,

THIS WORK IS AFFECTIONATELY INSCRIBED WITH THE
ARDENT HOPE THAT INTEREST IN MISSIONS
BY PRAYER, MEN AND MEANS WILL
STEADILY INCREASE.

PREFACE

History or fiction of which the American Indian is the subject has a peculiar fascination for many people. Those who remember the high privilege, while at school, of taking out a library book on Friday afternoons will, most likely, have a picture in their minds of the shelf upon which stood the "Leather-Stocking Tales" or other Indian books. Places made historic by having been haunts of the Indian or scenes of his special activity, good or evil, are invested with an unfailing glow of romance and Indian names are retained in spite of difficult spelling and pronunciation. The Indian's arrowheads and other relics never cease to charm.

The writer has experienced all these thrills, but wishes to record that, for him, the greatest interest attaching to the Indian has been to observe him responding to the Gospel. This is the best part of Indian lore.

Moravian mission history is particularly rich in this field, for the Indians ever lay near to the hearts of the Moravian Brethren—hearts filled with the great love of the Saviour. Histories of the labors of the Moravians among the northern tribes in the United States and Canada have been written, and it is fitting that this story of the Moravian missions among southern Indian tribes of the United States should be added, a history which has never before been written, except in outline. This mission, also, is a finished work of the Church, and, from that viewpoint, deserves to be written and read.

This story forms part of the early history of Wachovia, the Moravian settlement in North Carolina, which, in turn, is one of the main chapters in the history of that State.

The primary work of the Church of Christ is the spreading of His Gospel. Methods do and should change; people change; times change. Fifty years ago, the farmer plowed his field with an old-fashioned plow, drawn by a team of horses or a yoke of oxen. He reaped the grain with a cradle, bound it by hand, and separated the grain from the chaff with a flail. The grain was ground between two millstones, and then the dough was baked in the fireplace. The result of this difficult process was BREAD.

Today, the farmer plows with a tractor, reaps his grain with a binder, threshes the wheat in a modern threshing machine, has it ground in a modern mill, and the housewife bakes it in an electric range. But note again, the result of this new process is BREAD. Thus, spiritual truth abides unchanged and man's need of this Bread of Life is exactly the same as ever it has been. This work, therefore, is not a mere recital of the past, but lays claim to be an inspiration for the present and the future. What the Cherokee and the Creek needed was the Gospel; what every human heart today needs is the Gospel; the same Gospel in both cases—there is but one Gospel—the Grace of God in Christ for all men.

The composition of this work has been extended over several years, the most laborious part being the translating of the Diary and correspondence of the mission through the many years during which these were written in the German. The increasing demands of a busy city pastorate crowded this work into the hours of the night, when, in the quiet, it seemed as if the scenes of the history which follows were being re-enacted. The writer asks considerate judgment because the work could never occupy the main line of thought, time or strength.

Grateful acknowledgment for assistance received is heartily made to Miss Adelaide Fries, Winston-Salem, Archivist, American Moravian Church, South, for constant courtesy in granting access to the archives and much valuable help given; to Col. W. A. Blair, Winston-Salem, for securing books on general Cherokee history; to Miss Sarah A. Vogler, Winston-Salem, Mr. J. D. Bishop, Georgia, and Mr. Amos Clauder, New York, for kindness in submitting personal diaries of missionaries, of whom they are descendants; to Mr. E. J. Bishop, Bethlehem, Pa., for annotating, from the records of the Boards of the Northern Province of the Moravian Church in America, items pertaining to the Cherokee mission for the years 1892-1899, when the mission was under the care of these Boards; to Miss Lettie E. Green, Winston-Salem, who has spared neither pains nor time in carefully typewriting the book.

That the work may, though in an humble manner, glorify God and, in some measure, help forward His cause, is the earnest wish of the writer.   E. S.

Winston-Salem, N. C., 1922.

BIBLIOGRAPHY

1. "The Indians of North America in Historic Times," by Cyrus Thomas, Ph.D., being Vol. 2 of "The History of North America," by G. C. Lee, Ph.D., 1903. Geo. Barrie & Sons, Philadelphia.

2. "Historical Sketch of the Cherokee," by James Mooney; 19th Annual Report of the Bureau of American Ethnology to the Secretary of the Smithsonian Institution, 1897-1898. Washington, 1900.

3. "Travels," by William Bartram. London, 1792.

4. "Memoirs of Henry Timberlake," secured for the use of the writer from the Congressional Library, Washington, D. C., through the kindness of Col. W. A. Blair, Winston-Salem, N. C.

5. "The Encyclopedia Brittanica."

6. "The New International Encyclopedia."

7. "History of the United States," by George Bancroft, 1885.

8. "History of the North American Indians," by David Zeisberger, edited by Hulbert & Schwarze. Ohio State Archaeological and Historical Society, 1910.

9. "History of the Missions of the United Brethren Among the Indians in North America," by George Henry Loskiel. Barby, 1789. Translated from the German and published in London, 1794.

10. "The Moravians in Georgia," by Adelaide L. Fries, 1905. Edwards & Broughton, Raleigh, N. C.

11. The Springplace Diary, 1801 to 1836, and papers relating to the beginning of a mission among the Cherokees, together with all the correspondence between Springplace, Ga., and Salem, N. C., being the original manuscripts in the Archives of the Southern Province of the Moravian Church in America.

12. Letters and Reports from the missionaries in Indian Territory. Archives.

13. Minutes of the "Helfer Conferenz," Salem, N. C., for the years during which the Cherokee mission was carried on.

14. Minutes of "The Provincial Elders' Conference," for the same.

15. Minutes of "The Provincial Elders' Conference," and of the "Board of Church Extension," of the Northern Province, Bethlehem, Pa., for the years when the mission was carried on under the direction of these Boards.

16. "Gemein Nachrichten," Germany, for the years under review.

17. "Periodical Accounts Relating to the Missions of the Church of the United Brethren," London, for the years under review.

18. "The Moravian Church Miscellany," America, for the years under review.

19. "The Moravians in North Carolina," by the Rev. Levin T. Reichel. Lippincott & Co.

20. "A History of the Moravian Seminary for Young Ladies, at Bethlehem, Pa.," by William C. Reichel and William H. Bigler. Bethlehem, Pa., 1901.

21. "History of Wachovia in North Carolina," by J. H. Clewell, Ph.D. Doubleday, Page & Co. 1902.

22. "A History of the Moravian Church During the Eighteenth and Nineteenth Centuries," by J. Taylor Hamilton, D.D. Bethlehem, Pa., 1901.

23. "The Case of the Cherokee Nation Against the State of Georgia," argued and determined at the Supreme Court of the United States, January term, 1831. R. Peters. Philadelphia, 1831.

24. "Niles' Weekly Register, containing Political, Historical, Geographical, Scientifical, Statistical, Economical, and Biographical Documents, Essays, and Facts, together with Notices of the Arts and Manufactures and a Record of the Events of the Times." Vol. 42, March to September, 1832. Baltimore.

25. Copies of "The Moravian," for the years under review.

26. Diary of the Rev. H. G. Clauder, missionary among the Cherokees. By kindness of the family.

27. Diary of the Rev. Gilbert Bishop, missionary among the Cherokees. By kindness of the family.

28. Diaries of the Revs. John Renatus and D. Zeisberger Smith, missionaries among the Cherokees. By kindness of the family.

29. Incidents in the life of Mrs. Miles Vogler, wife of missionary Vogler among the Cherokees, as penned by her own hand in her 80th year. Through kindness of Miss Sarah A. Vogler, Winston-Salem, N. C.

30. Reminiscences of her father and mother and their service among the Cherokees, written and related by Miss Sarah A. Vogler, Winston-Salem, N. C.

31. "History of the Cherokee Bible," by Geo. E. Foster, Ithaca, N. Y., 1899.

32. An account of the labors of a Danish Lutheran Missionary, the Rev. N. L. Nielsen, serving for many years and at the present time among the Cherokees in the field formerly occupied by the Moravian Church, around Oaks, Okla. Kindly written by the Rev. Nielsen for the writer of this history.

TABLE OF CONTENTS

LIST OF ILLUSTRATIONS

These pages lay claim to a purpose beyond the historic
interest of the subject-matter. They have been written
with the profound and growing conviction that the great
needs of man are the things of the spirit; and that beneath
the civilization, progress and prosperity of today, lie spiritual fundamentals which are in the greatest danger of
being overlooked in our materialistic age. In some measure,
the peace, the safety and beauty of *our* life are due to that
spiritual work, done by our forefathers, herein recorded.
The pioneers of the Christian religion laid the spiritual
foundation for humanity—the foundation is Christ—and it
is the Christian Church which has ever held up before the
world the essential needs of life, which are spiritual. The
Church has looked to the foundation which, failing, would
topple the whole superstructure man has built into ruin.
Obedience to Christ's command to go into all the world
with His message is, at the same time, the strongest safe-
guard for a sound church at home which, in turn, under-
girds and makes safe social and economic life of any community. Lest the Church lose her vision in the blinding
glare of materialism; lest God's children, following the
fashion of the world, pile up THINGS so high that they
cannot see GOD; "His"-tories such as this should continue to be written and read, and above all, missions—
home and foreign—must continue to be the very life of the
Church; for, "O Lord, by these things men live."[*]

* Isaiah 38:16.

INTRODUCTION

This narrative is part of a continued story which goes back to the Moravian settlement of Wachovia in North Carolina in the year 1753. It goes back to the first settlement of Moravians in America in the colony of Georgia, in the year 1735. It goes back to the missionary impulse felt by the spiritually awakened Moravian congregation of Herrnhut, Saxony, whose first missionaries had been sent to the Island of St. Thomas in 1732. It goes back to the baptizing of the Brethren of Herrnhut* with the Holy Spirit, August 13, 1727, on which day the hearts of adherents of many different phases of religious truth, previously attracted to Herrnhut, having heard of a living church there, flowed together in true brotherly love, founded on a new kindling of love to the Saviour, and the Moravian Church was renewed by Divine power. It goes back to the movement of Pietism in Germany and spreading to other countries, in the latter part of the 17th and early part of the 18th centuries, in which was manifested that longing for personal godliness and genuine spiritual life which came like God's springtime upon an age made cold, spiritually, first, by a dead orthodoxy, which was self-sufficient, and, later, by a wave of rationalism which spread its barren doubt over these countries, completely paralyzing missionary activity and even the missionary idea, both of which were revived in the warm fervor of Pietism and could take deep root in this congenial soil. The story goes back to the "Hidden Seed" of the Ancient Moravian Church, when this church was seemingly extinct after the terrific convulsions of the Anti-Reformation in Bohemia and Moravia and the decree that all adherents of evangelical truth must leave these countries. It goes back to the widespread and influential Moravian Church in Bohemia, Moravia and Poland, dating from 1457, whose members, awakened by the evangelical testimony of John Hus, were reformers be-

---

* A colony of a large number of refugees from Bohemia and Moravia and Christian people from elsewhere seeking religious freedom, who had found a welcome on the Berthelsdorf, Saxony, estate of Count Zinzendorf. Count Zinzendorf was a young man of fervent spirituality and zeal for God to Whom he had consecrated his life in early childhood.

xiii

fore the Reformation. It goes back to the introduction of Christianity into Bohemia and Moravia. It goes back to the banner of the Cross established over the Roman Empire. It goes back to the Apostles and their companions on their missionary journeys. It goes back to the first church at Jerusalem which had all the marks of a true church—founded on the Rock; true in doctrine; separation from the world and association of its own members; service of mutual helpfulness; fervent worship and the powerful presence of the Holy Spirit—lacking only one mark of a true church, the missionary spirit, which was divinely supplied in the first persecution, when "they were scattered abroad went everywhere preaching the word."[*] This wonderful story goes back, finally, and rests upon the words of the Lord Jesus Christ in the meeting with the eleven disciples which Jesus had appointed upon the mount in Galilee, where He spoke as follows:

"All power is given unto me in heaven and in earth.

"Go ye therefore, teach all nations, baptizing them in the name of the Father, and of the Son, and of the Holy Ghost:

"Teaching them to observe all things whatsoever I have commanded you: and, lo, I am with you alway, even unto the end of the world. Amen."[†]

Going back thus far, and based upon the whole sufficient work of Jesus, the Christ, for the salvation of the whole world, the story, of which the following pages are but the smallest part, goes forward and is continued from age to age, until "the kingdoms of this world are become the kingdoms of our Lord, and of His Christ; and He shall reign for ever and ever."[‡]

That such a history as follows is part of the story of the Kingdom of God is the genius of the Moravian Church and the secret of her remarkable vitality—a small, seemingly weak church—which has carried her through vicissitudes and hours of trial which would have wrecked any other organization. The Moravian Church has been and is a real church of God, owned and used as such by her Lord. As such, the missionary motive has always run parallel with her own spiritual experience. That experience, spiritual life genuine and deep, has the inherent tendency to propagate itself. The Moravian Church has never been atrophied because she has always been missionary.

---

[*] Acts 8:4.   [†] Matthew 28:18-20.   [‡] Rev. 11:15.

xiv

Further, this narrative is based on the fact that the Moravian Brethren had a religious experience calculated to fit the real need of the world. The reason they *did* help in all parts of the world was because they *could* help. Their faith brought them and could bring others into that relation with Jesus Christ which elevates man temporally and spiritually. It was capable of producing a civilization which is the salt of the earth; it would lift men into a higher usefulness and that enlargement of their powers which rendered them valuable to the community. Chief and above all, the faith which the Brethren had experienced could bring souls to Christ and train them for eternal companionship with God.

From the beginning, the Moravian Brethren were conscious of and gave place to Jesus Christ as the Divine Head and Leader of the Church. Therefore, His unmistakable "go" was to them not a possibility, nor a suggestion, but a *command* to be obeyed; the obligation to which was undertaken when He was received as personal Lord and Saviour. Real fellowship with Him made devotion and duty real. Humble as this narrative may be among the chapters of that great story of the Kingdom; meagre as may seem, though they are not, the results of the extraordinary self-sacrifice and consecration of the servants in this field; let every line glow with the truth that this is a real church in the real business of her Lord. And may it be borne in upon us Moravians of a later date, that only a church so alive and so fruitful, bears the Divine stamp of reality.

That there were mistakes in the administration of these Indian missions and errors of judgment and of action by the missionaries themselves, it is hardly necessary to state. Some phases of the project were undoubtedly mismanaged. In other cases, the distinctive organization of the Moravian Church, with one far-distant executive center through which local machinery had to work, rendered a movement so slow that a strategic situation could not be grasped at the right moment. Possibly, methods of procedure in the care of souls were so thorough as to be over-weight and in the way of quicker progress; while other denominations seemed to be running, we were following on a slow walk. For all that, the fact remains, that this story, truthfully drawn from the actual records themselves, shows defects and errors and mistakes of the human instruments far in the background and graciously overruled in the development of a meritorious work among the aborigines of America. A work, to be sure, that is largely past and over, as our years run; but an accomplishment, nevertheless, whose results are permanently conserved and will be plainly visible in our Father's House.

Comes to all this the question which can never be answered finally to satisfy every opinion. What are the real objectives of Christian missions?

One method of work for and with souls in the foreign field may be carried on as is sometimes done in the church at home. Itinerant missionaries may establish preaching places; the Gospel may be preached with a consequent emotional stirring of the people; apparent results may be checked up. If this be meant as the aim of Christian missions, we of the Moravian Church have been slow of method and wasteful of means. But this method is superficial; often there has been no real change of heart in the "convert." Comes the time of temptation and the falling away.

If the aim of missions be not merely the evangelization of the heathen, but to live Christ among them so faithfully and preach Christ to them so intelligently that they will accept Him as their personal Saviour; if it include the careful instruction, training and grounding of converts in the Christian life, together with the establishment of the native church and the church school; if, likewise, the temporal interests and needs of new-born souls are added; in a word, if a mission is to build up the physical, moral and spiritual life of the native community and make its good influence contagious; then the missionary aims and general methods of the Moravian Church are correct and the following incidents are worthy mission annals. The thoroughness of Moravian mission work has already had the Divine seal of approval in the nature of its converts gathered from among the heathen. Pre-eminently, they have been of the type of Christian who "endureth to the end." A given community may be evangelized in several months' time; the Christianizing of it must be the toilsome and unfinished process of years. Often, a practicable combination of both methods would seem the most fruitful.

It must be admitted, that evangelistic journeys as mentioned in the preceding paragraph, in our judgment would have greatly increased the usefulness of the Creek and Cherokee missions The people were scattered and needed the outposts with stated preaching and visitation. Hampered as our Brethren were, with a large farm and an establishment that took nearly all their time and strength, the best they could do was simply to look after the station itself, and the opportunity for the aggressive pushing of the Gospel and reaching many ears was lost. Of a working mission combining both valuable ideas and reaching many souls outside of the regular stations through missionary journeys, native helpers, etc., the present Moravian mission in Nicaragua, Central America, is a notable illustration.

CHAPTER I

THE CREEKS

Broadly considered, the Creek Nation of Indians was a confederacy of tribes all belonging to the general family of the Muskhogee. The Uchees, Choctaws, Chickasaws, Natches and others, were all of this stock. The Creeks proper were the most populous and important of the Muskhogee family and second in importance only to the Cherokees among the southern Indian tribes. The name "Creeks" was given to this Nation by English traders because of the large number of creeks in their country. This tribe was located chiefly in northern Alabama and along the upper and middle valley of the Chattahoochie River in Georgia. They occupied a central position among the Indian tribes in the Gulf States, and their custom was to incorporate bands or parties from other tribes or entire tribes, when these were small, with themselves. These would drop their own peculiar customs and adopt those of the Creeks. Thus the Nation was continually strengthened.

One of these smaller tribes of Muskhogean affinity comes into prominence in connection with the earliest labors of the Moravian Brethren among the Creeks. It was the Yamacraw tribe, of whom Tomo-tschat-schi was Chief. Their location was on the banks of the Savannah River, near the site of the present city of Savannah. When found here by General James Oglethorpe, they appear to have come to these seats from beyond the Mississippi only a few years previous. Tomo-tschat-schi was the firm and true friend of the whites and was especially devoted to Governor Oglethorpe. When Oglethorpe undertook a journey into the heart of the Creek country, Tomo-tschat-schi, although unable to accompany him on account of advanced years, obtained for the Governor, beforehand, the assurance of a favorable reception by the Creek Chiefs. Tomo-tschat-schi died in 1739 at the age of 97. His death was mourned by both Indians and whites. After his death, his little tribe seems to have been absorbed by the Creeks.

As to the original home of the Creeks, their tradition* pointed to the country west of the Mississippi River as the primeval seat of this Nation. The Muskhogee, along with other tribes west of the Mississippi, were mound-builders. The building and occupancy of these structures was still going on at the time of de Soto's expedition and some mounds were still occupied when the French appeared on the scene. The Creeks had stories of a long and arduous journey incident to their emigration from the ancestral home and said they were opposed by numerous valiant tribes of Indians and had to fight their way through to their present abodes.

The Creeks were an agricultural people but warlike at the same time. Among the stories of the Cherokees was one to the effect that when they, the Cherokees, were driven farther south by the northern tribes, they found the Creeks in desperate struggle with the Shawanose, originally in Florida, whom they utterly vanquished, some of the remnants of the Shawanose fleeing to the north where they sought and obtained the protection of the Delawares.

There were Upper and Lower Creeks. The former inhabited the highlands in which their creeks and rivers found sources; the latter living on the lowlands nearer the seacoast. All of them lived in well-constructed log houses, "chinked" or plastered and provided with wooden chimneys lined with clay to prevent their burning.

Villages were permanent and arranged in a rectangular grouping of the log houses around a central space reserved for public gatherings and ceremonies and, especially, their annual "green-corn dance," of which we will record more later.

The Creeks lived on a comparatively high moral plane. The grosser forms of vice are not found among them until they have been corrupted by intercourse with wicked and unscrupulous whites. They were among the first of the Indian tribes to attain civilization, taking their place among the "five civilized Indian tribes." Their ideas of a Supreme Being were vague and their language destitute of any words properly to express spiritual conceptions. They held the immortality of the soul, though on a low and material basis. Conjurers, pow-wow physicians

* See Bibliography No. 1.

and charms were prominent in their religion. Eagerness to learn was a distinguishing feature of this tribe coupled with great ability to master arts and crafts taught them.

This tribe was given to hospitality and only in later years, through wrong dealings of the white people with them, became suspicious and unapproachable. Then they drew the lines against the white man even more strictly than the Cherokees, refusing permission for any whites to live among them save when white men married Creek women, or in case the full consent of the National Council for residence among them had been secured. This consent it was almost impossible to obtain.

When the English were establishing the Carolina colony, the Creeks sent envoys to Charleston with offers of friendship and alliance, which alliance was made and kept inviolable until 1773. Up to this time, the Creeks appear to have been generally quiet except for tribal wars with the Cherokees on one side and the Choctaws on the other. They had a curious custom of dividing their towns into two groups, white towns and red towns—marked by poles of the respective colors set up in the public square—the white denoting peace, the red, war towns. This division was of great importance in deciding the policy of the Nation. Whenever an occasion for war was brought before the Council, it was the duty of the white towns to bring forth all the arguments in favor of peace to be maintained, while the red towns would present all the arguments for war. Detailed information is wanting as to the actual working of this Creek Hague Tribunal!

When the English occupation began and calls were made for additional cessions of land, the usual results followed. In 1773, the Governor of Georgia succeeded in obtaining from the Cherokees and Creeks a large tract of land situated on the headwaters of the Ogeechee River. Creeks attacked settlers in this new territory and killed many. Punitive expeditions were sent against them.

During the Revolutionary War, the Creeks were generally hostile to the Americans. Parties of them would join their former enemies, the Cherokees, and make common cause against a new foe, and terrible attacks were made on the settlements in Georgia, Carolina and Tennessee. When Tarleton with his British forces prepared to invade North Carolina, he was joined by a party of Creeks under McGillivray. Peace between the United States and the Creeks by treaty came in 1795.

For several years they were at rest, but, roused by Tecumseh, the discomfited and disappointed Shawnee Chief, at the instigation of the English, the Creeks plunged into the War of 1812 under Weatherford, a young Chief of outstanding ability, but of very bad moral character. They perpetrated the fearful massacre at Fort Mims, on Lake Tensas, Alabama: the men of the garrison, being surprised by the Creeks, were killed in the desperate struggle in which the Indians outnumbered them ten to one, and the women and children, having taken refuge in a block house, were burned. In a sanguinary campaign for the Creeks, they were completely crushed by General Jackson, 1200 warriors having been slain in three battles. The Creeks were glad to sue for peace, in which contract they were obliged to give up about one-half of their former territory. Submissively, they retired to the reservations assigned them, and were ultimately removed to the west of the Mississippi.

CHAPTER II

THE MISSION AMONG THE CREEKS

This story introduces the beginning of the Moravian Church in America. Considered by itself, this attempted mission is merely a worthy enterprise that had, in time, to be abandoned; in reality, this movement, under the Providence of God, was the Moravian seed-plot of the whole North American field, developing into two Provinces of the Moravian Unity, thus providing the base for widespread missionary activity to the present day.

The events leading up to the beginning of this mission seem almost accidental; but, looking more deeply into the following incidents and the development which came, one sees the finger of God at work on a wonderful plan for the wider extension and usefulness of the Brethren's Church.

Some Schwenkfelders, followers of Caspar Schwenkfeld, a Silesian nobleman, contemporary with Luther, but whose doctrines on the Lord's Supper and other points were at variance with the teachings of that Reformer, seeking asylum from the persecutions of Lutherans and Jesuits alike, appealed in 1725 to Count Zinzendorf, upon whose estate around Ober Berthelsdorf, Saxony, some thirty families were given refuge.

Preceding the coming of the Schwenkfelders to his estate, a small company of descendants of the Ancient Brethren's Church had, in 1722, been hospitably received by Count Zinzendorf. Their numbers were greatly augmented by other Moravians who, hearing of the place of safety, left the lands where once the Unitas Fratrum had flourished, but where they could no longer worship God under the dictates of their conscience. The village of Herrnhut in Saxony, on the good Count's territory, was established for these exiles, and others who came seeking true religious liberty. Count Zinzendorf earnestly devoted more and more of his attention to these refugees and was providentially led to become the instrument for the resuscitation of the Brethren's Church among the settlers of Herrnhut, some of whom had come to the place of refuge with a vision of a renewed church in their hearts and had earnestly prayed God to accomplish this end.

On August 13, 1727, a wonderful outpouring of the Holy Spirit in connection with the celebration of the Lord's Supper divinely marked and sealed the Renewed Moravian Church. It was the birthday of the Moravian Church of modern times.

In April, 1733, an edict of banishment was issued against all Schwenkfelder living in the Kingdom of Saxony, and four men, representing those families which had been befriended by Count Zinzendorf, besought him to enter into negotiations with the Trustees of Georgia for a place of permanent refuge for them.

Georgia was that tract of land in North America, situated in the southern portion of the Carolina grant, between the Savannah and Altamaha Rivers, put at the disposal of General James Oglethorpe and twenty other English noblemen and gentlemen as a corporate body entitled, "The Trustees for establishing the Colony of Georgia in America." The purpose of the corporation and its liberal grant of land was to provide a place for a new beginning of life for imprisoned, insolvent debtors in England and for those on the continent enduring persecution, for conscience' sake, in their religion.

Count Zinzendorf, accordingly, sent detailed proposals to the Trustees in behalf of these exiles, which proposals to the Trustees already contained petitions for wider privileges than the needs of the Schwenkfelder required, indicating that the plan was even now forming in the Count's mind for a Moravian settlement in Georgia. The colonists were to build a town; they were to preach the Gospel to the heathen; they were not to bear arms but were to be willing, if necessary, to pay a double war tax. Count Zinzendorf's proposals met with a favorable reply and the Schwenkfelder left Berthelsdorf in May, 1734, for England by way of Holland, intending to sail for Georgia. In Holland, due to persuasion by another Protestant body of Separatists, they changed their minds and sailed under new offers for Pennsylvania instead, arriving in September, 1734.

This change of affairs did not defeat, but rather carried forward the plans of Count Zinzendorf and the Moravians, anxious as they were to make Christ known wherever in the world there was an open door. Missionary zeal was the characteristic trait of this Spirit-filled people. Seventeen Hundred and Thirty-two marks the beginning of Moravian missions; the Brethren Leonard Dober and David Nitschmann carrying the banner of the Cross to St. Thomas, West Indies, in that year. Three messengers of Christ from among the Brethren went to Greenland in the following year. And now here, in Georgia. was a door open to the Creek and Cherokee Indians. Some Brethren at once started a movement to send several of their number thither. In 1734, Divine approbation was given, through the lot, to go to Georgia as missionaries and, also, as colonists, to insure a home, should an edict of banishment ever be issued against the Moravians. Accordingly, Count Zinzendorf appealed again to the Georgia Trustees and received the promise of land. August Gottlieb Spangenberg was sent to London in the fall of 1734, as Zinzendorf's agent, to arrange for a grant of 500 acres.

The whole colonization project of the Moravians was not without bitter opposition. From the University of Halle, once the center of Pietism, and its adherents, what was considered a rival movement at Herrnhut and the possibility of a new church, was viewed with utter disfavor. Spangenberg, prior to 1733, a warm friend of the Moravians, some of whom he had learned to know while a student at Jena, was required either to quit his chair of professor of theology at Halle or to sever his connection with the Moravians. He did the former and became one of the ablest leaders of the Moravian Church; the leader, also, of the first expedition to America.

While Spangenberg was carrying on negotiations with the Trustees of Georgia and awaiting the arrival of General Oglethorpe from America, a party of ten Moravian colonists arrived in London, under the leadership of David Nitschmann, Syndic. (This Nitschmann and John Toeltschig, another member of the party of ten, were two of the five young men from Zauchtenthal, Moravia, who, in 1724, had resolved, God willing, on the resuscitation of the Moravian Church.) Nitschmann was to return to Herrnhut, once this company had set sail for Georgia. This group of Moravian Brethren were introduced to Oglethorpe and the Georgia Trustees, and after careful examination of the scheme and questioning of these men by them, on January 10, 1734, the grant of 500 acres of land was made to Zinzendorf. Fifty acres each were given to Spangenberg and Nitschmann personally, parts of which tracts lay in the town of Savannah.

General Oglethorpe, their warm friend, arranged for a loan of sixty pounds for the company; ten pounds for supplies bought in London and fifty pounds for passage-money. In addition, he collected as a gift for them, twenty-six pounds, five shillings, to help them buy the necessary supplies on their arrival. The Moravian colonists made many friends while in London. Their meetings—for they were a little congregation— attracted many visitors. Good seed was thus sown for the future Moravian Church in England.

February 3, 1735, this company of ten Moravian men, Spangenberg their leader, embarked on the ship, "The Two Brothers." Besides Spangenberg, there were John Toeltschig, gardner; Peter Rose, gamekeeper; Gotthard Demuth, joiner; Gottfried Haberecht, weaver of woolens; Anton Sciffert, weaver of linen; George Waschke, carpenter; Michael Haberland, carpenter; George Haberland, mason; Friedrich Riedel, mason. April 8, they disembarked at Savannah, the capital of Georgia, a town with a population of about 600. The Brethren had letters of introduction to one of the Magistrates there and were well received.

The town lots in the tracts given to Nitschmann and Spangenberg were at once assigned to them. Their belongings were moved into a cabin hastily erected and the first night in the new land found them holding a service of praise and thanksgiving. Soon the five-acre garden plots in Spangenberg's and Nitschman's tracts were surveyed and planted and by the middle of April a small house stood finished on the town lot of Spangenberg's grant. Later on, the tract of 500 acres on the Ogeechee River was surveyed, as agreed on in London. Owing to later adverse developments, this tract was never improved and occupied by the Moravian Brethren.

During the time of their strenuous labors to get settled, our colonists had several friendly visits from Indians. They were made more friendly by simple presents and by their gestures indicated that they wished the Brethren to visit them.

February 17, 1736, the second company of Moravians arrived; twenty-five persons under the leadership of Bishop Nitschmann, another one of the five Zauchtenthal young men who had left their ancestral homes with the burning desire for the renewal of the Moravian Church. He was Dober's companion in the West Indian mission of 1732. The face of the good Bishop* was to the members of the first company "as the face of an angel." Among those in the second company with Nitschmann were Martin Mack, later missionary among the northern Indian tribes, and the parents of that Moravian Apostle to the Indians, David Zeisberger.

The congregation was now fully organized and Anton Seiffert was ordained by Bishop Nitschmann as chief elder or minister. The congregation worked in common and had their living in common and had a common purpose: to preach the Gospel to the Indians.

Spangenberg left Georgia in March, 1736, having been commissioned to make a visit to the Schwenkfelder in Pennsylvania. Bishop Nitschmann followed him to Pennsylvania a little later, and both Brethren spent several weeks getting acquainted with the spiritual and material conditions there. Nitschmann sailed for Germany, June, 1736.

Having followed these companies of Moravian Brethren to their Georgia home and seen them settled there, living in their first homes, having completed the organization of their congregation, we must now turn to the main object for their coming, namely, mission work among the Indians.

The second band of Moravians to Georgia had among their companions on board the ship the Wesleys, John and Charles, and Benjamin Ingham, a clergyman of the Church of England, but a member of the "Methodist Society" as this movement was then called. The Wesleys had induced Ingham to accompany them to Georgia to engage in mission work among the Indians. From the first, Ingham was very anxious to begin work among the *Cherokees* and his inclination moved the Brethren likewise to think of that tribe as the object of their first efforts among the Indians. After careful consideration, it developed that a long journey would be required to reach the Cherokees as they were situated in the mountains at a considerable distance from the

---

* Nitschmann was ordained to the Episcopacy on March 13, 1735, by Bishop Daniel Ernst Jablonski, one of the last surviving Bishops of the Ancient Moravian Church, and at this time, Court-preacher at Berlin.

Moravian settlement. Such an undertaking was deemed dangerous.

Attention was then directed to the Creek Indians. In January, 1737, after deliberation and prayer, the lot did not yet give
the approbation of the Lord for a mission among the Upper
Creeks. In June of the same year, the lot was again appealed to
as to whether work among the Indians should now be begun.
The answer received was, that the language should be learned.
Ingham, their friend, already had some knowledge of the Creek
language and more could be learned as the visits to the settlement by Creeks were frequent, especially by the friendly Chief
Tomo-tschat-schi and his Yamacraw clansmen who lived around
Savannah.

In July, 1737, Peter Rose* and his wife† went to live among
the Lower Creeks with the intent to learn the language, and tell
the Indians what they could about their Saviour. Then came
another opening among the Creeks, described so particularly in
another work‡ as to call for the quoting of several paragraphs
here:

"On August 9, Mr. Ingham went to the Moravians with a new
plan. General Oglethorpe had agreed to build a schoolhouse for Indian children, near Tomo-tschat-schi's village, with the idea that it
would give opportunity also to reach the older men and women with
the Gospel message. The house was to contain three rooms, one for
Ingham, one for the Moravian missionaries, and one to be used for

---

* Gamekeeper by occupation, member of first company from
Herrnhut to Georgia. Missionary among the Creeks 1737-1739.
Settled at Germantown, Pa., 1739, where he died March 12, 1740.

† Sister Rose before her last marriage was Catharina Riedel, wife
of Friedrich Riedel, mason, of the first company to Georgia. She
had come with Bishop Nitschmann's, the second band of colonists, to
join her husband, but found, instead, his grave in Savannah! After
her marriage with Rose, she labored with him among the Creeks
until 1739, when the Moravians had to quit Georgia. The Roses then
left for Pennsylvania, and settled in Germantown, where Peter died
March 12, 1740. Catharina married John Michael Huber in 1742.
He died, 1747, while on a voyage to the West Indies. For the third
time a widow, she became one of the first occupants of the Widows'
House in Bethlehem, Pa., and served as Deaconess for many years,
dying in 1798.

‡ See Bibliography No. 10.

the school, and it was suggested that the Moravians undertake the erection of the building, the Trustees' fund to pay them for their labor. The proposition was gladly accepted, and preparations were at once made to send the necessary workmen.

"On Monday, the 13th, Töltschig and five others went to the spot which had been selected for the Indian Schoolhouse, usually called Irene. The site of this schoolhouse has been considered uncertain, but a short manuscript account of 'the Mission among the Indians in America,' preserved in the Herrnhut Archives, says distinctly that it stood 'a mile above the town (of Savannah) on an island in the Savannah River which was occupied by the Creeks.'

"When the carpenters arrived the first act was to unite in prayer for a blessing on their work, and then they began to fell trees and cut down bushes, clearing the ground for the hut in which they were to live while building the schoolhouse. The hut was placed on the grave of an Indian Chief. 'The Indians are accustomed to bury their Chiefs on the spot where they died, to heap a mound some 24 feet high above them, to mourn them for a while, and then to abandon the spot,' and this little elevation was a favorable site for their hut. Until the hut was finished the men lodged with the Indians, Tomochichi himself taking charge of their belongings. Töltschig returned the same day to Savannah, going back later with a supply of provisions. The Indians made them heartily welcome to their neighborhood, and the Moravians, even in the midst of their building operations, began to teach them the English alphabet, at the same time putting forth every effort to learn the Indian tongue, in which Rose was rapidly becoming proficient.

"By the 20th of September the schoolhouse was finished, and Ingham and the Moravians held a conference to plan the future work, and decide what duties each should assume, as he proposed to move thither at once, and, with the approval of the lot, Rose and his wife were to do the same. Morning and evening they were to read the English Bible, accompanied by silent prayer; morning, mid-day and evening an hour was to be given to the study of the Indian language; and Rose and his wife were to have an hour for private devotions. Mrs. Rose was to teach the Indian girls to read, and the boys, who had already begun to read, were to be taught to write. In their remaining time they were to clear and plant some land, that they might not be too long dependent on the Congregation at Savannah, and on the friendly Indians, who were giving them much.

"The next day Mr. and Mrs. Töltschig escorted Rose and his wife to their new home, and at Ingham's request united with them in a little prayer service. Four days later fourteen of the Moravians went to the schoolhouse, which was solemnly consecrated by Seifert, the Chief Elder. That evening, in Savannah, Rose and his wife were formally set apart for their missionary work, and the next day they returned to 'Irene,' as the school was called, to enter upon their duties.

"At first everything was encouraging. The children learned readily, not only to read but some to write; they committed to memory many passages of Scripture, and took special delight in the hymns they were taught to sing.

"The older Indians looked on with wonder and approval, which stimulated the missionaries to new zeal in mastering the language, and in taking every opportunity to make the 'Great Word' known to them. Zinzendorf wrote a letter from Herrnhut to Tomochichi, commending his interest in their message, and urging its full acceptance upon him; the Indians gave some five acres of land for a garden, which Rose cleared and planted."

On October 7, 1737, Seiffert and Böhner moved to Tomo-tschat-schi's village further to learn the language and begin their missionary work, these Brethren having been designated by the lot for this service. Peter Rose and wife went with them. The work was kept up until January, 1739, but under very discouraging conditions as the minds of the Indians were restless and they were indifferent and given to drunkenness, all these disorders growing out of rumors of war between Spain and England.

Already in the latter part of 1737 the threatened invasion of Spaniards from Florida called everybody to arms in Georgia, and when the Brethren insisted on their previous agreement with the Trustees, namely, not to be required to bear arms, troublesome times began for them; resulting, finally, in the declaration against them that if they would not remain in Georgia as citizens—i.e., do military duty if necessary—they might not remain as missionaries. The Georgia Trustees took the position that to allow the Brethren when they were not citizens, to send missionaries to the Indians, would be construed to mean that the English had no one to preach the Gospel. Thus, unexpectedly, the open door was shut. England declared war on Spain in 1739. Spain had long been jealous over English possessions in America, especially her southern colonies, and here the whole burden of the war in America fell.

Already the Moravian colony in Georgia had been decreased by death and removals due to disagreements or dissatisfaction and the remaining members were glad for the opportunity to sail for Pennsylvania with George Whitefield who had offered them free passage thither on his sloop "Savannah" sailing April 13, 1740. Possibilities for Moravian settlement and missionary labors were opening up in Pennsylvania through the evangelistic labors of Spangenberg.

Thus the first labors of the Moravian Brethren among the southern Indians came to an end.

The Brethren wished to preserve, if possible, some of the influence they had gained among the Indians, and an effort to this end was made by John Hagen who arrived in Savannah, May, 1740. He had come over from Germany desiring to go as a missionary among the Cherokees, not knowing the Moravians had abandoned Georgia. He was kindly received at Whitefield's house, where he worked about the establishment. He was much impressed with the prospect for the Lord's work in and around Savannah, for the people had been deeply stirred by Whitefield's preaching. Hagen wrote to Herrnhut urging that two married couples be sent to help reap the harvest, which was also the wish of Whitefield. Unfortunately, these cordial relationships between Whitefield and Hagen and the Moravians in Pennsylvania did not long continue, disputes over doctrinal differences having arisen.

Hagen went first to visit the Creek Indians at Irene, with whom the Brethren had lived, but found only the women at home. The men were all gone with General Oglethorpe to fight against the Spaniards. Tomo-tschat-schi had died the year previous.

The Cherokees never left Hagen's heart and mind, but the opportunity of going to them did not present itself. First of all, the Cherokees were still living far away from Savannah—the same difficulty which had hindered the first Brethren from going to them. Also, an account had been received that the small-pox had played havoc among them and in a short time destroyed a large part of the Nation. The survivors were much dejected, believing this calamity to be a punishment for having suffered themselves to be seduced by the whites to drink brandy, and on that account, they now abhorred all white people. Under these circumstances, Hagen reflected that even if he could go to them he would not be welcome nor could he accomplish anything. However, his ministry to Indians came about in another way.

Of the many Indians who had gone to war, numbers were brought to Savannah in a wounded and dying condition. These he visited, preached the Gospel to all who understood English and endeavored, even, to learn their own language for that purpose. Hagen* remained in Savannah until February, 1742, when he went to Bethlehem, Pa.

---

* Hagen was appointed Warden of the Nazareth congregation when it was organized. He went with Joseph Powell to Shamokin (Sunbury), Pa., June, 1747, to help in the establishment of a mission there at the request of Chief Shikellimy, after Martin Mack had aroused interest by preaching at this place. Hagen died at Shamokin, June, 1747.

CHAPTER III

THE SETTLEMENT IN NORTH CAROLINA BECOMES THE NEW BASE FOR THE MISSIONS TO THE SOUTHERN INDIANS

The determination to gather precious souls for the Saviour among the southern Indian tribes did not die out with the unavoidable abandonment of the first Moravian project in America. A new door was opening for the carrying out of the Brethren's cherished ideal to serve the Red man in the things of Christ. In the year 1749, negotiations by the leaders of the Moravian Church with England, which gained for the Brethren's Church its recognition by the British Government as a Protestant Episcopal Church and guaranteed for its members liberty of worship and service throughout Britian and her possessions, led, also, to the making of several influential friends for the church; notably, Lord Granville, Speaker of the House of Commons. Upon reasonable terms, he offered for sale to the Brethren a large tract of land which he held in North Carolina.

Meanwhile, the Moravian Church in the new world had come to a cross-roads. Was the Church to grow and develop in its own way on the new continent, by the preaching of the Gospel in various places in the colonies as hitherto, receiving those who were awakened, and desired admission into Moravian fellowship? This was one possibility. The other alternative was the system which had been begun on the continent of Europe, namely, Moravian retreats, or exclusive settlements, cut off from the world and even from other branches of the Christian Church; with a view to the development of spirituality in its members and a holy brotherhood sealed for service at home and abroad and each settlement closely linked up to and governed by the mother church in Herrnhut. The Brethren chose the latter plan, believing this to be the Lord's will for the Moravian Church. Beyond this statement of the policy adopted for the spread of Moravianism in other parts of the world, it is not within the province of this narrative to go. Reference is made to this Moravian mode of settlement in America because of the two fundamental ideas with which such a community was planted: holiness of life and separation for mission service, both of which are back of the Indian mission. Certain it is, in passing be it remarked, that here is to be found the initial and perhaps the main reason for the Moravian Church as a small church among the other branches of the great household of the Christian faith.

In line with this policy, the purchase of one hundred thousand acres of land from Lord Granville by Count Zinzendorf was consummated. The land was selected in the Piedmont section of North Carolina and the survey was finished in January, 1753. Thus, in the wilderness of North Carolina, there was now room for a settlement of the Brethren to work out several distinct aims: mission work among the southern Indians, Creeks, Chero kees, Chickasaws, etc.; evangelistic work among the colonists of North Carolina; a large territory or home where the Brethren might have undisputed authority and liberty to live and develop, to the highest degree possible, a Christian community. This tract was named "Wachovia;" the fine meadows reminding of the valley of the Wach in Austria, formerly in possession of the Zinzendorf family.

Necessary preparations having been made for the first beginning in Wachovia, a company of twelve single Brethren set out from Bethlehem, Pa., October 8, 1753, to establish a settlement. They arrived November 17, and Bethabara was begun. The settlement at Bethania followed in 1759, and Salem, the principal and central town, was built in 1766. In the year 1771, Salem became the seat of a distinct Moravian center and government of the Church in this southern section of the country. For the story of the development, through the years, of the Wachovia settlements into the Southern Province of the Moravian Church in America, the reader is referred to another work.*

One of the main objects of a Moravian settlement anywhere, i.e., missions to the heathen, was never forgotten with the settlement of Wachovia. The spiritual needs of the Creek and Cherokee Indians were ever carried in heart and mind. Parties from both tribes frequently passed through the Bethabara settlement and were well treated by the Brethren. In consequence, Bethabara became a place noted among the Indians as the "Dutch Fort, where there are good people and much bread."

---

* See Bibliography No. 21.

The Rev. John Ettwein[†] who came to Bethabara on a visit in 1758, took an especial interest in the Indians, and asked a party of them in a meeting held at Bethabara, whether they would like it if some of the Brethren should come to their country to learn their language; to which they replied that they would be proud of it, it would be a very good thing. In 1757 and 1758 more than five hundred Indians passed through the settlement at various times.

To be sure, nearness to the southern Indian tribes, for the Brethren's purpose one of the main advantages in the situation of Wachovia, was very dangerous during the years 1759 to 1761, as the Creeks and Cherokees were on the war path, embroiled in the French and Indian War. Bethabara had been stockaded already in 1756, so that there might not be here a repetition of the dreadful massacre in the north at the Gnadenhuetten mission station on the Mahoni, in 1754. Many refugees came to Bethabara and some of these were accommodated in the Bethania settlement. Every precaution was taken in each settlement, and by those who, almost daily, rode from one place to the other. Often, in the morning, the traces of Indians were found quite near the settlements and it was afterward ascertained, through some whites who had been prisoners among the Indians, that one hundred and fifty of their warriors had encamped for nearly six weeks about six miles from Bethabara, whilst a smaller camp was only three miles distant. They had planned, on a number of occasions, to attack and destroy the village. When approaching the fortifications, they heard the ringing of the bell and concluded that they had been discovered and withdrew. The bell, however, had been rung only for the customary evening service. Again, an attack had been planned, in the night, and, when the Indians were surrounding the fort, they heard a trumpet blast,

---

[†] Consecrated Bishop in 1784. First President of Society for Propagating the Gospel Among the Heathen, when organized, 1787, at Bethlehem, Pa. Ettwein was life-long friend of the Indians and may be classed as one of the missionaries among them, although his life was spent mainly in the administration of the Brethren's affairs, south, 1758-66 and, after that, in Bethlehem, Pa. In 1772, Ettwein conducted a company of Delawares from Friedenshuetten, northeastern part of Pa., to Friedenstadt, on the border of Ohio.

2

and, thinking their plans had been exposed, they hastily retreated. The night watchman, on this occasion, was merely announcing the hour with his horn. Thus did the Lord use "the things that are not as though they were" in keeping this settlement and Bethania, also, from all harm. A sharp watch was kept in Bethabara from the vantage point of the burying ground, a very steep hill to the rear of the church.

With the year 1760, the danger increased; Cherokees in strong numbers having invaded many parts of North Carolina, and encamped in two parties, three and six miles from Bethania, so that for some time none ventured to attend the daily meetings unarmed. In a short space of time no less than fifteen persons were murdered in the neighborhood.

"In 1761, the war with the Indians was brought to a close. The South Carolina Militia having entered, near Fort Prince George, the country of the Cherokees east of the mountains, burnt about eight hundred houses, and laid waste thirteen hundred acres of Indian corn. The Indians were forced to sue for peace, while, at the same time, the transmontane Cherokees were subdued by the Virginians. The latter were assisted by North Carolina troops, and supplied with large quantities of flour from the Bethabara mill."[*]

Brother John Ettwein, who had been called to Wachovia and served seven years up to 1766,—when he was appointed a member of the General Conference at Bethlehem,—continued to be deeply interested in the Creeks and Cherokees, and made several evangelistic journeys into South Carolina, preaching in the vicinity of the Congaree, Saluda and Broad Rivers, itinerating even as far south as Georgia, getting into frequent touch with the Indians.

---

[*] See Bibliography No. 19.

CHAPTER IV

THE CHEROKEES

This name of the largest and most important of the Indian tribes of North America, or in the form employed by themselves, "Tsaraghee" or "Chera-taghe" has no meaning in their own language and seems to be of foreign origin, though the tribal name may possibly be derived from the Choctow "chiluk-ki"—cave people—in allusion to the numerous caves in their mountain country. The proper name by which the Cherokees call themselves is Ani-Yun'wiya, signifying "real people," the word being closely related to "Onwe-honwe," the name by which the Cognate Iroquois know themselves. "Ani-Yun'wiya" properly denotes "Indians," as distinguished from people of other races, but in usage it is restricted to mean members of the Cherokee tribe.

The Cherokees have been styled "the Mountaineers of Aboriginal America," and it is quite reasonable to suppose that they were the original inhabitants of the southeastern portion of the United States, in the upper valley of the Tennessee River, (commonly known in early days of American history as the Cherokee River), and among the mountains of Georgia, western North Carolina, Tennessee, with large sections of country in South Carolina and Alabama.

Scientific research testifies to the antiquity of the Cherokees, and by some they are believed to be direct descendants of the Mound Builders. It is a curious fact that mounds are numerous in that portion of the country once inhabited by the Cherokees. While the Cherokees claimed to have built the mounds on the upper Ohio, they yet expressly disclaimed the authorship of the numerous mounds in their later home territory, and, although sometimes utilizing the mounds for their own town houses, they were as ignorant as the whites of their origin or purpose, having only a general tradition that their forefathers had found them in much the same condition on first coming to the country.[*]

---

[*] See Bibliography No. 3.

The Cherokees could not tell, when first found by the white man, whether they owned their land by right of discovery or by conquest; so long had been their occupancy. The Cherokees have seven clans, viz., Ani-Wa-ya (Wolf), Ani-kawi (Deer), Ani-Tsi-skwa (Bird), Ani-Wadi (Paint), Ani-Saha-ni, Ani-Ga-Tagewi, Ani-Gi-lahi. The last three cannot be translated with certainty. The Wolf clan is the largest and most important. The seven clans are frequently mentioned in the ritual prayers and are even in the printed laws of the tribes. They seem to have had a connection with the seven mother towns of the Cherokees, described by Cuming in 1730, as having each a Chief whose office was hereditary in the female line.

Not all the Cherokees lived in the mountainous sections of their ancient territory. They are distinguished into two great divisions: the Ottare, or Upper Cherokees, and the Airate, who inhabited the lower grounds and were known as the Lower Cherokees. They *were* lower than the Ottare, not only in situation, but likewise in intelligence. While the Upper Cherokees had a well-defined mythological account of their origin, the Lower Cherokees believed they had come from a hole in the ground! Intermarriage between the Upper and Lower Cherokees was strictly prohibited.

Great interest attaches to the Spanish expeditions in search of gold and their conquests in America at the opening of the 16th century, which constitute the first invasion of the Indian's territory by the white man and which brought the Spaniards into touch with the Cherokees. Even before de Soto came through the Cherokee country in 1540, a band of Spaniards made an expedition into what is now Florida. This company, under the command of Pamphilo de Narvaez, had obtained from Charles V the contract to explore Florida and reduce that country to Spain. In April, 1528, his fleet anchored near the outlet of what is now Tampa Bay. The natives having shown samples of gold and indicated, by gestures, that it had come from the country farther north, Narvaez directed his ships to meet him at a harbor with which the pilot pretended acquaintance and, having mustered 300 men, the march inland was begun. For the first time, Florida was traversed by white men. Scouring the country round for many days, in quest of silver and gold, the party were stricken with fever, their progress delayed, and they began to perish with hunger. Not until August, 1528, did they find the sea and came upon a small bay. Here they finished five boats and embarked for the Rio Grande. For four days the half-famished adventurers kept their course to the west when a storm overtook them and one of the boats, commanded by Cabeza de Vaca was thrown on the beach near Galveston. Subsequently, all the adventurers in the other boats perished and only Cabeza de Vaca with three companions survived, as prisoners of the Indians. For eight years Cabeza lived among the southern Indians, 1528-36. He was a devout Catholic. The Indians did not treat him like a common prisoner, but regarded him as divine. When he returned to Spain, he wrote an account of what he had taught the Indians, and said, among other things, he had taught them the stories of the Book of Genesis. It is not impossible, taking into account tribal migrations and the official story-tellers of the Indians, handing down these stories from one generation to another, that, when a century later the Cherokees were first heard of through the English settlers, and several centuries later when missionaries came to them, the traditions and legends of the creation, etc., found among them, so strikingly similar to those of the Book of Genesis, were a survival of this devout Catholic's teachings. Many of these traditions are preserved among Cherokee antiquities.

The Cherokees believed that there is an Almighty Being who created all things; among others, he built the first man of red clay, hence the red man! Yet they had no real word to express the Deity and their language, in general, is barren of expressions for any ideas outside the range of the five senses. They believed in a life after death; its nature, whether blessed or unhappy, determined by a good or evil life lived on earth. The Supreme Being was considered as good and merciful and could be propitiated when wrong had been done. Both good and evil spirits are recognized by the Cherokees and these may, and do operate in human beings. Sacrifices were made and religious festivals held among them, in charge of their sorcerers, who had the Cherokees very much in their power. Like other Indian tribes, the Cherokees had well-defined traditions of the Deluge. Whether these go back only to the days of the Spanish invasion, as above noted, or to remote antiquity, forever hidden with other mysteries about the origin of these children of the forest, is a matter of conjecture.

The Cherokees were a powerful people, but had many enemies among the Indian Nations and of these, the Delawares were most to be dreaded. The following is related of the contests between these Nations:*

"Years ago, the whites being already in the country and many of the Delawares having moved far up the Delaware River, a party of these Indians, with the cousin of a chief as captain, went on a hunt. They were attacked by Cherokees, at that time dwelling along the Allegheny and its branches, and some of them were killed, the captain among the rest. The survivors fled to their homes, related to the Chief what had happened and suggested that he give them more men in order that they might avenge themselves on their enemies. The Chief, however, put them off, and did not let them go, even though he sorrowed over the loss they had suffered. After the lapse of a year, the Chief sent out several hundred men to avenge themselves on the Cherokees (the Delawares at that time already having European arms). When they arrived at the enemies' first towns along the Allegheny, they found no one, for all had fled at the news of the Delawares' approach. The latter pursued, the Cherokees constantly retreating until they were overtaken at the great island ('Neville's Island? This is clearly the Delaware tradition.'—Ed.) at the fork where Pittsburg is now situated. Perceiving that the Delawares were strong in number, they had no heart to fight, though they stood ready with bow and arrow in hand; instead, their Chief called to the Delawares to rest their arms and not fight. Afterwards they had an interview with the Delawares and surrendered themselves as prisoners. About half of them, however, dissatisfied with the capitulation, refused to surrender and escaped during the night, going down the river to the mouth of another river, now named the Cherokee River (the Tennessee), where they landed and afterward settled along this stream, in the region in which they still live. After the Delawares had finished with the Cherokees, the Six Nations arrived, having heard of the expedition of the Delawares. When they realized that the Delawares were masters of the situation, they professed satisfaction and said that they had come to assist them, but recognized that their aid was not now needed. Thereupon the Delawares gave them some of their prisoners as a present for their trouble and suffered them to go to their homes."

As already stated, when found by the white man the Chero-kees had numerous and populous towns in the mountains of Vir-

* See Bibliography No. 8.

ginia, western North Carolina, Tennessee, etc. Itsati, or Echota, on the south bank of the Little Tennessee, a few miles above the mouth of Tellico River, in Tennessee, was commonly considered the capital of the Nation. The Holston River and its tributaries formed the water-courses along which these towns were built. Here they were attacked by the tribes from the north and driven to the Little Tennessee where they established themselves permanently. A large branch of the tribe, hailing from the neighborhood of South Carolina, settled upon the main Tennessee but the greater body occupied northwestern Carolina and northern Georgia. While the Upper Cherokees were thus engaged in warfare with the Delawares and other tribes of the north, the Lower Cherokees on the Oconee and Savannah Rivers were harassed by the Creeks. The last war of the Cherokees with the Delawares lasted until 1766 or 1767, when the Cherokees sought the friendship of the Delawares who had done them much harm. Accordingly, peace was made and the Cherokees recognized the Delawares as their grandfathers.* Through the intervention of the Delawares, the Cherokees secured peace with the Six Nations and others.

In 1700, the Cherokee Nation consisted of sixty-four large towns. Due to the almost continuous warfare, as noted, their numbers greatly decreased. At different times, too, they had to fight the French and English. The terrible scourge of smallpox likewise took a large toll from this tribe, so that in 1740, they numbered only 5,000 warriors.

The Cherokees themselves claim remote affinity with the Iroquois, who called them Oyata-ge-ronon, "inhabitants of the cave country." Linguistically, the Cherokees belong to the Iroquoian stock, though grammatical differences indicate that the separation must have occurred at a very early period. Some claim relationship with the Powhatans.

In physical appearance, the Cherokees were a splendid race, tall and athletic. Their women, especially, differed from those of other tribes, being tall, erect and of a willowy, delicate frame, with features of perfect symmetry and complexion of olive. The warriors' heads were shaved, except a patch on the back part which was ornamented with plumes. Their ears were slit

---

* Note letter of Chief Charles R. Hicks to the Delawares, page 110.

and adorned with large pendants and rings. The Cherokees enjoyed greater longevity than any of the Indian Nations owing, no doubt, to the pure mountain air they breathed and the clear mountain streams from which they drank. Their locations were generally high and healthful.

They lived in permanent villages of substantially-built log houses, and depended for a living chiefly upon agriculture, raising large crops of corn, beans and pumpkins.

Warrior was the highest title and honor they could confer apart from the Chiefs, and was obtained by merit. Besides this, they had some head men in each town who, by dint of eloquence or superior knowledge and ingenuity had obtained some influence among them, though the power of these head men never went further than to get their brethren by persuasion and representation, to do what they wanted them to do. Of all the Indian tribes, the Cherokees were the most proud and disdainful. Especially was this trait exhibited in their early intercourse with the Europeans, the soldiers and the lower class of whom they despised most cordially. The warriors would not associate themselves with anyone less than superior officers and generals of the English and French armies!

Unlike other Indian Nations, the Cherokees had no laws against adultery, and both sexes being unrestrained in this particular, marriage was frequently of short duration.

The idea that all Indian women were almost the slaves of their husbands is erroneous so far as the Cherokees were concerned. Possibly the difference between them and the other tribes in the matter of standing of the women was due, largely, to the fact that the Cherokees subsisted not by the chase, but by the tilling of the soil. Their women practically ruled the men and some of them did so with a rod of iron! This power rested chiefly upon their ancient customs: 1. Marriage could be dissolved when one of the partners so wished. 2. Man and wife did not have property in common; each kept what was his own and tried to increase it. 3. Children belonged to the mother and were connected with her clan; therefore, if husband and wife disagreed, his own children as well as his wife's tribe were against him and he could do nothing.

The Cherokees observed some singular rites in connection with the burial of the dead. When a patient was pronounced past recovery, his hair was anointed and his face painted; and, the grave being prepared beforehand, he was interred as soon as the breath had left his body.

It was in one of the mother settlements of the English, in 1730, that the first political convention between the Cherokees and the English was held and a treaty concluded. The English were especially eager for an alliance, it having become known that the French were planning to unite Canada and Louisiana, which plan Great Britain wished to counteract and, therefore, was anxious to enlist the Indians. Sir Alexander Cummings was the agent of King George II, and through him the alliance was brought about. He had traveled extensively among the southern Indians, but just how he won them over is not clear. On the day when they swore allegiance to Great Britain, there was a mighty gathering of the Cherokees and they seated Sir Alexander on a stump, well covered with furs. Then, with the same number of eagles' tails as there are stripes today on the American flag, they began to stroke Sir Alexander and sang around him from morning to night, at which time the Cherokee warriors bowed on their knees and declared themselves to be dutiful subjects of His Majesty, King George. A special agreement of this treaty provided that the Cherokees should not trade with any other people than the English. On the occasion of this meeting, also, by suggestion of the English, Moytoy was appointed head Chief and designated "Emperor" of the entire Cherokee Nation. In 1755, the Nation further ceded part of its territory to the English and consented to the erection of English forts within its domain.

This comity between Cherokees and English was interrupted during the French and Indian war, when in 1759, under the leadership of Aganstata, the Cherokees began war with the English of Carolina. But after the decisive victory of Colonel Grant over the Cherokees at Echoee, peace was again restored in 1761 and, in the following year, Henry Timberlake, a lieutenant in the British service, in order to cultivate friendly relations with the Cherokees, visited the towns on the Tellico and Tennessee Rivers and persuaded three powerful Chieftains to accompany him to England. These were Ostenaco, a Chief famous through many wars and a man of uncommon sagacity; Collanna (the Raven) and his nephew, Oconnestoto, Chief of the long-hair clan and great war Chief of the Cherokees, famous for having. in all his expeditions, taken such prudent measures as never to have lost a man. They were presented to King Geroge III, being introduced at Court by Col. Beamer. Before the King they exhibited a dignity and bearing in keeping with their rank and influence as representatives of a great Nation.

Timberlake's acquaintance with the Cherokees was extensive and his description of them goes back to the years when they had scarcely any contact with the whites:

"The Cherokees are of a middle stature. of an olive color, though generally painted; and their skin stained with gunpowder, pricked into it in very pretty figures. The hair of their head is shaved. though many of the old people have it plucked out by the roots. except a patch on the hinder part of the head, about twice the bigness of a crown-piece, which is ornamented with beads, feathers, wampum, stained deer's hair, and such like baubles. The ears are slit and stretched to an enormous size, putting the person who undergoes the operation to incredible pain. being unable to lie on either side for forty days. So soon as the patient can bear it. they are wound with wire to expand them, and are adorned with silver pendants and rings, which they likewise wear at the nose.

"They that can afford it wear a collar of wampum, which are beads cut out of clam shells, a silver breast-plate. and bracelets on their arms and wrists of same metal, cloth over their loins, a shirt of the English make. a sort of cloth-boots, and mockasons, which are shoes of a make peculiar to the Americans. A matchcoat thrown over all compleats their dress at home; but when they go to war they leave their trinkets behind and the mere necessities serve them.

"The old people still remember and praise the ancient days, before they were acquainted with the whites, when they had but little dress, except a bit of skin about their middles. mockasons. a mantle of buffalo skin for the winter, and a light one of feathers for the summer. The women are remarkably well-featured, and both men and women are straight and well-built, with small hands and feet.

"They are of a very gentle and amicable disposition to those they think their friends, but as implacable in their enmity, their revenge being only compleated in the entire destruction of their enemies.

"They are very hardy, bearing heat. cold, hunger and thirst. in a surprising manner; and yet no people are given to more excess in eating and drinking, when it is conveniently in their power; the follies, nay mischief, they commit when inebriated, are entirely laid to the liquor and no one will revenge an injury, murder excepted, received from one who is no more himself.

"They are particularly careful of the superannuated, but are not so till of great age. Ostenaco's mother is an instance. Ostenaco is about 60 years of age, and the youngest of four; yet his mother still continues her laborious tasks, and has yet strength enough to carry two hundred weight of wood on her back near a couple of miles.

"They seldom have their eyes on the person they speak of, or address themselves to, and are always suspicious when people's eyes are fixed upon them. They speak so low, except in council, that they are often obliged to repeat what they were saying, yet should a person talk to any of them above their common pitch, they will immediately ask him if he thought they were deaf?

"They generally concur in the belief of one superior Being, who made them, and governs all things, and are therefore never discontent at any misfortune, because they say, the Man above would have it so. They believe in a reward and punishment, as may be evinced by their answer to Mr. Martin, who, having preached the Scripture till both his audience and he were heartily tired, was told at last, that they knew very well, that, if they were good, they would go up; if bad, down; that he could tell no more; that he had long plagued them with what they no ways understood, and that they desired him to depart the country."

Here follows:

"A translation of the War Song: Caw Waw noo dee, etc.:

'Where'er the earth's enlightened by the sun,
Moon shines by night, grass grows, or waters run,
Be't known that we are going, like men, afar,
In hostile fields to wage destructive war;
Like men we go to meet our country's foes,
Who, woman-like, shall fly our dreaded blows:
Yes, as a woman, who beholds a snake,
In gaudy horror, glisten through the brake,
Starts trembling back, and stares in wild surprise,
Or pale through fear, unconscious, panting, flies.
Just so these foes, more tim'rous than the hind,
Shall leave their arms and only cloaths behind,
Pinched by each blast, by every thicket torn,
Run back to their own nation, now its scorn;
Or in the winter, when the barren wood,
Denies their gnawing entrails nature's food,
Let them sit down, from friend and country far,
And wish, with tears, they ne'er had come to war.' "

. There are some honorary titles among them, conferred in reward of great actions; the first of which is "Ontarity", or Man-

Killer; and the second "Colona", or The Raven. Old warriors
likewise, or war-women, who can no longer go to war, but have
distinguished themselves in their younger days, have the title of
Beloved. This is the only title females can enjoy, but it abundantly recompenses them, by the power they acquire by it, which
is so great, that they can, by the wave of a swan's wing, deliver a
wretch condemned by the Council, and already tied to the stake.

At the time when Moravian missionaries came to the Cherokees
during the latter part of the 18th century, this tribe had advanced in a remarkable degree to civilization. In great part this
was due to the intermarriage among them of white men, chiefly
traders of the ante-Revolutionary period, with a few Americans from the back settlements. The families that have made
Cherokee history were nearly all of this mixed descent.
The Doughertys, Galpins and Adairs were from Ireland; the
Rosses, Vanns and McIntoshes were of Scottish origin; the Waf-
fords and others were Americans from Carolina or Georgia.
Most of this white blood was of good stock. Those of mixed
blood who could afford it usually sent their children away to be
educated, while some built school-houses upon their own grounds
and brought in private teachers. Influential mixed bloods, in
the course of years, came to places of influence in almost every
town except in the middle towns, which, shut in from the outside world by high mountains, remained a stronghold of Cherokee conservatism.

During the Revolutionary War, the Cherokees remained faithful and were powerful allies of the British until the year following the Declaration of Independence, when they ceased hostilities and sued for peace, having been completely defeated, successively by troops from South Carolina, North Carolina and
Virginia. They entered into a formal treaty with the United
States Government in 1781.

To this interesting Nation at about this time in their history,
the Moravian Brethren felt constrained to come as messengers of
Christ. The story of the Moravian mission and of the missions
of other Christian denominations which followed many years
after the Brethren as pioneers had begun work among the Chero-

kees, is inseparably connected with and principally responsible for the rapid and remarkable rise of this Indian Nation in enlightenment, civilization and prosperity. The espousal of Christianity by the Cherokees brought them out as the most highly developed of all the Indian Nations.

CHAPTER V

THE FIRST FRUITS OF THE CHEROKEE NATION FOR CHRIST, AS THOSE "BORN OUT OF DUE SEASON"

A Cherokee Indian and his wife were baptized by Moravian missionaries twenty-eight years before ever the mission to that Nation was undertaken. It is not known whether the Brethren who labored for years among the Cherokees without seeing results knew of or remembered the first fruits gathered out of this tribe before their first fruits ripened for the harvest. The fact of the baptism of a Cherokee Indian and his wife by Moravian missionaries on July 4, 1773, is mentioned in an early history of Moravian missions among the Indians[*]

All this is explained in a letter of David Zeisberger[†] to Bishop Nathanael Seidel,[‡] dated Schoenbrunn,[§] August 26, 1773. According to this letter, the Cherokee Indian and his wife, by their baptismal names, were Noah and Wilhelmina.[||] Taken prisoner in the Delaware-Cherokee war, Noah had been brought into the Schoenbrunn neighborhood. Noah had received permission to return to his own Nation after peace had been concluded, but did not wish to do so at the time and had, consequently, remained in this vicinity and had married. Now he believed his remaining among the Delawares had been overruled by the Lord, so that he and his wife could hear the Gospel, through the Moravian missionaries, and be saved. The missionaries at Schoenbrunn baptized him and his wife on the date named.

Noah was familiar with the section of country in North Carolina wherein lay Wachovia, the tract of the Brethren. He said

---

* See Bibliography No. 9.

† Moravian missionary to Indians in New York, Pennsylvania, Ohio, Michigan and Canada for over 60 years, 1746-1808.

‡ Member of the Governing Board or Provincial Helpers' Conference, American Province, North, Bethlehem, Pa., at this time.

§ Settlement of Moravian Christian Delawares, Tuscarawas Valley, Ohio.

|| Wilhelmina was a Delaware.

it was in the neighborhood of the Pilot Mountain. Though a long time among the Delawares, he spoke Cherokee more fluently than that language. He said his tribe could be reached by going down the Ohio and up the Kanawha Rivers. Zeisberger wrote that he seemed anxious to make a visit to his Nation, accompanied by one of the missionaries. He thought the Cherokees would accept the Gospel if they had the opportunity to hear it.

Doubtless the confusion of the Revolutionary War made this intended, promising visit come to naught.

CHAPTER VI

THE BRETHREN TAKE STEPS TO BEGIN A MISSION AMONG THE CHEROKEES

The efforts of the Moravians to keep in touch with the southern Indians have already been noted. After Hagen had visited them in 1740, they were not heard from further until after the settlement of Wachovia began from Bethlehem, Pa., in 1753.

In a Helpers' Conference held in Bethlehem, September, 1755, when another band of colonists were making ready to leave for Wachovia, this settlement was again talked over and regulations to be established there were set down. Among other items, the minutes record that Christian Heinrich, probably in charge of the party, is asked to visit among the Cherokees, Catawbas, etc., when his duties permit him to leave the settlement. Further, the Moravian colonists are asked not to be afraid of the Indians but to treat them kindly and show them favors.

Next, we find Brother John Ettwein in 1759 holding a conference with several Cherokee Chiefs in Bethabara, when these Indians declare their approbation, in the most friendly manner, of a mission of the Brethren among them. Before Ettwein left, in 1766, for Bethlehem, Pa., to assume his executive duties there, he wrote for further information about the Cherokees and the likelihood of an opening for mission work among them to John Daniel Hammerer.* stationed at Fort Prince George, Cherokee ·

---

* John Daniel Hammerer, native of Strassburg, Alsace, a Lutheran who, under stress of civil and religious oppression, left his country and came to England. After living there for ten years, he became interested in the civilization of the American Indian. His scheme attracted the favorable attention of the Earl of Hillsborough, Commissioner for Trades and Plantations, and of Charles Witworth, M.P., of the Society for Promoting Arts and Manufactures, and a subscription was raised for the undertaking.

In 1765, Hammerer read in the papers of some Cherokee deputies who had come to England and in an audience with the Board of Trade had expressed the desire of their Nation to have some persons sent among them capable of instructing their youth in reading, writing and useful arts. He accompanied these deputies on their

country. The following reply was received by Frederic William de Marshall, Superintendent of the Brethren's affairs in Wachovia, under date of September 26, 1766.

"Dear Sir, Mr. Ettwein in his letter of the 7th of August tells me to write to you, as he is going to Pennsylvania. Mr. Ettwein expresses a desire to know 'something certain of the ways and manners, towns and dispositions of your neighbors, the Cherokees; how they would treat strangers that live among them still and quiet, only to learn their language and preach unto them without words.' Mr. Ettwein adds that he believes the Overhills are more engaged in wars, but perchance, the Lower Towns are more spoiled by their more frequent connection with the white people. To which several particulars I shall endeavor to give that gentleman all the satisfaction I am able, from my own knowledge and observation.

"First as to their towns. The whole Nation of the Cherokees is divided into four settlements, namely, the Upper or Overhill, the Middle, the Lower settlements, and the Valley, which lie in a kind of a cross.* These settlements are separated from one another by such craggy mountains and bad roads that it will ever be impracticable to make any communication by wagon-roads from one to another. On the other hand, communication between the Overhills and Virginia is easy and a wagon road might be made without great expense. There is one, also, between Charlestown and this place. The Valley, I believe, is surrounded by hills on all sides and the Middle settlements, if they have any opening, it must be towards your Province. Their towns consist of from 20 to 60 houses.

"Their number cannot be ascertained. They were thought, a few years ago, to have among them about 2,000 men capable of bearing arms and to amount in all to upwards of 16,000 souls; but the losses

---

return to America, arriving in Virginia on June 24, 1765. The Governor of Virginia encouraged Hammerer's plan, bestowing upon him a bounty of £40, and recommending him to Cherokee Chief Atakulla-Kulla or "Little Carpenter," who wished instruction for his people and who promised to take Hammerer under his protection. In his company Hammerer went into the Cherokee Nation. Already in August, 1765, he wrote to the Moravians at Bethabara asking their interest in his undertaking and offering any assistance he could render to Moravian missionaries who might be sent to the Cherokees. Later notices as to Hammerer's success are wanting.

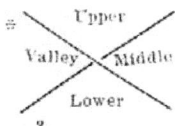

Upper Settlements 13 towns.
Lower Settlements 9 towns.
Middle Settlements 5 towns.
Valley Settlements 5 or 6 towns.

3

they have sustained must have diminished that number; and as their propensity for strong drink, in gratifying which they are but too much encouraged or indulged by the white people, and some other bad customs they are given to are too apt to prevent their recovering from these losses, they seem to me to be a fast-decreasing people unless they mend.

"They love strangers among them and are hospitable, but poor. However, a man who does not know their language is subject to many inconveniences. What I, therefore, would suggest to any person or persons from among you who should have it at heart to make a trial whether they could promote the knowledge of Christ and His Kingdom among these people, is, to come and live some time with me, where they shall be as welcome as I am able to make them, and apply to the learning of the Cherokee, in which I myself am yet but a small proficient. However, they might avail themselves of the small progress I have made, and they might, by the assistance of those youths who are to live with me soon, obtain a sufficient knowledge of it to venture to live afterwards in the midst of the people.

"I cannot think but that the Overhills are as much, if not more, corrupted than these Lower inhabitants. They have had a much larger garrison for several years among them and many of the traders and most of their packhorsemen are the worst sort of people for morals that breathe the vital air. They have too frequent opportunity to corrupt the manners of the Indians without being checked so much as those in these Lower towns. Add to this the natural ferociousness of the Overhills which has never been tamed as that of these Lower towns has by the last war, and the evil disposition of many of them toward the white people. It will make this part,—Lower— appear much more eligible for the purpose of instruction and reformation than the other.

"With sentiments of esteem, I am your most obedient, humble servant,   "John Daniel Hammerer."

Continued troubles between the French and English kept the Indians stirred up and at war among themselves, and the good intentions of the Brethren toward them had to be postponed to better times. In the meantime, Salem was built as the central town of Wachovia and became a flourishing settlement.

In 1775, a Cherokee Chief passing through Salem, assured the Brethren that missionaries would be welcome among them, provided they would instruct their children.

Then the Revolutionary War broke out and it was to be ascribed to God's merciful Providence alone that the settle-

ments of the Brethren were not destroyed, nor could the mission
be thought of during that disastrous period.

Peace having been concluded and the Government entering
into negotiations with the Indians in 1783, the Brethren remembered the visit of the Cherokee Chief in 1775, and resolved upon
an official inspection of the Cherokee villages along the Tennessee River. Brother Martin Schneider[*] volunteered for this
journey, which was carried out from the middle of December,
1783, to January 24, 1784. From his account of the visit, entitled, "*Journey of Martin Schneider from Salem to Long Island
on the Holston River and from there to Towns of the Upper
Cherokees on the Tennessee River*," we glean the following interesting and important particulars:

"I received instructions December 6, 1783, to travel with Col.
Martin Armstrong who would shortly leave for the Holston River
to make a treaty with the Indians, to ascertain more about those
regions and the needs of the Cherokees, so that the Brethren could
plan something definite about establishing a mission among them.

"On December 14th, I was commended to the Lord and blessed by
the congregation for the trip, and on the 15th, left by way of
Bethania and reached Col. Armstrong that night."

Armstrong decided he could not go on the journey because
all his family were down with the measles. He advised Schneider to return home, but Schneider, true Moravian that he was,
told him he had a commission from the Lord to go and go he
would! So Colonel Armstrong gave him a pass and a recommendation to Col. James Martin. Schneider found several companions going in the same direction. They found great difficulty
in crossing the Blue Ridge Mountains on account of depth of
snow. (They were on horseback.) On the third day out from
Col. Armstrong's, they crossed the New River, 80 miles from
Salem, and reached Col. Martin's house on December 26, and
found that " no signs of holding a meeting for a treaty existed."

---

* Martin Schneider was born December 18, 1756, at Friedensthal,
near Nazareth, Pa. He was married December 3, 1786, to Elizabeth
Dixon at Salem. Bro. Schneider was ordained a Deacon of the
Moravian Church and served the Friedland, N. C., congregation,
1787-1791; Friedberg, N. C., congregation, 1791-1804. His wife
died November 3, 1805, and on September 10, 1806, he was married
to Anna Williard, of Friedland. Bro. Schneider died November 14,
1806.

Col. Martin had gone to the Cherokee towns. Schneider decided to follow. He met a young Indian trader who told him Col. Martin's Indian name and the names of the towns, so that Schneider could tell Indians whom he wished to find.

By this time Schneider had no companions and his instructions from Salem said he should not travel unaccompanied, but he resolved "the Saviour should be his companion," and went on! He arrived at Col. Smith's establishment and hired a man and horse for $3.00 to accompany him to Island Ford on the French Broad River. (Joins the Holston River three miles above Knoxville, Tenn.) He and his companion forded this river on January 3, 1784, and reached the first house on this side of the Tennessee River. Here his guide left him and an Indian showed Schneider where he could cross the Tennessee. Once across he soon met Col. Martin who accorded him a very friendly reception and promised to render every assistance possible. Martin inquired about the Brethren in Salem and said he thanked God for bringing Schneider safely through the wilderness in the interest of the poor Indians. A call was sent out at once by Col. Martin for the Principal Chiefs to come to a Council at Chota, one of the principal towns of the Upper Cherokees.

Meanwhile, Schneider went up the Delequay River in a canoe and visited a Cherokee settlement. He met with a friendly reception, the Indians showing their hospitality by asking him to eat. They had bread made of broken corn, beans and roasted pumpkin. "The more thrifty Indians sifted their corn through a sieve of reeds and made real fine flour." They also gave Schneider some hominy "which was very bad as they allow it to sour."

"On January 5, about 20 Cherokee Chiefs assembled at a Mr. McCormick's house. First of all, other business was discussed by Col. Martin with these Indians who sat in a circle. Then he said to them that now he wanted to tell them why they had been called. (McCormick was interpreter.) Col. Martin said he had a letter from a man who belonged to the Assembly and had much to do with the Governor who said that this man (Schneider) had been sent by the chief ministers of certain people who wished to know whether the Cherokees wished to be instructed about their God and Creator and whether for this purpose a few of these good men could live among them and be given some land for cultivation?"

The Head Chief, Tayhill, answered by asking time to consider the proposition. After two hours, he got up and said he remembered that their Father—the King of England—years ago sent two men as ministers to them. One died and the other did not remain long as the war broke out. He—the Chief—was sorry about this and believed that this man—Schneider—was a good man sent by higher men to tell them about God, the Great Man who lives above. He was glad about this and the other Chiefs also. But he could give no definite answer until the other Chiefs returned from the hunt. There would be a big Council meeting, to be held on Long Island, about the treaty, and then they would take this matter up and give their decision. "McCormick encouraged the Indians to accept and held them a real sermon. McCormick is a good and righteous man." (McCormick was an old man at this time. Schneider found him sickly and cupped some blood after which McCormick felt better.)

Schneider then did some more visiting in the Cherokee houses and, although he could not talk with them, the people were all very friendly. He found their houses, on the average, about 14 x 10 feet, 7 feet high. The doors were very small and chimneys were attached to the houses on the outside.

"Every family has, besides the dwelling, a 'hot' or 'sweat-house,' built tight with only a small opening to creep in. This is used in cold weather. Fire is made in the center of the floor, and, after it is burned out, ashes are raked over the glowing embers. Bunks are built around the walls in which they sleep till 9 a.m., the next day."

Schneider says these houses are necessary in cold weather because the adults have little and the children no clothing!

"Each town has a little house elevated on a hill of earth, where, in time of work in the fields, the Principal Chief calls the people together with their corn-hoes and they begin work in common. Although each family has a field of its own, the work is done by all together and, since all must work, there is seldom any want to any. They stay in the fields until night—the women bring out the midday meal. At night, especially in time of war, the Chief calls all together and asks each what he has done or heard during the day and what he wants to do tomorrow."[*]

---

[*] Paragraphs in quotation marks in Schneider's account as well as in other documents which follow—except letters from Government officials—are translated as literally as possible from the German. Shortly after the removal of the mission to the Indian Territory, the records began to be written in English.

Each house, Schneider found, had, also, a small orchard, though these were in a very neglected condition.

The Cherokees have no expressions of profanity, but must borrow English words!

They do not make much ado with their dead. If the deceased is poor and has not much house, the body is put in and the house set on fire. For a Chief, a coffin of tightly woven reeds is made and set up on posts 10 feet above the ground where it stands until it falls together.

After a strenuous return journey, Schneider reached Salem January 24, 1784.

Before the expiration of the year, new disputes arose involving the Cherokees in war with the neighboring States. The towns where Schneider had visited were destroyed and negotiations with the Cherokees were broken off for another long interval of 15 years, during which time, after peace was concluded, North Carolina and Tennessee became separate States, and the care of Indian affairs devolved upon the Government of the United States. White people were strictly forbidden to settle among the Indians—this had been the occasion of so many disturbances—except upon special license from the Government. Regulations were made to promote peace and quietness; others prohibited the introduction of strong drink and contained provisions to prevent the further corruption of the Indian. The Indians now looked upon the President of the United States as their "Father."

In 1787 there had been reorganized in Bethlehem, Pa., "The Society for the Furtherance of the Gospel," dating from 1745, into "The Society of the United Brethren for Propagating the Gospel Among the Heathen," having in view, more especially, the Indians of North America. Many Brethren from Salem joined this Society and thus the interest in the Indian mission was kept alive and fostered for more favorable times. As Bishop Ettwein, friend of the Indians as we have seen him, and first President of this reorganized Society, said of its object:

"Every member of the Brethren's Unity is bound to take part in furthering the missionary work of the Church; but those who join this association pledge themselves in a particular manner to do all within their power to further Christ's Kingdom among the heathen nations, and confess before the world that they love the whole human race and take a deep interest in the eternal salvation of such as still sit in the darkness of heathenism."

The Brethren in Salem communicated with David Zeisberger, Apostle to northern Indians, in 1797, seeking his advice as to the best manner to enter in among the Cherokees for the beginning of a mission. He wrote to Frederic Wm. de Marshall from "Fairfield, Upper Canada, Sept. 22nd, 1797," in answer to the questions laid before him, and extracts of his letter follow:

"I do not consider it best to seek to gain entrance to the Indians through whites who are living among them or are dealing with them. Even if such whites seem friendly and show themselves willing to aid our purpose to preach the Gospel to the Indians, they are not the people to render the proper assistance nor is it to their interest in trading, etc., to have the Indians converted. Towards us they may be very friendly, but among the Indians they may work against us all the while we are thinking they are with us. A certain English preacher came to the Shawanose and wished to preach to them, but came in jeopardy of his life over it and sought protection among the traders who were around and found out they would have helped to get him out of the way had he not secretly left.

"Since the Brethren in Wachovia live far away from the Indians and are little acquainted with them, their customs, habits and government, but yet would gladly bring them to Christ their Redeemer, I think one should not start hastily with preaching before seeing that there will be an audience, for by nature, there is a thorough and strong antipathy among the Indians to the preaching of the Gospel. Their idea is that the Gospel is only for whites and that God has destined the Indian for something different and intends that they should bring sacrifices and not forsake the customs of their fathers. Just as a fish cannot live on the ground and birds cannot live in the water, so the Indian should and could not adopt the white man's manner of living.

"My advice would be, if one or several Brethren are willing, first to learn the language of the Cherokees. The Indians are always agreeable to a desire to learn their language and like to see it written down. This would give opportunity to become acquainted with them, win their confidence and tell them of the love of Christ.

"I cannot remember that the Brethren ever asked permission of the Chiefs to preach the Gospel. If one begins with the Chiefs, the answer may be known in advance: 'We will think about it, and, if we agree, we will let you know.' That will never happen. But Brethren have often done this: when they came to an Indian town, they went to the Chief's house—that is the place for everyone who has something to say to go—the Chief called together the Indians without knowing what they would hear and, when they were gathered, the Brother preached a sermon which the Lord accompanied with blessing, without danger and attracting attention. The Indians would then meditate upon what they had heard."

A mission among the Cherokees was considered, also, by Dartmouth College* about the year 1799. The Conference in Salem had a copy of a letter from Captain Edward Buttler, written July, 1799, from Tuskegee† to "The Little Turkey," Principal Chief of the Cherokee Nation, in part, as follows:

"Friend and Brother. A number of good men from the eastward have formed a plan to have a number of your young men taught our language and to read and write without putting them to any expense.

"Indeed, they wish to have an opportunity of doing it amongst yourselves, that, in arriving to necessary information your young people may not entirely forget the simplicity of their own manners nor inculcate the depraved habits of bad white people.

"Their friendly disposition towards you has been communicated to me by a man sent especially for that purpose. Being a stranger, he has requested me to secure of you your opinion, and that of the Nation generally, respecting the business, and to write him what you will answer me on this subject.

"For my part, I cannot help but believe that the Great Spirit has directed them to offer you this humane service, and I cannot help recommending to you to think seriously of it and write me all the minds of the head men."

The good offices of the Rev. Wheelock for the Cherokees did not materialize. However, this school did train many valuable native Indian missionaries, notably Occam and Kirkland, who achieved permanent results among the Six Nations.

The annual meeting of the Society for Propagating the Gospel Among the Heathen, held in Bethlehem, Pa., in August, 1799, recorded in its minutes an item which was transmitted to the members of the Society in Salem and there aroused great interest. The Rev. Joseph Bullen, from Vermont, had been sent

---

* Dartmouth College originated in Moor's Indian Charity School for the teaching of the Indian youth. Organized about 1750 at Lebanon, Conn., by the Rev. Eleazar Wheelock, Puritan Clergyman, and endowed, at first, by Joshua Moor. This school was soon enlarged so that both whites and Indians might be taught, was further endowed and placed upon a legal and permanent basis in 1769 by Charter from King George III and named in honor of the Earl of Dartmouth, a liberal patron.

† Now in Macon County, Ala.

on a missionary journey to the Chickasaw Indians by the New York Missionary Society in March of that year. He wrote under date of April 24, 1799, from Knoxville, Tenn., being on his return journey. "That the Cherokees who reside in the vicinity of Tennessee are desirous of having missionaries among them."

This portion of Rev. Bullen's printed report to his Society, when it reached the Brethren in Salem had an immediate effect on them in kindling the old-time interest in a mission among the Cherokees. On October 17, 1799, came the annual meeting of the Salem branch of the S. P. G., at which several members expressed their warm disapproval, because there was business of no more importance than some questions relating to the Society's land on the Muskingum River. Speeches were made to the effect that Salem had Indian tribes nearer, yet no attempt had been made from Wachovia to bring the Gospel. Among those who expressed themselves in this manner, Brother Abraham Steiner*

---

* The Rev. Abraham Steiner was born in Bethlehem, Pa., 1758, and educated in Nazareth, Pa. After he had attained his majority, he went to Bethlehem and was employed for some time as teacher in the Boys' Day School. Next, he was called to Hope, N. J., to take charge of the Church store for several years. From childhood Brother Steiner had been greatly interested in the Indians and it was a great joy to him to be allowed to accompany the Rev. John Heckewelder, Moravian missionary to the Indians, on a missionary tour along the Muskingum in 1789. After this, Brother Steiner was called to Bethabara, N. C., to take charge of the Church store there. In Salem he married his first wife, Christina Fisher, who died after a short married life of 16 months. Steiner's second wife, Catherine Sehner, was also of Salem. In 1798, Bro. Steiner felt a great desire to serve the Indian mission on the Muskingum, but the lot did not give approbation for this. In 1799 he was deputed to make the first visitation among the Cherokees and later went out again to begin the mission. His health was in very precarious state in the Cherokee country, due to repeated attacks of fever. Finally, he was compelled to leave this work, so dear to his heart, in other hands.

He was ordained a Deacon of the Moravian Church in 1801 and took charge of the congregation of Hope, N. C. From here he was called to be Principal of Salem Academy, which position he filled with great ability for 10 years. Declining health made him resign his position in 1816, but he still assisted in the work. In 1822 he took up the work of the Negro congregation of Salem. He was continually active in Church and community until his life drew to a close in 1833, when he passed away at the age of 75 years. He lies buried in Salem Graveyard.

was particularly insistent. He was told in the meeting that there must be some cause for going and to wait for an opening. Steiner answered this by saying that the Lord's command, "Go ye into all the world," etc., did not have the extra clause, "if they call you." The Rev. Bullen's statement about the Cherokees was read in the meeting. This had, as Steiner writes, the effect of an electric spark upon the Brethren assembled, going through many at one and the same time. More earnest talks followed with the purport that the Moravians had not done the duty for which originally they had settled in these parts, and that now an effort should be made to work among the Cherokees under such favorable circumstances.

The upshot of the meeting was a recommendation to the Helpers' Conference to consider the matter and to act. The Conference met and called to mind the incidents of Martin Schneider's visit sixteen years previous; the fact, also, that several Moravian families now lived in the Cumberland settlements in Tennessee, not far removed from the Cherokee country, and these should be visited. After thorough discussion, it was resolved that the best and only way to obtain more information was to send one of the Brethren on a reconnoitering journey across the mountains into the neighborhood around Knoxville, Tenn. Then the Brethren, according to their custom, having deliberated as best they knew how, laid the matter before their dear Lord in the lot and received His approval for the proposed journey. Available Brethren for this business were likewise put before Him in the lot but none had the approbation until someone suggested to place before the Lord the Brother who had spoken most warmly in the meeting. Accordingly, Abraham Steiner was proposed and the lot answered in the affirmative. Christian Frederic de Schweinitz, of Salem, volunteered to accompany him.

At this time, 1799, the situation of the Cherokee Nation was this: only a few years ago, the Cherokees had been at war with the United States along the frontiers, especially around the Carolina territory in the section which North Carolina, under the name of Southwest Territory, ceded to the United States. (Now the State of Tennessee.) Everything was upset with the Indians, until by formal treaty, made first at the place where Knoxville now stands and ratified two years later at Tellico, a military station on the Tennessee River, all hostilities were laid down and boundaries were fixed. The United States adopted the Cherokee Nation; appointed an Agent among them; started a factory at Tellico and did many other things for their civilization. In 1787, Col. Benjamin Hawkins came through Salem. He was special Government Agent for the Creeks and had the oversight of Agents of Government among other southern Indian tribes. He was on his way to the frontiers as one of the Commissioners to measure and designate the boundary lines of the Cherokees, Creeks, etc., and had a chart of that region with him which he permitted to be copied in Salem for use in missionary enterprises.

It was a memorable service, held in the Salem church on the night of October 28, 1799, in which the two Brethren designated for the missionary journey were solemnly set apart for this service before the congregation and the blessing of God was invoked upon them! As in Apostolic days, when "the Holy Ghost said, Separate me Barnabas and Saul for the work whereunto I have called them,"* those of Antioch prayed and laid their hands on them, so did the Brethren in Salem bless their deputies to the southern Indians and sent them away.

The journey was begun early the following morning on horseback. Several Brethren accompanied Steiner and de Schweinitz as far as Bethania and there bade them an affectionate farewell. The missionaries carried the following paper by way of credentials:

"Salem, N. C., Oct. 28, 1799.

"To David Henley, Esq., at Knoxville,
"Supt. of Indian Affairs.

"Sir: Supposing that you are not unacquainted that the United Brethren, otherwise called Moravians, have a mission among the Delaware and Mohican Indian Nations in the Northern States, which has been of happy effects, both for their civilization and to render them Christians, for which they are respected in that whole country. I take the liberty to address you upon a similar occasion.

"Sixteen years ago, one of our ministers, the Rev. Martin Schneider made a visit from hence to the Cherokee Indians living at Chota and the neighboring towns, who signified a desire that he should

---

* Acts 13:2.

come and live among them, but the war which since broke out prevented its taking place.

"Some accounts lately received mentioning their having still a desire to be instructed and that somebody might come to live among them, the bearers of this, Abraham Steiner, Esq., and Frederic de Schweinitz, Esq., going to Tennessee and perhaps further to Cumberland, will be glad to see some of them or to go to their towns, to be more particularly informed of their mind.

"The importance to this whole country of the Indians being brought to a true knowledge of Religion, whereof civilization is a necessary consequence, seemeth to be particularly noticed by the Government of the United States, and that the endeavor of the United Brethren have met with the approbation of the different legislatures is sufficiently evidenced by the Acts of Incorporation passed in the States of Pennsylvania and New Jersey, in favor of their Society for Propagating the Gospel among the Heathen.

"The bearers of this, members of said Society, not doubting your best wishes for the matter, will make free to apply to you for advice and protection and I beg leave to recommend them to you for that purpose.

"I am, very respectfully, Sir,

"Your obedient, humble Servant,

"F. W. Marshall."

The Brethren arrived in Knoxville, Nov. 6, after a journey particularly hard on the horses. On the next day they intended paying their respects to Col. Henley. They had spoken to people on the way of Christ but found those along the road too much occupied with temporal concerns. (The old difficulty the sower experienced with the seed which fell by the wayside!) De Schweinitz likewise wrote to Marshall—his grandfather—of his experiences. He had much trouble with his horse which stumbled often, even on good road, and threw him. The horse has no virtue except a good appetite! Fine weather attended the Brethren all the way from Salem and both were in excellent health. As yet they had seen no Indians. "Col. Henley," both wrote, "has a good name all through this section of the country."

The next news from the travelers came on Nov. 19, and was written from Tellico Blockhouse. Col. Henley had received them with great kindness; had given them a pass through the Cherokee Nation; written a letter of recommendation to Captain Buttler, commanding officer at Tellico, also, one to Major Lewis, another Agent of the Cherokees. At Tellico, they were received most kindly by Captain Buttler who made their stay with him exceedingly pleasant. But, alas, they found they had come their long journey to their destination about three weeks too late! Three weeks before there had been about four thousand Cherokees at Tellico to receive their annual presents, (which had not yet taken on the form of an annuity). Now all the men were on their hunt and would not return until the end of winter.

Much disappointed, Steiner and de Schweinitz, nevertheless, resolved to "spy out the land." They made a considerable tour in the Cherokee country, over one hundred miles in the circuit, visiting the towns Toka and Chota and got along famously except that they had no interpreter and had to use signs exclusively. Everywhere they were well received and remarked on the good order kept among the Indians by the Government—no disorderly conduct and no strong drink imported! Also, they found the Cherokees instructed in spinning and weaving and learning other useful arts. However, they were unacquainted with Religion and both missionaries felt that the Moravians had come to a time like this for their evangelization.

One Indian Chief, (Kulsatahi,) entertained them for supper and then accompanied them to a trader, there through interpretation, to learn the exact purpose of their visit. After Steiner had rehearsed their errand and his words had been interpreted, Kulsatahi expressed himself that he was glad the Great Spirit had prevented him from going on the hunt up till now so that he could hear these words. He would tell them to all he met while hunting. He was sure their old Chief, Little Turkey, would be very well satisfied if Brethren would settle among them.

Before their departure, Captain Buttler desired Steiner and de Schweinitz to express their mission in writing and was handed the following paper, under date of Nov. 19, 1799:

"The undersigned, members of the Society of the United Brethren for Propagating the Gospel among the Heathen, having been sent by the Directors of said Society into this country to enquire into the present state and circumstances of the Cherokee Nation; and,

"WHEREAS the said Society hath got advice by their friends, the Missionary Society in New York that the Rev. Mr. Bullen, whom they had forwarded into the Chickasaw country, in a letter to his Society expresses himself thus:

" 'That the Cherokees who reside in the vicinity of Tennessee are desirous of having missionaries among them,' and

"WHEREAS, the Society of the United Brethren is desirous that the Gospel of the grace of God might be propagated among all the heathen nations and particularly among the Cherokees, but have as yet been quite unconnected with the Cherokees and ignorant of their present situation, as to their manners, customs, state of civilization and their relation with the Government of the United States, etc., the Directors of said Society have thought proper to send the undersigned to inquire into all the above matters and, more especially, to see what can be done among the Cherokees in preaching the Gospel and, at the same time, in teaching their children to read and write and to turn their education, by the grace of God, into a moral and Christian life. Whether the said Directors shall think proper actually to send missionaries among them, or how soon, the undersigned cannot say, and it will probably depend on circumstances, but the undersigned pledge themselves, should such missionaries be sent, that they will always cheerfully conform to the Rules and Laws of Government as good and peaceable citizens ought to do.

"In the meantime, the said Society of the United Brethren will take it as a favor and be particularly thankful to Captain Buttler if he will condescend, from time to time, as he thinks proper, to communicate to them what he finds proper touching said subjects and about the desire of the Indians to be instructed in Christianity as likewise of their next meeting at Tellico or other grand meeting.

"The undersigned beg leave to take this opportunity to give their warmest thanks and acknowledgments to Mrs. Buttler and Captain Buttler for the kind reception and particular attention paid to them, which they are not able to reciprocate but by praying God to pour His blessings upon them and their family.

"With great respect, we are Sir,

"Your very humble Servants,

"A. Steiner,
"Fr. de Schweinitz."

This rather unfruitful visit among the Cherokees, due to the absence of the Chiefs did not deter the Salem Society and the Brethren who had made the tour from pursuing their object. In the spring of 1800 we find Steiner in charge of the Bethabara store, temporarily, from which place he writes to Col. David Henley at Knoxville asking whether the Cherokees are at peace with the neighboring Nations? Whether they would be likely to consent for several missionaries to live among them to preach the Gospel and instruct their children? Would they be apt to disturb preaching by force? Would the sending of missionaries be agreeable to the wishes of the officers of the Government in charge of Indian affairs? Would a piece of ground for cultivation be assigned such missionaries? Must the consent of the Chiefs of the Nation be obtained for the residence of missionaries among them or is the consent of the Agent sufficient? Steiner's letter closes with the following paragraph:

"The happiness of the poor Indian is a weighty matter to our Society and the establishment of a mission among them to teach them the Way of Salvation is seriously thought of. With that view, Sir, the above questions are made to you and permit me to confide in your goodness that you will answer them and add what other information it may be in your power to give concerning Indian affairs."

Brother Steiner directed a similar letter to Captain Buttler[*] at Tellico. To both Col. Henley and Captain Buttler, he transmitted, at the direction of the Society in Salem, copies of the history of the missions of the Brethren among the northern Indian tribes. Captain Buttler evidently read his copy carefully, referring to it in his "Talk" to the Principal Chiefs which will be found farther on.

Col. Henley replied, April 23, 1800, in a very friendly and encouraging letter, to Brother Steiner's series of questions which we have noted. The following extracts are important:

"The Indians do not appear to be in perfect peace and the Cherokees threaten war against the Chickasaws respecting the right to the Muscle Shoals, which, I believe, the four southern Nations claim each as their exclusive property.

"I do believe the Cherokees would consent to one or more missionaries among them and would be glad to have their children instruct-

---

[*] Captain Buttler, who showed the Brethren every kindness, considered himself under obligation to the Moravians as indicated in the following extract of a letter to Steiner:

"I promise, should you proceed with the contemplated mission and we tarry in the neighborhood, we will try, at least, to pay the interest of the debt of gratitude I owe the Brethren of Salem for assisting me when I was sick, poor, and a stranger among them."

Also, Brother John Heckewelder, Moravian missionary among the Delawares, had one of the children of Captain Buttler and a child of Col. Thos. Buttler, of Southwest Point, with him for education and training, when he left for the new settlement of Moravian Christian Indians on the Muskingum, middle of the year 1800. Little Caroline, Captain Buttler's daughter, is much attached to Heckewelder and has written her father for a Cherokee pipe to present to him.

ed in Reading, Writing, etc., and I have no doubt they might, after that, be brought to like the preaching of the Gospel, and that the teachers would be undisturbed.

"The sending of the missionaries would, I have no doubt, be agreeable to the officers of Government in this District.

"I also am of the opinion that they would live in peace and that a piece of ground would be allotted them for cultivation, the situation and distance made convenient.

"I am of the opinion that the Chiefs should be consulted because, whatever is their own act, like other people, they would be most likely to be satisfied, or in any disappointment, more patient with.

"To seek the happiness of the savage nation is certainly humane and laudable, more so, because in such an undertaking those that persevere therein are not to look so much for the praise of men as for the approbation of the Supreme Being and an approving mind."

In sending copies of his letters to Col. Henley and Captain Buttler and the reply received from Henley, to Christian Lewis Benzien* in Salem, Brother Steiner makes some interesting comments on paragraphs quoted above. The fact that the Cherokees threaten war on the Chickasaws does not seem very alarming to him as the Muscle Shoals lie about 300 miles southwest of Tellico. He feels, also, that the respective Indian Agents will not permit this dispute to result in actual warfare. However, it would be well not to go too far south or west in settling for the mission.

The point which Henley makes, that the instruction of the children should come first and "they might, after that, be brought to like the preaching of the Gospel," brings this illuminating remark from Steiner:

"We should not think hard of people nor argue with them over the notion that heathen nations can grasp the conception of the Gospel only after they have learned to read and write. If the Saviour commands us something, we should do it in simplicity, with the grace, insight and experience which he has given us."

Steiner agrees with Col. Henley that the consent of the Chiefs must be secured, and, also, the approval of the Agent. They may preach anywhere without asking for permission but no one can dwell in any locality without the consent of those in authority. As to the selection of a site for the proposed mission, Steiner is uncertain whether this consideration is to be left to the

---

* Successor to F. W. de Marshall as Administrator of Wachovia.

direct leading of the Lord* or whether it is to be picked out "by good judgment." In the latter event, someone should soon be sent to view the country.

Captain Buttler's reply to Steiner's letter of inquiry—a duplicate of the one sent Col. Henley—is dated May 11, 1800, from Tellico, and is attached to a copy of a "Talk" given by Buttler to the Principal Chiefs of the Cherokee Nation which is here given first before noting some comments of Captain Buttler:

"Talk from Captain Edward Buttler, Commandant at Tellico, to the Principal Chiefs of the Cherokee Nation, delivered to 'Little Turkey' and 'Bloody Fellow' at Tellico, 9th of May, 1800."

"Friends and Brothers, I am happy to see you, my friends, Little Turkey, Principal Chief of the Cherokee Nation, and you, my friend, the Bloody Fellow, whom I know to be a principal man in your

---

* Upon the promise of Christ, Mark 11:24, and the practice of the Apostles, Acts 1:23-26, in selecting one witness of Christ to be numbered with the eleven, in the place of Judas, the use of the lot in the Moravian Church was founded. This institution, in its correct use, was never allowed to displace careful consideration and the use of good common sense and sound judgment in deciding any question of Church government or problem of individuals. The guidance of God through His Holy Word, His Holy Spirit, His general and particular Providence was to the Brethren pre-eminent and the lot never ran counter to these great sources of guidance. Nevertheless, there were cases when, after the best deliberation, the Brethren felt convinced of the insufficiency of their own insight and, therefore, they referred the matter directly to the Saviour through the lot, using slips with "yes" or "no" or other words, or sentences stating the affirmative or negative of the matter in question, these usually accompanied by a blank. Requisites for the legitimate use of the lot were prayer, childlike faith that the Lord would thus express His direction, and cheerful and implicit obedience to the result.

"We regard the lot with thankfulness, as a means granted to us for the time, by the Lord, for learning His mind, and acting under His direction, when He does not give us to know His will in any other way. Should filial confidence in this special guidance of our Lord become more and more weakened among us, it would be time to lay aside a usage, which must be devoid of blessing, as soon as it ceases to be grounded on the innermost conviction of the heart." (Results of General Synod, 1857, Par. 41.)

Through the years, the use of the lot, at first very general, as illustrated in the inception of the Cherokee mission, became more and more restricted and was at last used only in the selection of Bishops and, finally, abolished many years ago.

4

Nation. I am sincerely glad to see you both as friends whom I have long known and respected. You know I have always received you both as friends, and have still endeavored to assist and accommodate you in your little wants, as well as in giving you my opinion on your great National concerns whenever you asked me. I thank you for the confidence you have put in me by calling for my friendly advice in sundry instances. Having now the pleasure to see you in my quarters which I purposely built large for the reception of my friends, I have a serious business to communicate to you, and which, I hope, will greatly tend to the civilization and well-doing of your people; and I now call on you, as old and experienced men, who, I know, wish well to your children, the Cherokees, to hear favorably what I have to offer and to communicate the good tidings to your Grand Council so soon as it convenes and after having their explicit answer to everything I shall propose, that you will write me a full account of the same, in order that I have it in my power to put the good work in train, through the Commanding Officer, in Tennessee, as quickly as possible.

"Friends and Brothers, I have received a letter from a number of good men who wish to know if the Cherokees would receive one or more of them, favorably, into the Nation, to teach the young people to read and write, to be industrious in farming, etc., and above all, to teach both young and old, to know the goodness of the Great Spirit, and what He can do for them if they will follow the straight path which He will tell His servants to point out to them all. I have received a large book from these good people which has told me of much good they have done amongst your Red Brethren in the North. Indeed, I have been a witness to much of their good deeds myself and, therefore, believe you ought to be very glad to receive them among you. They wish to come and live at some distance from any town where those who come to have their instruction and hear their good talks may not be interrupted by great numbers of your people who might not wish to follow their sober, beneficient and plain manners.

"They wish to know if you will grant them a sufficient piece of ground to cultivate, in order that they may, occasionally, work thereon, raise food for themselves, and to assist the needy, and in doing of which they will set a pattern of industry to your young people. They must have the promise of perfect protection to themselves. You are to understand that they will come to live by their industry; therefore, they will have no presents to make to your people. They will come to do you service, by educating your children, by telling you good tidings from the Great Spirit, by setting your people an example of honesty, sobriety, and brotherly love. I am not disappointing you when I tell you these things of those people because I known them and know that you will thank me ere long for having even a small share in bringing them to you. And I now advise that you. Little Turkey, you Bloody Fellow, my brothers, The Glass, Doublehead, Dick Justice, etc., be the first to encourage these people coming amongst you and that each of you send a son to them as soon as they arrive and are fixed to receive them. My friend, The Little Turkey, is very old and he has been so much employed in doing public business that I fear his circumstances are not very good. I, therefore, promise while I stay in this country, to assist his son all in my power.

"Friends and Brothers, I will thank you to be particular on every subject I have mentioned to you that I may not deceive my good friends who have employed me to speak to you. The good men from the east (Dartmouth) who formerly offered you their assistance, which you agreed to receive, may probably continue in the desire to assist you. I do not think your receiving these good men I have now told you of ought to form any objection to receive both as they will all labor for your good.

"I am your sincere friend and Brother,

"Edward Buttler."

"Note: You may expect that any persons who may come to settle amongst you for the purpose above mentioned, will come with the knowledge and approbation of the President, your father, and will be amenable to the Laws and his orders."

This "Talk" all through reveals the man whose heart is in sympathy with the undertaking of the Brethren; a man who is interested and highminded as to the temporal and eternal welfare of his Indian charges. The "Talk" shows he has modified some of Steiner's queries but only to gain a more favorable ear for the whole project as his experience in dealing with the Cherokees would teach.

Captain Buttler writes Steiner, on the same sheet with the "Talk," that it was well received by the two Chiefs, who acquiesced in the desires of the Brethren and faithfully promised to lay the business before the General Council, strengthening Buttler's points with all their rhetoric. They promised to report the reception the plan would receive and did not hesitate to say beforehand that it would be favorable. Major Lewis, the Agent, told Buttler the Brethren might count on his exertions in their behalf as did also Col. Buttler of Southwest Point. The good Captain finally advises the Brethren of Salem to apply to the Secretary of War for the President's approbation and permission for their undertaking. This would probably be answered by the President's orders to the Commanding Officer in Tennes-

see—Captain Buttler—in which case he would be under orders
to render every possible assistance which, already, it is in his
heart to give, and which his own wishes would dictate.

Correspondence between Steiner and Buttler was kept up during the summer of 1800, the latter advising that the Brethren
who came on the first visit, a year ago, should by all means be on
hand when the next annuity would be distributed at Tellico in
September. The Helpers' Conference considered another visit
to the Cherokees and the proposition received the affirmative
through the lot.

Thus Steiner and Frederic de Schweinitz again set out, arriving in Knoxville on September 3. Brother Steiner had repeated
attacks of malarial fever on the journey and was obliged to keep
his bed for several days after arriving in Knoxville. September
7th, the missionaries went on to Southwest Point, whither Captain Buttler had gone on business, and here they met both him
and Col. Thomas Buttler. Together, they journeyed to Tellico
where Agent Major Lewis received the Brethren very kindly and
said they had come at the right time as he had called the Chiefs
to gather for a Council in a few days. While they were waiting,
Major Lewis rode about with Steiner and de Schweinitz viewing
sites for a settlement. He advised them to locate among the
Upper Cherokees as the lands of the Lower were very unhealthful for white people; fever appearing among white settlers already early in the spring. Among the Lower Cherokees, also,
were more half-breeds, more whiskey and more disorder!

The Chiefs began to arrive on the 18th—Doublehead, Little
Turkey, Glass, Bloody Fellow, Boot, etc., and on the 23rd the
Council was held. Dick Fields was interpreter. The meeting-
place was one mile below Tellico across the Tennessee River.
About thirty Chiefs were present and the Council "sat" in the
form of a square, on fence rails, under the open sky. The
Brethren's business was taken up first. Doublehead asked to
know their errand and by whose authority they had been sent.
Steiner answered that they had been sent by their Society and
with the consent of the Government—which Major Lewis affirmed—and that their object was to speak with them about the
Great Spirit, to instruct them in the Word of God, and then to
teach them and their children Reading, Writing, and useful arts.

Finally, Steiner requested to know if they would permit missionaries to live among them on a plot of ground assigned them by the Nation for this purpose and where such Indians also might live who, after the example of the Delaware, would accept the Word of God and desire to live thereby.

In their answer, the Chiefs said nothing about the Word of God—naturally—but wanted to know whether the Society which sent them would board and clothe the children sent to school. Steiner said: "No! we will instruct them gratis, but no board and clothes!" Said the Chiefs: "Go home, ascertain the mind of the Society about this, and come back." Steiner pointed out that it was not necessary to do this for they knew the "mind of the Society" perfectly well, and, to as many Nations as the Society had gone, this had never been expected of them; the Society could and would not do it! Finally, after much palaver, Steiner asked whether, if he and another Brother would come next year, they would allow them to settle among them and make a trial according to their principle. Doublehead said, "You are welcome, make a trial." To this, all agreed.

On the 24th, when the Brethren and a Mr. Carey were ready to set out to look over locations, they were told that another Council was being held, probably to determine where they should settle. Steiner went to the meeting and told the Chiefs they were about to cross the river to look for a place and asked had they anything further to say? The Chiefs said they should not go across the river and their father, the President of the United States had forbidden them to receive whites among them. Steiner said he had the permission of the President* and also a pass from the Agent, whereupon the Chiefs answered that they prohibited their going. After much confused talking, Bloody Fellow began again to talk about board and clothes for the children!

---

* This was true. Although Steiner had no direct paper from the President, Congress, already in 1785, had passed an Act in favor of the Society for Propagating the Gospel Among the Heathen in reserving the sites in Ohio, where flourishing missions of the Brethren among the Indians had been destroyed, for the benefit of the Christian Indians and their children forever. Also, by 1788, the Society had been incorporated in the State of Pennsylvania. Steiner therefore, as a deputy of the Society which had the recognition of Federal and State Government, was correct in this statement.

In vain, Steiner reminded them of yesterday's decision that they might come and live among them; the Chiefs averred that must be a misunderstanding! Even Steiner lost his calmness at this and said if they could not get clear on this point they would go home! With all serenity the Indians replied, "All right, no damage has been done." Agent Lewis advised waiting for a few days, because, as so often the case, the minds of the Indians might change completely within a short time. So the Brethren composed themselves with the best grace they could and commended themselves and the whole matter to the Lord. To be obliged to stay at this place, where the cost of living was high, at the expense of the Society worried them not a little. De Schweinitz drew portraits of several Chiefs and soon everyone wished to have a sketch made of himself! Steiner asked Doublehead when the Brethren might talk to the Chiefs again and he said that in two nights they would be willing to listen to them once more. Col. Buttler, at Southwest Point, to whom Steiner had written of their predicament, wrote sympathetically:

"I assure you that I am disappointed in finding the Cherokees so indifferent as to the future welfare of their children and Nation. The idea of your being obliged to feed and clothe the children is out of the question. I assure you I am quite at a loss how to advise."

At the same time, he cautioned the missionaries not to attempt a settlement without the full approbation of the Chiefs.

Came another Council, September 30. Col. Henley who had arrived at Tellico and Major Lewis had long conferences with the Chiefs. At the close of their discussion, Henley said, "Now I have another matter to talk over with you," and spoke of the Brethren's mission. He told them much of the Society's work among northern Indians; but the Chiefs brought out continual objections and excuses. Col. Henley continued: "I earnestly advise you, as an honest man as you know me and know I would never advise you but for your best, receive these people among you. You will not soon again have such offers for your best welfare."

Doublehead answered, "There is no hurry, let us wait until the other Chiefs are here."

At this point, Charles Hicks, a half-breed, who was Interpreter at this meeting, asked Steiner to tell him the connection of the whole matter and Steiner carefully explained that the Brethren's main object was to preach the Gospel to the Cherokee Nation.

"If that is the case," said Hicks. "I will help you all I can."

Hicks lived in Oostanaula among the Upper Cherokees. At supper he said, "If the Lower Towns will not take these people, we 'pipemakers' will receive them."

Steiner replied that he would as lief go to the "pipe-makers" and "frog-eaters" as to the others. (These nick-names were given by the Lower Cherokees to the Upper because the Upper Cherokees made long clay pipes and were said not to be averse to eating frogs.)

During the time of these parleys, the Brethren also met with another encouragement. A man named James Vann asked whether the main object of their coming was to teach Religion.

"Yes," said Steiner.

"Then come to me in my section among the Upper Cherokees." Vann invited, "you can accomplish more among them than in the Lower Towns."

At last on October 6, after the annuity had been distributed, the last Council was held and the Brethren were invited to sit with the Chiefs. Again, Lewis laid the matter of the mission before them. Chief "Gentleman Tom" was speaker for the Upper Cherokees; Doublehead, the spokesman of the Lower. Gentleman Tom addressed Little Turkey as follows:

"From what has been said respecting the missionaries of the Moravians, we consider their intention as laudable. Let them come and make the trial; we hope it will prove beneficial. We ask our beloved man, Little Turkey, his sentiments on the occasion."

Answered by Doublehead for Little Turkey:

"Respecting those missionaries, it has been nearly twelve months since they paid us the first visit. Now I address myself to the Chiefs of my Nation. I hope it will be well understood. I have already mentioned these gentlemen have been here some time. Their desire appears to be good, to instruct us and our children and improve our and their minds and Nation. These gentlemen, I hope, will make the experiment; we will be the judge from their conduct and their attention to us and our children, this will enable us to judge properly. Should they not comply as now stated, the Agent will be the judge for the Red people.

"We advise them to live at Mr. McDonald's and, that both Upper and Lower may have the benefit, we think it best if one goes to Mr. McDonald's; the other, to James Vann."

Steiner thanked them heartily and said the Society had not, as yet, empowered them to accept a location. Hereupon, all the Upper Chiefs came and shook hands with both Brethren as a token of friendship and the sign of reception into their country. The Lower Chiefs remained seated and our missionaries had to go to them to shake hands. After another address by Little Turkey, the Council came to an end. Doublehead came up to Steiner and demanded a bottle of whiskey because he helped get the proposition through Council. (It is not said that Steiner complied with the request.)

Bloody Fellow said, "All this talk and trouble could have been saved if you had had a paper from the President."

Steiner and de Schweinitz now determined, as the Chiefs were breaking up to return to their homes, to accompany one or the other into their country to become better acquainted in the land. James Vann was very willing for them to go with him and waited for them to have their horses shod, etc. Although Vann was a wild and dissipated man, he showed the missionaries every kindness and charged them nothing. At his place in the Upper Cherokee country they stayed several days. Vann took them to Oostananala, on the Chickamauga, and other places where they explored the territory and made notes about suitable localities; then the Brethren went back alone to Tellico on October 19. The end of the month found them safely in Salem to the great joy of their loved ones and of the congregation which had sent them forth.

The following extracts, commenting on locations for a mission settlement they looked over, are taken from their report:

1. **James Vann's place.** About 80 miles form Tellico, not far from the Connesauga River, a branch of the Coosa. This place lies on the trail between South Carolina and Georgia and is counted in with Oostananala, which belongs to the Upper Towns. The Connesauga River is the boundary between the Upper and Lower Cherokees. Here in this locality lives James Vann, a half-breed with two wives, very dissipated and drunken, yet kind and hospitable. He is a trader going often to Charleston and Augusta; is wealthy, has much land, cattle and many negro slaves. The soil is good; there is much limestone and many fine springs. The woods abound with Oak, Hickory, Chestnut and Pine trees. Two miles south of James Vann's is a large plantation occupied by a Mr. Brown who wishes to move away. Vann thinks he could buy Brown's improvements for about

820. Indian Towns near are: Sumach Town, 7 miles; Rabbit Trap, 15 miles; Coosawattee, 17 miles; Oostanaula, 15 miles.

Steiner objects to this plantation near Vann's because it lies too near the road and they would be troubled by traveling Indians who would help themselves to what was in the fields. There is too much whiskey in the neighborhood and immorality and drinking around Vann's. Also, the Indians in this section are very much scattered, living on large plantations.

2. Mr. McDonald's place at Chickamauga is 100 miles southwest of Tellico and 13 to 15 miles south of the Tennessee River. McDonald is a white man with an Indian wife and a large family; is wealthy and influential with the Lower Cherokees. The land is good.

Steiner's objections: The missionaries should locate on no man's property but should be independent. This section is not healthful, the Agent Lewis having contracted fever thrice in one season. McDonald does not seem very anxious to have them near. Major Lewis advises, also, that this place is too far removed from the frontier. He thinks the missionaries should not be too far from Tellico.

3. A section not far from the Hiwassee River, located 40 miles south of Tellico, 40 miles north of James Vann, 60 miles east of Chickamauga and 5 miles west of a long chain of mountains in which are nestled the Valley Towns of the Cherokees. Steiner and de Schweinitz were much impressed with this section, a high and seemingly healthful country. Good water and real good soil. Mr. Burgess, who lives here, a nice man, acquainted in Salem. He is a great enemy of Tom Paine's writings.

What commends this locality to Steiner is the fact that it lies about equidistant from Upper and Lower Cherokees. Also, the whites and half-breeds seem to be better and Burgess would like to have the mission near. There is easier correspondence with Salem because only one stream, the Tennessee, need be crossed, while from Vann's there are several. Already a year ago Steiner and de Schweinitz had viewed this location and were drawn to it.

4. A place hard by the main trail, somewhat nearer Tellico and four or five miles north of Mr. Burgess' improvements. A splendid spring there, good land and a better site for a building. Steiner would choose this if a congregation already existed; now there were two strong objections: it was too near the main highway and too far from the Indians.

The Helpers' Conference in Salem met on November 17, and the report of the two deputies was thoroughly gone over. The plans above mentioned were carefully considered and Steiner's statements about each, pro and con, were duly weighed. The location at the Hiwassee River which Steiner particularly recommended did not receive the approbation of the Lord and when the Conference, in full assurance of faith, submitted the next question, whether the place should be definitely fixed after the Brethren had arrived in the Cherokee country, they received instruction that the place should be decided on before. Thus each of the situations in the report was laid before the Lord and the lot affirmed that in the neighborhood of James Vann a beginning of a mission among the Cherokees should be made, and the Text for the day was especially suggestive and comforting to Conference: "I will instruct thee and teach thee in the way which thou shalt go; I will guide thee with mine eye."*

The Indians being desirous that the consent which they had given might be confirmed by the President of the United States, applications were accordingly made to him as follows, dated:

"Salem, in North Carolina, 18th Nov., 1800.

"Samuel Dexter, Esq., Secretary of War.

"Honored Sir, The undersigned beg leave to lay before your Honor a matter which is to them of importance and which, in their humble opinion, may become so to the public.

"Probably your Honor is not unacquainted that the Church of the United Brethren in America has missions among the Indians, and that Congress has granted to their 'Society for Propagating the Gospel Among the Heathen,' working among the Indians, the tracts where the three towns lay which their Indians formerly inhabited and now are settled again by an Act, entitled: 'An Act regulating the Grants of Land appropriated to military service and for the Society of the United Brethren for Propagating the Gospel among the Heathen.' Also, that the States of Pennsylvania and the Jerseys have, by Acts of Assembly, incorporated the said Society.

"From the first arrival of said Brethren in North Carolina, the conversion of the Cherokees was one of the chief reasons for their settling there, the execution whereof was, however, delayed by the wars and similar obstructions that happened since, until last year, as well as this, they deputed two of their members, who, under favor of Mr. Henley, Agent of the War Department, and Mr. Lewis, Agent of Indian Affairs, informed themselves concerning the mind of the said Indians, at their great meeting near Tellico, when in Council their Chiefs consented to their living among them if properly authorized—as they express it—by their Father—meaning the President of the United States—with his seal to it.

---

*Psalm 32:8.

"Not doubting that the same has already been mentioned to Government, we make bold to beg of you, Sir, to procure the said Society leave to send, from time to time, persons upon such mission as may be wanting for it, whereto, for the present, we propose the Rev. Abraham Steiner, who would be willing to go with his family and such assistants as may be required to instruct them and their children in the principles of our Holy Religion as well as in useful arts, whereby it is hoped that their real happiness may be effected.

"The Government of the United States having already taken such ample measures for the civilization of these people and, we flatter ourselves, the endeavors of the said Society, for the improvement of the poor heathen will be correspondent to the same, we are the more encouraged to urge this matter which has been of anxious concern to us these many years.

"Not doubting that your Honor will view the premises in the same salutary light, we trust that you will recommend it to the President of the United States, on whose paternal care the Indians make so great dependence, to grant the sanction to the undertaking in the manner which they wish for. The Indians expecting our final determination concerning the place where a beginning may be made, we shall be much obliged to you for a favorable answer.

"Please to accept the assurances of our respect and best wishes as, Honored Sir,

"Your most obedient and humble servants,

"Frederick Wm. de Marshall,
"Christian Lewis Benzien, p.t.,
Directors of the Society for Propagating the
Gospel Among the Heathen."

To which came the following reply under date of December 9, 1800, from the War Department:

"Messrs. F. W. Marshall,

"Christian L. Benzein, Gentlemen, I have received your letter of the 18th ulto., and submitted it to the President of the United States. Under his direction I enclose a permission for the Rev. Mr. Steiner to reside among the Indian tribes for the purpose of diffusing a knowledge of Christianity as well as of the useful Arts.

"Wishing you success in your laudable undertaking, I remain, Gentlemen,

"Very respectfully, your most obedient servant,

"Samuel Dexter."

The document read as follows:

"To All to Whom These Presents Shall Come, Greeting:

"Frederick William Marshall and Christian Lewis Benzien, the present Directors of the 'Society of the United Brethren for Propagating the Gospel among the Heathen,' having represented to me that the Rev. Abraham Steiner is desirous of being permitted, under the direction of the said Society, to reside with his family among some of the Indian tribes within the United States, to instruct them and their children in the principles of Christianity as well as in useful Arts, and the President of the United States approving of the intentions of the said Society, as above cited:

"These are to enjoin on all Officers, Civil and Military and all other, the good citizens of the United States, to permit said Abraham Steiner to pass and repass on the objects of his mission; he, on his part, well and truly observing the Constitution and Laws of the United States and, particularly, the provisions of the Law entitled: 'An Act to Regulate Trade and Intercourse with the Indian Tribes.'

"Given under my hand and the Seal of the War Office of the United States, this, the 9th day of December, in the year of our Lord, One Thousand Eight Hundred, and of the Independence of the United States the Twenty-Fifth.

"Samuel Dexter, Secretary of War."

[SEAL]

Thus after years of waiting and months of special effort which often seemed worse than useless; after strenuous and fatiguing journeys amidst sickness and difficulty; after long interviews and consultations with Government officials and the Chiefs themselves, the Brethren received full consent of the Cherokee Council, in the presence of Officers of the United States, for their Society in Salem to send one or more missionaries to live among the Cherokees. The return journey seemed easier to Steiner and de Schweinitz because they were glad of heart; they were carrying careful reports showing the object of their journey accomplished; the way to the Cherokees was open for the Gospel.

CHAPTER VII

THE BEGINNING OF THE MISSION AMONG THE CHEROKEES,

OR

"THEY THAT SOW IN TEARS"

The year 1801 marks the reestablishment of the Moravian mission among southern Indian tribes of America which mission, as we have seen, was begun in 1735, disrupted in 1739, re-attempted in 1753 and re-agitated in 1784.

Abraham Steiner, whose heart was ever warm for the Indian, is to be considered the first missionary of the reestablished work, though his actual time of service in that field was not long.

The first problem confronting the Brethren in entering the newly opened door to the Cherokees was the finding of another missionary. In casting about for available men, the Conference deliberated over Gottlieb Byhan.* He was a young, unmarried Brother and "a good spirit was in him," also, he had proficiency in weaving and baking and some knowledge of music. His name was taken into the lot which affirmed that the call should be extended to him to serve the Lord with Steiner among the Cherokees. Byhan accepted the call with humility of heart, trusting in Divine grace, and was at once ready to go.

At eight o'clock on the night of April 12, 1801, an inspiring service was held in the Salem church at which all the members of the congregation who could possibly attend, were present, for the solemn sending forth of the Brethren Abraham Steiner

* Gottlieb Byhan was born at Herwigsdorf, near Herrnhut, Saxony, on August 4, 1777. His parents were Frederick Byhan and Elizabeth, m.n., Ay. He arrived at Salem in 1796. In 1801, he accompanied Bro. Abraham Steiner on a mission to the Cherokees and on Nov. 10, of that year was married to the Single Sister Dorothea Schneider at Salem. Their first term of service among the Cherokees was 1801-1812. Returned to Salem. Byhan served the congregation there, first as keeper of the Hotel and then as Warden of the Congregation. Their second term of service among the Cherokees was during the years 1827-1833. After this Byhan served as pastor at Bethabara and Friedland, N. C., successively, and in 1842, took charge of the colored congregation at Salem, which charge he served until declining health in 1853 compelled him to retire. He died Oct. 17, 1861, at Salem, aged 84 years.

and Gottlieb Byhan to the Indian country. Brother Benzien led the meeting. In his address, he stressed the fact that the Brethren and Sisters of this day were not the first to have a desire to preach the Gospel to the Cherokees, for 60 years ago the same desire had existed in the congregation, namely in 1740, when the sainted John Hagen had come to Georgia with a view to going into the Cherokee country. At that time, he could not carry out his desire. An epidemic of smallpox was raging which carried away about one-half the tribe. He ministered to the sick and dying and spoke the Gospel to as many as understood. There seemed little response, although the Cherokees believed the smallpox had come on account of their evil life.

Brother Benzien referred to the last visit of Steiner and de Schweinitz to the Nation, the approval of the Chiefs to live among them, and the permission for this from the President of the United States. He said, further, that he did not know whether the mission could be started at once but that the Brethren who had accepted the call should go and make ready by preparing a dwelling and planting the fields.

Next, in the service, came Byhan's reception as an Acolyte of the Moravian Church with prayer and the Right Hand of Fellowship, marking his entrance into this particular service of the Brethren's Church.

Both Brethren were admonished by Brother Benzien carefully to nurture their own spiritual life and to hold their united devotions daily. Steiner was charged particularly with the preaching the Gospel, wherever he found an opening, to both Indians and negroes on Vann's estate.

Whereupon all knelt in prayer and asked of the Lord the Spirit's anointing of the two Brethren and that He would be their guide and stay in all the labors and difficulties of the new undertaking. For the Cherokees, the petition was, that He, the Saviour of all men, might now let this be the time of visitation for this poor people; to save them from all bonds of the arch-enemy and receive them into His Kingdom of Grace, and to this end, to give them open ears and willing hearts to hear and receive the Gospel.

A hymn and the Old Testament benediction closed this service, after which the members of the Helpers' Conference, several Brethren in the service of the congregation and the two missionaries had another meeting, uniting themselves around the Cup of Covenant in the resolve ever to remain servants of the Lord and to carry on His work in spite of all difficulties and to remain united in deepest bonds of love. At the close, they gave one another the kiss of peace.

Accordingly, the Brethren Abraham Steiner and Gottlieb Byhan set out on horseback and with one pack horse April 15, 1801, "to prepare for the settlement of a mission, by planting some ground with provision and providing an habitation." Instructions were given them by Conference to begin their Diary at once. A letter of credit was given them to Mr. Hooker, in Tellico. They reached Tellico in safety and spent several days there. Major Lewis loaned them another pack horse and Captain Buttler gave them a pack-saddle and thus outfitted they left Tellico on April 28th with an Indian guide, reaching Vann's two days later. They found he had gone on a journey to the frontier of Georgia, and Brown, whose improvements Vann had promised to buy for them, had not yet moved.

The only thing to do was to stay at Vann's, awaiting developments. They learned that Vann had cultivated Brown's plantation himself, leaving one field for the missionaries. While waiting for Vann to return, Steiner contracted malaria and lay ill for several days, Byhan nursing him faithfully while much kindness was shown by the members of Vann's household. When he was better, both began to clear their field of stubble and stumps. They had left their plow in Tellico awaiting an opportunity to have it sent with other freight and thus could not begin the cultivation of their garden immediately.

On May 10, the first service in the Cherokee country was held for the blacks on Vann's plantation. A good company listened with great interest to Steiner's sermon on First John 4:9-10.

Vann returned May 11, and assured them they should have Brown's plantation, "Springplace,"* for the same amount he would have to pay for it. He generously insisted that they

---

*Springplace was built on the site of the present town of that name in Murray County, Ga.

should stay with him until Brown had gone, working meanwhile on their field of nine or ten acres, ground enough for their first season.

May 12. Little Turkey arrived with a letter from Captain Buttler who wrote that he had recommended the missionaries to the protection of Little Turkey and told him to speak a good word for them at the coming "Talk" to be held at Oostanaula. Steiner showed Little Turkey the pass from the Secretary of War and was invited to come to the "Talk" which would take place in six nights.

May 20, they had finished planting their field with corn. James Vann rendered them splendid assistance in this work, coming with six teams and many negroes, so that it was accomplished in a short time.

On that day Steiner left with Vann to attend the "Talk," going a distance of 18 miles to destination. The Talk was held in the Indian Town House of Oostanaula—an open shed with seats of plank—and when the proceedings were about to begin, an Indian stood by a high pole and beat on a drum for a long while until all the Indians had gathered and were seated, fanning themselves—great heat prevailed—with turkey wings. About seventy Chiefs of the Upper Cherokees were present. Charles Hicks was Interpreter.

After their other business had been attended to, which consumed much time, Little Turkey made an address, and, pointing to Steiner, recommended him and his family to the friendship and protection of the assembly. Steiner expressed his thanks and had occasion to use the title: "Society for Propagating the Gospel among the Heathen." Hicks had a terrible time trying to interpret this; finally, he put "Indians" for "Heathen" and made a long detour around the rest! One of the Chiefs came from the center of the group and gave Steiner his hand. With these friendly overtures the "Talk" came to an end.

Came Whitsunday and Steiner preached to half-breeds, blacks and whites. The Brethren lost no opportunity to speak of Christ to individuals of the tribe who were continually coming and going at Vann's. More and more they realized the almost insuperable difficulties connected with the learning of the language. Most of the half-breeds understood English but the

Brethren noted with heavy hearts how indifferent they and all the Indians were. In personal conversation on spiritual themes they would say "yes" just to evade the issue. During preaching, the Indians, especially, would stay a while, then walk away. Vann, too, showed the greatest indifference to the object of the Brethren's presence. Sundays at his house were usually given over to drinking. All these discouraging features the Brethren laid before the Throne of Grace with many a sigh and tear; their only comfort being mutual encouragement of one another before the Lord.

In June, the missionaries had begun to fell trees, splitting them into boards for a hut on Brown's plantation which Vann, meanwhile, had bought for them. Three months after leaving Salem they moved into their little cabin. That same day Brown left with his family, his possessions loaded on many packhorses. At night, July 13, after the missionaries had lit their pine torch, they dedicated the place and themselves anew to the Lord. The Text for the day, "I will make thy name to be remembered in all generations; therefore shall the people praise thee for ever and ever,"* was a great comfort to them.

Let us look about a little on the "mission premises." Springplace† is two miles east of the Connesauga River, two and one-half miles south from Vann's, seven miles south of Sumach Town, sixteen miles north of Oostanaula and on the road which leads from Oostanaula to Tellico. Forty acres of the land are clear, mostly bottom lands with red, fertile soil. The missionaries' field which has been cultivated for thirty years, still grows fine corn. In the woods are pine, hickory, black, white, and post oak, chestnut, walnut, mulberry, poplar and sourwood trees. In the lowlands stand maple, beech, elm and sweetgum trees, with a thick underbrush of sassafras and sumach. In the early summer there is much grass and clover in the meadows. Three fine springs flow out of beds of limestone. Brown's buildings are in very bad repair and infested with fleas and vermin. In general, Springplace is a camping ground for Indians.

* Psalm 45:17.

† Springplace was about 400 miles from Salem, by way of Knoxville, Tennessee.

5

The Brethren lived in the first months mainly on corn bread, eggs and coffee; meat they had none. Once several Indians came to remain over night and they shared with them what they had to eat and it was only bread and water. They fared better when their garden yielded an abundance of fresh vegetables. Wayfaring Indians also made use of the garden, helping themselves to anything they pleased and the Brethren dared not speak a word against it.

August 31st Steiner set out for Southwest Point where a Treaty between the United States Government and the Cherokees was to be concluded. He describes his experiences on the trip very graphically; coming first to Tellico, then Trimble's Ferry —where he found the Trimble family staunch Presbyterians and held prayer for them at night—arriving in Southwest Point September 3rd. Vann had already come. Steiner was rejoiced to find a package of letters from Salem, containing, among other items, the advice for Steiner and Byhan to return to Salem as soon as possible.

About 300 Indians had gathered for the Treaty proceedings. Little Turkey did not come and for this reason: the President of the United States did not come in person but sent deputies; therefore, Little Turkey, the Head of the Cherokee Nation, did not come in person, but sent deputies!

Steiner and Vann paid a visit to the camp of the Commissioners, where they found General Wilkinson, Col. Hawkins, General Pickens and the present Agent of Indian Affairs among the Cherokees, Col. Return J. Meigs. All received Steiner in a very friendly manner; Wilkinson and Meigs at once asking about Heckewelder. Steiner "fell in love," as he puts it, with Col. Meigs as a "brave, lovable man." Meigs knew Heckewelder, having visited in Gnadenhuetten and Goshen; he had been, also, in Zeisberger's house. Steiner was introduced, likewise, to Governor Roan of Tennessee and two gentlemen from England who were with him; one of them, a Mr. Sharpe, knew Bishop La Trobe personally.

The following day Steiner had an interview with Col. Hawkins, Superintendent of Indian Affairs for the southern States, and he told Steiner that never had he seen the Indians so full of mistrust toward the Government of the United States

and all its laws and so full of bitterness against the white people.
They were very ungrateful for what the Government was doing
and were continually demanding more and Hawkins said he
would not be surprised, if the dissatisfaction continued, to see
them take up the Tomahawk if opportunity offered. In regard
to the Moravian mission among the Cherokees, Hawkins advised
to proceed in a small way and not to enlarge the plans without
the consent of the Chiefs.

At noon, September 4, the beginning of the Treaty proceedings was announced by sixteen cannon-shots. The Commissioners
went into a large booth prepared for the meeting and soon forty
Chiefs came marching, single file, with "The Glass" at the head,
into the booth, shaking hands with the Commissioners as they
entered. All sat down in a circle on benches. Doublehead was
speaker for the Indians, General Wilkinson for the Commissioners. Charles Hicks was Interpreter. All smoked in silence for
a season then Wilkinson made an address in which he assured the
Indians of the protection of the President and told them to be-
ware of the talk of unscrupulous whites—traders, etc.,—with
whom he urged them to deal honestly but not to heed their
advice. Thereupon he asked the Indians if they had any land
for sale? If so, the Government would buy it and pay them
faithfully; if not, no more should be said about it. Then he
mentioned the fact that the white people in the Mississippi Territory and in the States of Tennessee, South Carolina and Georgia
were complaining that they lived so far apart with no communication as the trails were so narrow and often blocked with
fallen trees, etc. They wished to make the roads wider and
passable so that they could have more intercourse among themselves and their Red brethren. Doublehead answered, that the
Chiefs would give their reply tomorrow.

When they met again, Doublehead made a long declamation
against the injustice of the whites: they always wanted the Indian's land; only a short while ago an Indian woman had been
murdered by a white man. He flatly declined the road proposition and said, evidently the narrow trails were wide enough for
the white people to find the Red man's land! General Wilkinson, in reply, said only, that all they had spoken would be faithfully laid before their father, the President. Whereupon the
meeting broke up.

On his return journey to Springplace, Steiner had occasion to hear from several quarters that the feeling of the whites against the Indians was growing bitter; one assertion predicted that the Cherokees would be allowed to remain only ten more years in their country. Little Turkey stopped at Springplace for a brief visit right after the meeting and the missionaries learned from him that there was to be held soon, a great meeting of Cherokees, Creeks, Chickasaws and Choctaws and the Brethren could gather that the plan was to make a confederation among them to oppose any orders of the United States Government and to allow no roads through their territory.

After Steiner returned to Springplace, preparations were made to journey to Salem whither they had been called to come. Mr. Vann saw that Steiner was weak and made him accept a good horse to ride to Salem. He also arranged that Ned, one of his negroes, should live at Springplace in the absence of the Brethren. In spite of Vann's personal shortcomings, he was uniformly kind to the Brethren and it is hard to see how they would have fared without his friendly assistance. The journey was begun September 21, after the Vann's had loaded them with provisions. They reached Salem, October 8, without any mishap whatever.

Steiner's health at this time was precarious; he was sick in Salem for several weeks and very weak, so that it became evident he could not at this time return to his post. Byhan signified great desire to return, and Conference deliberated over a suitable Brother to return with him. Martin Schneider, who had visited the Cherokees eighteen years before and was now Pastor of Friedberg congregation, expressed a willingness to go but the lot did not give approbation. This was the case with other Brethren proposed. After much deliberation and prayer Conference came to the conclusion that Brother Byhan should marry and he and his wife should be permanent missionaries among the Cherokees. This plan seemed feasible inasmuch as Byhan felt sure there was no danger for a couple to reside alone at Springplace. This proposition was approved of the Saviour and the Single Sister Dorothea Schneider,* when approached by Conference with this call, found herself willing to follow the

---

* Born Jan. 6, 1769, died July 8, 1854, at Salem, N. C.

direction of the Lord. They were married, Nov. 16, 1801, and preparations for the journey were made without delay on account of approaching winter. Brother Jacob Wohlfahrt, Pastor at Friedland, was chosen to accompany them to Springplace and to remain with them temporarily until the Byhans were well established in their home among the Indians. Up to the last moment, Steiner had hoped to be able to return, but about this time became really dangerously ill.

Thus on November 24, 1801, Brother Gottlieb Byhan and wife, Dorothea, and Brother Jacob Wohlfahrt left Salem for Springplace, undertaking the journey in a large wagon, driven by John Krause. They were accompanied as far as Bethania by the Brethren Benzien, Gambold, Pfohl, Eldridge, Fetter, Zevely and Meinung. Arrived at Bethania, a little farewell service was held at Peter Hauser's home; then the missionaries went on. They crossed the Little Yadkin and came over the Blue Ridge and New River, next to the South and Middle Forks of the Holston River, reaching Abingdon on December 2; Knoxville was reached December 9. At their next stop, Tellico, they were received with much kindness by Mr. Hooker. The good road ended at this place, hence the driver set out on the return journey for Salem, and the missionaries hired a packhorse and an Indian guide for the rest of the way. The nights found them encamped in the woods under the open sky, and several times they were thoroughly soaked with rain, having no tent for shelter. Coming to the Hiwassee, they found the water very high. Wohlfahrt managed to get across on his horse and the guide took Mrs. Byhan over in a canoe. Wohlfahrt called to Byhan not to venture into the flood with the packhorse and went back in the canoe and transferred the horse's load into it. This was a blessing, for when Byhan, on the horse, was in mid-stream, the girth tore and the pack-saddle went into the water. After a hard struggle Byhan and horse landed safely and the saddle was rescued.

On December 16, the missionary party heard the sad news that the Indians had driven away Ned, Vann's negro left in charge of the Springplace premises, and had robbed the house. That same day they reached their destination and found many articles stolen and things generally in bad condition. One can imagine somewhat how they felt, tired out from the long, arduous and most uncomfortable journey, arriving in the desolated cabin. We would expect our fatigued missionaries to come down with a heavy attack of the blues, but their diary records a praise service held that very night, thanking God for preservation on the journey and praying for an open door for the Gospel among the Cherokees! Praying, too, to be given perseverance when no results of their work could be seen! This service of praise was followed on each successive night during many years with a similar meeting for prayer, praise and the study of the Word of God.

Wohlfahrt preached at Vann's the following Sunday to Indians and blacks on John 3:16. Also, on New Year's Day, 1802, a New Year discourse at the same place. A Mr. Austill had invited the missionaries to come and preach at his house in Oostanaula, which was done on January 2. Their host took them into a cave, entering on one side of a mountain and emerging from the other; in this cave they saw many strange rock formations.

On January 26, after Wohlfahrt had rendered great help in getting the Byhans settled, he began his return journey to Salem.

January 31, Nancy Vann, sister of James Vann, came to live with the Byhans at Springplace. She brought with her two cows, as the cows of the missionaries were still at large in the woods. Vann's negroes built a cabin for her and her presence soon became a great help to the missionaries as a companion and, chiefly, because Nancy could speak with the Indians who often came by. Nancy Vann had a cousin, likewise a half-breed, and both came very faithfully to the devotional meetings in the mission house, being especially delighted with the singing.

In February, something stirred in the consciences of certain Cherokee Indians within the neighborhood. "Standing Turkey" and two others came and brought back several of the articles which had been stolen; plates, spoons, etc.!

March 17, 1802. Abraham Steiner arrived from Salem and was received with unbounded joy at Springplace. On March 24, the first official Mission Conference of the Moravians in the Cherokee country was held. Present, Abraham Steiner, Gottlieb and Dorothea Byhan. Resolutions were set down in the minutes as follows:

"1. One of the houses is to be repaired and a floor laid in it. This, in preparation for an additional missionary family. To be done when the work in the fields is more slack.

"2. Re school. Scholars cannot be boarded, but such as would come would be instructed several hours each day. Steiner will communicate this to Vann and his sister.

"3. Since some of Vann's negroes usually stay around the mission premises over night, decided to read something every night in their hearing. Spangenberg's 'Idea Fidei Fratrum' chosen.

"4. Will preach at Vann's any time there is opportunity, but the effort is to be made to hold more and more services at Springplace.

"5. When strangers are present the night meetings are to be conducted in English. Tuesday, Prayer-meeting; Wednesday, Bible study; Friday, Passion Litany.

"6. Several pastoral calls are to be made, especially to Nancy Vann as she seems a little distant and suspicious."

A very cordial letter from Col. Return Jonathan Meigs, Southwest Point, who was now United States Agent for the Cherokees, cheered and encouraged the missionaries. The good colonel praised their undertaking and urged them to call on him for any assistance in his power. He felt sure, though the beginnings of the undertaking were discouraging, that the Cherokees would eventually respond to the message of the Gospel.

School opened at the mission station March 26, 1802. Sally, Vann's youngest daughter, was the first scholar; the second, Polly Vann, Sally's cousin, came April 14. The first schedule was one hour of instruction each day.

A final Conference was held before Steiner left for Salem. The situation appeared very discouraging so far as the real object of the mission was concerned; not knowing their language, it seemed that years must elapse before the Cherokees could be reached. Steiner was requested to lay before the Conference in Salem two suggestions to remedy this great difficulty: Would a young Brother volunteer to go and live in the Indian Towns where he would hear only the Cherokee language; or, should they try to get an elderly, honest Indian and his wife to come and live with them to give instruction?

Steiner started back May 29, leaving the Byhans well supplied with fine garden produce and the mission fields promising good harvests. The missionaries had two horses, six head of cattle, eighteen hogs, twenty chickens and nine ducks! In the outer circumstances, therefore, they were comfortable; but the farewell found both sides somewhat heavy hearted over meagre prospects for the progress of the Gospel. Steiner reached Salem safely, June 7.

Even before his arrival, Conference had considered the advisability of sending one of their number to look over the field and to cheer the missionaries. Brother John Gambold had been designated for this official visit, largely because he felt a great desire to be of service in the Gospel to the Cherokees. He was to carry the heartening resolution of Conference to the lonely Byhans, that another missionary couple would, ere long, be appointed for the Cherokee mission. Gambold awaited Steiner's return, when the two suggestions he brought from the mission Conference were duly considered. In their efforts to secure an Indian or an Indian couple to live with them for the sake of the language, the Byhans were to be encouraged. At the same time, the suggestion that a single Brother be sent to live in the Indian Towns for the same purpose, was deemed excellent. Every effort was made to secure a fit subject. In Salem, at the time, there was no man capable for this in the Single Brethren's Choir; hence, Conference applied to Bethlehem. In due time came the answer that the Brethren there could not even supply the same need for the Fairfield, Canada, mission. Neither could the Unity's Board help the Salem Brethren in this matter; all of which did not tend to brighten the prospects for the future of the Cherokee mission.

However, Gambold's visit of about six weeks to Springplace did inject new life and hope into the situation. He was a man after God's own heart, combining whole souled consecration and devotion to the Lord's cause with a persistent optimism and sound judgment. Also, he imbibed more and more love for the Cherokees and on his return to Salem in August expressed a desire to serve the Lord among them. His name was forthwith taken before the Lord but the Saviour's sanction was, for the present, not given.

Reinforcements to Springplace came in the persons of Jacob Wohlfahrt[*] and his wife Elizabeth, December 19, 1802. Their children were left behind in Salem, one married daughter and three sons: the oldest to learn a trade, the others to be in school.

Previous to their coming and in preparation for the enlarged missionary staff, important building operations were carried out at Springplace. The first cabin was sadly out of repair and inconveniently located with regard to the spring. At first, one large house, adequate for two families was considered, but this plan was changed to two houses, each 20 x 24 feet, 9 foot ceiling, built with the roofs in a straight line, but with a 20 foot space between, intended to be roofed over later for a meeting house.

Early in 1803, when the new missionaries were settled,[†] a mission Conference was held in which arrangements were made

---

[*] John Jacob Wohlfahrt, born August 9, 1755, Broadbay, Maine, died August 4, 1807, Hope, N. C. He was son of Johann Jacob Wohlfahrt, and Sophia Barbara, m.n. Voight. He came to Wachovia, in 1769, with his mother and stepfather, Adam Shumacher. Was apprenticed to the mill-wright, Jacob Van Der Merk. Settled in Salem in 1772. Married August 15, 1788, at Salem, to Elizabeth Schneider (born September 30, 1759, Friedensthal, Pa., died August 26, 1812, Salem, N. C.). He was ordained a Deacon in 1788; served as Pastor at Hope, 1788-1792; pastor at Friedland, 1801-1802; missionary to the Cherokee Indians, 1802-1805; pastor at Friedland 1805-1806; pastor at Hope, 1807. His Memoir says: "His humble and unassuming character, his true and faithful heart toward his Brethren, by which he became so generally beloved, and what else adorned him amongst the children of God, will be long remembered amongst us."

[†] Wohlfahrt was fitted out at Salem with the following articles for the Cherokee mission:

59 lbs. iron and steel	1 draw knife
1 plowshare	1 wood saw
1 shovel	1 carpenter saw
1 tomahawk	3 taper bits
1 hatchet	1 doz. awls
1 hoe	1 mallet
6 lbs. nails	3 chisels
1 large butcher knife	1 plane
4 cabbage knives	1 harness
4 hanging locks	1 saddle
2 iron lamps	6 pack girths
1 grindstone	1 side saddler leather

for the joint household and services were arranged for Sundays and week nights. The Brethren no longer went to Vann's house to preach; there was little interest among the blacks there and usually much disorder on Sundays with drinking, etc.

Nancy Vann was much impressed with a picture the Wohlfahrts had brought with them. It represented the suffering Saviour. As best they could, the missionaries tried to explain to her the meaning of it and on one such occasion noticed tears in her eyes. In other ways, she showed many hopeful signs of com-

4 lbs. glue
2 large saddler needles
1 doz. awls
2 doz. shoe awls
6 pr. men's shoes
6 pr. women's shoes
1 pkg. buckles
3 wool hats
7 yds. red flannel
2 blankets
7 yds. cloth for overalls
7 yds. cloth for mantle
1 doz. scarfs
4½ yds. cotton strips
11 yds. muslin
9 bolts tape
2 yds. dimity
12½ yds. fine muslin
3 caps
1 tin cream ladle
1 tin blowpipe
1 large coffee pot
1 tin sausage stuffer
1 tin grater
2 tin snuff boxes
1 tin candle-mold
6 gal. Teneriffe wine
1 bbl. flour
20 lbs. butter
25 lbs. coffee
60 lbs. sugar
4 lbs. chocolate
3 lbs. tea
2 lbs. pepper
1 lb. pimento
2 oz. cinnamon

12 lbs. rice
1 lb. indigo
2 lbs. gun powder
10 lbs. shot
1 gun
1 bottle white drops
1 bottle mint extract
1 syringe
1 bleeding instrument and sponge
3 Liturgy books
2 Gregor "Prayers for Every Day"
1 Daily Texts
1 "Word of the Cross," Rissler
1 Life of Pastor Reichel
1 Songs of Pastor Reichel
1 "Something for the Heart"
1 pocket Dictionary
1 North American Almanac
½ Ream writing paper
2 pkgs. ink-powder
8 window panes 7 x 9
4 tin plates
4 cook pots
1 lb. twine
40 yds. rope
2 gross shoe binding
2 gross quality binding
1 gross shirt buttons
1 gross white corals
50 darning needles
1 gross sewing needles
6 pkgs. pins
6 thimbles
4 pocket knives
4 pen knives
2 razors

ing to the light and the missionaries began to entertain the hope that she might be the first, under their ministry, to accept Christ. Unfortunately, at this stage, she married a half-breed and moved away to the town Coosewattee. However, the good impression made on her was not lost. She begged the missionaries to come to her house and hold a meeting for which she promised to gather the neighboring Indians. To many other Indians who came and went at Springplace, the missionaries by gestures endeavored to convey the idea of God's love for them. Their ignorance of the Cherokee language was felt by them to be tragic.

Imagine the consternation of the missionaries when on June 10, 1803, they received the following letter through Major W. L. Lovely, Asst. Agent for the Cherokees, an outcome of a Talk held at Oostanaula, June 5, and addressed to Wohlfahrt:

"Dear Sir, I have to inform you by the request of the Cherokee Chiefs of the result of their Talk at Oostanaula, June 5th.

"They observe that a long time has elapsed since a school was to be erected for the instruction of their youth in order to prepare their minds to receive the doctrines of religious worship which was proposed to be taught them, and they received the offer of the friendly Society with much satisfaction. At that time some of their people had children of a proper age to receive instruction, but are now grown up and we now consider that the Society have fallen through their good intentions towards us, as we discover no prospect of such business going on.

"We have, therefore, thought it necessary to acquaint you through our Agent that you continue in your present situation till the first day of January next, as by that time you may know from your people whether their friendly intentions toward us will be put in execution.

"We are your friends and brothers in behalf of the Council.

"Chuleoa and
"The Sour Mush."

"Signed by Major Lovely."

The missionaries were greatly disturbed over this letter. It seemed that everything in the Cherokee Nation was against them. They told some of the Chiefs at Vann's that they had not come to teach school but to tell them the Word of God. The Chiefs replied, they had no ears to hear it! After conferring together, it seemed best to send Wohlfahrt at once to Salem with the dis-

tressing news that the Chiefs had all but told them to vacate the
Nation, having misunderstood the proposition about the school.

June 30, Conference had a long deliberation over this sudden
turn of affairs and it was decided to send several members of the
Society to the Chiefs with a message from the Directors reminding them of their agreement to permit the Brethren to live in
the Nation without any obligation to board and clothe their
children when a school should be begun. The Chiefs' attention
was to be directed to the main purpose the Society had in mind
in sending missionaries to them. At the same time Conference
thought wise to begin school in a small way, that is, in addition
to the one or two scholars now in the missionaries' care, to
receive three or four sons of the Chiefs, to regain their good will.
Incidentally, the missionaries might learn some Cherokee from
their scholars.

Armed with a message of this purport, the Brethren Abraham
Steiner, Martin Schneider and Jacob Wohlfahrt set out for the
Cherokee country on July 24. On August 16, after a talk with
Major Lovely, it was decided to call together the Chiefs who had
sent the disconcerting message, to Oostanaula in ten nights.
Vann at once sent out a courier to notify them. Previous to the
meeting, Steiner went to Charles Hicks, the Interpreter, to give
him the message of the Directors for his careful study to get his
Cherokee words in line for unusual expressions in the message.
Colonel Meigs, who had been notified from Salem of the dilemma,
sent a splendid exhortation to be read at the Council.

August 27, the Chiefs arrived at the Vann house, led by Sour
Mush and Chuleoa. From a distance one could see Chuleoa
coming with large red feathers in his cap. In addition, he was
adorned with several hundred silver bracelets! After they sat
around in order and had smoked in silence for a while, Major
Lovely read Col. Meig's letter, as follows:

"Southwest Point, July 22nd, 1803.

"Brothers, Mr. Wohlfahrt has been to see that good Society of
Christians who sent him first into this section; he carried your
message with him; he will now make you an answer by which you
will see that his powers are something enlarged with respect to the
education of children. That Society is not rich; they expend all
their money for the good of mankind. They will take as many of
your children as they can.

"Your old friend, Mr. Steiner, has come to speak to you from the Society. You will see that they take great pains to do good wherever they can; they are not speculators, nor merchants; they do not want your lands, nor your money; they wish to give that to you which is worth more than lands or money. They want nothing but your good will.

"Brothers, you know that it takes time to bring about any valuable thing. Brothers, we must plant and hoe the corn before we can have the harvest; we must plant the tree before we can get the fruit. I hope you will receive them with great good will. The Great Spirit will be pleased to have his children treated kindly—they are his children and you are his children, we are all brothers. Mr. Steiner will explain everything better than I can; you may rely on his words; what he tells you, he will tell his Society and will also tell his Society what you shall say to him, that everything may be short and plain.

"Your friend and brother,

"Return J. Meigs."

"P.S.—I hope you will not be hasty in what you do. Do not refuse the good things they are sent to do for your Nation. Give them time; in the course of a year or two years, you will be able to judge better than you can now. I have been amongst the Delawares who have been instructed by these people. They have three towns on the waters of the Muskingum River where they live very happily. I think if you should send some of your people to see the Delawares they would return home much pleased and would not afterwards be willing to part with the missionaries."

"To Chuleoa and Sour Mush."

The message of the Directors was next communicated, but the Chiefs became impatient and said it was too long! Steiner abbreviated it, whereupon Chuleoa and Sour Mush gave a combined Talk, in part as follows:

"I shall now make proposals, that is to say, as our good friends the missionaries have taken us under their consideration, they must not think too hard of taking care of our people. (That is, boarding and clothing the scholars. The impression among the Chiefs seems to have been that the missionaries were too proud to deal directly with the Indians.—Writer.)

"This is now the second time we are to make a trial, and we hope those who are now to be instructed by our Brother may be well used, so that, when they return, they may be able to render a good account. And as the Red People are slow in learning, we do agree that one year from next Christmas shall be given to make a begin-

ning by the teachers with four scholars, agreeable to the proposal
of the Society.

"Signed.

"Chuleoa,

"Sour Mush."

"Charles Hicks, Interpreter."

"I do hereby certify that the Talk as above was given by the
Chiefs in Council held at Oostanaula, August 27, 1803.

"Wm. L. Lovely, Asst. Agent for the Cherokees."

Almost endless discussion preceded this final decision; the
Indians, Major Lovely and even Steiner became heated at times
in the argument. The Chiefs adroitly avoided any reference to
the preaching of the Word of God which was reiterated in
the message of the Directors. When the Talk had been given,
the Chiefs came up to the Brethren and some of them shook their
hands, and others shook them by the arm, whereupon Council
broke up.

While awaiting the session of the Council at Oostanaula, lodged
with Standing Turkey near the Town House, the Brethren had
opportunity to observe some of the Cherokee dances. They saw
five different varieties of Indian dances, all very simple, but some
distinguished by great regularity. Each dance was accompanied
by the song of two men who also beat time with calabashes filled
with small stones. Their principal dance was the "Green Corn
Dance," really intended to be a religious exercise of Thanksgiving to "the Man above," for the new crop of corn. Men and
women were decked out in their best for these dances, at which
good order prevailed. The dancing ground was in front of the
Town House, a large, level place swept clean. In the center
stood a high pole with green boughs tied to it to afford some
shade. At the pole stood a bench upon which were seated those
who beat time. One dance is carried out by two groups of men
who appear out of the bushes on opposite sides of the dancing
ground with loud shouts and advance towards the pole in the
center around which they dance in opposite directions. Another
dance is done by one group of men who are led by their singer.
They carry guns and after they march a little distance to calabash time, the singer quickly turns and bows down to the earth.
The whole group then sing with him and likewise bow to the
ground and begin to dance around the singer; next, the guns

are fired and then they begin all over again! A third dance, in which men and women assist, is carried out in a slow movement around the pole. The singers dance in front and somewhat to one side of the ring, looking very serious and solemn. Another dance employs about sixty Indians who start dancing at the pole and then widen the circle more and more with an interwoven, spiral movement until they reach the limits of the ground, then closing up to the pole again. The last dance the missionaries witnessed was done by women only, dancing around the pole, the men beating time. The female leader of this dance wore leather shoes with turtle backs fastened thereto with which she mightily rattled!

Arrived at Springplace August 28, the missionaries held a praise service, thanking God for having delivered them out of their difficulty. They determined to erect at once another house near their present habitation.

In October, 1803, Byhan and Wohlfahrt felled trees and, with the assistance of Vann's negroes, erected two new houses at Springplace with the aid of Schneider, a carpenter by trade, who remained at Springplace until the houses were finished. Meanwhile, Steiner had reached Salem in safety.

Vann's mother came, one day, to the missionaries and they could see at once, from the expression on her face, that she had something disagreeable to tell them. The Chiefs Chuleoa and Gentleman Tom had visited her and said that all the Chiefs wished to get the missionaries out of the country. They claimed to have information that several other denominations had agreed to send three or four teachers and that each one of them would board and clothe 25 to 30 scholars.* The Chiefs were dissatisfied because our missionaries had been there already four years and had not yet fulfilled the promise about the school and now would take only four scholars. This intelligence caused the good spirits of the missionaries to descend to the depths, working hard as they were on the new buildings. Chuleoa said to Mother Vann, too, that it was all right for the missionaries to build busily, but they would never live in the houses.

---

* The Presbyterians began a school under Rev. Gideon Blackburn in 1803, on the Hiwassee River, with 21 scholars, and good progress was made within one year. This school was abandoned in 1810.

January 26, 1804, the first missionaries' child was born in the Cherokee country to the Byhans, receiving the name Nathaniel.

Provisions were very low at Springplace during the winter 1803-4, and the Brethren decided that it was impossible to take on four boarders before new corn came in. Those were dark days for the missionaries. In their distress, they appealed to Col. Meigs to reason with the Indians. Another Talk was to be held April 4, at Oostanaula. From this their friend Col. Meigs returned on April 10, stopping at Springplace, with the good news that the Indians had relented somewhat, owing to circumstances; whereas, they had stipulated the school must be in good progress by Christmas, 1804, they now said that if the school were actually begun by that time, the missionaries might remain within their borders.

October 8, who should come to bring the first boy to school but Gentleman Tom, who had expressed himself so bitterly against Springplace! The poor missionaries were considerably "helped up" over this. Another boy, nephew of Chief Bark, who had been staying at Vann's came also; thus, with Sally Vann, three scholars were in the mission school. Gentleman Tom stipulated that his eight-year-old hopeful should be taught English, not German, and that he was to be treated well. True, one of the boys complained to passing Indians that he was not getting enough to eat; the other ran away several times; nevertheless, the school was under way; the mission was saved! In November, "Big Halfbreed" brought his nephew, George Hicks, to school. Wohlfahrt taught the school in the morning and Byhan in the afternoon. The scholars were at once taken to all the meetings, except the Holy Communion, and the services were held for the most part in English for their benefit.

George Hicks, their most promising scholar, could now help them many times by interpreting messages about Gospel pictures, etc., to visiting Indians of whom there were many warmed, fed and lodged at the mission.

During these days their friend and benefactor, James Vann, was rapidly traveling the downward road, with incessant drinking. The Brethren visited him often, remonstrated with him and told him of Jesus Christ, the Saviour both from the guilt and power of sin, but seemed to make no impression upon him.

Vann did not believe in any such person as Jesus Christ, the Scriptures were fables to him. He was unspeakably sinful and cruel when under the influence of liquor. When sober, he was kind and generous; when intoxicated he was a veritable fiend. One of his negroes he burned alive because he had robbed him; another he shot, because he had heard that he was plotting against his life. Vann got into trouble with his brother-in-law, John Falling, the husband of Nancy Vann in whom we have noticed gleams of the light of a new life. Falling sent a challenge to Vann which he accepted. They met in the woods, on horseback and both discharged their pistols. Vann's sleeve was torn by Falling's shot, but Vann's bullet entered Falling's breast and he dropped dead. The plot now thickens around Vann. Falling's relatives, among whom there is an Indian Chief, have sworn revenge. Finally, in February, 1809, came the terrible news of Vann's murder while on a trip to punish some thieves who were in the country at that time. He had had several shot, including an Indian who would not surrender. All the while, he was drinking heavily, and one day, standing in the doorway of a house, a shot was heard and he dropped dead. He was forty-one years of age. Always he had been friendly to the missionaries and had rendered them great assistance. During one winter the missionaries could not have subsisted without his constant aid for which he would accept no pay. Humanly speaking, the mission could not have been started or continued without him. The missionaries shed many a tear over his sad end and there came into their hearts a quite natural fear as to the future of the mission without their patron. However, before this stay was removed God was Himself preparing the way for other friends. To finish Vann's story we have run ahead several years and said nothing of the mission. Brighter days were dawning, and we enter them with the next chapter.

CHAPTER VIII.

THE ESTABLISHMENT OF THE MISSION AMONG THE CHEROKEES,

OR

"THEY SHALL REAP IN JOY."

Ofttimes, God brings the brightest blessings to His children out of the experiences of life they most dread. Thus it proved in the Cherokee mission, when the school, which had been such a bugbear to the apprehensive missionaries, turned out to be the real means of the success of the work among the Cherokees. Christmas Eve, 1804, when they met, ten persons in all, to celebrate the Saviour's birth, their scholars were able to sing some English verses of Christmas hymns which they had learned during the Advent season. The meaning of the Lovefeast was explained to them and the lighted Christmas taper was given to each. They were very attentive and happy. This made the missionaries very thankful and happy! "A little child shall lead them."

February 3, 1805, the school children were able to pray the Lord's prayer in the Litany for the first time.

The year brought changes in the personnel of the mission. Wohlfahrt and wife having asked to be released from the service among the Cherokees, Brother John Gambold* was again brought

---

* John Gambold, born June 16, 1760, at Shechem, State of New York. Parents labored in the church there. At age of four he was brought to Nazareth Hall. The work of the Spirit in his heart began at a tender age and he often prayed for forgiveness of sins. In 1773, he came to Bethlehem to learn the hatter's trade. He retained the tender heart that dreaded sin. In 1782, he returned to Nazareth, worked several years at his trade, and then removed to Bethlehem as master of the hat-making establishment of the Brethren's House there.

In 1790, he was called to Lititz as leader of the Single Brethren and next year called to the same office in Salem. In 1802, June, he was commissioned by the Helpers' Conference to make a visit to the mission among the Cherokees. He stayed until August and said this was one of the happiest times of his life. Became "Mitgemeinvorsteher" in Salem, 1802. He then married Catharina Lanius. They were called to Friedberg in 1804, where she died of fever. One day, a letter came from Salem inviting him to come thither. He said he felt it was for a call to the Cherokee mission which is turned out

into consideration for the place and received a call to the field which he at once accepted. October 19, 1805, Brother Gambold arrived with his wife, Anna Rosina Kliest,† having come from Salem in a covered wagon. John Hartman and Jacob Lanius were teamsters. There was unbounded joy in the little mission house at Springplace when the party arrived. The Gambolds brought with them a negress, named Pleasant, who had been bought for service in the mission. This relieved the mission Sisters of much of the hard manual labor incident to caring for the ever increasing number of passing Indians.

---

to be, and he accepted the call with joy. He was married in 1805 to Anna Rosina Kliest in Bethlehem and came to Springplace in October of the same year. Dark time then among the Cherokees! The Moravian mission was the first among them. The mission existed five years and no fruits were visible. First church at Springplace dedicated by him in 1819. In 1821 he was called to Oochgelogy and while preparing to move his wife died. Yet he went and with the assistance of his brother Joseph, got settled as well as possible. In April, 1823, he married the widow Anna Maria Schultz, nee Grabs, in Bethania, and went back to his post. In 1825, the meeting hall was finished in the second story of the dwelling and another house finished for the Indian school. In 1827, he baptized the first Indian woman at Oochgelogy and this was his last official act. Dropsy of the heart set in from which he was released November 7, 1827, aged 67 years, 4 months. He had been for 22 years in the service of the Cherokees. Always cheerful, always trustful and restful in faith, steadily he labored on with no sign of complaint in his long and interesting letters to Salem.

† Mrs. Gambold, nee Anna Rosina Kliest, was born May 1, 1762. She was married late in life, having served for many years, 1788-1805, as principal tutoress in the Boarding School for young ladies in Bethlehem, Pa. She was remembered in love by many students all over the country. Her interest and love for the Indians she probably imbibed when she accompanied George Henry Loskiel—historian of Moravian missions to northern American Indians—on a visit to the Indian mission on the Muskingum. "She connected herself with Mr. Gambold chiefly from a willingness to assist him in missionary labors among the Cherokees." Her eminent talents and gifts were of particular benefit to the Springplace scholars. With her coming to Springplace the school at once moved up to a high level which was maintained for many years. Mrs. Gambold died in 1821 at Springplace, Cherokee Mission, where her mortal remains rest beside those of her first Cherokee Sister, Margaret Ann Scott, who was brought to the Saviour largely through her efforts. The

Mrs. Gambold at once began her labors in the school with much enthusiasm. Frail in physique, she was, nevertheless, indefatigable among her Indian children. For this work she was especially gifted and could make little desert hearts blossom like the rose. The number of scholars had now increased to six.

On the first Sunday in Advent they sang "How Shall I Meet My Saviour!"* with splendid effect. For Christmas, the room was prettily decorated and a gilded inscription said "Christ is Born!" For the Lovefeast, they had real wax tapers and when the children sang.

> "Praise the Lord, for on us shineth
> Christ the Sun of Righteousness;"†

following is a tribute to her genius as a teacher which made her so valuable at Springplace:

"Gifted with talents of a high order, of amiable and winning manners, a deep sense of the responsibility of her calling prompted this lady to devote the powers of a versatile mind to the welfare of her charge, among whom her memory is cherished to the present day. Sprightly in person as well as in fancy and imagination, she was the genial spirit of the institution—(Bethlehem)—in which she dwelt,—willing at all times to vary the monotony of its routine by the offerings of her fertile inventions. To plan an island excursion, a ramble on the mountain, or a moonlight transit across the ferry,—complete with all their attendant circumstances,—was with her only an exertion of thought. The details were no sooner conceived than executed. Her willing muse, ever at hand, was invoked, and granted the desired boon. As she walked out in the fields, she taught her joyous flock the lessons of wisdom from the great book of nature spread open before them. The flowers, the trees, the stones, the clouds, the stars,—these were chapters in the manual she consulted in her teachings. When in the class-room, she gave from the stores of her mind the knowledge she would have her pupils retain, in a happy manner, leading them unconsciously into the secrets of science by practical and familiar illustration.

"In 1805, Sister Kliest was married to Brother John Gambold of the Cherokee mission, and entered on a new sphere of usefulness with faithfulness and marked success.

"In 1821, she finished her earthly career, to the sorrow and regret of her beloved Indians, many of whom now risen to eminence in their nation, ascribe their standing and usefulness in civilized Society to the instruction received at her hands."

See Bibliography No. 20.

* J. Mueller.

† Paul Gerhardt.

the missionaries felt amply repaid for all trials and tribulations they had undergone during the dark days of the beginning of the mission.

New life and joy in service was in the air in the mission household. Great spiritual fervor was manifest in the Sunday and week day services, and, through the school, the mission's circle of influence was widening. Indians had frequently attended the meetings in former years but walked and talked in and out indifferently while the service was in progress: now they sat quietly through the entire service, reverent in prayer and awed when the children sang.

Yes, the missionaries were beginning to see that their labors were not in vain in the Lord. They were comforted and strengthened to persevere in their work and, especially in their instructing the children, took great pains to acquaint them with Christ and His love. Of the Christmas of 1806, the following paragraph from Gambold's letter will bear witness to the new day which had come:

"Even in this dark region the Day Spring from on high has visited us, during this festival season, with rich grace and unction. Our children sang the Christmas hymns they had learned in school with cheerful voices, and we doubt not but that Jesus, who was made partaker of flesh and blood and appeared as a child in the world for their sakes, graciously heard and received the praises of these little ones. Brother Byhan had put together a small organ which accompanied the voices and pleased the children very much."

Also of the Passion and Easter season they write:

"We celebrated these solemn days with our school children in blessed contemplation on the sufferings of our Saviour. When we read to them on Maundy Thursday, the story of his agony in the garden of Gethsemane, they were so much affected that many tears were shed."

During the summer no week night meetings were held. They were resumed on October 1. Scholar Tommy heard of it and asked, "Will there be meeting tonight?" Answer, "Yes." Said Tommy, "O, that's good: I love the meetings, good meetings."

The mother of John Gut-Se-ye-di, one of the Springplace scholars, with her daughter, visited for several days at the mission. She was much delighted with the singing. The missionaries told her, by interpretation of the children, that they did

not sing like the Indians, for merriment, but to praise and pray
to God. She inquired whether God heard and attended to it.
The children replied, "God sees and hears all things and knows
even the inmost thoughts of our hearts, and those who love Him
here will after this life be received by Him into Heaven." While
the children were explaining the Gospel to her the poor woman
sat weeping and, taking Mrs. Gambold by the hand, expressed
the wish that she lived nearer the missionaries that she might
often hear the Word of God.

Another reason for thankfulness to God at this time was the
favorable disposition of the Chiefs towards the mission, particularly of Chuleoa, once a decided and bitter enemy. When in
March, 1806, the Chiefs held a Council at Mr. Vann's, Chuleoa
lodged four days at Springplace and delivered a Talk to the
children at parting—his son was one of the scholars—reminding
them how well they fared with the missionaries, better than any
other children. Every day they had enough to eat and drink,
while many of their countrymen were starving; besides which,
they learned nothing here but what was good; therefore, they
should be very obedient and do everything with alacrity and
cheerfulness, and love and revere the missionaries as their parents. He asked them to remember that he—Chuleoa—and other
Chiefs had called the missionaries to this place to instruct them
in every useful art and that he would ever consider the missionaries as his own children. The missionaries thanked him for his
good will toward them and assured him that they prayed God to
bless him and give him grace, which seemed to affect him very
sensibly.

Three scholars were now boarding and living with the missionaries: Tom A-ca-ru-ca, son of Chuleoa; George Vann, nephew
of Chief Bark; John Gut-Se-ye-di, son of Du-a-i. Five scholars
boarded with Mr. Vann.

The number of traveling Indians who came to Springplace for
food and shelter often greatly inconvenienced the missionaries.
At such times they must quit their firesides and stand or sit together in some cold corner of the room, leaving the fire for the
visitors. Frequently they experienced dearth of provisions,
especially meat, as their cattle and pigs continued to stray away
or were stolen. But never did they experience suffering from

hunger. When most needed, help would often come from quarters least expected.

The missionaries found it exceedingly difficult and well nigh impossible to learn the Cherokee language. Even with the help of all the letters and sounds, both English and German, many Cherokee expressions could not be written. They asked Nancy Falling to express the idea "God, the Creator of all." The nearest she could come to this in Cherokee was to say "Our Daddy above," which the missionaries learned.

For the festivities at the end of the year 1806, the children had learned to sing the Te Deum. They were taken into the Watch Night services, which they greatly enjoyed.

In May, 1807, when the Brethren Christian Burkhardt and Karsten Petersen came from Salem to Springplace, where they stayed for several months before going to the Creek country, whither they had been sent to renew a work among that tribe, the school children welcomed them with a well-written hymn, composed by Mrs. Gambold, which, having learned by heart, they sang for the Brethren. How Petersen and Burkhardt felt may be gathered from their account:

"It is not to be expressed in words, how sweet their voices are and how attentive and devout they appear at school and when met for worship. Their whole behavior is such as to insure the love of all who know them. Whatever, even by the glance of the eye, they guess to be our wish, they do directly. Both at the baptism of Brother Byhan's child and on Ascension Day, they were deeply affected and shed many tears. Truly, the Lord is present with this small congregation, and fulfills his promise that where two or three are gathered together in His name, He will be in the midst of them."

Petersen and Burkhardt, master craftsmen, before leaving Springplace for their new field, built a complete loom and set it up in a little house for weaving on the Springplace premises, for the use of the missionaries.

Here we will leave the first bright gleams of the coming harvest, resuming the story in the chapter after the next. Meanwhile, we shall speak of further labors of the Moravians among the Creeks.

CHAPTER IX

THE MORAVIANS' RENEWED EFFORTS AMONG THE CREEKS.

A new attempt for a mission among the Creeks, objects of the Brethren's first settlement in America, as we have seen in Chapter II, lay upon the hearts of the Salem members of the Society for Propagating the Gospel Among the Heathen, and they were praying and watching for an opening for the Gospel among them. Reports from the mission among the Cherokees seemed hopeful for such a work among the Creeks also, and an official visit to the tribe seemed warranted, especially since the Brethren had heard that Colonel Benjamin Hawkins, United States' Agent for the Creeks was well disposed toward any effort for the betterment of that tribe.

The emergency visit of Abraham Steiner to Springplace in July, 1803, when that mission was in jeopardy because of the attitude of the Chiefs on the school question, seemed a good time to spy out the land and people of the Creeks for the Lord. Accordingly, Steiner was instructed before leaving Salem that if the school matter could be amicably settled at the Cherokee Council, he should proceed on to the Creek Indians to obtain the desired information.

Steiner accomplished this business in the month of September, by means of a visit to Col. Hawkins. Arrived at Fort Wilkinson, he learned that Col. Hawkins had gone about sixty miles down the Flint River, whither a Mr. Hill, assistant to the Colonel, accompanied Steiner. On the way, Steiner observed much long-leaf pine and sandy soil, also saw Catalpa trees for the first time.

Hawkins received Steiner in a most cordial way and was presented with a History of Moravian Missions Among Northern American Indians, with compliments of the Salem Society, for which he was very grateful. Steiner delivered, also, the special letter from the Society for Propagating the Gospel Among the Heathen, which elicited from Hawkins the hearty response to do all in his power to aid the Brethren. He gave Steiner, first of all, the following information about the Creeks, which throws additional light on our First Chapter, dealing with this people:

The stronger part of the Nation call themselves Muscogulgee, the weaker part, Seminoles. The Muscogulgee live mostly beside the Chattahoochie and the Mobile with its tributaries. The Seminoles live eastward from the Gulf of Mexico on the Achalopicola River and Florida Point.

The Creeks said they originated west of the Mississippi River and came into this country conquering the weaker tribes and uniting them with their own. Others they drove out of the country. Then they settled along the water-courses. At the time of Steiner's visit there were about 37 Towns and Hawkins estimated the number of Creeks at about 70,000.

Fewer whites live among the Creeks than among any of the other Indian tribes.

The Creeks are of a lighter brown than other Indians, are of medium height, built straight, have regular features and a noble appearance. Their sins are jealousy and a suspicious disposition. Their language is well-sounding and said to be more easily learned than the speech of other tribes. The Nation is divided into many families designated by names such as "Wolf," "Eagle," etc. Persons of the same family may not marry. The children belong to the family to which the mother belongs and she alone has full jurisdiction over them. If a man wishes to marry a woman he does not ask her direct, but her family, who ask her and if she consents, the man must provide a year's support.—(This is not a bad idea!—Writer.)—then they may marry. A man may have more than one wife but most of them have one only. Should the couple become dissatisfied, they separate and the mother keeps the children. Adultery is one of the greatest sins with them and is severely punished.

Chiefs of the Creeks are called Micalgee; singular, Micco, of which each Town has seven. The Micco is the highest civil officer and judge and he makes peace treaties. The Nation has its Great Speaker, who leads discussions with whites and also among Indians. There is, also, a Great Keeper of records and history who must keep in mind all events of importance referred to him by Micco and Speaker, and rehearse them briefly once each year. Each of these National officers have several assistants; the most apt of which will be successors to Speaker and Historian.

They have doctors, or "medicine makers," who are little more than pow wow conjurers.

Creeks believe in a single Supreme Being, called the "Father of Breath." There are no subordinate deities. Man has a soul which is immortal and there is another world where those who have lived well will live in glory while those who have lived the opposite will have a hard time.

Their big festival comes each year in July or August when the corn is ripe. It is held in every Town and is called "Busketaw," i.e., Day of Purification. It is a time of reconciliation and thanksgiving, and every inhabitant is expected to be present. They fast and cleanse the body internally by means of emetics. All fires in the Town are extinguished and a new one is kindled by rubbing two dry sticks briskly. Pipes are lit with this new fire and the smoke is blown upward on each others breast. The women prepare of the new corn and concoct a black drink out of herbs and then there is moderate eating and drinking. At this festival all crimes are forgiven and every fugitive may return home. (Murder is excepted and must be paid with blood.) Asked the reason for these customs, they say God has commanded them thus to do. Of the Christian Religion they are suspicious, having heard of cruelties perpetrated by Catholic priests and because of certain ministers who mixed in with their political affairs.

At first, the Creeks did not want any improvements. Hawkins had achieved great changes in this direction, having introduced plows, cattle-raising and simple manufactures of baskets and pottery. Some of the men now even made spinning-wheels and looms.

Steiner found Hawkins willing and eager to assist in a missionary enterprise among the Creeks. He offered to take one or more of the Brethren along on one of his trips through the Creek country. Having an establishment of his own at Hawkins' Springs, he volunteered to give the use of this to any missionaries who might come. Col. Hawkins was strongly of the opinion that the missionaries sent should be artisans—carpenters, smiths, etc., —the reason he gave being that the Creeks were very anxious to take up the crafts of the whites; therefore, men with a trade would find more ready entrance to them.

Col. Hawkins himself had worked along these lines to bring the Creeks to civilization. For eleven years, he had endeavored to get their minds away from hunting, fishing, etc., trying to train them to agriculture, simple manufactures, knowledge of weights and measures and the like. His had been a wonderfully successful administration among these Indians; hence, also, his suggestions as to what kind of missionaries should come.

Steiner brought home a most interesting and encouraging report which incited the Brethren to pray and work for a beginning among the Creeks. To make some definite arrangements, Brother Steiner was again commissioned to undertake a trip into the Creek country during the months of June, July and August, 1804. His companion was to be a younger man, Nathanael Schober.

Commended to God in fervent prayers at a special meeting of the congregation in Salem, these Brethren set out on June 4, passing through Rowan and Iredell counties, crossing the Catawba River in Mecklenburg County. Came to York district, South Carolina, crossed the Broad River, thence to Spartanburg, crossed the Pacolet, thence to Petersburg, Ga., and Fort Wilkinson. Provisions were very scarce in the country owing to crop failures. Even at Fort Wilkinson they could not buy a sufficiency of supplies. They bought a loaf of corn bread made with spoiled flour, paying for it one-half dollar. June 23, they reached Col. Hawkins, and his kind treatment was especially grateful to them after the difficult trip.

They had come at a favorable time. A Council for a treaty was to be held in a few days, to which the Brethren were invited to come. Steiner, however, became very sick of fever and Schober had to nurse him in Hawkins' headquarters. Meanwhile, fortunately, the treaty was postponed because not all the Chiefs came.

By the time the Council was convened, Brother Steiner had recovered sufficiently to be able to attend; thus he and Schober had a first-hand experience of an important Council among the Creeks. It had been called for the purpose of considering the purchase of some of the Creek lands by the State of Georgia. With Colonel Hawkins were several Commissioners, empowered to act for that State.

From Col. Hawkins' establishment the party went to the Town House and public square of Tookaubatchee, five miles distant, across the Tallapoosa River. The public square was enclosed by four long, rectangular buildings of thatch-work, with an entrance at each corner. Of these buildings, the outside and roofs were closed tightly, but on the inside, facing the square they were open, so that one could hear what was carried on in each. In these buildings, raised seats of cane ran the length of the house, and upon these the Indians either sat or reclined. Posts, inlaid with stones on the top, were set in the ground at regular intervals along these seats, upon which small fires were kept burning for the lighting of pipes. The open square was used for fires and, especially, for dancing. One of the buildings was fitted with an alcove for the Micco, or Principal Chief.

Outside this quadrangular structure stood the Town House, a rotunda covered with bark. Upon a high pole without was affixed a carved eagle, the emblem of the Town.

The Commissioners and Steiner and Schober on entering the square, were welcomed by about 80 Creek Indians. The former were taken to the house of the Micco; the Brethren, into the building of "The Great Warrior."

In the open square was a fire over which an Indian was cooking the so-called "Black Drink" in a large earthen vessel. This drink had the color of dark beer and was prepared from the leaves of the Cassia bush regarded as sacred by the Creeks. "Black Drink" was peculiar to the Creeks and was used on all solemn occasions and regarded as a mystic drink of purification, by the partaking of which body and soul were cleansed and prepared for the festivities or solemnities, as the case might be, to follow.

When the delegation was seated, "Mad Dog," an old and prominent Indian, formerly the Speaker, rose and welcomed the white visitors, saying they were glad for the visit and thankful to the Great Spirit who had brought them all together. The Creeks were poor people, he said, but glad to share what they had with their white brethren who, he hoped, would be able to make the best of what they had. Thereupon, Col. Hawkins introduced each visitor to Mad Dog. When he came to Steiner, the Colonel gave a long description of the Society which had sent him and companion and told the purpose for which they had come. Mad Dog shook hands with both, followed by the other Indians, all with the utmost gravity.

During which time the "Black Drink" had boiled sufficiently and was carried to the seat of the Micco who, with a calabash, poured it back and forth between two vessels until it foamed up like new beer. He poured the foam upon the ground, then filled three calabashes with the drink which three Indians handed first to the Commissioners and went through the following ceremony: bowing frequently, then stepping back, they stood erect and sang two notes, one much higher than the other, holding the last until breath failed; then they took the calabashes with more profound bows and brought them to the other white visitors, with the same ceremony except the song. Then they went to the Indians. Meanwhile, another quantity had been boiled and was passed around. Steiner says it was not very bitter and not hard to take. After a few minutes, the Indians brought it up again as easily as they had drunk it. It did not have the same effect with the white men, who retained "Black Drink" without bad effects.[*]

Next, calabashes with water which stood ready in large vessels, were passed around for the cleansing of hands and mouth. In the meantime, the squaws had prepared dinner outside the square and brought it to the four entrances to the building where it was received and set down by the Indian waiters. By command of the Micco, the servants put the dinner into large earthen dishes, several of which were so placed in each building that about ten persons could sit around each spread of victuals. A supply of large, new, wooden spoons were equally distributed but there were not enough to go around. Steiner describes their meal as follows: One platter of very good boiled beef, not salted; one dish of Osaufke;[†] one dish of beans. No bread was served, as the corn crop of the last year had been a total failure. The meat was gotten out of the dish with the fingers, after which each one proceeded further with his pocket knife. Of the other

---

[*] It is barely possible they did not imbibe enough of it!

[†] The writer could not ascertain and, even with the help of a vivid imagination, cannot conjecture what this dish was.

dishes each ate several spoonfulls, leaving the spoon in the dish for his neighbor.

The business of the Council was successfully dispatched and certain lands of the Creeks were purchased from them, by their consent, for annexation to the State of Georgia.

Col. Hawkins was a landholder among the Creeks and some of his property lay in that strip which the Creeks ceded to Georgia. Upon part of this land he promised to build a log house for missionary Brethren should they be sent. This location was on the Flint River, about fifty miles from Milledgeville, Baldwin County, Georgia. While this land was situated right in the Creek Nation, by the purchase, as noted, it was no longer under their jurisdiction; hence Hawkins' offer was perfectly legitimate, and no formality of asking the Creeks whether missionaries would be permitted to reside among them needed to be gone through, on which point the reverse situation among the Cherokees had caused so much trouble and delay.

After the Council, the Brethren had planned to explore the country a little, but, owing to the fact that Steiner was very weak from fever and because the horses had become very thin from lack of grain, they decided to return to Salem at once, via Springplace. The horses suffered much on the journey from weakness, and, when the Brethren reached Hawkins' quarters on the Flint River, Steiner came down with a bad attack of fever, remaining abed for over a week. Very slowly they wended their way into the Cherokee country, arriving at Springplace, July 28, where they enjoyed a good visit. Leaving again August 6, they came to Salem on August 22.

The reports which the deputies brought to their Society in Salem were very encouraging. A beginning of mission work among the Creeks was heartily resolved upon. Unfortunately, there were lacking in the congregation, Brethren who would volunteer for this service. Others, who considered it their duty to go wherever the Lord called, lacked necessary qualifications or were hindered by untoward circumstances. Recourse was taken to the Unity's Elders' Conference in Herrnhut, Saxony,

and this body called Christian Burkhardt* and Karsten Peter-
sen† to mission service among the Creeks. These Brethren arrived in Salem in 1806. Both labored earnestly to perfect themselves in trades other than those in which they were already proficient, agreeable to the advice of Hawkins, that missionaries as
tradesmen would find best entrance to the Creeks.

In the year 1807, these Brethren were sent from Salem into
the Creek country, making the journey in a three-horse wagon.
They came first to Springplace whence, after a very happy and
helpful visit with the missionaries there, they continued their
journey under the care of Brother John Gambold who took them
to Colonel Hawkins. Here they were received most cordially,
the Colonel and his wife taking them into their own family until
the mission house would be completed.

This house which, it will be remembered, Hawkins had offered
to build, had two large rooms, each 18 x 20 feet with a passage
12 feet wide between, and had one and one-half stories. One
room was intended for the dwelling, the other was to be fitted
up for the workshop.

Hawkins soon reported to Salem that the conduct of the missionary Brethren was exemplary and it had gained for them a
favorable impression among the Indians who frequently visited
his establishment.

Meetings were held regularly in their house, attended by
whites, blacks and some Indians. It soon became evident that
the missionaries would not get into touch with many Indians,
for it was Col. Hawkins' policy not to permit them to lounge

* Johannes Christian Burkhardt was born Dec. 19, 1771, at Ten-
germuende, Alt Mark, Prussia. His father died when he was 13
years of age and Christian was put out to learn the weaver's trade.
He became a journeyman in 1792 and met with some members of the
Moravian Church in Berlin. Through their influence he came to
Christiansfeld where he was converted and received into the
Brethren's Church. After his service among the Creeks he lived in
Bethabara, N. C., working at his trades, coming to Salem in 1818,
where he died August 28, 1846.

† Karsten Petersen was born in 1776 near Flensburg, Denmark.
By trade he was a joiner and turner, and when he came to Salem,
1806, he worked with the Salem gunsmith and learned that trade
also. After the close of the Creek mission, Petersen established himself in Salem where he lived to be over eighty years of age.

about the Agency for any length of time. Both Petersen and Burkhardt did much work at their respective trades, and their services were constantly in demand by whites and Indians. This good work of their hands, accompanied with testimonies for their Saviour which they were usually able to slip in with a business transaction, was their preaching.

Both missionaries made extended trips into the Creek country beyond the Chattahoochee River. It was almost impossible for a white man to settle among the Creeks unless he married an Indian woman; hence missionary trips were the only expedient for reaching them. They faithfully preached Christ wherever they could be understood or an Interpreter could be secured.

In 1809, from August to the end of the year, Burkhardt and Petersen suffered greatly from dangerous attacks of fever. End of November, Burkhardt seemed to be very near his end. Col. Hawkins and his lady cared for them in the most faithful manner, lending, also, their negroes to assist in the housekeeping. The Colonel showed his medical skill in the application of blisters in Burkhardt's case which produced a good effect and brought him again to himself, after having been unconscious for several days. As long as the Brethren were in this helpless condition, some of the white people in their neighborhood sat up with them every night. When the news of their distress came to Salem, it awakened deep sympathy. Two Brethren were sent at once to their assistance: John F. Holland, to help them in housekeeping, and Dr. Fred Henry Schuman, from Bethania, to render medical assistance. The latter had been consulted by the Salem Brethren but did not venture a diagnosis and a remedy at such a distance from the patients, hence generously volunteered to go. These two Brethren reached Flint River, January 8, 1810, to the inexpressible joy of the patients. Dr. Schuman's treatment proved most salutary and by the end of the month, he was able to leave. Though the missionaries were still weak, they were able to do their daily work. Brother Holland remained with them for some time and was a valuable help. He had begun to make clay pipeheads, an article much in demand by the Indians. Also, he instructed some of the Creeks in the making of earthen-ware.

In July, 1811, while Burkhardt was visiting the missionaries at Springplace, Petersen had a very friendly visit from Alie

Colonel, Head Chief of the Creek Nation and Assistant Agent and Interpreter. His daughter, with whom Petersen had become acquainted on a missionary tour along the Chattahoochee, was with him. On Sunday, she came to say that she understood that on that day he taught the Word of God and that she, also, wished to hear it. When the time came, her father accompanied her to the place of meeting and both were very attentive hearers. After the service, Petersen conversed much with them. The Colonel said that the Chiefs, especially the old Chiefs, often spoke of the Saviour, and he had dreamt of Him. They could not, indeed, "read the Old Book," but they were not wholly unacquainted with the subject.

Six years passed in this way. While they had done hard manual labor, preached wherever and whenever they could, and endeavored to learn the Creek language, Petersen and Burkhardt felt they had never been able properly to follow the real object of their mission among the Creeks. Even their hard evangelistic trips showed no tangible results. Consequently, they drew up a careful survey of the situation and sent the following points to Salem for consideration:

1. The Indian Agency was no place for a mission.

2. Col. Hawkins, with his fixed ideas on civilizing the Indians with arts and crafts, was no real patron of the preaching of the Gospel.

3. They could not learn the Creek language, having no frequent communication with the Indians, and further, no linguistic ability.

4. In order to settle in the Creek country beyond the Chattahoochee, the permission of the Chiefs must be secured. They were very strict in their prohibition of whites living among them; practically only those who married Indian women were allowed to settle.

The Helpers' Conference in Salem disagreed with point two and four of the report. They felt that Hawkins would further any attempt to preach the Gospel. They believed that, with the good reputation Burkhardt and Petersen had won among the

7

Indians by the work of their hands, the consent of the Chiefs might readily be secured. On the other observations, they concurred with the Brethren.

However, what made the situation still more difficult was the fact that the Creeks were again on the warpath. Having concluded peace with the United States in 1790, they were, for several years, at rest; but instigated by the English, now engaged with the United States in the War of 1812, they again took up arms against the latter, beginning hostilities by the terrible massacre at Fort Mims. In a sanguinary campaign for the Indians, they were completely crushed by General Jackson. In three battles over 1,200 warriors were slain and the Creeks were glad to sue for peace, in which contract they were obliged to give up about one-third of their former territory.

The rumors of this warfare were followed by the actual commencement of hostilities, and the two Brethrens' condition was very dangerous, hence the Helpers' Conference hastened to lay before the Unity's Elders' Conference the precarious situation of the Creek mission. As soon as advice could come under the slow means of communication of those days, the following instructions were received:

1. The War of 1812 made communication between Europe and America very difficult.

2. No Brethren had volunteered for mission service either in Salem or Pennsylvania, and several would again have to be called from Europe if the mission were continued.

3. Having taken the matter before the Lord, sanction was no longer given for the continuation of the mission among the Creeks.

Of these, No. 2 was the point really fatal to the mission. Was mission interest waning? Had the joyous spontaneity for the Lord's work ceased? Were the Brethren leaving their first love? God alone knows; but here the story ends, as there were no more men, for the time being, who said, "Lord, here am I, send me."

In 1813, following their earnest petition, Burkhardt and Petersen were recalled from the Creeks. Earnest and whole-souled men for Christ they were, though not particularly fitted for work among the Indians. It is of interest to note that when this Nation had been transported to Indian Territory and a visit to them was made by a Moravian Brother of those later years, he found quite a number of Creeks who held Burkhardt and Petersen in affectionate remembrance. Much good seed of the Word had they sown; this, according to promise, shall not return void unto the Lord of the harvest. Doubtless, real and surprising results of this effort among the Creeks, this expenditure of strength and means, these prayers and tears, will appear in the day of His glorious Kingdom. For 'twas done IN HIS NAME!

CHAPTER X

PROGRESS AMONG THE CHEROKEES—(Continued)
"JOY OF HARVEST"

Encouraging progress in the Springplace school continued to gladden the hearts of the faithful workers. May, 1807, they began to instruct the children in writing, to their great delight. The teachers enjoyed the utmost confidence of their Indian pupils. There was an added source of encouragement to them in the comments of a Mr. Lyon who visited at the mission station while on a trip through the land of the Creeks and Cherokees. He was in the employ of Dr. G. H. Muhlenberg, Lutheran Clergyman and celebrated botanist, whose letter of recommendation he carried. Mr. Lyon looked over the work in Springplace very carefully and told the Brethren "they were on the right track." He said that to learn the language of the Cherokees sufficiently to preach to them with any degree of satisfaction was well nigh impossible, because the Cherokee language was one of the poorest for terms to express spiritual conceptions. His opinion, therefore, was, that instructing the children and having them tell it over to their elders was the solution of the difficulty of a mission work among these Indians.

Col. Meigs was another welcome visitor. Having seen the work in its inception when the first Cherokee children were admitted to the school, this warm-hearted friend of Indian and missionary alike, could scarcely believe his own eyes over the progress he noted. He wept when the scholars read and sang for him. He said, "What great men these children will some day be in the Cherokee Nation!"

Witness, also, Chief "The Flea." He made several visits and was deeply impressed with the school and the religious meetings. Flea understood enough English to be able to follow the songs of the children and said, it seemed to him like heaven.

June 5, 1808, was the fifth anniversary of that dark and sad day when the Indians sent the letter which seemed to aim at driving the missionaries from their country. It was marked by an occurrence which showed the esteem in which the missionaries were now held. "Tus-ge-di-di," a very earnest Indian, came and said the children had told him the objects for which the missionaries had come. He said, all the Indians loved them! The missionaries replied that they, on their part, loved the Cherokees and wished to bring them to the knowledge of Him who is Love. Tus-ge-di-di said, that was very good, then reverently, he looked on high.

Two other Chiefs, after seeing the school, wished they were children again in order to be able to attend.

With great joy, a distinct work of grace was noticed in the hearts of the children. Their eager conversations with the many Indians who stopped in at Springplace were about the Saviour.

The dark cloud which lowered over the mission in 1809, when James Vann was murdered, has been referred to. Into this darkness shown rays of a new light when God Himself brought forward another patron in the person of Charles Hicks, a half-breed Cherokee and a man of splendid character and great influence among his people. Hicks told the missionaries not to worry over the future even though they had lost, in Vann, a generous friend of their school, for he would speak for the school at the coming Council and insure protection. O! there were joy and thanksgiving in the mission house then! Another, wholly unexpected, blessing followed. April 5, 1809, came a letter from their good friend, Cherokee Agent Col. R. J. Meigs, who had, unknown to them, advocated their cause before the Secretary of War and secured an annual grant of $100 from the Government for the school. Truly, God hath not left Himself without witness wherever they labor in His name! When Gambold journeyed to Col. Meigs to receive this annuity, the latter made him a present of Primers and Bibles for the school.

Among the most welcome letters from Salem which Col. Meigs had received for the missionaries was one for Brother Gambold which contained a written ordination, executed by Bishop Reichel in Salem, for Brother Gottlieb Byhan as a Deacon of the Moravian Church; this Brother having approved himself as a servant of the Lord in blessing among the Cherokees.

In a letter to Salem September 3, 1809, Brother Gambold writes of some interesting visitors:

"We had here a very agreeable visit from four Christian Mohawk Indians. Among them was Captain John Norton, by birth a Cherokee, but adopted by the Mohawks. Four years ago he was sent as a deputy to England in concerns of his Nation. There he became acquainted with many worthy characters of various classes, from whom he received much benefit. He had traveled with the other three partly by water, down the Ohio, and over land for the rest of the way to the Cherokee country, that he might, according to the custom of the northern Indian tribes, cover the grave of his father with wampum. On this journey, also, he wished to declare to his tribe by birth, the love of God in Christ Jesus, if he could find an interpreter who would venture to translate his speech. He appears to be a man who loves the Lord Jesus Christ in sincerity, and we were particularly struck with this circumstance, that though he is an Indian of an uncommon share of talents, and stands in the highest esteem with the Mohawk Nation where he assists in preaching the Gospel, yet he thinks and speaks humbly of himself. We spent Sunday with these worthy people most pleasantly and continued our conversation with them between the services of the day and till late at night. I accompanied them next morning on the road towards Oostanaula. O! how much we wished Captain Norton had understood the Cherokee language! Doubtless, it would have made a great impression if the Indians could have heard one of their own countrymen declare what happiness there is in being a follower of Jesus."

November 5, Gambold adds:

"We have been informed that Captain John Norton, as he could not find an interpreter at the Council at Willstown, and the Treaty was put off from December 1, to January 1, for which he could not wait, had returned to his own country, without executing the well-meant purpose of his journey, to preach the Word of Life to his countrymen. We have, with much pleasure, read an address to the Six Nations, sent by him from London, recommending to them the translation of the Gospel according to St. John into the Mohawk language and printed by the British and Foreign Bible Society. From this paper may be gathered that this worthy man received the grace to love Jesus as his Saviour and earnestly to seek the salvation of his fellowmen."

The close of the year 1809 found seven scholars in the school and Mrs. Margaret Vann, James Vann's widow, living near them in a small house. She was evidently growing in the knowledge of Christ and was very faithful in attendance upon the meetings. Often she was in tears during prayer and preaching.

The Salem Brethren wrote to Springplace asking whether, in view of the Government assistance received, they could take a few more scholars. This it was resolved to do, in spite of the fact that it involved more hard work on the Sisters in the housekeeping, sewing and mending.*

Talks with visiting Indians grew more and more satisfactory. The Spirit of God was opening their hearts. Some of the older Chiefs loved to have long talks about "the Great Man in heaven." Mrs. Vann was daily growing more interested, eagerly listening when Scripture was read and explained. She was able to interpret many messages of the missionaries to visiting Indians.

Then on June 16, 1810, came a red-letter day! It was John Gambold's 50th birthday and he received a most "acceptable present" in the request of Margaret Vann for Baptism. In tears, she made a very clear confession of faith in Jesus Christ. It was a day of pure joy; scholars and all rejoiced together. A Conference was held and she was declared a Candidate for Baptism.

According to Moravian custom, such Candidates are carefully instructed over a considerable period of time in the essential doctrines of Christianity. At that time, the special instruction was continued even after Baptism up to the time of the first partaking of the Lord's Supper. It is to the thoroughness and conscientiousness of this teaching—never perturbed by the desire merely to get more members into the church—and to the personal dealing with individual souls that the remarkable perseverance of Moravian converts from heathenism is principally to be ascribed. In this case, Brother Gambold was directed to impart the necessary instruction.

Great joy prevailed in the mother congregation at Salem when letters from Springplace arrived telling that the Good Shepherd had led one of His sheep from among the Cherokees into His fold!

---

* The missionary Brethren, too, found time not hanging heavily on their hands. They were carpenters, joiners, coopers, weavers and Gambold, at 50, learned to make shoes for himself and his wife! Besides all this they were missionaries in the truest sense and of the finest sort.

Provisions were again very scarce in the first months of 1810. In June, the missionaries had a clear instance of the particular Providence of God. They had no more wheat flour and the mill in the neighborhood was out of commission. Their corn was not fit to be made into flour and the available supply of meal was limited to several baking baskets full. Early potatoes had not turned out well owing to drought. In the greatest embarrassment the missionaries sat together not knowing what to do—and the school children must be fed—when a strange man appeared at the door. "Do you want to buy a barrel of freshly ground flour?" The Brethren said they lacked money, whereupon the man said that would be all right as Captain McNair had directed him to tell that he, the Captain, would advance the price in case they needed money. He sold the barrel to them very reasonably and there followed fervent prayers of thanksgiving. The acute shortage of flour was relieved when 1810 brought the finest harvest of wheat since the beginning of the work.

And a fine harvest of precious souls was ripening in the school! On June 24, 1810, the regular Moravian Children's Festival was held, with a Lovefeast, when, for the first time, the children sang their parts in the program entirely unassisted, to the great joy of the missionaries. Before this day each of the scholars had been spoken with individually, and they had promised, moved to tears, to give their hearts to the Saviour.

CHAPTER XI

AUGUST 13, 1810

Always a great day for true Moravians everywhere; the day when in 1727, the Holy Spirit sealed the covenant of the Brethren with their Saviour and the Renewed Moravian Church was born; the 13th of August, 1810, witnessed a similar experience of Grace, wrought by the same good Spirit of God, in the Cherokee Nation, through the instrumentality of the Brethren's mission among that tribe.

Previous to this day Brother Gambold had finished with his special instruction to Mrs. Vann through which he had become convinced that she had experienced regeneration of heart and been born of the Spirit. He announced before the Mission Conference that she was ready for Baptism. The Saviour's approbation for this solemn act was received for August 13th.

It was decided, since the houses at Springplace were inadequate for the crowd that would be in attendance upon the baptismal service, to make ready the barn* for this occasion. It was beautifully decorated with the scholars' assistance, and its large floor space proved too small for the great, reverent company which assembled.

The Candidate had spent most of the preceding night in prayer. She was radiantly happy when the great morning of her life dawned, and the light in her face on that morning was prophetic of the Sun of Righteousness arising with healing in His wings upon the whole Cherokee Nation. Dressed in white, she entered before the large congregation and the service began. The school children sang heartily with their teachers and Brother Gambold delivered a short, earnest address and poured out his heart in prayer to God for the Candidate, the whole assemblage, the entire Cherokee Nation. Many persons wept during the entire service. Clearly and from her heart Margaret answered the questions directed to

---

* The barn had been built with the assistance of Joseph Gambold, older brother of the missionary, who had come from Salem in 1808 to help in the outer work of the mission and who continued to serve in this capacity for many years.

every Candidate for Baptism in the Moravian Church, whereupon she knelt and was baptized, by Brother Gambold, in the name of the Father, the Son and the Holy Ghost, receiving the name, Margaret Ann.*

The service made a deep impression upon all present. Especially moved was Mr. Charles Hicks to whose friendly offices towards the mission, after Vann's death, reference has already been made. He said he would never forget what he had seen and in private asked many questions about the significance of Baptism.

When at night the missionaries met for the private service of the Lord's Supper† it was in the satisfaction, joy and peace which always mark the close of one of God's perfect days.

---

* Her maiden name was Scott and she was born August 20, 1783. Her late father was Walter Scott, a Scotchman, at one time Royal Agent among the Cherokees. Her mother was a Cherokee.

† The newly-baptized convert could not, according to Moravian rule at that time, be admitted to Communion before receiving further instruction and the Lord's approval through the lot.

CHAPTER XII

PROGRESS OF THE MISSION SCHOOL AT SPRINGPLACE TO 1819

In August, 1810, the news reached Springplace that Rev. Gideon Blackburn's school* among the Cherokees had been abandoned. Thus the Moravian school, though small, which had been the first, was now the only school in the Nation.

The following letter is in the nature of a first official report of the school to the Government assisting in its maintenance:

"Hiwassee Garrison, August 4, 1810.

"Dear Sir, Having again been favored with a donation towards the maintenance of our little school from your generosity, which I this day received from our friend and patron, Col. Meigs, I humbly beg you to accept my most sincere thanks for the same.

"A year has now elapsed since last I had an opportunity to thank you for a similar favor. I then promised to give a statement of the use I should make of your bounty. The first great use of it was to provide each of our scholars with a good, warm blanket; next, strong, home-made clothing; some medicine; beef, venison and wheat flour when our stock of corn was at an end.

"Since last I wrote you our scholars have advanced in Arithmetic as far as the Rule of Three,† made further progress in Reading, Grammar and Writing; learned by heart a little of sacred history and, likewise, the first rudiments of Geography. They advance but slowly and great patience is requisite to lead them on by degrees. Steadiness or perseverance in matters which require exertion of mind is not natural to the Indian, unless it regard those pursuits which are and have been habitual with them from generation to generation. Yet, I must say they are willing children whom we love sincerely and would gladly sacrifice our days in their service.

"Our girls excel the boys in writing at present, of which I enclose a specimen to you, trusting you will kindly take their good will.

"Commending ourselves and our dear little Indian charges in this country to your kind patronage and imploring our dear Lord to shower upon you, our generous benefactor, His choicest blessings day by day, I have the honor to subscribe myself,

"Your most obliged humble servant,

"John Gambold."

"Wm. Eustis, Esq., Sec. of War."

---

* Presbyterian.   † The Theory of Proportion.

The Byhans with their youngest child returned to Springplace in December, 1810, after having been away on a visit to
Salem since September; the chief object of their journey was to
take their two oldest children to Salem and place them in school
there. A Mission Conference was held immediately upon their
return, for which meeting they brought the main topic for discussion; namely, the building of a separate house for school purposes and religious services. There was great need for this forward step. The whole establishment at Springplace still consisted of two 20 x 18 feet dwellings, each a story and a half, and
a little cabin which the scholars occupied. The Byhans occupied
one of the dwellings; Gambolds, with Joseph Gambold, the
other. The 20 x 18 foot space was divided in each house by a
partition. Christmas, 1810, found 36 persons in Gambold's small
room! The houses were provided with wooden chimneys, lined
with clay, and the roofs were constructed of clap boards held
down by heavy poles. Evidently, there was urgent need for
more equipment and Gambold was asked to go over the business
more particularly with Brother Benzien of Salem.

The proficiency of some of the scholars, already in 1808, may
be judged by the following extracts from a letter sent by the
Rev. Jacob Van Vleck, Nazareth, Pa., to Springplace:

"My dear Johnny Gut-se-ye-di, Tommy A-ca-ru-ka and George
Vann:

"O! you don't know what a great pleasure I have had to receive
such fine verses for my birthday from such a distance, the Cherokee
country, written by the scholars of my dearly beloved Brother and
Sister Gambold. I had no idea that you already could write so well
and spell so well. * * * Your teachers teach you out of love to
God and to yourselves; love and respect them, they are your best
friends. Follow their advice, it is for your own good."

September 27, 1812, the teachers had the sorrow to lose one of
their scholars by death; "Dawnee," a little Indian girl of eleven.
She died very suddenly, before the missionaries could find out
what ailed her. They feared what the parents might say or do
and sent a messenger to bring them the sad news. A touching
funeral service was held, and when the parents were ready to
start for home they asked if they might send a younger daughter
to school. The missionaries were very happy over their confidence and gladly consented.

In the course of years, many distinguished visitors stopped at Springplace in their journeys and looked over the school. Among these, there came, in May, 1813, the daughter of General Nathaniel Greene, of Revolutionary War fame. She was now a Mrs. Littlefield, making a journey to Tennessee with her husband. She had been a former scholar of Mrs. Gambold in the Moravian Female Seminary, Bethlehem, Pa., and Mrs. Gambold found her true to the principles and traditions taught her in that school.

In August, 1814, the mission school had a visit from Dr. Golding, of Franklin College, Athens, Ga., who was well pleased with methods employed and results achieved. He gave hearty admonition to the scholars to make use of the opportunities they now had. With him was General Flournoy, with his staff, who rejoiced over the progress made in Reading, Writing, Arithmetic and Music, and gave presents to the scholars.

Several of these were so promising as to warrant higher education with a view to future usefulness in the Nation. At Cornwall, Connecticut, was conducted a Seminary for the education of the heathen youth of all races, under the auspices of the Congregationalists. Hither, Leonard Hicks and "Buck," Springplace scholars, had been sent in 1818. The following year, three more boys came to this institution; John Ridge, who had studied at Brainerd Congregational school, Cherokee Nation, after finishing his studies at Springplace in four years; David Steiner Tauchee-chee, a fine boy and good student—named after Abraham Steiner—in whose heart a work of grace was going on; John Vann, son of the former benefactor of the Cherokee mission. Missionary D. S. Buttrick of the Brainerd Congregational* station and Brother Gambold together fitted out these boys for their journey and entrance into the school. Buttrick procured some money for Tau-chee-chee to which Gambold added $10 out of his meagre treasury; giving him, beside, two of his own shirts. Buttrick took off his own coat and put it on Tau-chee-chee and Mr. Crutchfield† added vest and trousers! Thus, Springplace

---

* In 1801 a plan was agreed upon between the Presbyterian Church and the Connecticut General Association, for mutual help. Presbyterian ministers might serve Congregational churches and vice versa. Thus, while Brainerd was begun by the A. B. C. F. M., it developed into a Presbyterian mission.

† More of him in a later chapter.

had five scholars on the road for a higher education—probably future assistants and native Helpers in the mission work.

When Gambold was writing to Salem the good news about these five scholars setting out for Cornwall, his eyes were blinded with tears of emotion and gratitude to God. Thirteen years had they labored, often under the greatest discouragement and with apparently no results; but the day when the boys set out in pursuit of higher education, holding in store a bright future when they would return as leaders of their people, was worth all labor, prayers and tears—many times over.

The boys had quite a triumphal tour to Connecticut. A Mr. Cornelius had them in charge for the journey to Cornwall. At Salem they tarried several days, were shown marked kindness and received many gifts. There was great rejoicing and, also, great strengthening of faith and encouragement to prayer and further service, over these living, tangible, promising results of the Cherokee mission.

Mr. Cornelius reported the boys much gratified with their journey during which time they enjoyed perfect health and were very good and gentle all the way. At Washington, all visited ex-President Jefferson, dined with ex-President Madison and were introduced to President Monroe. They visited the tomb of Washington at Mt. Vernon.

Arrived at their destination, they were much pleased with the school and were left in charge of the Rev. Mr. Daggett, the President. It did not take the school authorities long to ascertain that these youths had had excellent training. From our observation of the Springplace school and consideration of its teachers in previous parts of this history, we are not at all surprised but, indeed, gratified to learn that the Prudential Committee on its first visit of inspection of the Cornwall school after the Moravian boys from Springplace had arrived, voted $200 for the support of the Moravian mission among the Cherokees. A fine tribute to the work that had been done by the Moravian missionaries in the first school ever established in the Cherokee Nation.

"Buck" fell in with a remarkable good fortune at Cornwall which at once started him on a career. Dr. Elias Boudinot,*

* 1740-1821.

Philanthropist, Statesman, Author and first President of the
American Bible Society, was much pleased with all the boys and
especially with "Buck," and gave him his name with the promise
of caring for him by annual support. "Buck" also received a
medal from him.†

A letter each from "Buck" and David Tau-chee-chee at Cornwall to their friends, the missionaries at Springplace, are illuminating as to the progress they have made in the mission school
both in mind and heart. Buck writes:

"Dear Friends, It was with grief and sorrow the last letter I wrote
you. I said that my sorrow was more than I could bare. But what
alteration has taken place since that time. The joy that brakes from
my wounded soul is more than I can express to you with my pen.
The loving Saviour that has so long been concealed, I hope is now
reveiled to my soul. O my beloved friends, little did I think the
love of God, when you told me daily, the preciousness that is in
Christ Jesus. But now I feel Him to be the chiefest among ten
thousand and the one altogether lovely.

"Pray for me that my faith fail not, and that I may be useful to
my countrymen and also pray for my countrymen who are in this
school that they all may be adopted into Christ's family. Methink
I hear the Saviour say, 'Son, go and work today in my vineyard.'
Lord, I obey. here am I, send me among the heathen.

"This letter need correcting but as it is vacation and our Instructor is not well, I will send it as it is."

Following is the letter of Tau-chee-chee:

"Dear Friends, I write you this time a few lines. I am hoping that
you are all well. I am very happy indeed to receive your letter. I
am very happy that our Good God has provided a place for the poor
heathen to get their education, so they may be useful. The Lord
will help us that we may return to our own country to teach our
Nation.

---

† Anticipating later reports from this boy it may be noted here
that "Buck", i.e., Elias Boudinot, after finishing his schooling,
married a white lady of Cornwall. He delivered "An Address to the
Whites" on behalf of his Nation May 25, 1825, in Philadelphia. He
edited the "Cherokee Phoenix", the first paper published in the
Nation, and was a man of talent and influence among the Cherokees.
Being, with others, persuaded to make a treaty with the United
States in December, 1835, for the expatriation of the Cherokees, he
was accused of having sold his country, and was killed by adherents
of the John Ross party, west of the Mississippi.

"There are at present 27 scholars in the school and 10 different languages. I am very much pleased here in this school. The master is very gentle in his way. I am but yet a poor wretched creature under the sun and very often I shed my tears about my soul. I hope my studies will be more benefit to me than all worldly employments. If I could live in this world happy in religion, I should not wish for anything more."

Several donations of One Hundred Dollars to the Springplace school by the United States Government have already been referred to. On September 3, 1819, came the following circular letter sent to all mission schools among the Indians from the War Department and signed by John C. Calhoun, the Secretary:

"In order to render the sum of $10,000 annually appropriated at the last session of Congress for the civilization of the Indian as extensively beneficial as possible, the President is of an opinion that it ought to be applied in co-operation with the exertions of benevolent associations, or individuals, who may choose to devote their time or means, to effect the object contemplated by the act of Congress.

"But it will be indispensable, in order to apply any portion of the sum appropriated in the manner proposed, that the plan of education, in addition to reading, writing and arithmetic, should, in the instruction of the boys, be increased to the practical knowledge of agriculture and such mechanical arts as are suited to the condition of the Indian; and in that of the girls, spinning, weaving and sewing.

"Such associations or individuals who are already actively engaged in educating the Indian and who may desire the co-operation of the Government, will report to the Department of War, to be laid before the President, the location of the institution, their funds, the number and kind of teachers, the number of pupils of both sexes and the objects which are actually embraced in their plan of education and the extent of the aid which they require. This information will be necessary to enable the President to determine whether the appropriation of Congress ought to be applied in co-operation with the institution, and to make a just distribution of the sum appropriated."

Brother Gambold duly forwarded the information requested and the entire Society of Salem were gratified by an answer in the most friendly terms, granting an allowance of $250 per annum, containing an agreement to pay two-thirds of all future building expenses and holding out the prospect of an increased allowance if the work would be expanded.

It was decided, in 1819, to confine the school, for the time being, to boys only. Experience had shown that it was very difficult to have both sexes at school under the circumstances of liv-

ing together at Springplace. Later on, it was hoped to start a
second, and separate, school for girls only.

The following comment on the mission school among the Cherokees was found with the papers relating to that mission. Its
writer was Henry Steinhauer,* and it gives a clear insight into
what was really going on at Springplace:

"The Moravian mission at Springplace, on the borders of Georgia
and South Carolina, in the country of the free Cherokee Indians, has
now been conducted for some years with unparalleled perseverance
by Brother John Gambold, ably assisted by his wife. They have
kept school with ten or twelve Indian youths, who have, under their
care, attained to a respectable degree of education. Three or four
of them give hopes of having attained to a practical knowledge of
the Truth and two, "Buck" and Leonard Hicks, will probably pursue
their studies in the mission college in New England with a view to
future usefulness among their countrymen.

"The indefatigable exertions of Brother Gambold and his wife are
almost beyond credit. Besides providing food, raiment, shelter and
fuel for themselves and their scholars, attending to the school daily,
acting as advisers and physicians to the whole neighborhood, entertaining every visitor—and they are numerous who draw on their
hospitality—writing letters, and on Sundays teaching, admonishing,
etc., they find time, even, to oblige their friends in various ways.

"On my expressing a wish to see some of the botanical products
of that country, Sister Gambold sent me, last autumn, between twelve
and fourteen hundred specimens of dried plants, besides near a
hundred packets of seeds, several minerals, specimens of all the
Indian manufactures of cane, etc., and a number of other curiosities,
apologizing for not having done more as the season was unfavorable,
whereas I should have thought the collecting of these a good half
year's work for one person's undivided attention, under the most
favorable circumstances. And yet this person, banished as she is
from civilized society, cheerfully laboring year after year with
scarcely any promise of success, yet undauntedly persevering, was
the first teacher in the Bethlehem Young Ladies' Seminary, and
seemed its main support by the excellent qualities of her mind and
heart and her abilities natural and acquired. To any not devoted
to the cause of God from the same principle, the sacrifice might appear almost too great; but not to one who 'loves Him because He
first loved us'."

* A distinguished scholar acquainted with nearly every subject in
literature and natural history. Principal of the school in Fulneck,
England, for the training of candidates for the Moravian ministry,
1802-1816, when he became principal of the Young Ladies' Seminary,
Bethlehem, Pa. He died in 1818.

8

A similar testimony from an entirely different source is the following in the report of Correa de Serra, a Catholic Abbé,[*] on a tour of the United States, who came to Springplace and abode there for a day and night:

"Judge of my surprise, in the midst of the wilderness, to find a botanic garden, not indeed like that at Paris, or yours at Kew; but a botanic garden, containing many exotic and medicinal plants, the professor, Mrs. Gambold, describing them by their Linnean names. Your missionaries have taught me more of the nature of the manner of promulgating civilization and religion in the early ages by the missionaries from Rome, than all the ponderous volumes which I have read on the subject, I there saw the sons of a Cherokee Regulus learning their lesson, and reading their New Testament in the morning, and drawing and painting in the afternoon, though to be sure, in a very Cherokee style: and assisting Mrs. Gambold in her household work or Mr. Gambold in planting corn. Precisely so in the forests of Germany or France, a Clovis or a Bertha laid aside their crowns, and studied in the hut of a St. Martin or another missionary."

Abraham Steiner came out to the Cherokee mission for an official visit in October, 1819, remaining at Springplace for six weeks. He wrote back to Salem, among other observations, that he could clearly see the influence the school at Springplace had had on the Cherokee Nation. The training there received by the scholars[†] was reflected in the homes of their parents. In these homes there were well-being, contentment and purity. In addition to their studies, the boys learn to cultivate the land and the girls, spinning, weaving, sewing and knitting. More teachers and better equipment are urgent necessities. Regular religious instruction is held, as part of the curriculum, and each Christmas a public examination in Bible and Christian Doctrine takes place and awards are given.

Let us, in spirit, live a day at Springplace. In the morning, when all are up and dressed—in the winter, at daybreak; in summer at sunrise—we meet for family prayer, all kneeling. After breakfast school begins, remaining in session till dinner. Several hours' intermission are followed by school from three

---

[*] Minister from Portugal to the United States and a distinguished naturalist and linguist.

[†] About 70 had been instructed here to date.

o'clock until toward evening. In the hours of intermission the
scholars either help in the garden and field, chop wood, etc., or,
when no work is pressing, take exercise together; go out with
their blow-guns—tubes of cane, 7 or 8 feet in length, fitted with
arrows which are blown out—or bows and arrows, to shoot birds
and squirrels. After supper is evening-song and prayer and
early to bed. Mrs. Gambold does all the teaching except the
class for religious instruction which is taught by Mr. Gambold.
The school opens and closes with song.

This chapter has dealt with the school as such. In conclusion,
it should be remembered that the spiritual interests of the
scholars were *always* the first concern of the missionaries. Besides the class instruction in the Bible, the scholars were individually dealt with, lovingly and prayerfully, as to personal
salvation. Of this, the following letter is a touching evidence.
Johnston McDonald was taken home from school by his mother
who needed him at the time. The boy was loath to leave and
wrote his teachers, in part:

"O how happy I was in hearing the Saviour's Word preached by
you! We who lived in darkness now hear the Saviour's Word
through which we can come to His light. May he grant that all who
have been educated by you may come to Him. One thing I yet lack:
I wish that my Saviour would take my heavy load of sin away from
me. I pray daily that Jesus would cleanse me with His blood, that
my sins might not abide on me until that great day when He shall
demand an account, and that, when He calls, I may lift up my head
with joy to live with Him forever."

CHAPTER XIII

EVENTS IN THE MISSION LEADING UP TO AND INCLUDING THE REMARKABLE YEAR OF GRACE FOR THE CHEROKEES, 1819

Our narrative of the beginning of the spiritual harvest among the Cherokees has told the events of the glad day of Margaret Ann's baptism. Early in 1811 she expressed a desire to be admitted to the Lord's Supper. This was another point upon which the Brethren of that day consulted the Lord directly; that is, when converts from heathenism, after Baptism, should come, for the first time, to the Holy Communion. Careful instruction regarding this sacrament was accordingly given Mrs. Vann and finally, on March 17, approbation was received for her participation. The Communion service that night, when the faithful missionaries together with their first convert presented themselves before the Lord in the common bond of the Spirit was filled with indescribable blessing.

In the year 1811 the mission was put on a more stable footing through much-needed financial assistance. Gambold regarded this help as a clear instance of the particular Providence of God. Just when they were in need, and there was almost a famine in the Cherokee country, a certain Brother Godfrey Haga* and his wife, on her birthday, happened to read in a missionary journal of the Springplace mission and its needs. At once they sent $100 to Brother Gambold, at the same time asking for information how they might be of further assistance.

The mission was growing deservedly popular among the Cherokees. At this time, the Chiefs sent a message to Brother Gambold that the missionaries might enlarge their fields as much as

* A wealthy merchant of Philadelphia, member and office-bearer of the Moravian church there. He was a member, also, of the Society for Propagating the Gospel Among the Heathen, and the particular friend of its missions. After this first donation, the Cherokee mission received stated assistance from him. In 1825 he bequeathed the bulk of his estate to the Society and thus enabled that organization to carry on the Cherokee mission for many years and to enter other fields. Part of this legacy he stipulated to be funded for the education of ministers and missionaries.

they wanted and could dwell in their land in perfect safety, since the Indians were convinced they were here for the good of the Nation. This action was the more encouraging to our Brethren, coming at a time when the Cherokees were growing more and more distrustful of the whites and their ambitions and were hedging about residence of whites in the Nation with severe restrictions.

The years 1811 and 1812 were marked by seismic disturbances in the southern and western parts of the United States. Frequent and violent earthquake shocks were experienced in the Cherokee country which caused great consternation among the Indians. Many of them came to the mission and asked the cause of these commotions, which gave the missionaries a desirable opportunity of speaking to them of Him, the Rock of Ages, upon Whom His people stand firmly built though heaven and earth should pass away. Several Chiefs begged earnestly to know more about God. When told of the Creation, Fall, God's promise of Grace, the Saviour's life, death, resurrection and the Day of Judgment, they listened with rapt attention, sitting by the hour with folded hands. When the missionaries had done, they begged to hear everything over again. "Tell us all you know about God." One of them exclaimed: "I cannot forget it; I will think of this all the time." The Gambolds endeavored to teach them short, ejaculatory prayers, such as aroused our Saviour's instant sympathy and brought His help, when sincerely uttered.

"The Ridge," concerned about the earth tremors, took occasion to visit at Springplace and asked if the end of the world was near. He was told that the end was unknown, but it behooved men to be ready at all times. He said, "It is true, we are very bad; God make us better!" When told of the Saviour's love and sufferings, he remarked, "They treated him too badly." Thereupon the missionaries showed him how Christ suffered all this willingly and he exclaimed, "O, how much he must love us!" His difficulty was to comprehend how God could forgive one who had long lived in wickedness, and he cited instances of special hard-heartedness and wickedness, and asked, "Can God forgive that?" When Gambold said, "Yes," he was very much touched.

Margaret Ann, too, labored faithfully to point out "The Way" to inquirers. Two Chiefs, especially, seemed deeply in earnest and to them she related the story of the Crucifixion, showing them a picture. Both were greatly concerned not to come into the place of condemnation. "Peggy," as the missionaries affectionately called her, confidently looked for them to be saved.

A man by name of Joseph Crutchfield, for a while overseer on Vann's estate, was becoming very much interested in Margaret Ann. One day, he approached Brother Gambold with the desire to help him in the effort to win her for his wife. Several times had she rejected him! After an earnest conversation, Gambold was convinced the man was not hankering after her estate but, as Crutchfield said, really concerned over that happiness which Margaret Ann had found in the Lord. She respected him and he seemed a man of good character. To the missionaries, in Conference, such an alliance seemed not undesirable, especially since certain evil persons were seeking Margaret in marriage. The Helpers' Conference in Salem was asked to consider the matter and approval came from this Body for the step. Then it was that Margaret decided to accept him, and the marriage took place on July 9, 1812, John Gambold officiating. Mr. Crutchfield became more and more interested in the services. The couple lived hard by the Springplace premises and came regularly to the meetings.

The year 1812 was memorable for the mission by the coming-forward of Assistant Principal Chief Charles Hicks with the request for Baptism. With heartfelt joy he was accepted as a Candidate and taken into special instruction. On Good Friday, April 16, 1813, he was received into the fold of the Brethren's Church by Baptism at a most remarkable service, held again in the barn which the audience filled to overflowing. Hicks answered the questions before Baptism with great conviction. He received the name "Charles Renatus." His full-blood Cherokee wife wept much during the service and testified that the Holy Spirit spoke to her own soul. The school children were moved in an especial manner; from their corner came the sound of loud weeping and sobbing. Charles Renatus was at this time 46 years of age. In his youth he had had some education and was able to read and write English well. He was almost constantly employed by his Nation on business.[*] While one soul, in itself, is not of more value than another in God's sight, one may be more valuable than another so far as service is concerned. Hicks was a distinct acquisition to the Cherokee mission, because he was a man of great influence. After his baptism, he said, "Your cause is now my cause; it will be a joy to me to help you whenever it is in my power."[†]

Hearing of Hicks' baptism, good old Col. Meigs felt constrained to write:

"Mr. Charles Hicks' being added to the Church of Christ is an acquisition and will have an effect to strengthen your hands. His example will, I hope, be followed. The enemies of religion cannot say that the weak and ignorant only are made converts; for it may with truth be said that the most intelligent of both sexes have been added to the flock of the Redeemer in the Cherokee Nation."

On October 14, 1812, the Brethren Abraham Hauser and Benjamin Wageman arrived at Springplace, having come from Salem in a wagon for the purpose of fetching the Byhans who had petitioned the Helpers' Conference to be released from ser-

---

[*] Hicks made a very good impression in Washington, when, in 1819, he headed a delegation to protest against the encroachment on the Cherokee lands by the State of Tennessee. That State had already measured out the part of the Cherokee country which would fall to its share if the Indians were driven out. On his return from Washington, Hicks reported a very satisfactory agreement entered into with the United States, by which over two-thirds of the Cherokee lands east of the Mississippi were secured to them. Speaking of this delegation of the Cherokees, Thos. L. McKenny, United States Superintendent of Indian Affairs, says, "In conversation at Mr. Calhoun's Secretary of War—the other evening, I adverted to the successful efforts now being made to improve our natives; when Mr. Calhoun replied: 'We need never despair when we can show such an evidence as Charles Hicks.'"

[†] Shortly after this, the missionaries one day gave Brother Hicks a $20 note to take along to have it changed. When the roll came back they found $30 and wrote Hicks he had made a mistake. He replied that he had made no mistake, but was contributing $10 towards the church to which he now belonged.

vice in the mission owing to Mrs. Byhan's impaired health. This left the Gambolds alone in the service of the Cherokee mission, with work enough for several missionary couples.[*]

In the War of 1812, the British induced the Creeks to take up arms against the United States and they began hostilities late in 1813. The Cherokees were invited by the United States Government to join with the United States forces in an expedition against the Creeks, which they decided to do. Charles Hicks was asked to go. Needless to say, the missionaries were very anxious about him and sent up many prayers to the Throne of Grace for his safety. November 12, 1813, they heard from Brother Hicks that the United States forces had been victorious thus far. Before the end of the year the Creeks had sued for peace, and in the negotiations again lost a section of their territory. The cessation of hostilities between Cherokees and Creeks was celebrated at Springplace with a special service of thanksgiving. Hicks returned from the expedition in time to be present at the Christmas Eve Lovefeast which was held with the mission house crowded to its utmost capacity.

Col. Meigs sent a letter, early in 1814, in which the following sentences are significant: "I rejoice with you at the termination of the Creek war. I never told you that I had at times some apprehension of your not being perfectly safe; but I hope your fears from that quarter are at an end forever."

June 16, 1814, Brother Hicks was admitted to the Holy Communion. He was greatly moved and fell on his knees in prayer whenever the missionaries did although he was troubled with a lame leg. He was steadily growing in grace and was a joy and comfort to the missionaries.

Joseph Crutchfield, husband of Margaret Ann, having made application to be received into the Brethren's Church—he was a Methodist—soon after his marriage, and the Gambolds having satisfied themselves as to his state of heart, his name was laid before the Lord and approval received end of August, 1914. He was admitted by the Right Hand of Fellowship on Septem-

---

* Joseph Gambold, an older brother of the missionary, was at this time living with them at Springplace, having come to help them in the outer work about the mission—Born Feb. 13, 1753.

ber 7. Thus the close of the year found three full communicant members, besides Brother and Sister Gambold, connected with the Church of Christ among the Cherokee Indians.

The missionaries were holding on to God in prayer and were gaining victories. Repeated examples of remarkable answers to prayer are cited by Gambold. Two are given, showing "the Lord working with them, and confirming the word with signs following."*

"Darky," a little Cherokee girl, the youngest of their scholars in 1813, broke out, one day, with a dangerous-looking eruption over her whole body. High fever set in and the child lay unconscious by nightfall. The missionaries could not diagnose the disease and all remedies they tried had failed. It appeared certain that Darky could not live till morning. At her bedside, the two missionaries united in intercession, prayed fervently that she might be spared, for the child was precious to them. Also, they feared the effect her sudden death might have on her heathen parents. The father had been hurriedly summoned to Springplace. In the morning, the child's skin was perfectly clear; the fever had left her; she was completely restored! Subsequently, the father brought large quantities of provisions to the mission out of gratitude.

May 1, 1815, the meal in the barrel and the oil in the cruse had all but failed. Provisions were almost gone and there was no money to buy. In full assurance of faith, Gambold and his wife just told their Father about it, laying the whole situation before Him. On the very next day, supplies came in from all sides, including two barrels of flour; by night, their larder was well stocked.

An interesting diversion for the missionaries was furnished by their observing a Cherokee doctor treating one of "Peggy" Crutchfield's sick negroes. He used herbs for medicine and seemed to diagnose and prescribe correctly, for the patient improved. Gambold saw some red and white corals with the doctor's things and noticed that he threw these into a vessel of water before he started with the sick man. Upon his inquiry, Gambold was told that the doctor did this whenever he was called to a

---

* Mark 16:20.

patient; if several corals floated, it was a good sign and there was hope; if all sank, the patient was declared incurable. Corals and herbs; a strange combination of superstition and good sense!

Brother Gambold was an occasional contributor to journals other than the regular publications of his own denomination.* Having read an article from his pen in "The National Intelligencer," on "The Origin of the Cherokees," Mr. Thomas L. McKenny, of the Government office for the Indian Affairs, wrote to Brother Gambold a letter of appreciation and added the following thoughts on the subject:

"The questions, 'Where Originated and From Whom Descended the Aborigines of this Country?' will never, in my opinion, be conclusively answered. They will recur, however, whilst an artificial mound remains in the wilderness or a relic of antiquity is to be found. Yet none of these will be found to contain the record of their creation, or to disclose the history of those remote people to whom they owe their existence. Time, which seems to delight in burying all things, has closed in upon the evidence of this case and shut it up forever. One thing, however, appears certain; the interminable wilds that have been considered as being frequented only by the beasts of the forest, have been inhabited by human beings of a race anterior even to the Indians themselves. But, as you remark, it cannot be known when and from whence these ancestors came, who those nations were which the Indians expelled from their country or what has become of them."

McKenny asserts that the Indians are endowed with the highest human endowments and fitted for the exercise of those qualities which the Christian religion imparts. He cites the instance of "Skenandon," celebrated Oneida Chief who died in the year 1815 in the 110th year of his age, having lived as a Christian man for over 50 years after conversion to God under the min-

---

* Gambold was convinced that it was indispensably necessary for the preservation of the Indians that they learn the English language, rather than be ministered to in their own, and that they should adopt the laws of the United States Government, and especially, our most holy Religion. He understood the plan for their civilization, steadily pursued by the Government, to have for its ultimate object the fitting of the Indians to become members of the family of free men and useful citizens of the United States and not merely to feed and clothe these poor creatures. Only through progress in civilization and education could the aboriginal man be saved from the destruction which awaited his race.

istry of a Rev. Mr. Kirkland. A short while before his death, Skenandon uttered the following remarkable words:

"I am an aged hemlock. The winds of an hundred winters have whistled through my branches. I am dead at the top. (Skenandon was blind.—McKenny.) The generation to which I belonged have run away and left me. Why I live, the Great Good Spirit only knows. Pray to my Jesus that I may have patience to wait my appointed time to die!"

Patiently they prayed and toiled, that lone Moravian couple at Springplace in the land of the Cherokees, their hands strengthened in the Lord by the growing in grace of their first converts, who were their joy and crown. Over the genuineness of these there could be no question. In April, 1816, Hicks wrote to them as follows:

"The waters were so high here on the 11th of this month that I thought it would be an act of imprudence to attempt to cross them; and yet, the thought of being absent from my brethren and sisters on that solemn evening (Maundy Thursday) affected me much and, on that account, I felt low-spirited all day. In the evening I called all my black people and charged them to do no labor whatever on Friday, as our Saviour suffered on this day and told them He suffered for our sins and whosoever believes in His name, black as well as others, will be saved."

Also, Margaret Ann's face continued to shine with the joy that was in her heart and her husband was walking worthily of the Gospel and rendering much assistance to Brother Gambold on the mission premises.

Meetings at this time were attended, on an average, by thirty persons; whites, Indians and blacks. Several times, when the attendance was much larger, the barn was used for meetings.

Another man and his wife were beginning to show signs of concern for their soul's salvation. Clement and Mrs. Vann, parents of James Vann who had befriended the mission in the early years, had caused the missionaries much trouble; particularly Mrs. Vann, a full-blooded Cherokee, had caused them grief by her disagreeable words and actions and had brought disrepute upon the work by her misrepresentations. Clement, a white man, in the past had been found to deviate often from the truth. Steadfastly, Gambolds had prayed for these people, and it proved that the direct line to their hearts was by way of the Throne of Grace; whereas, in years they had not attended any services, though they lived close by, now they came regularly.

And now came the year 1819, *annus mirabilis;* year of grace; a particularly acceptable year of the Lord among the Cherokees; a year of spiritual awakening felt over the entire Cherokee Nation.

Nearly 20 years had elapsed since the beginning of the attempt to impart the saving light of the Gospel to the Cherokees. During the greater part of this period, all efforts seemed without result and the situation must, at times, have seemed most discouraging to missionaries and the church which had sent them forth. Not only did the work seem hopeless, but it was costly. Then came the great joy of the first converts and, with this encouragement, Brother and Sister Gambold continued to preach patiently, to the benighted Indian heathen, salvation through Christ Jesus and endeavored to impress upon the minds of the youths entrusted to them, besides much other useful knowledge, the truths of the Gospel, waiting for the time, known to God alone, when the good seed would sprout and grow. At Salem, among the members of the Society most faithful, "some doubted" whether, under the peculiar plan of the mission and the extremely limited means at its disposal, even faithful labor, persevering prayer and patient waiting could bring results.

Nothing short of a powerful revival of religion which came in 1819 could dispel doubts and misgivings. Then there was great gratitude to God and the renewed assurance that toil with Him and for Him shall not be in vain. As Mrs. Gambold wrote, "The Dayspring from on high" did, indeed, appear among the Cherokee Nation and the power of the Holy Spirit was in such evidence as even to abase the faithful missionaries over their conscious lack of faith. During the year, the little flock increased from two to fourteen, earnest, sincere, growing Christians; numbers of Cherokees were coming, asking what they must do to be saved. Ofttimes, conversations and prayers with individual inquirers continued until late at night. Indians who have shown persistent and special enmity to the mission and hostility to the word of the Cross are now among those most deeply under conviction of sin.

The human instrumentality for bringing about this new day among the Cherokees were the undaunted perseverance and the unwearied pains bestowed by the missionaries on the education of the heathen children. The hand of the Lord was pleased to use these as the principal means for the visitation of Grace. Springplace had, by this time, attracted the attention of the whole Cherokee tribe and there was manifest that thirst, so uncommon and unusual in the Indian, for something better and greater than their fathers knew, which indicated that a new day had, indeed, come.

Early one morning in January, Mother Vann started the good year aright by coming happily, before breakfast, to beg for Baptism. She testified that for about a year she felt her heart had been changed; she detested her former ways and heathenish life, and now wanted to live only for the Lord. After a talk with her and prayer she was received as a Candidate for Baptism. By March, she had finished her instruction, and on the 14th day of that month her baptismal service was held. It was a real Pentecostal experience; the Holy Spirit working mightily in many hearts. The Candidate was dressed in white, which dress she had already designated for her burial. Her Indian name, "Wawli," was exchanged for "Mary Christiana." Among those most deeply touched, were the wife of Brother Charles Hicks and their daughter.

Shortly after her baptism, mother Vann had a letter written by Brother Gambold, and copies made of it to be sent to her relatives. She dictated as follows:

"I let you know that God has changed my heart. I have been received by Baptism among the Christians. I am so happy as I have never been all my life. Formerly, for many years and up to within a short time, I thought as you do and lived as you live. God has had mercy on me. May you all make the same experience. Take my words to heart! Pray to God that He may give you a change of heart and mind! I am much concerned for you."

Clement Vann, her husband, was received into the congregation June 27.

The Cherokee Nation is awaking. From a distance of thirty miles they come, William Hicks, his wife, Sarah, and others to receive instruction towards Salvation. Sarah soon declared that she had found the Saviour and two months later, in September, she witnessed a good confession at her baptism; and her husband, greatly moved, came forward in that service to give his heart to Christ. Others followed,

The joy occasioned in Salem when Gambold's reports of the spiritual awakening were read before the congregation can be imagined. (Gambold drew attention to another encouraging feature of the harvest, namely, that among the converts were several mothers of families. According to the peculiar customs of the Cherokees, we have already seen that the chief influence in the home, both as to external arrangements and in the way of thinking, rests with the mother. Gambold noted that most striking evidences were already apparent that the Lord was blessing this peculiarity of the Cherokee home to the salvation of souls within the household.)

The Book of the Acts of the Apostles—in reality, the Acts of the Holy Spirit—was never finished. New chapters have been added to it from the days of the Apostles even unto this day whenever men have followed the call of the Lord and permitted Him to work with them in the spread of the Gospel. What happened in the meeting at Salem when the good tidings from the Cherokee country were communicated, may be fitly expressed by a slight paraphrase of several verses of that Book:

"Then tidings of these things came unto the ears of the church which was in (Jeru)Salem; and they sent forth (Barnabas) Steiner, that he should go as far as (Antioch) Springplace.

"Who, when he came, and had seen the grace of God, was glad, and exhorted them all, that with purpose of heart they would cleave unto the Lord."*

Steiner arrived at Springplace, October 6, 1819, in company with the young Brother, Thomas Pfohl. On the very next day came Mrs. Delila McNair with a sweet expression of faith in Christ and was declared a Candidate for Baptism. On October 16, Steiner had the great privilege to administer the Rite of Confirmation to Clement Vann and his wife. Of this experience he wrote home as follows:

"It is wonderful what grace can do! I learned to know Mother Vann and others 19 years ago, and where at that time there was darkness and indifference, if not hostility, now they look bright and happy and are enjoying the merits of the Saviour's death and life. What was opposed of the Gospel now has become evangelist; especially Mother Vann tries to lead all her relatives to Christ."

* Acts 11:22, 23.

The growth in grace and usefulness of those who had come to a saving knowledge of Jesus was astonishing, as attested, both by the letters of Gambold and Steiner's report. The Spirit of God was working on the hearts of some who did not understand English, and Charles and William Hicks and Mrs. Crutchfield were extremely active in imparting to such the instruction which they needed, by careful translation of the words of the missionaries and by their own comments on Scripture or exhortation given. This assistance they rendered not only at Springplace at the gatherings there, but in the homes of their respective vicinities which they visited. An altogether unusual incident occurred when "The Ridge," commonly called "Major Ridge," although expressing himself as not yet ready to devote himself wholly to Jesus, carefully translated the instructions of the missionaries to his wife, who understood not a word of English, and she became a true Christian! The "Major" expressed his joy over her conversion, and added, of his own accord, the warmest exhortations to perseverance in the truth she had found! Then he expressed the hope that his time might come soon.

A similar circumstance occasioned much joy for the faithful Gambolds. Many of those who had learned to read at Springplace read diligently out of the Scriptures to those who had not enjoyed the advantage of an education, explaining to them what they had been taught about various passages. At festival seasons and, indeed, on most Sundays between meetings could be seen a little group here and there whose center was such a reader and expounder. Frequently, those who read had themselves, as yet, no saving experience of Christ, and the missionaries were simply amazed how the Spirit used the Word only, thus transmitted, for the salvation of souls. And it was astounding to them to find out when it came to instructing such converts, through an interpreter, how much real understanding and grasp of spiritual truth they already had without human instrumentality, save the reading of the Word.

A proof of the real hunger of souls after God was afforded by the fact that Indians now made use of every opportunity to hear the Gospel, though some lived 30, 40, or even more miles from Springplace.* Often, some who had traveled 50 miles missed the time for services because they could not read nor find anyone who could read the numerical figures signifying the day and the hour, which rendered almanacs and Text Books useless. Special services were often held for such who had come too late for a meeting.

Some of the Indian converts from among the Cherokees were tried and found faithful under bitter persecution for Christ's sake. Of one of these Mrs. Gambold writes to a friend, in part as follows:

"In my last, I mentioned the case of a poor woman who had been most cruelly treated by her wicked husband. (After she came to the mission.) The narrative of her sufferings is hardly to be exceeded either by the reports in Fox's 'Martyrs,' or the annals of the Inquisition and is too horrid to admit of being transcribed. At length, she took refuge in the house of one of our Sisters, scalped, and her whole body covered with sores. Her name is Keren-Happuch Sandford Turner Haskins.† She is still at Sister Crutchfield's, happy as a child, industriously earning a living by spinning, weaving, sewing, etc., and is very neat and cleanly. To encourage her in reading, we presented her with a Testament. 'O, thank you! Thank you!' she exclaimed quite enraptured. 'I will work, I will spin for you in return.' She now employs every leisure moment in reading her dear Testament."

A letter from Margaret Ann to the Helpers' Conference in Salem gives a view of what God's grace could accomplish in a Cherokee heart. It was written in 1819, doubtless under the inspiration of the great things for God that were then taking place:

"I have for some time had a thought to write to you whom I love as parents and tell you the situation of my mind. When I reflect on my former situation, I think I have lost a great deal that I had not these good brethren and sisters here when I was young, but I am thankful to our dear Saviour that He sent them when He did. When they did come my heart was so bad that it could not receive anything that was good. My dear Sister Gambold has taken a great deal of pains with me; she

---

* The Cherokee mission was different from other missionary settlements of the Brethren. Usually a mission was built up by the converts settling around the Station. The Cherokees, living on plantations, necessarily lived far apart; thus the mission work among them resembled a country congregation with its disadvantages; but with the advantage, for the Cherokees, of being far removed from the evils of the Indian Towns.

† Yes, this was an INDIAN woman!

spoke to me incessantly of that dear Saviour who suffered for us. Then He made me feel that He was my Saviour at length and when I felt that, I thought, is it possible that I have crucified the Son of God and He still is so good and still calls to me to come unto Him? I cannot thank Him sufficient for His goodness to me. When I think of the grace, that I was received into the Church of God and am become a member of the Brethren's Church, I have no words to express my thanks.

"I only wish that our Church would have beside ours here another place in my Nation, where they might hear the glorious Gospel that our dear Saviour will receive all that believe and come to Him.

"I have been at other preachings beside my brother Gambold's, but their doctrines seem a mystery, they are not so clear as those of the Brethren's Church. Brother Gambold speaks to my heart."

November 14, 1819, the church at Springplace was consecrated to the worship and service of God.* All these years, hitherto, meetings had been held in Brother Gambold's house which had, with increasing interest, been of late utterly inadequate to accommodate the congregations. The day of dedication was a day which the Lord had made and His people were glad in it. Seventy persons were present. A beautiful Ode was used at this service, having been prepared especially for the occasion. Mrs. Gambold, in all probability, was the author of the verses, which the school children sang from memory. Part of this Psalm of Praise follows:

> "1. Praise, honor, glory unto Thee,
>   Almighty God and Lord,
>   That we have lived a house to see,
>   Wherein to preach Thy Word.

> "2. We dedicate it unto Thee,
>   On this auspicious day:
>   With grateful hearts, we fervently
>   For thy blest entrance pray.

---

* Absolutely nothing could be found, either in the Springplace Diary or the letters of Brother Gambold, descriptive of this church building. The map of Springplace while probably accurate as to the general outline, gives no scale to judge the size of any of the buildings. Its general location, therefore, is all that can be shown of the church. From references in the diary, it is evident that the building was used for school also; consequently, two-thirds of the cost of the building must have been met by the United States Government, as per agreement of 1819. The building was erected by hired laborers and one carpenter, all under the supervision of Brother Gambold.

9

"3. Come, enter Thou, blest Trinity,
   Fill with Thy peace Divine
   This Tabernacle; let us see
   Therein Thy glory shine."

"MISSIONARIES:
"Think, O think, how great the favor,
   In Jehovah's courts to dwell!
   There poor sinners meet their Saviour,
   There, the sin-sick souls grow well.

"Admire the deeds our God hath done,
   What mercies to this Nation shown!
   'Tis twenty years, now, since His powerful hand
   Led the first missionary to this land.

"CONGREGATION:
"With him,* first messenger of Peace
   To the poor, wandering Cherokees,
   We now with grateful hearts here meet,
   And him, our benefactor, greet.

"The seed which he then sow'd with tears
   Has sprung; and, after twenty years,
   Each eye, rejoiced, the fruit now sees,
   And we have hopes of great increase.

"CONGREGATION:
"We humbly, on this blessed day,
   For our kind friends in Salem pray;
   'Twas love to Jesus, which them moved
   To send us teachers whom they loved.

"They richly all our wants supply;
   Tho' distant, still regard us nigh;
   In all their prayers we have a share;
   We are the objects of their care.

"O, gracious Saviour, bless them all!
   Hear the joint prayers of great and small;
   Thy servants, as their God and Lord
   And kind Director, do reward!"

After this service of song, the 84th Psalm was read as the
Scripture Lesson and Brother Steiner preached the dedicatory
sermon on the Text: "In all places where I record my name I
will come unto thee, and I will bless thee."† He followed the

---

* Abraham Steiner.

† Exodus 20:24.

discourse with a fervent prayer, after which Charles Hicks translated most of Steiner's address into Cherokee, to the great edification of all.

In the second meeting, held in the afternoon, the church was for the first time used for a sacramental service: the baptism of William Abraham Hicks, married brother, and Susanna Catherine Ridge, wife of "Major" Ridge. The Lord's presence was deeply felt. Mrs. Gambold writes of the day of dedication: "It was a most blessed day which many will not forget. By us it will always be remembered."

The year 1819, with its signal outpouring of the Spirit of God upon the Cherokees through the instrumentality of the Moravian Church, may be said to have marked, likewise, a new era in their advance in civilization. A new Council House, on the site of a new Town, called New Echota, stood finished, about thirty miles south of Springplace on the Coosa River, and was to become the capital of the Nation. The National Government is zealous for the improvement of the Cherokees; the President of the United States has made a visit among them. Col. Meigs is a powerful friend of the Nation, always at work for its welfare. A new system of internal government has been perfected for the Nation and the whole management of its public business has been adapted to the remarkable degree of progress already attained by this tribe. English has been adopted as the official language; the Nation's records are kept in English and it is more and more coming into use with the average man. Not a few Cherokees have altogether discarded their Indian language and customs. More of them are becoming agriculturists; some with considerable property differ but little from the substantial planters among the white people. All the Chiefs, and, more especially the younger, zealously espouse the cause of civilization and education, a thirst for which has become well-nigh universal.

Steiner had the high honor to preach in the new Council House, at the meeting of the Grand Council, before ever any business was taken up. For this ceremony, the Chiefs, sixty in number, had assembled at some distance from the building, and rode up, under the leadership of Major Ridge, in the best of order. Steiner was then called upon, and he opened the proceedings with fervent prayer, invoking God's guidance upon the

Council meetings to be held here. Thereupon he spoke on John 3:16, Charles Hicks translating into Cherokee. Complete quiet and reverence prevailed and the message was well received. The Chiefs spoke of this religious exercise as the dedication of their Council House. Steiner was greatly moved when he remembered how, sixteen years ago, he had stood before the Council of the Cherokees, before an audience of surly and disapproving faces, pleading for the missionaries to be allowed to remain in the country. "What hath God wrought!"

Major Ridge lived near New Echota and gave Brother Steiner an urgent invitation to preach at his house. His wife, it will be remembered had just been baptized. Ridge and his wife were full-blood Cherokees and were living a good life in a splendid home. Steiner was royally entertained here and, after his sermon, which Mrs. Crutchfield interpreted, was asked by Ridge to represent to his Society that missionaries were needed in their section; he, his family, his neighbors were seeking salvation. John Ridge, son of this couple, erstwhile scholar at Springplace, was now at Cornwall, studying science.

Steiner closes the report of his official visit to Springplace with these words: "What love, simplicity and sincerity prevails in the little congregation at Springplace, can be felt but not described. The hunger for the Gospel is strong in the Cherokee land. Pray that God may carry out His counsels of love for this people through us!"

The happy events of 1819 gave wonderful encouragement to Brother and Sister Gambold who had long labored in faith and with much love. They endured through all the seemingly barren years, "as seeing Him who is invisible."[*] Now, in spite of advancing years and diminishing strength, they felt called upon to persevere in the work committed to them and to devote the remainder of their lives to the service of the Cherokees who were endeared to them by so many ties and who, in turn, highly esteemed, loved, yea, reverenced them. To a friend, Mrs. Gambold wrote, "We are lost in amazement and bowed in the dust when we behold the wonders of God's grace now displayed among us." Their own report to Salem, the diary of the year 1819, closes with these verses:

---

[*] Hebrews 11:27.

"Dies war ein Jahr!
Ja, das ist wahr!
Dergleichen wir
Noch keins erlebet hier
Der Herr warf Funken aus,
     Manch Haus
Ward angesteckt;
Manch Herz erweckt;
Manch Auge weint
Nach Ihm, dem Suenderfreund!

"So wirkt die Gnad!
Und, in der That,
Wir sahen nur zu
Was Jesus Gutes thu'!
Wir fuehl'n uns arm und schwach,
     Und ach
Gar weit zurueck!
Doch macht der Blick
Auf Seine Treu,
Sein Lob hier taeglich neu!" †
                    —GAMBOLDS.

---

† The following translation of these really beautiful verses is given, merely to convey their meaning and with sincere apology to the authors:

This was a year
In verity.
The like which we
Had ne'er experienced here!
The Lord spread sparks of grace,
     And many a place
Was thereby set afire;
Awakened hearts' desire;
And many, weeping, bend
Before the Sinners' Friend.

Thus *Grace* proceeds!
In what was done
We just looked on
Beholding Jesus' deeds.
Ourselves, we poor and weak confess;
     We have, alas,
Remained far back;
And yet, one look
Upon *His* faithfulness,
Daily renews our praise.

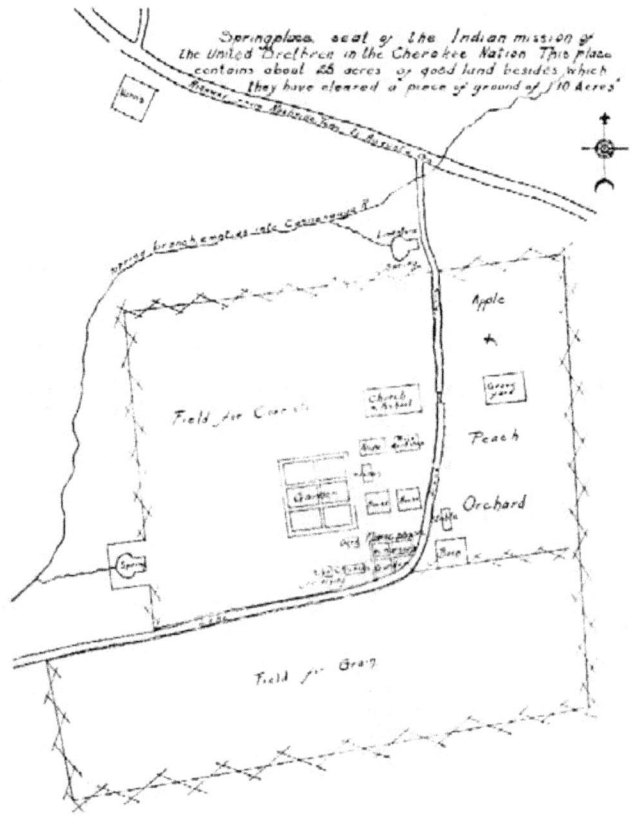

CHAPTER XIV

IMPORTANT EVENTS OF 1819–1821 IN THE MISSION

Abraham Steiner's report of his official visit to the Cherokee mission in 1819, contained notes indicating some important changes which had taken place within the Cherokee Nation and its internal government. Connecting his observations with items gleaned from other sources, the following statement will give a general idea of the situation of the Cherokees at this time.

The Upper Cherokees had made the greatest advance in civilization and were now no longer hunters and trappers but agriculturists and manufacturers. Among the Lower Cherokees, who still subsisted chiefly on the proceeds of the chase, there was much discontent over the growing scarcity of game. Accordingly, a party of the Lower (Town) Cherokees started out for the White River country in Arkansas where the United States Government had set apart lands on the White and Arkansas Rivers for them, with a view to finding better hunting ground. In this they were successful, and in eight years from the date of their first settlement, there were three thousand members of the tribe located on the White River and its tributaries. By a later agreement, the United States Government furnished each Indian with a rifle, trap and blanket and the promise of land in the west in lieu of his home claim east of the Mississippi, and transported him, free of charge, west of the Great River to join his comrades. Thus, a large part of the Nation, by gradual emigration, had, already at this time, found a home across the Mississippi. Each part of the tribe, east and west of that river, claimed to be the stronger.

Cherokees east of the Mississippi are judged at about 12,000 in number. Their lands now seem secure, by settlement with the Federal Government, and aggregate ten million acres. By the year 1820, a fully civilized form of government has been adopted. The annual Council of the Chiefs, which is attended by an Agent of the United States Government for reference and counsel, has sole legislative, executive and judicial powers. The results of Council are printed in English in sufficient quantities to supply each Cherokee house. (Those of the older generation have grown up without educational advantages and are much concerned that their youth shall be educated. The next generation will speak English.) "Pathkiller," an old man, is Principal Chief at present. Second in power is Charles Hicks (our Moravian Brother) who really does all the official business.

No land can be held in fee simple by anyone; all are tenants in common, although improvements on the land can be bought and sold. Land is assigned to any Indian who wishes to cultivate it. Private property is safeguarded. In general, the Cherokee Nation is becoming more and more settled and orderly.

White people, especially blacksmiths, mill-builders and tradesmen generally, may reside in the Nation after having received a Permit, which Charles Hicks is authorized to issue, on good judgment, between sessions of the Council. If such white men marry Cherokee women, they are thereby nationalized and belong to the tribe. Henceforth, no white man may marry an Indian woman without proper ceremony before a minister or other duly authorized official. The last step taken by Council in this direction was to forbid the marrying of more than one wife. Missionaries and school teachers are highly honored, and the mere word "missionary" is as good as a pass anywhere within the Nation.

Of missionary establishments among the Cherokees there were in 1819, four, of which the Moravian at Springplace was oldest, having been established in 1801, its beginnings going back, as we have seen, many years prior to that date. The second, Brainerd, thirty miles west of Springplace, on the Chickamauga, in 1816; third, Tallony, a new station thirty miles east of Springplace. Both Brainerd and Tallony were under the management of the "American Board of Commissioners for Foreign Missions."[*] Fourth, a station in the valleys of southern North Carolina, ninety miles northeast of Springplace, new in 1819, maintained by the Baptists. There were, in addition, several private schools, kept by individuals, paid by individual Cherokees.

---

[*] Closely co-operating with the New School branch of the Presbyterian Church. In fact, Brainerd and Tallony were Presbyterian.

Small and unassuming as seemed the work of the Moravian Church at Springplace, at the close of 1819 its influence had spread far and wide in the Nation. In the vicinity of the new Council House, the capital of the Nation, about thirty miles south of Springplace, in Gordon County, Georgia, several souls had been awakened, probably through children attending the Springplace school, and aroused to deep concern over their spiritual condition. Here lived William Abraham Hicks and his wife; both happily united to the flock of Christ by Baptism in 1819, as we have seen. Major Ridge and wife lived here; the latter a member of the church also. Quite of their own accord, these Indians who had found salvation and others who were seeking the Way of Life, gathered frequently at Brother Hicks' house where he would read from the New Testament, translating as best he could. Often reader and auditors had to pause, overcome by deep emotion! Many times they made the trip of thirty miles to Springplace, to receive new help and inspiration there. Early in 1820, these earnest people sent the following letter of appeal to the Society in Salem:

"To the Directors of the Society in Salem.

"DEAR FRIENDS: We take this opportunity to write you about the settlement at Ooch-ge-lo-gy and the prospects for a mission and school here, which we conceive would be an advantage for usefulness to our rising generation. Besides, it will be the means of bringing some of our red brethren and sisters to our Lord and Saviour and without doubt it will be a populous settlement near here in a short time. We trust that this plea will occupy your minds in your deliberations in sending some of the Brethren and Sisters who may live near to us to teach and instruct us, as some of us have already joined the Brethren's Society who now lives at this settlement. We deem it our duty to inform you that we have mentioned of these our wishes to the Chiefs in Council at our New Town, for we find difficulty to obtain suitable schoolmasters to instruct our children.

"We might say much on this interesting subject, but must refer you to the information of Brother Steiner who have visited our settlement and no doubt has formed his opinion on this place.

"With much esteem and love, we remain yours affectionately.

"WILLIAM HICKS,

"RIDGE   X. (his mark)

"WAYIFF   X." (his mark)

The effect of this letter telling of another door opened by the Lord to the Indians, objects of the Brethren's solicitude for near a century, is shown by the result it produced, namely, a decision in April, 1820, to enter the open door at once and take this people for the Lord. In fact, the beautiful day which had dawned for the Cherokees, the new day of harvest, had already called for additional laborers to come into this promising field. The necessity for a girls' school at a separate place from the school for the boys likewise commended a new station, and Oochgelogy seemed the logical location.

How it grieves us, even at this late day, to write that there were no volunteers in Salem for Oochgelogy who would eagerly say, when the letter was read with its petition, "Come down and help us," as of old, "Here am I, send me!" Neither were there volunteers in Bethlehem at this time for the field. The harvest was plenteous but the laborers were few.

A call to service among the Cherokees extended to Johann Renatus Schmidt, assistant in the Moravian mission among the Delawares at New Fairfield, Ontario, Canada, was accepted by him. A wagon was sent for him from Bethlehem and brought him there. Advice had been received from Salem that he should come by steamboat from Philadelphia to Petersburg, Va., and from thence by the mail route over Raleigh, N. C., to Salem.

Meanwhile at Springplace such as believed were added to the Church. Nancy Tally made a good confession of Christ as her Saviour on Easter Sunday, 1820, and was received as a Candidate for Baptism. Likewise Betsy Lasly was so received a few weeks later, to her inexpressible joy.

On May 14, came great news from Salem. John Renatus Schmidt had received and accepted a call to the Cherokee mission, this was one item; the other, an announcement that a second station was to be begun at Oochgelogy, to which new work Brother and Sister Gambold were assigned when Schmidt and his wife had entered upon their duties at Springplace. When these matters were communicated to the Cherokee flock at the next service, these dear souls wept for joy.

June 10, Captain McNair's Cherokee wife arrived at Spring-place from her home over the Tennessee border. A letter had been sent her by the missionaries telling that June 11 had been fixed for her baptism. She related that when she read the letter she ran out into the garden, laughing and weeping at the same time, lifted her hands to heaven and said, "Dear Lord, here am I, do with me as thou wilt!" July 23, Nancy Tally and Betsy Lasly followed her into the Saviour's fold in the Sacrament of Baptism. On each occasion, over 100 persons were present in greatest reverence. A second service was held on the latter date, at which the following were confirmed in their Baptismal Covenant: William Abraham Hicks and his wife, Sarah Bithiah, and Susanna Catherine Ridge.

July brought a very acceptable present of 100 yards of cotton goods to Springplace, the gift of Christian friends in and around Athens, Ga. A Mrs. Cole, friend of the Gambolds, was instrumental in securing this material which was utilized in making garments for the scholars.

A decade had passed, August 13, 1820, since the first fruits of the Springplace mission among the Cherokees had been added unto the Lord. What intervening years of grace and blessing the faithful missionaries—not once on furlough—were able to remember before God and what new joy the Festival Day of the Renewed Moravian Church brought to them when two more precious souls of this Nation knelt for Baptism: Mrs. Catherine Maria Gann and her mother, "Zau-e-n-eka," who received the more euphonious name "Lydia."

Testimony as to the type of work done by the Moravian missionaries, all by the grace of God, came again, at this time, from two sources. In October, 1820, a Rev. Mr. Porter, Presbyterian minister, native of Buncomb County, N. C., stopped at Springplace on his return journey from a missionary tour through Alabama. He had seen most of the members at Oochgelogy, preached at Mrs. Lasly's house and was overjoyed at the grace of God and the work of the Holy Spirit as manifested in these converts. Particularly pleased was he with old mother Vann whom, he said, the Lord had called in her eleventh hour to Salvation. The other word of commendation came from that dear and now aged man of God, Col. Meigs, still Government Agent for the Cherokees. He wrote, "You have succeeded as far as you and your Society could possibly expect. The persons you name as new members of your church are amongst the first characters in the Nation for understanding and respectability."

Finally, on October 13, 1820, came the long-prayed-for reinforcements to the Cherokee mission. John Renatus Schmidt and wife, arrived in company with Philip Rominger, of Friedland, N. C., congregation, and John Lick, of Salem, their drivers who had been instructed, also, to help the new missionary couple to get "fixed" in their new home. The Schmidts were welcomed in a happy Lovefeast given in their honor. They brought special greetings from the Indian congregation in New Fairfield, Canada, expressed in a letter from the Delawares and then translated into English. The congregation heard these greetings with great joy and satisfaction. Brother Schmidt further edified them by singing several of the Moravian hymns in Delaware.

The letter which Brother Schmidt brought from the Delawares seems to be no longer in existence, but an interesting answer to their greetings, admonitions, and exhortations addressed to the Cherokees is at hand. Brother Charles Hicks undertook to reply to the friendly sentiments of brotherly love which now united Indians of different tribes and erstwhile engaged in continual, bitter warfare; love generated in the Delaware and Cherokee by the same Jesus Christ whom the Brethren had proclaimed to these and other Indian Nations. It will be remembered, from the chapter descriptive of the Cherokees that they had, when finally subdued by the Delawares, applied the term "Grandfathers" to the latter after peace was concluded as indicating the veneration and superiority which the Cherokees henceforth would ascribe to them. Now read Brother Hicks' letter:

"*To the Delaware Christians at New Fairfield, in British Canada.*

"GRANDFATHERS: Your salutations have been most cordially accepted which were delivered to the believing brethren and sisters of the Cherokees assembled at Springplace in October last and rejoiced our hearts when your words sounded in our ears; that you had not forgotten your grandchildren, but had kept in remembrance of us who have become as one with you in believing the Gospel of Jesus Christ and have much reason to be thankful to Him for the instruction given to our children as well as ourselves in the Way we should all follow, obeying His words to the Salvation of our souls.

"Grandfathers. We sincerely unite with you in our hearts, in considering all men, believing in the doctrines of the sufferings and death of our Saviour, as brethren, for they are all one in Him and ought to love one another, as He did love us, by suffering in our stead, that we might become children of God through His merits, that all His believers should once meet in His presence, although now far distant apart.

"Our Grandfathers know already we are but as little children in the knowledge of the Gospel of God, which has begun to be taught us but few years since, when some began to believe the Gospel that our Saviour had purchased us with His blood, that all might be saved who believed in Him. Seeing then we were unable in ourselves to merit His favors, except we come to Him for the remission of sins through His merits, but otherwise could not be saved, so have we believed by grace and it is our wish to abide in Him as the children of God and feel assured that we shall grow in grace more and more strong in our hearts and by the influence of His Holy Spirit be led from strength to strength, that the blessed effects of the Gospel of God may be clearly seen in us from day to day.

"The admonition of our Grandfathers, for which we sincerely thank you, to abide in Him with faithfulness, we take to heart and trust our Saviour will enable us to remain and abide in Him at all times and so walk as is worthy of His Gospel, that its effects may be seen as an example to our growing children as well as our neighbors, and we are much gratified in our minds to find that you still retain in memory that appellation, 'Grandchildren,' which had rose and had its use among our ancestors in their intercourse with each other. But the relationship attached to Christians is far above any earthly appellation retained among us, for we have now become as one, united as brethren and sisters through the sufferings and death of the Son of God, and may we all abide in Him in confidence as little children and not be ashamed at His coming!

"It was with much love we took Brother and Sister Smith by the hand and welcomed them into our country who have come a long way to serve us and, we sincerely hope, will be the means of doing a great deal of good to our people as he has been to you all. But how has it happened, Grandfathers, that you say, 'We who live on the lands belonging to the English,' which would seem you had none of your own? We that live here got a country left to us* that has descended to us from our forefathers and secured to us by the American Government by Treaties for the protection of it to us and our descendants and we wish to hear from you the situation of your country.

"We will now take leave with our cordial love to you all.

"CHARLES R. HICKS, and in behalf of others."

---

*It seemed secure, but was soon to be relinquished.

And now, October 18, 1820, brought an experience of quite another sort to the little congregation at Springplace. For more than a year preceding this date, Sister Margaret Ann Crutchfield had been in declining health. She perceptibly grew weaker from day to day and realized that she was approaching the time of her home-going. Meetings were held around her sick bed, where, also, the Holy Communion was administered several times to her inexpressible joy and comfort. When it seemed that the time for her departure had almost come, a special service was held with her—she was fully conscious—and the final blessing pronounced with the imposition of hands, as was the custom at that time. She greatly rejoiced over the prospect of soon seeing her Saviour who was all to her, and death held no terrors, nor the grave. Her face was lit up with the light and joy of the Christian hope, her heart was filled with the blessed assurance of faith. Calling on her Saviour, "O, my blessed Lord come soon and fetch your poor child," and bidding her beloved missionaries and loved ones an affectionate "Good night," after the manner of the early Christians, "until the day break," she peacefully "fell on sleep," and the first fruits of this mission to find Jesus was the first, likewise, to see Him "face to face!" The missionaries upbraided themselves for shedding so many tears over one who had exchanged the earthly lot for an infinitely better one, but, humanly speaking, they felt their own great loss. She was, indeed, one of them. Since the day of her conversion she had caused them naught but joy as she steadily ripened in Christian experience and approved herself not only a consistent follower of Christ, but as an accurate interpreter and a real evangelist. Many Indians came to see her body, prepared for burial, and were quick to note the sweet, peaceful expression on her face which gave the missionaries opportunity to point them to Jesus. An immense throng attended the funeral, listened attentively to the words of both missionaries and then joined the procession as the body was born to God's Acre, which the Brethren had laid out in the fenced orchard. "Forever with the Lord," was sung as the company walked to the grave where only that which was mortal was deposited, awaiting the day when the gloriously fashioned resurrection body would be united with its immortal spirit at Christ's coming.

The year 1820 at its close found the Springplace flock increased by six souls and the first day of 1821 was auspicious as Susanna, wife of "Waytee," came forward seeking Baptism.

A deep sorrow is sometimes accompanied by another. For several months, faithful Anna Rosel Gambold, frail in body but ever strong in spirit, had been ailing. To poor Brother John Gambold, sitting at her bedside came the alarming realization that he could not much longer hold this earthly treasure—for such she had been to him,—and the light of the mission. She had actually been kept alive by her indomitable will to do for God and in this spirit she kept the Diary of Springplace to within one day of her death, which occurred February 19, 1821. Her peace and joy in anticipation of "going Home" were dimmed but by one thought of sadness as she contemplated her aging husband and the Cherokees weeping about her bed. The attacks of *Angina Pectoris* recurred more frequently and became more severe, leaving her breath sufficient only to call upon the Lord. She could not recline, and during one of the attacks while Brother Gambold held her in his arms, she passed over. Weeks afterward, when John Gambold was sufficiently composed to write his friends in Salem, he speaks of his grief as indescribable, and thus is must have been for she was an unusual woman in mind and heart, in wealth of talents and completeness of consecration. She had the power to choose among many careers which her ability fitted her to follow, but she had one passion, and only one, Jesus Christ her Saviour, and only one life to live for Him. Following this, to the worldly mind, seemingly narrow path, her life became unusually wide and rich in its influence. Appeared the following in "Traits of the Aborigines of America," by Lydia (Huntley) Sigourney:*

---

* An American poetess and philanthropist of Hartford, Conn. She was one of the first women in America to plan for higher female education and maintained a select school for young ladies at Hartford. She published many books of poetry and prose and contributed to many periodicals. (1791-1865.)

"Thou mild Moravian sister! Thou wert decked
With what the giddy, unreflecting world
Might call accomplishment, but thou didst own
A pearl it could not purchase. Thou didst cleanse
Thy knowledge in the Fount of Jesus Christ
And pour it to the poor; even as the hand
Of the blest Angel moved Siloam's pool
To heal the impotent. And thou didst die
E'en as thou liv'dst, serene, unmurmuring, pure,
And ardent in thy faith. Thou hast obtained
Eternal gain for sublunary loss
And tribulation; for thy robes are white
In the atoning blood. Say, shall we shed
The tears for thee, blest Sister! When thy lot
Is better far than ours?"

Beside her Cherokee Sister, whom she loved as her own flesh and blood, was she tenderly bedded in the Springplace graveyard amid the sobs and tears of her little Indian boy-scholars who would not be consoled.

CHAPTER XV

THE CHEROKEES READ IN THEIR OWN TONGUE THE WONDERFUL WORKS OF GOD

In the diary and in the letters of the missionaries are found frequent allusions to the difficulty of learning the Cherokee language. With regard to the mastery of this tongue, the first visitors of the Brethren to the tribe were sanguine; as time wore on, the workers in the field reported that the task was hopeless unless some young Brother could be found who would be willing actually to live with full-blood Cherokees for several years; in that event, it was thought, Cherokee speech could be acquired. No action was taken on this suggestion; either the young Brother was not forthcoming, or the plan was later deemed not feasible.

The first ten years of missionary labor in the Nation were practically barren of visible results. With all allowance of time for the new and spiritual concepts of the Gospel to take root in the minds of a heathen people, years were necessarily lost because the messengers could not speak at all to the Indians except by gesture and, in later years, through awakened half-breeds.

When Charles Hicks became a member at Springplace, he gave the missionaries considerable information on the construction and inflection of the language. He said it could not be learned by writing it down as the pronunciation was different. Hicks tried to show them how words and syllables were expressed partly through the nose and partly in the throat. The sounds were so peculiar (naturally!) that no combination of English vowels and consonants could fully express them. D. S. Buttrick, missionary of the American Board, located at Brainerd, was commissioned by his Board to learn the language, and had put several years into the endeavor with the result that, up to date, he had found 9 modes and 15 tenses and 3 numbers, singular, dual and plural. No prepositions or auxiliary verbs were employed; these adjuncts being in the verbs themselves. Pronouns were seldom used; instead, the nouns were repeated. With all his study, Buttrick could not yet express himself to the comprehension of Cherokee Indians.

Hicks, after much patient, persevering labor, translated the Lord's Prayer into Cherokee, expressing the sound of the syl-

10

lables as best he could with English vowels and consonants and rendering the meaning of the prayer as faithfully as possible. "Our Father which art in Heaven," became "Eh, ghee, to,

Sequoya.

taugh-ae-cho-lar-Cal-le, lo- ch." Translating Hicks' Cherokee prayer into English, it read as follows:

"Our Father, resident in the firmament, unblemished be Thy name; Thy kingdom come: Thy word will be done here on earth as is done in the firmament. Give us this day our daily food; pity us of our misdeeds as we pity them that do us wrong. Do not lead us into danger, but assist us from it. For Thine is the Kingdom, great is Thy mind, Thy beatitudes without End."

In the year 1821, a remarkable man, mixed-blood Cherokee, named Sik-wa-yi, commonly called Sequoya, came forward with a Cherokee alphabet which he had invented and which was destined to bring the Nation forward by leaps and bounds, making the Cherokee a literary Nation. Sequoya had reached middle age before the establishment of the first mission in the Nation,

SEQUOYA'S ALPHABET.

by the Moravians, never attended school and in all his life never learned to speak, read or write the English language. Of a contemplative disposition, he observed, while on a trip to a neighboring village, that white men had a method of conveying thoughts on paper by a series of signs or marks, and he conceived the idea of inventing characters intelligible to the red man. He took up a stone and began to scratch figures on it with a pin, remarking that he could teach the Cherokee to talk on paper like the white men. He was heartily laughed at and his attempts ridiculed, but this seemed only to make him more earnest and he worked on until he had invented 86 characters, a complete Cherokee alphabet, by a system in which characters represented sounds out of which the words could be compounded—a system in which single letters would stand for syllables.

In 1821, he submitted this Cherokee syllabary to a public test by the leading men of the Nation. It is said that the leading men assembled, placed Sequoya and one of his sons at some distance from each other, had them write sentences dictated to them, and, having carried them by trusty messengers, had the writing of each read by the other, and in that manner tested the correctness of his claims.

The alphabet was soon recognized as an invaluable invention for the elevation of the tribe, and in little over a year, thousands of hitherto illiterate Cherokees were able to read and write their own language, teaching each other in cabins or by the roadside. The whole Nation became an academy for the study of the system. Letters were written back and forth between the Cherokees in the east and those whom we have mentioned as having emigrated to the lands along the White River in Arkansas.

In 1824, a young native convert, "Atsi," made a manuscript translation of a portion of St. John's Gospel, which was copied hundreds of times and distributed widely through the Nation. In September, 1825, David Brown, a half-breed preacher, completed a translation of the New Testament in the new syllabary, and this work was handed about in manuscript.

Meanwhile, Sequoya had visited the Moravian mission, and, while he never abandoned his native religion, he became imbued with a friendly feeling towards Christianity and its attendant new civilization. In 1823, the Cherokee National Council made public acknowledgment of the great service Sequoya had rendered his people by sending to him, through John Ross, then President of the National Committee, a silver medal with a commemorative inscription in both languages. Sequoya visited Washington, D. C., in 1828, as one of the delegates from the Arkansas band, attracting much attention, and the treaty made on that occasion contains a provision for the payment to him of Five Hundred Dollars, " for the great benefits he has conferred upon the Cherokee people, in the beneficial results which they are now experiencing from the use of the alphabet discovered by him."

Within a few years after Sequoya had given the Cherokee alphabet to his people, or in 1827, the Cherokee Council resolved to establish a national paper in the Cherokee language, and an iron printing press of improved construction, fonts of Cherokee and English type and all the appurtenances of a press in those days were made in Boston, under the supervision of the Rev. Samuel Austin Worcester,* through whose labors the letters made by Sequoya were made to express the Word of God. Early in the next year, the press and types arrived at New Echota, and the first number of the new paper, "Tsalagi' Tsu'lehisanun'hi," or "Cherokee Phoenix," appeared on February 21, 1828. White men were the printers and Elias Boudinot, "Galagi'na." or "The Buck," being our Springplace scholar Buck, back from Cornwall, was the Editor. Thus, again, we see the humble Moravian school bearing noble fruit! The sheet on which the "Phoenix" was printed was 16 x 24; paper, in those days, was molded, each sheet separately. The office was a log house. The

---

* Noted missionary of the A. B. C. F. M., or "American Board." First at Brainerd in Tennessee, and then in Indian Territory he labored for the Cherokees, devoting 34 years of his life to them. Died at Parkhill, I. T., April 20, 1859. At the time of the forced removal of the Nation from Georgia to the Territory, 1831, Worcester, refusing to leave his flock, was arrested, tried and imprisoned for many months like a common felon. Worcester pleaded the unconstitutionality of the Act, and by writ of error the case was brought before the Supreme Court in 1832. That body confirmed Worcester's plea and found judgment in his favor—Chief Justice John Marshall delivering the opinion—and Worcester was set at liberty. After his release, he worked early and late in translating the Scriptures into Cherokee. For 23 years he published the "Cherokee Almanac," printed mainly in Sequoya's alphabet and partly in English, "to promote knowledge, virtue and piety among the Cherokee people." Painful sickness in his last years caused him to work often in agony and many passages of his Cherokee Bible were translated while he was flat on his face, the only position in which he felt some ease. On his death bed, he said, "I would willingly live years of this suffering, if I could only finish the work of giving to the Cherokees the Bible."

Worcester was a warm friend of the Moravian missionaries and through his and Elias Boudinot's efforts, the Moravian Litany, Easter Morning Litany and several hymns were printed in Cherokee.

Miss Alice Robertson, present member of the House of Representatives from Oklahoma, is a granddaughter of the late Dr. S. A. Worcester,

hand-press and types, after having been shipped by water from Boston, were transported 200 miles by wagon from Augusta to their destination. Cases and other equipment had to be devised and made by the printers, neither of whom understood a word of Cherokee, but simply set up the characters as handed to them, in manuscript, by Worcester and the Editor. Such was the beginning of journalism in the Cherokee Nation. Wrote Worcester, "Their enthusiasm is kindled. Great numbers have learned to read and write, they are circulating hymns and portions of the Scripture, they are eagerly anticipating the time when they can read the white man's Bible in their own language."

Within five years of the acceptance of Sequoya's invention, the presses—now three in number—in the Cherokee forests, had turned off 733,800 pages of good literature, which was eagerly read and re-read by the Cherokees. Among all the remarkable forward strides made by the human race in civilization wherever the printing-press has appeared, none is more wonderful than the rise of the Cherokee people, attributable largely to the printed page. That Sequoya should invent an alphabet just at a time when the Cherokees were hungering for education and beginning to turn to God, under the labors of the faithful missionaries, these two facts fit together in a remarkable piece of evidence of that particular Providence of our God Who hath not left Himself without witness, and Who would have all men to be saved.

A partial estimate of the results of Sequoya and the press follows:

"Such a general distribution of good literature among those Indians, where it was so eagerly read, could but have a civilizing effect in all ways upon the people. They began to abandon superstition, they gradually adopted the white man's dress, they put themselves in the way of religious teachings; they began to produce grain for the market, instead of raising only for their own use; they practiced more frugality, they favored law, order, morality and temperance. Records show that nowhere in the Cherokee Nation did the cause of temperance spread so rapidly as in the immediate vicinity of Sequoya's home, and it was not long before a missionary wrote from that vicinity that the traffic in drink had almost ceased. In an incredibly short time they doubled the number of their horses and cattle, while small agricultural implements were in greater demand. A few mills were put up, public roads were established, more schools were started."*

* See Bibliography, No. 2.

After a precarious existence of about six years the "Cherokee Phoenix" was suspended, owing to the hostile action of the Georgia authorities, who went so far as to throw Worcester into prison. The journal to succeed the "Phoenix," after the removal

ᏓᎴᏯᏔ XVII. 65

ᎠᎴᏯᏔ XVII.

1 ᏫᏓᎿᎯ ᏔᏲ ᏏᎤ SᎪᎾᏃᏴ ᎤᏎ ᏂᏃ ᏀᎿᏃ ᏫᎧ ᎠᏬᏃᏨ, ᎠᏍ SᏔᎹᏬᎣᎨ ᏔᎧ ᏔᏍᏃ ᎠᏈᏔᏔ.

2 ᎣᏫᎠᏨᏍᏃ ᏫᏂᏨᏨᏔ, ᎠᎹᏁᏃ ᏒᏍᏊᏋ ᏴᏫ ᏊᏛᏫᎠᏔ ᎤᏴ ᏔᎫᏔᎮᏁ, ᎤᏊᎠᏃ ᏔᏍ SᏍᎹ ᏂᏊᎠᏴᏍ ᎠᎠᏴᎯᏔ.

3 ᎬᎤᏫᏍᎠᏃᎯ ᎥᎤ ᎬᏂᏢ ᏂᎬᏨᏍᏁ ᎤᏍ ᏔᏫᎤᏃ ᎬᏯᏍᏯᎢᏁᏔ.

4 ᏫᏂᏃ ᎤᎪᎮ ᎠᏍ ᏔᏍᏞᎤ ᏂᏴ; ᎬᏍᏫᏔ, Ꮲ ᏍᏴ ᏂᏂ ᏂᎠᏫᏔ, ᏔᎡᏃ ᏍᏂᏫ ᏍᎦᏍᎠᏬᏍ, ᎤᏂ ᎦᏔ ᏍᏫᏂᏕᎩᏍᏊ, ᏃᏍᏥ ᏂᎠ ᎦᏫᎿᏍ, ᏍᏯᏃ ᏔᏫᏬ ᎤᏮᏍ.

5 ᏫᏫᏍᎹᏃ SᎤᏂᏫᎯᏔ, ᎬᎤᏫᏍᎠᏯ ᎤᎠᏍᏟᏫ ᎤᏴᎢᏫ ᎤᎤᏫᎠᏊᎠᏫᎠᏔ, ᎬᎤᏫᏍᎠᏃᎯ ᎥᎤ ᎤᎠᏴᎤ ᎫᎠᏔᏔ, ᎠᏍ ᎤᎫᏫᎤᏔ; ᎠᏍ ᎠᏊᏂᏞ ᏂᏂᎤᏔ, ᎤᏍᎥ ᏔᏫᎤᏊ ᏂᏊᏔᏔ, ᎤᏍᎥ ᏃᏔᏢᏫᏘᏍᎠᏞᏍᎢ.

6 ᎤᏫᏟᏍᎤᏃ ᎬᏣᏫᏛᏬᎠᎢᏯᏃ SᏂᎠᏣᏍᏞ SᏍ ᎢᎤᏔᏔ, ᎤᏯᎠᏃ ᎤᏂᏍᏍᎿᏔ.

7 ᎢᏊᎤ ᎤᏴᎢᏕ SᎡᏂᏍᏔ, ᎠᏍ ᏈᏊᏔᏔ; ᎠᏊ ᏍᏯᏍ, ᎠᏍ ᏎᎿᏂ ᏍᎮᏍᏔᎢᏍᎢᏞᏂ.

8 ᏍᎤᏫᏍᎤᎦ ᏂᎤ ᎩᎤᏫᎤ ᎤᏂ ᎠᎢ ᎻᎤ ᎤᏍ

CHEROKEE BIBLE: THE TRANSFIGURATION.
(Matth. 17:1-8.)

of the Cherokees to the west, was the "Cherokee Advocate," of which the first issue appeared at Tahlequah, capital of the Nation, in 1844, with William P. Ross as Editor.

It was but natural that "Buck," i.e., Editor Elias Boudinot, should remember his school and his missionaries, when he identified himself with the press for his Nation, and make him quick to see the immense benefits that would come to their work if assisted by Gospel and song in print. He came to Springplace with Worcester and there they worked out the manuscript for the hymns. They had brought with them, already printed, copies

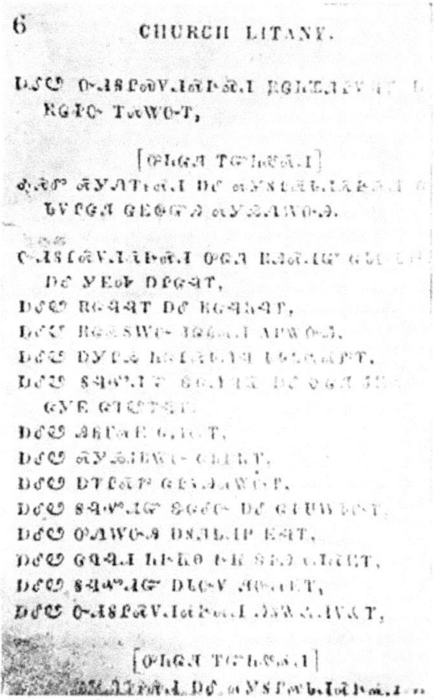
6 CHURCH LITANY.

MORAVIAN LITANY IN CHEROKEE.
(Section described is below asterisks.)

of the Gospel according to St. Matthew for use at Springplace. In April, 1830, Boudinot came again to Springplace, bringing copies of the Litany, beautifully printed! At once these were put into use in the congregation and gradually the missionaries learned to read aloud the Cherokee version.

The particular page of the Moravian Litany here illustrated in Cherokee print reads in the Moravian "Liturgy and Hymns," as follows:

"By thy agony and bloody sweat,
"By thy bonds and scourging,
"By thy crown of thorns,
"By thy cross and passion,
"By thy sacred wounds and precious blood.
"By thy dying words,
"By thy atoning death,
"By thy rest in the grave,
"By thy glorious resurrection and ascension,
"By thy sitting at the right hand of God,
"By thy sending the Holy Ghost,
"By thy prevailing intercession,
"By the holy sacraments,
"By thy divine presence,
"By thy coming again to thy church on earth, or our being called home to thee.
"Bless and comfort us, gracious Lord and God."

This same portion of the Litany translated accurately from the Cherokee into English, shows the excellence of the translator's work:*

"On account of thy extreme distress of mind and bloody sweat,
"And of thy being bound and scourged,
"And of thy being crowned with sharp pointed things,
"And of thy pains upon the cross,
"And of thy honorable wounds and the shedding of thy precious blood.
"And of thy dying words,
"And of thy having paid for us in dying,
"And of thy having rested in the grave,
"And of thy having risen and ascended,
"And of thy sitting at the right hand of God,
"And of thy never unsuccessful intercession,
"And on account of thy being present.
"Make our hearts ever happy, gracious Lord, and our God."

The Litany in Cherokee was soon followed by "The Doxology," from the Moravian Hymn Book and "The Easter Morning Litany." The latter was very valuable to the mission, aside from the beauty of the early service that could be carried out on

_____

* Petitions Nos. 11 and 13 were omitted. The Cherokee clause in brackets in the illustration (opposite page) means, "Congregation Responding."

Easter day, because it contains a real Moravian confession of faith or doctrinal statement of Moravian belief.

From the Cherokee Hymnal has been selected for illustration the hymn beloved by all Moravians: "Sing Hallelujah, Praise

"SING HALLELUJAH, PRAISE THE LORD."

the Lord."† The measure of eight and six syllables in the English can be counted in the Cherokee lines.

This hymn, in English, brings to a fitting close the story of the works of God through man as told in this chapter, and expresses the thoughts of our hearts as we, in spirit, behold the Cherokees reading their Bible:

> "Sing hallelujah, praise the Lord.
> Sing with a cheerful voice;
> Exalt our God with one accord,
> And in his name rejoice.

---

† J. Swertner.

Ne'er cease to sing, thou ransomed host,
Praise Father, Son, and Holy Ghost;
Until in realms of endless light
Your praises shall unite.

"There we to all eternity
  Shall join the angelic lays,
And sing in perfect harmony
  To God our Saviour's praise;
He hath redeemed us by his blood,
And made us kings and priests to God;
For us, for us, the Lamb was slain:
Praise ye the Lord! Amen."

CHAPTER XVI

OOCHGELOGY,* THE SECOND MISSION STATION, 1821–1829

From the digression in which we have followed the Cherokees in the beginnings of their literature, we return to the main narrative of our particular mission, now greatly helped and blessed by books and papers in the Cherokee language in Sequoya's characters—which were never used to print anything but what was pure, noble and uplifting. The letter of appeal for missionaries to the Salem Society in 1820, from certain Cherokees living in the Oochgelogy† neighborhood and the decision reached the same year at Salem to open a second mission station, will be remembered.

Already in 1816, several souls in the vicinity were moved by the Spirit of God, probably through some children, scholars at Springplace, and came, anxious to hear the Gospel. During 1819, three from this community were baptized and added to the church. These wished ardently that some missionaries might live among them for their further instruction and guidance; others, while not yet troubled over their soul's salvation, were very desirous to have a school for their children. In addition to the letter asking for help, these Oochgelogy people had laid their wishes very near to Brother Steiner's heart, on his visit in 1819, and begged him to support their plea for missionaries, which he did and prevailed. Johan Renatus Schmidt‡ had been

---

* Many different spellings of this name have been encountered. The writer has retained that used in the Diary and in the correspondence between the station and Salem.

† On a creek by the same name near Calhoun, Gordon County, Georgia.

‡ Johan Renatus Schmidt was born Feb. 11, 1784, at Bethlehem, Pa. He was descended from pure Moravian stock; his grandfather, Melchior Schmidt, having come from Zauchtenthal, in Moravia—David Zeisberger's ancestral home. Johan Renatus Schmidt was admitted into the Moravian congregation at Nazareth, Pa., in 1802 and taught for some years at Nazareth Hall, beginning 1807. In 1815, he received a call to the Indian mission in New Fairfield, Canada, where he served as assistant missionary with great success. In 1820 came the call to the Cherokee Indian mission which he cheerfully followed. Coming through Salem, N. C., he remained there several months and married Salome

called from New Fairfield, Canada, and had been married in Salem, en route to Springplace. At the same time, Brother John Gambold and his wife had been called to undertake the work of a new station at Oochgelogy.

After the Schmidts had become a little acclimated in Springplace in body, mind and heart, Bro. and Sr. Gambold were ready to set out when the symptoms of her last illness developed. In spite of sickness, she was filled with her characteristic zeal and wished to go to Oochgelogy, if possible, to win a few more souls there. She helped with the packing and counseled in the planning, both, with great enthusiasm, when, in the midst of these preparations, her summons came.

And here is a fine example of Moravian heroism. Gambold was almost prostrated—his own strength was failing in the latter years—when "Anna Rosel" left him, and even at this day we can imagine how he felt, when the first impact of grief had spent itself and the thoughts of Oochgelogy came to him. For him to go alone in sorrow and loneliness seems almost impossible to us; we could not have blamed him but considered it perfectly natural had he requested a rest in Salem to regain composure in the company and ministrations of loving Brethren and friends. Not so John Gambold. He considered his call to Oochgelogy as from the Lord, and, although he realized that alone he could be useful only to a limited extent, he felt he ought to go, *and he went,* fixing his tearful eye on Him and trusting in His grace.

On April 11, 1821, Bro. Gambold left Springplace, accompanied by Bro. and Sr. Schmidt and all the scholars for a distance of three miles to the Connesauga River, where they met the big flat which had come down the river, destined for a point below Oochgelogy, and had stopped here by appointment. Gambold embarked after an affecting farewell, the scholars sobbing and clinging to him. On the boat, Gambold met with Captain McNair, good friend of the Moravian mission, who lived across the Tennessee border from Springplace, coming often to the ser-

---

Gertraud Spaenhauer—born Dec. 23, 1794, Salem, N. C.—August 29, 1820. On September 18, 1820, he was ordained to the ministry. He served in the Cherokee mission 1820-28; served several charges in the Home Congregation and helped to establish the Cherokee mission in Indian Territory, journeying thither with the younger missionaries. Schmidt died at Salem, Dec. 14, 1852.

vices with Mrs. McNair, a Cherokee, who had recently applied for Baptism. It was through the kindness of McNair that Gambold had free passage to Oochgelogy with all his baggage.

The next morning, the boat tied to the landing at Oochgelogy and here was Bro. Crutchfield, waiting with a wagon for Bro. Gambold and his things. Crutchfield will be remembered by the reader as the late Margaret Ann's husband. After her death, he had moved into this neighborhood, built a house and fenced-in the land he wished to cultivate. He now drove Bro. Gambold to his house where he had invited him to stay until the house then in building by the Oochgelogy members and friends for their missionary, would be finished. As yet it had no roof.

Temporary arrangements were made with Brother William A. Hicks to have services in his house which was a roomy structure. Here a most blessed Passion Week and Easter season were celebrated with the first observance of the Lord's Supper on Good Friday.

In June, 1821, on his 62nd birthday, Gambold moved into his mission house and henceforth the meetings were held here. Brother Gambold says nothing of the lonesomeness and difficulty of his housekeeping, but in September he came down with such a severe attack of fever that he believed himself at the end of his earthly journey. His faithful Indians cared for him very tenderly and efficiently, and Bro. Schmidt came from Springplace as soon as he heard of his illness, prayed with him, and used the remedies at hand with such good results, that towards the end of the month Gambold could be about again. In the meantime, Schmidt had kept the services for him. In every way, the work now opened up most encouragingly and the Christmas season and close of the year 1821 found the house crowded.

Brother Crutchfield having decided to remove from the community, Gambold decided to negotiate with him the purchase of a two-story house 20 x 36 feet, which Crutchfield had begun to build but was leaving unfinished. He was willing to sell the house as it stood for $547.00. It was surrounded by 12 to 15 acres of cleared land and seemed a most favorable location for the mission. The matter was referred to Salem, and in May, 1822, Gambold received instructions from the Helpers' Conference to buy the house for a mission establishment. The first story

OOCHGELOGY MISSION PREMISES.

was designated for the missionary's dwelling, while in the second, school sessions and church services were to be conducted. As yet there were no windows or doors framed in the new house, only walls, roof and chimneys were completed. The accompanying photograph is a copy of a pencil sketch of the Oochgelogy mission premises. The original,* framed, hangs in the rooms of the Moravian Historical Society, Nazareth, Pa. The inscription beneath the sketch reads as follows:

"Sketch of the house built by Mr. Gambold at Oothkeloge—15 miles from Carsville on the road to Newton. Mr. Gambold died in 1827. The house was afterwards occupied by another missionary, and then by the Indians. Captain Thomas Stevens moved into it in 1834. He died in 1839. The log house on the left of the sketch was the first house built by Mr. Gambold. It fronts the North. The two-story house fronts the East. The great Tennessee road runs immediately in front of the Settlement and between the house and the foot of the hill on which Mr. Gambold is buried. The Oothkeloge Creek runs immediately in the rear of the Town as seen on the sketch. The houses, doors, shutters, and all were built without a nail. The sketch was originally made by Jos. R. Batts, Esq., Aug. 2, 1845. The right hand building was occupied in later years by Judge John G. Pothill."

In May, 1822, Johann George Proske,* of Salem, arrived in Springplace, and came to Oochgelogy, having accepted a call as assistant at the latter place. Chiefly he was to be employed as teacher in the school soon to be begun there. Shortly after his arrival, Gambold was taken so violently ill with another attack of fever that he had to be removed by wagon to Springplace, where he recuperated under the faithful and splendid care of Bro. Schmidt and his wife.

Gambold left for a visit to Salem in October, 1822, and did not return until the following spring. Bro. Proske, meanwhile, held the meetings, Schmidt coming down occasionally for the administration of the Lord's Supper. When Gambold returned, he came not alone, for Conference had decided that for his own good and that of the mission he could not remain single. His

---

* Loaned, through the kindness of the custodian, The Rev. W. H. Vogler, for this photographic copy to be made. The original is backed with wood which has stained the sketch, hence the imperfections of this copy.

* Born Sept. 7, 1794.

new wife was Maria Schultz,† nee Grabbs, of Salem. Their journey from Springplace to Oochgelogy, in a small wagon, was slow by reason of the fact that a cyclone several weeks before had uprooted great trees and several of these at intervals blocked the road. On reaching the bank of the Oostenaula River, they found the river very high and did not cross that day, camping for the night in the woods. (It was May.) The river was negotiated the next morning and at several places the wagon began to swim, but they managed to get across safely with all their goods. They moved at once into the unfinished house at Oochgelogy and Gambold himself completed it before cold weather set in. Eight hundred dollars was sent to Gambold from the Treasury of the United States for the new school building at Oochgelogy. This amount was used towards finishing the house which served both purposes of dwelling and school. A good harvest of corn from the field and produce and fruit from garden and orchard had been gathered in and the missionaries were well provided for their first winter.

The room for the school was completed in July of the following year and George Proske began with 10 scholars, 3 boys and 7 girls, Mrs. Gambold also teaching. In due time, one of the Oochgelogy scholars was ready for higher education, namely, Sally Ridge, daughter of Major Ridge and his Christian Cherokee wife. Her father took Sallie to Salem where she entered the Female Academy.

Situated four miles from New Town or New Echota, Oochgelogy was overrun with Indians at the time of the annual Council;

† Anna Maria Schultz, née Grabbs, was born in Bethania, April 10, 1783, and baptized on the same day by Bro. Ernst. She was reared in a godly home and received into the congregation on March 19, 1802. She was married to the Single Brother Christian Gottfried Schultz, of Salem, on Feb. 9, 1812. In the year 1816, she was left a widow with two daughters, and returned to Bethania to keep house for her father. The unexpected call to marry the widower John Gambold of the Cherokee mission came in 1823. It was hard for her to leave her children, but she decided to follow the call. Her daughters were brought to the Salem Female Academy and Sr. Schultz was married to Bro. Gambold on April 6, 1823. She was unaccustomed to the rigors of the Cherokee country, but served with great faithfulness up to and after the death of her husband. In Sept., 1831, she returned to Salem and served for eight years as "Vorsteherin" of the Sisters' House. She died Oct. 7, 1854.

11

for at this time, in addition to the regular business, was held the
Supreme Court of Appeals for the Cherokee Nation. As yet,
there was but one resident family at New Echota and no buildings besides the Council House, consequently the hospitality of
the Oochgelogy mission house was much in demand and frequently overtaxed.

Christmas Eve, 1825, the first service was held—the customary Moravian Christmas Eve Lovefeast—in the completed second
story of Gambold's house. It must have been commodious, for
100 people, mostly Indians, were present.

Brother Proske having left Oochgelogy in November, 1825,
and returned to Salem, the young Single Sister Maria Rosina
Gambold, usually called "Polly Gambold," a daughter of old
Bro. Joseph Gambold, still living at Springplace, came from
Salem to take up the work in the school. She was in company
of Brother Henry Clayton and wife who were sent from Salem
to Springplace to assist in the work of farm and household. With
her outfit came a bell sent from Salem for the Oochgelogy mission.

The first years in the new station reminded of the early years
in Springplace of "sowing much and reaping none." There was
no numerical increase in the years 1821-1826, but an encouraging
growth in grace among the members already living there could
be noted. The Rev. Theodore Schultz, having been sent from
Salem on an official visit to the Cherokee mission in 1826, mar-
velled over the progress made at Oochgelogy. Large congregations
were attending the services and Gambold, in spite of advancing
years, was heart and soul in the work, faithfully assisted by his
wife. Late in 1826, an aged Cherokee woman was happily converted, mother "Qualiucka," considered to be over 80 years old.
She was baptized on February 25, 1827, at a largely attended
service in which was experienced a gracious outpouring of the
Spirit of God. Her great-grandson received Infant Baptism at
the same service. "Qualiucka" became "Hannah." Of her, it
may be said, that she was permitted to suffer the reproach of
Christ. She had lived with her Cherokee husband, "Big Half-
breed," for 50 years; now, when he found out her determination
to become a Christian, he drove her away from home. After a
while, he fetched her back, but when he saw she was firm in her

resolve to be baptized, he pushed her out again and kicked her off the place. Her relatives provided a little house for her. She decided rather to suffer for Christ's sake then to give Him up. On the day of her baptism, another precious Cherokee soul found Jesus in the forgiveness of her sins: Susanna Fields. In gladness of heart, Gambold wrote to Salem that again he felt like in a dream, seeing these wonders of God's power and grace, just as he had felt in 1810, when he was permitted to pour the baptismal water upon the head of the first Cherokee convert of the Springplace mission.

In connection with the case of Susanna Fields, who was accepted as a Candidate for Baptism, there is some correspondence which illustrates the care the Moravian missionaries exercised in receiving new members:

"Ridge's Ferry, 3 February, 1827.

"Rev. John Gambold. Dear Sir, I take this method to let you know that I have a great wish to see you and will come at your next meeting if I am well, to have some conversation with you. I think and hope that I have found an interest in our dear Redeemer. I have long sought the dear Saviour, and I hope he has suffered me to find Him. I wish to make a profession of His Religion and openly now declare that I am His follower. For this purpose I wish to be admitted in the church of the United Brethren under your pastoral care.

"Please accept my best wishes for yourself and Mrs. Gambold.

"SUSANNA FIELDS."

"Oochgelogy, 4 February, 1827.

"Mrs. Susanna Fields. Dear Madam, Your letter of yesterday I have received, and the contents gave me sincere joy. You say, that after long seeking the Saviour, you think and hope you have found Him and obtained an interest in Him. This indeed is the only one thing needful for every human soul, to have an interest in Christ's Salvation, to be by grace enabled to believe that by His blood and death we are reconciled unto God. Oh! may He who began the good work in you, fully accomplish it to the glory of His saving Name! May you be fully rooted and grounded in Him and may your faith in Him be strengthened and established.

"You further say, that you wish to make a profession of Religion and to declare now openly that you are a follower of Christ. To this end, you wish to be admitted into the church of the United Brethren and it is your intention to come up at our next meeting.

"I shall be very glad to see you at any time and converse with you on this important subject, but I would advise you not to delay your coming here to the time of our meeting, for two reasons: first, because something may prevent you, time after time, on such occasions; secondly, because it is not customary in our Church to receive new members hastily, but we are required to obtain, as much as possible, a satisfactory acquaintance with such as desire to come into connection with us, before we admit them as members of the Church. Come, then, whenever you find it convenient.

"Mrs. Gambold cordially joins us in the ardent wish that you may become a true follower of Jesus here and a partaker of His glory in the world to come.

"Your sincere friend,

"JOHN GAMBOLD."

Susanna came, and the interview was satisfactory to her own and Gambold's great joy, and she became a Candidate, as stated, on Hannah's baptismal day. Her faithful missionary and adviser did not live to see the day of her baptism.

An invitation for Moravian missionaries to come to the Choctaws was received at this time. The letter, written to Gambold, was as follows:

"Choctaw Nation.*

"Rev. John Gambold,

"Cherokee Nation.

"Dear Sir: From reading and conversation I have been induced to form a high opinion of the zeal, perseverance and success of the Moravian missionaries generally and particularly of yourself among the Cherokees. This is the reason why I write to you, although we are strangers. I hold the station of one of the Principal Chiefs of the Choctaw Nation and I am sincerely anxious, as far as is in my power, to promote the civilization of my people. One great means to effect this desired object is to encourage pious and educated men to come among us to teach our children letters and set examples of industry to our people generally. We have already several schools in different parts of our Nation which are doing well. But there is still a great opening for other missionaries and I should be glad if they could turn their attention to my people.

"Should your society be willing to send one or more missionaries to the Choctaws, they will be cheerfully welcomed and respectfully treated. Lands shall be assigned to them for cultivation and I will give them every assistance and protection in my power. Our good wishes and every friendly assistance necessary shall be given them.

"I am induced to think that the example of neatness and industry

---

* The territory of the Choctaw Nation lay largely within the State of Mississippi.

which would be set by a Moravian family settled among us would have a strong and beneficial influence.

"I would thank you to communicate with your brethren, the Moravians, on this subject and let me hear from you as early as convenient.

"I am, with respect, your friend and brother,

"DAVID FOLSOM."

This letter was forwarded to Salem, with Gambold's annotations and the Brethren decided to lay the matter before the Unity's Elders' Conference in Herrnhut. For two reasons, evidently, no work was undertaken among this Nation; in the first place, there were no available missionaries. Efforts had been made to secure them in America, Germany and England, but it was a difficult matter, even, to secure sufficient workers for Springplace and Oochgelogy where they were sorely needed; secondly, the Brethren realized that the Choctaws were not without messengers of the Gospel and teachers, the Presbyterians having several stations in the Nation. The Choctaw Chief's letter again furnishes evidence that the Moravians were making good among the southern Indians, and shows the high regard in which our missionaries and their work were held among them.

After 22 years of loyal, heroic and blessed service among the Cherokees, John Gambold came to the end of his earthly service. During the first months of 1827 he toiled on in weakness and sickness. In June of that year an entry in the Diary of Oochgelogy states that there is an awakening among the people and a great hunger for the Word of Life, and Gambold is hurt because he cannot accomplish what should be done in this promising situation. On August 11 was celebrated the Moravian Festival day of the 13th of August and Gambold, in great physical weakness, administered the Holy Communion to his congregation and this was his last service. Brother Schmidt came from Springplace to conduct the services as Gambold could scarcely speak audibly on account of shortness of breath.

In the meantime, in 1827, Brother Gottlieb Byhan and wife, of Salem, had expressed willingness to serve again in the Cherokee field. It was high time that additional workers should come, and Byhan at once received a call to Springplace which he accepted. Brother J. R. Schmidt and wife were then called to Oochgelogy. These changes took place in the fall of the year while father Gambold was still living. One day when Schmidt had prayed with him and asked him what message he wished written to Salem, Gambold said: "Greet them heartily and tell them I give you my blessing for your work here with all my heart, and now I wish nothing more than that the Saviour would hasten to my Home-coming." Gently he passed away on November 7, 1827, at the age of 68, an old, tried servant of the Lord, faithful to the last. His funeral, held two days later, November 9, was attended by over 150 persons, the great majority of them Cherokee Indians whom he had loved so well. Brother Schmidt's funeral discourse was based on Revelation 7:9-17, after which the body was laid to rest on the knoll east of the mission house.

Brother Schmidt and his family now moved to Oochgelogy. Mrs. Gambold decided to remain for a while in the field, having become very much attached to the work, and she was needed in the school which now took on new life, for during Brother Gambold's illness it was impossible to attend to the school properly.

Susanna Fields was baptized on the first Sunday in Advent of this year, bringing the total number of Communicants and children in the Oochgelogy mission, at the close of 1827, to 31.

In 1828, the awakening in this section which Gambold had noted in his last days went forward mightily and many Cherokees came, saying, "What must we do to be saved?" On Easter Sunday were baptized Alexander James Copeland and George Augustus Hicks, and on Whitsunday, "Chinasee,"* the second wife of Joseph Crutchfield who had come back into the Oochgelogy community. After the service on Whitsunday, five full-blood Cherokees remained, of their own accord, to talk with the missionaries concerning their soul's salvation.

Brother Schmidt having asked to be relieved from service among the Cherokees, was given permission to return to Salem with his family in November, 1828. He preached his last sermon to the Oochgelogy flock on the first of that month and a very touching farewell service it was, for the Indians loved Schmidt and he and his wife enjoyed the confidence of all.

---

* Received the name Maria Rosina.

The vacancy at Oochgelogy was immediately filled by the arrival of Franz Eder† and wife Caroline‡ and the young unmarried Brother, Henry G. Clauder,§ these having arrived in Springplace from Salem already in September. Clauder's work at Oochgelogy was to be more especially the school in which a new arrangement was made, conjointly with the workers at Springplace, by which the latter school was now devoted to boys only and the Oochgelogy school to girls. Clauder instructed the girls, 12 in number, in the morning and Mrs. Eder taught the household arts in the afternoon. Under these conditions, the school made encouraging progress.

---

† Franz Eder, born April 26, 1798, at Woltsegg, near Linz, Austria. In 1818, as a journeyman, he came to Gnadenfeld, where he found his Saviour and united with the Moravian Church. He answered the call to the Cherokee mission from Niesky, Silesia. Coming to Salem in 1828, he remained there for several months for the purpose of learning the English language. Here he was married to Carolina Fredericka Eberhardt, and they set out for the Cherokee country in the fall of the year. From the first, Eder felt that he was not fitted for the mission among the Cherokees, and upon his urgent request, was relieved after a year and accepted a call to the Danish West Indies. Here he served until his death in 1836.

‡ Caroline Fredericka Eberhardt was born in Salem, N. C., May 5, 1801, and reared here. She was well fitted, by her training in home and school at Salem, to teach domestic arts in the Cherokee mission school. She was a member and officer of the Female Missionary Society at Salem, an organization which kept in constant, helpful touch with the Cherokee mission. This Society, in 1922, rounded out one hundred years of existence as an auxiliary to Moravian missions.

§ Henry Gottlieb Clauder was born November 26, 1805, at Salem, N. C., the son of Charles Gottlieb Clauder, a native of Zwickau, Germany, and Anna Rosina Transou, of Bethania, N. C. He learned the plumber's trade, but when he grew into manhood, was inclined to teaching and mission service after remarkable experiences of God's grace to his own soul in 1822. For a while he taught in the Salem Boys' School and then volunteered for the Cherokee mission in 1828. Going out at first as a Single Brother, he returned in September, 1829, to Salem, where he was married and then took his wife to his field of labor. He served for nine years in the Cherokee mission with great success and then was forced to relinquish his post when the Cherokees were removed from their lands to west of the Mississippi. Clauder was then called to service in the home congregations, notably at Hope, N. C., and Staten Island, N. Y.

Bro. and Sr. Eder were called to the Danish West Indies in October, 1829. Already in September, Brother Clauder had been called to Salem for consultation with the Helpers' Conference regarding Oochgelogy. Clauder was found willing to become missionary proper at that place. A written ordination for him as a Deacon of the Moravian Church had already been executed

HENRY GOTTLIEB CLAUDER.

by Bishop Hueffel of the Unity's Elders' Conference and sent to Salem to be presented to him should he accept the call. September 20, 1829, Bro. Clauder was united in marriage to the young Single Sister, Charlotte Elizabeth Ruede* and shortly after, they left for Oochgelogy in company with Nathaniel Byhan, destined for Springplace in the work of the school there.

Bro. and Sr. Clauder's labors at Oochgelogy were owned and blessed of the Lord and Cherokees were turned to God. With

---

* Born Sept. 25, 1807, at Friedberg, N. C. Well fitted for her work as missionary and teacher by previous life and training. She died at Bethlehem, Pa., June 28, 1883.

Clauder labored Alexander Copeland and wife, née Maria Rosina Gambold, Joseph Gambold's daughter; the former in the outer work of the station, his wife, in the school where she had already taught before her marriage.

"Stand Waytee," one of the signers of the petition for missionaries at Oochgelogy, the father of "Buck," or Elias Boudinot, editor and publisher, as we have come to know him, was soundly converted under Clauder's ministry, and baptized in December, 1829, receiving the name "Christian David." After his baptism, he laid his hand over his heart and said to Clauder, "Here I am feeling very good." The close of the year found 34 souls in the care of the mission and 13 girls at school. One of these, "Margaret Mary," had given her heart to the Lord and received Baptism.

CHARLOTTE (RUEDE) CLAUDER.

CHAPTER XVII

SPRINGPLACE, 1821-1829

Right heartily did the members of the Springplace Cherokee flock stand by their new missionaries, John Renatus Schmidt and wife, although they missed the sainted Sister Gambold and Brother John Gambold, now missionary at Oochgelogy, more than they could tell. Schmidt and his wife soon won the love and confidence of members and scholars and the work went forward under the smile of God.

In July, 1821, Nancy Adair was received into the congregation, followed, in October, by the wife of Brother Charles Hicks, a full-blood Cherokee, who received the name Anna Felicitas. Her husband could not attend this service, to which he had looked forward ever since his own baptism, on account of his injured limb which gave him great pain. Mrs. Hicks was brought to the Saviour principally through prayers and efforts of her husband, for she understood not enough English to follow the Gospel message of the missionaries. In April of the following year, Mrs. Hicks' mother, "Ajosta," applied for Baptism.

When Bro. George Proske arrived in Springplace, May, 1822, on his way from Salem to Oochgelogy, having accepted a call to the work of the school there, he brought for each Springplace scholar—there were 18—a present of a booklet, sent by a little girl in Philadelphia, who, having read of the poor Cherokee children and the school begun among them, had denied herself the use of sugar in her tea and saved enough money in this way to buy the books. "Of such is the Kingdom of Heaven!" Her gifts caused unbounded joy among the little Indians.

Bro. Schmidt wrote to Salem that they were noticing a distinct work of grace in the hearts of their scholars of which there were, in 1822, 15 boys and 3 girls. Also, this testimony of the result of former work in the school: on a visit to Charles Hicks to give him the Holy Communion because he could not come to Springplace—his limb grew steadily worse—Schmidt ascertained that one of Mrs. Gambold's former scholars, Richard "Dijuntoheesy," who left school a pretty bad boy after causing her much grief, had died in the neighborhood, but, before his death, had called to mind the teachings of the Gospel heard in his boyhood, and requested the nearest missionary to be summoned at once. The pastor from Brainerd station came, to whom Richard made a full confession of faith in Christ, after which he fell asleep in sweet peace. Another proof of the promise of the Lord concerning His Word, "It shall not return unto me void."[*] In August, 1822, another of the scholars, Nancy, with many tears, applied to Bro. Schmidt for Baptism and was accepted as a Candidate. Moses, a scholar who had been taken home for a while by his parents to help with the work, took violently ill and soon died, but not before he had thanked God in a childlike prayer for the blessing received at Springplace and begged the Lord to receive him, in Jesus' name.

Other former scholars were turning out well. A company of Cherokee Light horsemen one day galloped up the Springplace lane and stopped for a visit. George Hicks, one of the first scholars in Jacob Wohlfarth's time, was Captain.

With great joy, the missionaries welcomed home some of the old scholars returned from the mission school in Cornwall, Conn., where they had finished their course: Elias Boudinot, John Vann, John Ridge and David Taucheechy. When the latter stepped into the house at Springplace, he broke down and wept aloud for joy.[‡] These boys had grown up into fine men and be-

---

* Isaiah 55:11.

‡ David Steiner Taucheechy was an especially fine boy who was soundly converted under our missionaries and developed great talent as an Interpreter. One cannot follow up his story without keen regret over the way in which he was lost to the Moravian Church and its Cherokee mission, one of the weaknesses of which was the lack of native assistance and conscientious and careful Interpreters. Taucheechy applied for membership in the church upon his return. the Lot was consulted and several times said "No," after which, Taucheechy, not willing to remain without church connection, applied at Brainerd— now Presbyterian—and was promptly accepted. So *our* church, more and more, was compelled to depend upon the indifferent services of paid Interpreters. Taucheechy lived a faithful Christian life; walking humbly with his God, and remained a friend of the mission up to his death, interpreting for our missionaries on special occasions whenever his services in his own mission were not needed.

come followers of Christ and each took a prominent part in religious or civil affairs of the Nation.

Two more baptisms could be performed in 1822, that of "Ajosta," who received the name Anna, and Susanna, "Waytee's" wife, who was named, Susanna Charity.

Christmas, 1822, was enjoyed by 150 people at Springplace.

In January, 1823, the missionaries learned to their great sorrow of the death of Colonel Return Jonathan Meigs, United States Agent for the Cherokees and always a warm friend and benefactor of the Moravian mission. Already 40 years ago, he had made the acquaintance of Moravian missionaries among the Indians in the mission settlement along the Muskingum River.* He knew missionaries Heckewelder and Senseman personally. To his good offices in their behalf, when the Moravians sought to establish a mission among the Cherokees, the permission given by the Chiefs was largely due. Himself a good Christian man, he was fully persuaded that the Gospel was the strongest means to uplift the Indian spiritually, mentally and physically.

The winter during the first three months of 1823 was unusually severe. Provisions at the mission ran low on several occasions, but the school boys, with their bows and arrows and blow-guns, shot so many rabbits that the table was always bountifully supplied with meat.

The church could not hold all the people who came for the services at Easter time. Nancy "Tussewallety," the school girl who had made profession of faith in Christ several months before, received Baptism under the name, Anna Johanna.

A great Lovefeast was held at Springplace, May 21, 1823, the occasion being the return of Bro. John Gambold from Salem with his new wife, Anna Maria. Everybody belonging to Oochgelogy had come up and everybody from Springplace was on hand for this welcoming Lovefeast. Through the kindness of the Female Missionary Society of Philadelphia, the Gambolds were supplied with a large number of Bibles to bring along for their Indians. There were enough to go around for each member and scholar and several could be given to persons deeply interested in Salvation. The joy and gratitude which prevailed and were expressed

---

* Eastern Ohio.

in a letter of thanks to the Female Missionary Society, must have been very gratifying to that organization.

Sister Nancy Adair died at her home, some miles from Springplace, quite suddenly and without any of the missionaries present with her. From the testimony of those who had stood about her it was evident that she had faced the end in full assurance of faith, trusting in Jesus and calling upon Him. Bro. Schmidt did not receive word in time to be at her funeral, but on the last day of May, 1823, preached a funeral discourse at her grave, using 1 Cor. 2:9. Over 70 auditors were present. Mrs. Adair left a 10-year-old daughter, Delila, whom Brother and Sister Schmidt decided to take into their family to raise and educate. By coincidence, we may as well say Providence, when Schmidts brought this litle girl home, there was a letter forwarded to Springplace from Salem stating that a woman in Boston, a friend of the Brethren's work among the Indians, had promised to contribute $20.00, annually, for the education of an Indian girl, who was to be selected by the missionaries and given the name "Elisha Hubart." Gratefully, the missionaries at once chose Mrs. Adair's little daughter for this "scholarship," though it is not stated whether Delila retained the superimposed name when she grew up into sweet, young womanhood. Another friend in Boston promised to contribute $25.00, annually, for the education of an Indian boy, to be called "Gardiner Green," and Brother Schmidt chose a scholar named "Wolf" as recipient of this benefaction.

Constantly, there were more requests for scholars to be received than could be accommodated at Springplace. Several were boarded and lodged on the Vann place two miles distant. The school was constantly growing in favor in the Nation in spite of some Indians who remained hostile. One of this kind came to the scholars one night, without the knowledge of the missionary, and said to them, in effect: Why have white teachers in the country? Their teachings are not correct and not suited to the Indians who have been better instructed by their ancestors. Some time ago, he himself had been 4 days in a seemingly dead condition. During this time, he made a visit in heaven and found everything very nice; corn growing without labor, plenty of deer of unusual size, and everyone fat and happy and in one continual round of pleasure. Their faces were like the full moon. He had found there all the Indians who had ever lived on earth, but not a single white person.—The scholars who reported this to the missionaries themselves laughed over this ridiculous tale.

Christmas, 1823, was made very happy with the baptism of "Oskeyah," wife of Richard Sanders. Her name in Baptism was "Salome Elizabeth" and, with her accession to membership, Springplace had a total of 25 souls in its care at the close of the year.

Special trials for the Nation and our mission came in 1824. A great famine prevailed through the Cherokee country. Hardly any corn could be obtained and many Indians were living on roots and greens. A great drought in the first half of the year cut off those garden and field supplies which usually eked out the corn-supply until the new harvest could be gathered. Now many Indians were coming to the mission for food, and Schmidt writes that not one was turned away, for God had laid a special blessing on the mission-garden and fields and they had a large supply of vegetables. Schmidt writes this curious phenomenon when, later in the year, abundant rains fell: the cherry trees blossomed a second time in August and fruit was gathered in due time! Toward fall, the great abundance of chestnuts on the hills somewhat relieved the food shortage. In order to gather the chestnuts more readily, the Indians lit the leaves covering the ground; often the woods caught on fire and wolves were driven into the neighborhood of the mission, and one Indian woman was torn up by them. But the fire brought more useful animals, also, within range, and many turkeys and some deer were secured by the Indians. A Springplace Indian Brother had the good fortune to shoot a large deer and he brought a great quantity of venison to the mission.

The other great trial was an epidemic of smallpox which ravaged fearfully among the Cherokees in this year. Most of the Indians believed that this disease was spread by a monstrous serpent of the thickness of a man and with a white head. To catch even the odor of this serpent is fatal. Therefore, the Indians sought refuge with their sorcerers. One of these arranged a so-called "Physic-dance" at Tallony. For seven nights this dance must be continued, the Indians drinking a tea, brewed

from certain herbs, along with this exercise, while the sorcerer
prays either to a great eagle whom he pretends to see, or to the
black dog in the north, the white dog in the east, the gray dog in
the south and the red dog in the west. The sorcerer's fee is
seven deer hides from the community in which the dance is held
and a string of beads from each family. The missionaries, on the
other hand, obtained cow-pox vaccine from Knoxville, vaccinated
themselves, all the scholars, also, all Indians who wished to be
vaccinated, which amounted, in a short time, to about 150 cases,
and the epidemic in the vicinity was checked. Some sorcerer or
other, no doubt, received most of the credit for the staying of the
disease.

The year 1824 brought its great blessings too. "Tussewallety," Nancy's father, became "Joshua" in Baptism, and a
noble Christian, worthy of the name, he proved to be. Sally,
"Jack's" wife, a relative of Joshua, witnessed a good confession
in Baptism and her name was called "Sarah Deborah." There
were two Candidates under instruction for Baptism. The missionaries found out that what helped these dear converts most,
and what appealed most widely to the Indians who were now attending the meetings in large numbers, was the story of the
Saviour's sufferings. This seemed to grip their hearts. Therefore, whenever the opportunity presented itself and the Indians
were gathered and there was an Interpreter at hand, the missionaries repeated this precious story.

> "Lamb of God belovéd, once for sinners slain,
> Thankful we remember what thou did'st sustain;
> Nothing Thee incited but unbounded grace,
> To bear condemnation in the sinner's place."[*]

On one such occasion, after a particularly earnest discourse on
the sufferings of Christ, Joshua got up voluntarily and delivered
a strong exhortation to the congregation while the missionaries
were speechless over this new manifestation of the grace and
power of God.

The reader will not need to be told that we are in the midst
of another revival of religion among the Cherokees. Schmidt
writes, in 1825, that he has never seen such a desire for hearing
the word of God as is manifest at this time. From Oochgelogy,

---

[*] J. Cook.

the other station, Gambold writes of encouraging signs of the quickening of spiritual life among the Indians. Many of them came on foot 10, 20, yea, even 30 miles, to hear the Gospel. Sumach Town, 30 miles away, has been stirred by the Indians who come to Springplace. During the week, they talk of what they have heard on Sundays. Richard Sanders'† baptism, early in the year, was an occasion of outpouring of the Holy Spirit; in the large company which packed the church for that service, there was not an eye-witness without tears.

A visitor to sense this incoming tide of grace was Stephen Grellet, Friend's missionary and philanthropist who, since 1800, had been touring the United States and Canada, preaching the Word. He was a friend of the Moravian Church* and a lover of the Saviour and he rejoiced exceedingly over what he saw at Springplace and Oochgelogy. The missionaries had no compunctions in asking him to preach and this he did with blessing to all, admonishing the school children and the Indian members in a manner which made a deep impression.

One Sunday afternoon, some Indians came asking the missionaries to sing with them some of the hymns which had recently been translated into Cherokee and written down in the Cherokee characters. Gladly the missionaries complied and had a blessed song-service with this company and Schmidt found opportunity to fit in a short talk and close with a prayer.

More, now, of Brother Joshua. Since his baptism a year ago, he has brought about a great interest and desire for spiritual things among the men. More men are attending the meetings and follow the service with the closest attention. Usually, after service, a group of men will go home with Joshua, sit around his fireplace and sing and talk over what they have heard at the service, also instruct one another in the art of writing with the Sequoyan alphabet.

Later in the year, "Zauejucka," who with her husband had been frequently coming from Sumach Town to services, humbly petitioned for Baptism and her husband followed her in the re-

---

† He was from Sumach Town.

* He had been with the Moravians in Salem several months before this time. Also, he had visited Moravian congregations in England, Germany and even Sarepta.

quest. Both were accepted for instruction. Another token of revival: on going into the school room early one morning, Schmidt found one little fellow on his knees praying, with hands uplifted and so absorbed in his devotion that he did not notice the missionary's presence. "O dear Saviour, be with us today in our school!" was the petition Schmidt overheard.

Times of spiritual revival are usually marked, likewise, by special activity on the part of the powers of darkness. Around Springplace the evils in connection with the frequent ball-playing among the Cherokees were especially marked. The game, innocent enough in itself, was generally attended with much bad behavior, drunkenness and licentiousness. At one such game in 1825, not far from Springplace, Schmidt estimated the crowd in attendance at about 3,000, and he had information, on good authority, that the bets made during the game aggregated $3500. At such times the Indians went wild, putting up against a bet anything and everything in their possession: horses, cattle, hogs, guns, copper kettles and clothing.

From their friend, Captain McNair, came the information at this time that the Creeks, neighbors of the Cherokees, had sold a good part of their territory to the State of Georgia for a consideration of $400,000. From the United States Government, they were to receive, in addition, an equal tract of land west of the Mississippi. Some of the Cherokees are beginning to fear for the tenure of their own lands; times are growing uncertain. The missionaries notice that those Indians who have awakened to spiritual interests, grow more earnest under the special stress of the times; others, without spiritual concern, are growing more reckless.

The mission was officially visited by the Rev. Theodore Schultz,* from Salem, in April, 1826. He was royally welcomed and soon endeared himself to all the Indian members and children at both stations. Large congregations greeted him and when he expressed good wishes from the Directors of the Society

---

* Theodore Schultz was, at this time, Administrator of the American Moravian Church, south, President of the Helpers' Conference, and of the Salem branch of the Society for Propagating the Gospel among the Heathen.

of Salem, Joshua arose and answered for the Indians, expressing gratification over Brother Schultz's visit and asking him to thank the Society for all that had been done for them.

Springplace, and its work, through the eyes of Schultz, looked somewhat as follows: Located 600 steps from the main road between Nashville and interior Georgia and barely three miles from the main Tennessee road, also leading to Georgia. A very healthful location, good soil, plenty of woods, good pasturage and wonderful springs. The mission buildings are blockhouses, placed in a square, enclosing a yard. The church stands about 50 steps from the dwelling. The yard is very pretty with china trees, catalpa, cherry, peach and apple trees. There is an orchard, in fine condition, in the midst of which lies the graveyard holding the graves of Margaret Ann Crutchfield and Anna Rosina Gambold.

Brother Schultz is much impressed with the school and the decorous behavior of the scholars. He finds them well advanced in Reading, and most of them write a clear, legible hand. In Arithmetic, several have advanced as far as Long Division. The school is opened with prayer and opens and closes with singing. Bible instruction is given regularly, once each week, and in connection therewith some English hymn-verses are learned, to be recited next Sunday at the preaching service.

Over spiritual conditions at this time, Brother Schultz could not cease to make mention and to thank God. The care exercised in the admission of new members and in the instruction which was given those who were to be received, in one way or another, showed everywhere in the walk and conversation of the Christian Indians. Shultz noted the effects of their conversion in their own homes and also in the homes of the unconverted which everywhere seemed to have felt the influence of higher, better things. There were clean homes and industrious housekeepers in them surrounded by happy families. Bibles and good books were in the majority of homes. Plantations were in better shape and industries, looms, mills, etc., were increasing. Charles Hicks, Moravian Brother from among the Cherokees, honorable and venerable Chief, assured Schultz, that the missionaries had done untold good and held the respect of the whole Nation, at the same time pleading with him to represent to the Society the urgent need of more assistants, as doors for the Gospel stood open everywhere. Indeed, this was Schultz's own main impression; the greatness and the readiness of the harvest and the crying need for more workers.

The distinguished visitor had the high privilege to baptize one of the full-blood converts, on the last Sunday in April. He was a single man, "Juijacka," radiant in his new-found Christ, and received the name "Jeremiah."

There was now one who was working among the women, as we have noted Joshua influencing the men. Anna Johanna told the missionaries that she had meetings at her house for members and friends. They spoke of the love of the Saviour and sang hymns! Another woman who comes regularly to service, but cannot understand a word of English, tells the missionaries, through an interpreter, that whenever the "teacher" prays, she asks God to hear and to permit to come to pass the things for which he is praying.

"Fishinghawk," a full-blood, had experienced a complete change of heart and was showing the fruits of it. Said he, "I am such a great sinner that I have often thought it would be impossible there could be any salvation for me and that the Lord would accept such a sinful person as I am. O, how happy I am to testify to His mercy."

Fishinghawk received Baptism on August 13, 1826. "James" was prefixed to his name. With him were baptized "Canaquiaqua," who received the much simpler name "Samuel," and his wife, "Wally," now "Mary Magdalene." During the singing of the hymn, "How great the bliss to be a sheep of Jesus,"[*] weeping and singing were mingled as was the case almost 100 years ago on the 13th of August, the spiritual birthday of the Moravian Church.

Reader! the Cherokees are coming to Jesus! November 12th, "Uweluchy,"—"William Henry," and the single woman, "Aly,"—"Rebecca," were added, by Baptism, to the flock, while "Nick," and "The Young Wolf," brothers and scholars at Springplace, applied for Baptism and were received into the instruction group.

---

[*] J. J. Rambach.

Well might the bell, brought from Salem by Henry Clayton and hung in a bell-tower erected before the church, ring happily for the first time on the first Sunday in Advent! It was a time of refreshing from the Lord, and the clear tones of the bell— Schmidt writes that the tone carried for several miles—invited all now to come to the Lord who would have mercy and abundantly pardon and save!

When, before Christmas, the brothers mentioned above were ready and had been baptized—"Nicholas Ignatius" and "John Jacob," respectively, it was quite fitting that the school children should sing the "Hosanna,"* for the Christmas celebration, rendering this antiphonal chorus wonderfully well, a fitting tribute to the Lord who had indeed come and visited His people. In this eventful year 1826, about to close, 42 souls, exclusive of missionaries, were now numbered to Springplace.

January 20, 1827, marked the new year as beginning with a great sorrow which was, at the same time, a glorious victory. Charles Renatus Hicks, Principal Chief of the Cherokee Nation, a principal man of God and a principal trophy of the mission of the Moravian Church among the Cherokees, passed into his eternal reward. Leaving his important biography to a footnote,† we go on to consider for a moment the best part of his

---

* Gregor.

† Charles Hicks was born Dec. 23, 1767, at Thomaatly, on the Hiwassee River. His father was a white trader, his mother, a Cherokee. When a small boy he injured one leg which gave him constant trouble through his life. He acquired a liberal education through reading and study. He married a full-blood Cherokee and raised a family of five sons and three daughters. For 30 years, he had served the Cherokee Nation as Interpreter most acceptably, for he knew both English and Cherokee languages well. For several years he was Secretary of the National Council and did most of the official business. In 1817, he became Second Principal Chief. Virtually he was Principal Chief, for "Pathkiller," First Chief, was old and infirm and turned over all but nominal duties to Hicks. Pathkiller died just 13 days previous to the death of Hicks. So that the latter, even if for only a few days, enjoyed the distinction of being Principal Chief of the Cherokee Nation. Hicks was a man of sound judgment and great strength of character. After his conversion, he came to see that the civilization which follows genuine Christian religion was what his Nation needed, and bent all his efforts in that direction.

life, namely from the day of 1812, when he began to live anew in Jesus. Since that time he had been a tower of strength to the mission. Nought but joy, encouragement and inspiration over his consistent, convincing Christian life and over his constant purpose, by prayer and effort to strive for the conversion to God of his countrymen, had he ever given to any of the missionaries. He loved Steiner as a friend, honored the Gambolds as spiritual parents and respected and cherished the other missionaries. In the last two years his crippled condition had prevented him from coming to Springplace, hence he was frequently visited by the missionaries and such visits were always red-letter days for him and for them. Always, he gave sweet and intelligent testimony to the faith that was in him and on him death had no power. Two days before his death, Samuel, an Indian Brother from Springplace, paid his sick Chief a visit and to him Hicks addressed these words:

"Brother, I am happy to see you once more. My time, it appears, is run out, and I must go away. I am not afraid of death. 'I know that my Redeemer liveth. I know in whom I have believed and am persuaded that he will keep what I have committed to Him against that day.' I trust alone in the redeeming merits of my Saviour. I am His, and He will accept me as a poor sinner. We must all die, we all have to go the same road, we are of earth, and must return to earth; God has ordered it so. If we believe in Jesus Christ, the Son of God who came into the world to save sinners, if we seek with Him the forgiveness of sins, we need not be afraid of death, but shall inherit eternal life. Also, there will come the time when our mortal body shall be made like unto His glorious body."

These were his last words. According to his own wishes, he was brought to his beloved Springplace for burial. Dressed in white and reposing in a walnut casket, his remains rested for several hours in Springplace church and were viewed by an immense concourse of people. Schmidt[*] preached from the words: "Father, * * *; glorify thy Son, * * *: As thou hast given him power over all flesh, that he should give eternal life to as many as thou hast given him."[†] Then six Christian Indians carried him to his last resting-place in the Springplace graveyard.

---

[*] Gambold was too weak to come.

[†] John 17:1, 2.

Meanwhile, other Cherokees were coming to life! "Keech-leeskeeny,"—"Boas," and "Tiunah,"—"Rachel," on Easter Sunday were followed in Baptism by two scholars, "Benjamin," and "Ruth," on August 13th.

In October, advice was received from Salem, that Brother Gott-lieb Byhan and wife, former missionaries at Springplace, had accepted a call to serve again in the Cherokee mission. With them would come Nathanael, their son, to help in the school and Rachel, their daughter, to assist in the large housekeeping. These were to serve at Springplace, while Schmidt and his wife were called to Oochgelogy, where Gambold passed away November 7th, as noted in a previous chapter.

In October, also, the Cherokees chose their principal Chiefs to fill the vacancies caused by the death of Pathkiller and Hicks. William Abraham Hicks, member of the Moravian church at Oochgelogy, was chosen Principal Chief, and John Ross, who be-came a firm friend and patron of the Moravians, was elected 2nd Principal Chief. It may be readily inferred that the Moravian mission had done a noble work and stood in high esteem through-out the Cherokee Nation when two of its principal men were made Christians through the human instrumentality of this mis-sion‡ and manifested the excellence of the Christian life to such a degree that they were chosen to these offices of high respon-sibility and honor.

The Byhans arrived on November 11, and on the following Sunday, a service of double interest was held. "Caselawi"—"Israel," and "Nelly"—"Esther," having shown to the satis-faction of the missionaries that they were added to the Lord, were added to the church. "Israel" will be seen at later dates faithful to the end. In the second part of the service, Byhan was introduced to the Cherokee flock as missionary and teacher. During the singing of an appropriate hymn, all present came forward expressing welcome and pledging love and loyalty by giving their new missionary the Right Hand of Fellowship. The close of 1827 found at Springplace 27 baptized adults, a total membership of 46 souls and 13 scholars in the school.

‡ Of W. A. Hicks it was said that it could be plainly seen how Christi-anity had turned a wolf into a lamb.

The mission was greatly helped by the type of men whom the United States Government employed as Indian Agents. We have noted the desire and willingness to co-operate with missionary societies and their representatives for the good of the Indian, on the part of the Buttlers, Major Lovely, Col. Meigs and Thos. L. McKenny. Mr. Hugh Montgomery was appointed successor to Col. Meigs and he, too, was an earnest Christian man who did all he could for the mission, particularly in securing from the Government annual appropriations for the school. It was by Mr. Montgomery's advice and help that the new arrangement for boys at Springplace and girls at Oochgelogy could be carried out successfully.

Encouraging religious experiences continued in 1828 and 1829. On all festival days there were baptisms and often between these special seasons were members added. Byhan writes that at the baptism of one Indian woman there was a special demonstration of the Spirit's power. When the Candidate knelt on the white cloth to be baptized, other Indian women voluntarily came forward and knelt with her, praying, weeping and singing. Church attendance continued to increase and there was rapt attention when the Word of God was expounded. At one service a temperance-petition which had been drawn up in one of the other mission stations, was circulated. It had been sent to Springplace to have the Indians there express themselves on the issue of banishing whiskey from the Nation. All the Brethren and Sisters either signed or made their mark. The party of new missionaries appointed for Oochgelogy, Brother and Sister Eder and Henry G. Clauder, with their companions,[*] arrived at Springplace just as the morning service of October 26, 1828, was in progress. Clauder wrote in his personal diary: "It was Sunday, and the Indian congregation was assembled in worship when we arrived and I had the indescribable pleasure of seeing, for the first time, a congregation of converted heathen listening with

---

* In the party were the Eders and Clauder, Aug. H. Schultz and Lewis Eberhard from Salem, Chas. Grabs from Bethania, the Single Sister Anna Margaret Becker from Friedland and Matth. Retch, the driver. Sister Becker had come to assist in the Springplace household. The others come as companions of the three missionaries and returned home after a brief visit.

profound attention to the tidings of Salvation. I felt a love for
these people at once and praised and thanked the Lord for His
goodness in bringing me here." More of the Cherokee members
feel freedom to pray and testify when opportunity is given.
"Samuel" often leads in fervent prayer in Cherokee and Polly
Vann tells the missionaries that the burden of the prayer is that
God may strengthen their faith in Jesus Christ. All these encouraging indications pointed to the brightest possible future
for our and other missions if the Cherokee Nation could have
remained undisturbed in their lands.

At the close of 1829, a total of 64 souls were connected with
Springplace, of which number 40 were baptized adults in good
church standing. Another accomplishment of the year was the
completion of the new and commodious dwelling for the missionaries. It was a double house, built for two families, and arranged so as to afford many comforts and conveniences which the
two-room dwellings, used up to the present time, lacked.

CHAPTER XVIII

GATHERING CLOUDS FOLLOWED BY THE STORM OF THE EXPATRIATION OF THE CHEROKEE NATION

The territory and sovereignty of the Cherokees were transmitted to them from their ancestors or gained by conquest from their predecessors, whoever these may have been; at any rate, they were in the enjoyment of both before the first settlement of Georgia. No better right or title to territory and national sovereignty can exist, either by the law of nature or nations.

The standing of the Cherokees as a sovereign State is further proved by the fact that Treaties were made with them by European nations, colonies and the United States, after the adoption of the Constitution. Never was their power as a Nation to negotiate Treaties, make war or peace and regulate trade and intercourse, questioned. While they were not an independent foreign State, they were an alien State and under the protection of the United States Government as were the other Indian Nations concerning all of whom it had been stipulated in the provisions under which a State was admitted into the Union, that "the utmost good faith shall always be observed towards the Indians; their lands and property shall never be taken from them without their consent; and in their property, rights and liberty, they shall never be invaded or disturbed, unless in just and lawful wars authorized by Congress; but laws founded in justice and humanity shall from time to time be made, for preventing wrongs being done to them, and for preserving peace and friendship with them."[*]

But when it came to the point where individual States became more thickly settled and it became necessary to extend jurisdiction over their chartered limits, the Indian Nations and, in our particular study, the Cherokees, occupied a unique and anomalous position on account of which trouble between the United States and Georgia and trouble between Georgia and the Cherokees were almost certain. It is not in the mind of the present writer to express a sweeping condemnation of the action of the Georgia authorities in the Cherokee case nor to criticise the steps

* Ordinance of Congress, July 13, 1787.

taken by the Federal Government to remove this Nation to a new territory. That there were injustice and wrong to the poor Indians is evident, and the story of their sufferings must ever fill right-minded citizens of the United States who consider it, with shame and grief. Surely, in the common desire of a great State and a great United States to do the right thing by the Cherokees, in the calm and thorough deliberations of great statesmen whom State and National Governments possessed, a way could have been found with justice and mercy to deal with these Indians to the satisfaction of all parties concerned. The facts of the case are lack of understanding between State and Federal Government, lack of patience on the part of both, no co-ordinated plan when the removal did take place, inconsiderate officials who acted with high-minded injustice, violence and cruelty, unscrupulous white people who wanted the lands of the Cherokees and wanted them *now*, regardless of consequences to the Indians. The brunt of all mistakes fell on the Cherokees and there was a heavy toll of suffering and death. These are the writer's views and criticisms on the case which can now be stated.

Originally, all the land lying between the Atlantic Ocean and the Mississippi River, now comprising the three States of Georgia, Alabama and Mississippi, was within the chartered limits and jurisdiction of Georgia. At the close of the 18th century, the settled part of Georgia was small and the balance was occupied by Indian tribes, namely, Creeks, Cherokees, Choctaws and Chickasaws. Before the adoption of the Constitution of the United States in 1788, Georgia came into frequent collision with the Cherokees and, more frequently with the Creeks, from which resulted wars, out of which Georgia usually acquired a piece of the Indians' territory, in the settlement. After the adoption of the Constitution, Georgia could no longer make treaties with the Indians nor receive land from them; all such negotiations must now be carried on by the Federal Government. In the year 1802, Georgia entered into a convention with the United States which resulted in an agreement as follows: Georgia ceded to the United States all the territory west of the Chattahoochie River—out of which the States Alabama and Mississippi were formed—the United States promising to pay Georgia $1,250,000 out of the sale of these lands and to gradually extinguish, by purchase and treaty, the claims of Indians to lands within the new boundaries of Georgia. Probably neither party to the contract at that time thought that Georgia would be settled so rapidly and insist on the carrying-out of the conditions of the pact so quickly. Nevertheless, it had been ratified and the United States must fulfill its promise sooner or later since Georgia has lived up to her part of the agreement.

At the time of this agreement, the Cherokees occupied a large part of Georgia to the east of the Chattahoochie and westward to the boundary of the State; of Tennessee, the whole southern portion from the Tennessee River to the boundaries and a large section between the Cumberland and Clinch Rivers; a large portion of that territory which Georgia had relinquished to the United States; the western corners of North and South Carolina. Since that time up to 1830, the United States had extinguished the title of the Cherokees to the following lands: Everything in North and South Carolina, the larger portion of the lands in Tennessee, nearly all in the section which is now Alabama and in Georgia everything east of the Chattahoochie. Some land remained for the Cherokees in the Alabama section, a small strip in Tennessee and the far greater part in Georgia.

Since the Federal Government had acquired so much of the Indian's territory for the other States and extinguished only so small a part for Georgia, the State to which it was especially pledged so to do, while it had no compact with the other States, Georgia was greatly roused at this time, especially since the $1,250,000 received from the United States was only a trifle of what the lands were worth to the Government. More and more vigorously, the State began to insist on the carrying-out of the terms of the contract. Georgia really needed the territory and needed the roads, for trade with other States, which would lead through the Cherokee country. Several times the Cherokees had refused permission for such roads to be opened. There were other considerations on the Georgia side of the case:

"The discovery of immense mineral wealth, within the limits of the nation, acting upon the avarice and cupidity of men, had brought into the territory a numerous body of men, lawless, abandoned, and hostile to the policy of the State.* These circumstances imperiously asked of

* Already in 1824, so called "Intruders" were coming into the Cherokee country and settling along the Chattahoochie River. Generals Turk

the State decisive and prompt action, and on these accounts she enacted laws, abrogating the Cherokee Government, making it penal to dig gold, and punishing a residence within the territory, unless the resident would take an oath to observe the constitution and laws of the State. The exclusion of all white persons from the Cherokee lands was the dictate of policy and necessity. * * * The law which has excited so much feeling is not partial or exclusive in its operation. The first citizen of Georgia, the most abandoned of the refugee adventurers for gold, as well as the meek and law-abiding Moravian missionary, are within its provisions—all classes, all grades, and all professions, are alike liable to its penalties. Our law in this, as well as other cases, aims at no individual or individuals, and recognizes no exceptions. And had the most talented, or the most dignified of our sons resided within the limits of our lands in the possession of the Cherokee Indians, without having taken the oath, the law would have been administered upon such an one with unsparing vigor and unrelenting severity."†

The emigration of 3,000 Cherokees to west of the Mississippi into Arkansas along the White River in 1818, has already been noted. In the subsequent years, exodus followed exodus. The lands of the Cherokees who remained in the east had been reduced by successive cessions, as we have seen, to about 8,000 square miles situated almost altogether in the mountains of Georgia. The aggression and the oppression of Georgia extended the jurisdiction of the State over the Cherokee country according to Act of Assembly of December, 1829. While annihilating the tribal government of the Cherokees, the State refused them citizenship.

On the 27th of December, 1830, and 1st of January, 1831, a notice was served on the Governor and Attorney General of the State of Georgia, signed by John Ross, Principal Chief of the

_____

and Williams received instructions from the United States Government to take a company of militia and drive them out of the country, in which undertaking they met with stubborn resistance. Often the Georgia settlers helped the "intruders," and one of the settlers was shot, after which there was a general fight and Col. Williams was made prisoner.

† From the report of a Committee appointed by the Legislature of Georgia to investigate the merits and the enforcement of the law enacted by which all residents within the State must take the oath of allegiance to its constitution and laws. The report of the Committee was unanimously adopted by the Legislature, December 24, 1831. See Bibliography No. 24.

Cherokee Nation, stating that on Saturday, the 5th day of March, 1831, at the city of Washington, D. C., the Cherokee Nation would, by their counsel, move the Supreme Court of the United States, expected to be then in session, for an injunction to restrain the State of Georgia from executing and enforcing the laws of Georgia within the Cherokee territory as designated by treaty between the United States and the Cherokee Nation. This case was carried before the Supreme Court under the provision of the Constitution of the United States which gives to that Court jurisdiction in controversies in which a State of the United States and the citizens thereof, and a Foreign State, citizens or subjects thereof, are parties.

The case was argued before the Supreme Court at great length and with much ability, but the motion for an injunction was denied by the Supreme Court on the ground that an Indian Tribe or Nation within the United States is not a Foreign State in the sense of the Constitution, and cannot maintain an action in the courts of the United States.

In the meanwhile, the final treaty was drafted and concluded in December, 1835. This treaty was a clear release of all lands owned by the Cherokees east of the Mississippi, for the sum of $5,000,000. John Ross, the Principal Chief, who had been at Washington for three or four winters, exerting every possible influence towards the welfare of his people, pronounced a decided disapproval to the treaty, and opened a correspondence with the President in the hope of relief, but there was none forthcoming.

Andrew Ross, a member of the Cherokee delegation, on the other hand, was favorable to the emigration, and suggested to the Commissioner of Indian Affairs his willingness to bring together a sufficient number of leading Cherokees with whom a treaty could be effected. A preliminary treaty was therefore concluded on the 19th day of June, 1834, but it was never ratified, although the enrolling books were opened and several names subscribed.

Early in February, 1835, two rival delegations, each claiming itself representative of the Cherokee Nation, arrived at Washington. One was headed by John Ross, who had been Chief for over eight years, and the other by John Ridge, a sub-Chief and a man of considerable influence among his people. The Ross delegation was implacable in its opposition to removal, while the Ridges, perceiving the futility of further opposition to the demands of the Government, were agreeable to accepting the treaty. Rev. J. T. Schermerhorn was authorized by the President to treat with the latter and effected a preliminary treaty on the 14th of March, with the express stipulation that it should receive the approval of the Cherokee people in full Council assembled. Such were the terms upon which Ridge, Boudinot and others signed the contract which terminated so fatally for them a short time afterwards.

In October following, the Cherokee people in full Council at Red Clay, rejected the Ridge treaty. Ridge and Boudinot, strong partisans and signers of the Schermerhorn agreement, abandoned their support of the measure and coincided with the mass of the people.

However, at a meeting the December following at New Echota, Mr. Schermerhorn concluded arrangements with the Ridge party, and the treaty was ratified by the United States Senate, May 23, 1836. John Ross and his delegation, who had left for Washington soon after the Red Clay Council, returned home to commence a vigorous campaign of opposition to the execution of the treaty. They openly refused to recognize the action of the Ridge party, and protested forcibly through the medium of their Chief against the unconstitutionality of a contract made by a few unauthorized parties to the detriment of a Nation.

Doubtless Ridge and Boudinot were under the impression that they were doing that which was for the best interests of their people. The latter was a man of culture and a Christian, and those who knew him best, invariably agree in the belief that his action on this occasion was not prompted by any selfish consideration whatever.

One of the saddest stories on record, is that of the removal of the Cherokees from their eastern homes. Between sixteen and seventeen thousand men, women and youths, left Brainerd late in the fall of 1838, with a winter's journey of nearly half a year before them. The severity of the weather, together with the number of old and infirm emigrants, rendered them unable to make over five to fifteen miles a day. As the season advanced, so did disease attack them with dreadful fatality. Numbers lay down by the roadside never to rise again. Soon the great caravan became a monstrous funeral procession, the average of deaths reaching thirteen per day.

The time taken to accomplish the journey increased from six to ten months, and when roll was called at the terminus of the trip, over four thousand persons were missing—one-fourth of the great exodus having left their bones by the wayside.

Immediately after the arrival of the Cherokees in the Territory, June 10, 1839, Chief Ross called a Council meeting at Takuttah, having in view the unification of the old and new settlers. Nothing was accomplished, but a time was set for a similar meeting with the same design.

A few days after the adjournment of Council, three of the leaders of the treaty party—John Ridge, Major Ridge (his father) and Elias Boudinot, were brutally murdered. The latter was assassinated beside his house at Parkhill, and within a few miles of the Chief's residence.

Major Ridge was waylaid and shot close to the state line, while John was taken from his bed and hewn to pieces. There are some who reflect with great severity upon John Ross, the Chief, for permitting these coldblooded murders, but it seems hardly fair to accuse him of sympathy with acts of which, in all probability, he was ignorant. Chief Ross had been several times heard to say: "Once I saved Ridge at Red Clay, and would have done so again had I known of the plot."

No sooner had the Ross party arrived in the new country than hostilities commenced between them and the old settlers, together with the treaty party—that is to say, the Ridge faction. It was several years before these factions compromised and there was again a united Cherokee Nation.

Having taken a view of the political side of this distressing situation, the question will arise, How did the Moravian and other mission stations fare in these troublous times before and during the removal of the Nation?

Already on November 5, 1829, the missionaries received a letter from the Secretary of War, Hon. John H. Eaton, telling that there seemed a great change impending for the Cherokee Nation; in all probability they would be forced either to leave

their lands and be transported west of the Mississippi River or
to come under the jurisdiction of the State of Georgia.

There is an event to record in the year 1830 which shines like
a great light in the darkness of distress settling over the Cherokee people. A day of fasting and prayer for the Nation was appointed by the Principal Chief in view of the dangers which
threatened the very existence of the Cherokee tribe. Who could
have predicted, when the Moravian Church made its humble
beginning among these Indians, followed by other denominations,
that in less than one generation this heathen tribe would be
Christianized to the extent that a day of prayer could be appointed for the whole Nation! The proclamation follows:

"WHEREAS, The crisis in the affairs of this Nation exhibits the day
of tribulation and sorrow,—and the time appears to be fast hastening
when the destiny of this people must be sealed; whether it has been
directed by the wonted depravity and wickedness of man, or by the
unsearchable and mysterious will of an allwise Being, it equally becomes us as a rational and Christian community, humbly to bow in
humiliation and prayer before Him who can alone relieve the afflicted
and protect the fatherless; and there to implore His gracious pleasure
to avert the dreadful evil, that wisdom may be given to direct the
Chiefs in the deliberations of their Council, and that the people may be
united in sentiment and action for the good of the Nation; therefore, I
have thought proper to set apart Thursday, the 19th of this month, as a
day of fasting and prayer, and to request the religious community of
every denomination, and all other well disposed citizens of the Nation,
to unite in observing said day with all due solemnity.

"Given under my hand at Head of Coosa, Cherokee Nation, the 3rd
day of July, 1830.

"By the Principal Chief,
"JOHN ROSS."

Brother Wm. A. Hicks, a member of the delegation sent to
Washington in 1830 to lay a memorial in behalf of the Cherokees
before Congress, returned with a letter from President Jackson
the gist of which was, that if the Cherokees remained where they
were, they must come under the Laws of the State of Georgia
and they would do that on their own risk as the President had
no power to interfere with the laws of individual States. He
assured them that if they moved westward, they would come
under the jurisdiction and protection of the United States. As
he and the Secretary of War were going on a journey to the

west, he invited the Chiefs to meet them at Nashville, to talk matters over.

Precious fruits—souls saved for Christ—continued to ripen in the Moravian fields among the Cherokees; there were frequent baptisms during 1830 and 1831. The missionaries found it easy to deal with individuals in these days of stress and uncertainty. With gratitude to God they noted, too, that while the Cherokees became increasingly distrustful of whites generally, their common national danger drove them nearer to their missionaries and teachers.

Brother Byhan attended the Council at New Echota in 1830, at which meeting the Cherokees decided *not* to remove to the west, but to remain and to bear patiently whatever the State of Georgia might lay upon them. They resolved to appeal to the Supreme Court of the United States, which appeal, as we have seen, proved fruitless.

Special blessings were experienced in Oochgelogy during 1830. Brother Clauder, in speaking with individuals privately before one of the Communion services, heard testimonies such as these: "I seek to draw ever nearer to the Lord and to have Him ever before me." Another, "He always helps me through." Another, "I feel often my sinfulness, but the Lord recalls me each time." Still another, "I desire nothing but to follow Him and to grow in grace."

Major Ridge, for whom prayer and supplication without ceasing had been offered up, came to Oochgelogy, one day, saying:

"My brother, Waytee, and my friend, Wm. Hicks, both belong to your church and I am still a bad man." He remembered the first visit of Steiner and de Schweinitz. "They are gone," said he, "and I am still here. I am now old and gray and many of my countrymen have found Christ. I will now also seek Him who is good."

With joy and thanksgiving to God, Ridge was accepted for careful instruction.

Margaretta, daughter of W. A. Hicks, is baptized and George Hicks is becoming a real personal worker, talking with individuals who seem interested, after the services. Clauder gives him charge of a service now and then which he holds in the Cherokee language with evident blessing to all.

13

In January, 1831, the missionaries were greatly alarmed, when a copy of the "Georgia Journal" was sent them in which appeared the new laws adopted by the Legislature, to read under Section 7 as follows:

"And be it further enacted by the authority aforesaid, That all white persons residing within the limits of the Cherokee Nation, on the first day of March next, or at any time thereafter, without a license or permit from his Excellency, the Governor, or from such agent as his Excellency, the Governor, shall authorize to grant such permit or license, and who shall not have taken the oath hereinafter required, shall be guilty of an high misdemeanor, and upon conviction thereof, shall be punished by confinement in the penitentiary at hard labor, for a term not less than four years."

The oath was this:

"I, N. N., do solemnly swear (or affirm, as the case may be) that I will support and defend the Constitution and Laws of the State of Georgia, and uprightly demean myself, as a citizen thereof, so help me God."

Hurriedly the Brethren met in a Mission Conference. They decided unanimously that they could not take the oath of allegiance to Georgia for the reason that the new laws were framed for the eviction of the Cherokees and to swear to uphold these laws when the missionaries had come for the sole purpose of helping the Cherokees would make them traitors to their cause. The second point acted on was an invitation from their friend, Capt. David McNair, residing in the Cherokee country of Tennessee, 18 miles from Springplace, for the missionaries to come and live with him. This was help come from God! With heartfelt thanks to Him and the good Captain, the invitation was accepted for Brother Clauder and Nathanael Byhan at once. Gottlieb Byhan was Postmaster at Springplace, and this was deemed sufficient protection for him as he was an officer of the Federal Government. The laws did not include women and minors, so the Sisters were safe, and it was decided that Sister Clauder and Sister Gambold remain at Oochgelogy for a little while to get movable things in order against the day of departure. These Sisters were to be commended to the protection of the Indian Brethren at Oochgelogy. These decisions were submitted to the Helpers' Conference at Salem for advice or approval, but the Brethren on the ground had to act, as the time was short. In due time came word from the Conference approving of the action taken, advising Byhan to send in his resignation as Postmaster, telling all the missionaries to take refuge at McNair's as soon as Byhan was relieved of the office, urging them to impress upon the Christian Indians, in case they were removed, to settle close together in the new territory beyond the Mississippi, as the Salem Society had determined to follow them with missionaries to renew the mission.

Our missionaries had not taken their precautions too soon. On March 4, they received the news that the Georgia Guard had come to New Echota and arrested the Rev. Samuel A. Worcester, D.D., Presbyterian missionary—friend of the Brethren and the man who, with the aid of Sequoya's characters, gave to the Cherokees their hymns, had translated the Moravian Litany and Easter Morning Litany into Cherokee and was now working on the Cherokee Bible. Among others arrested was Dr. Butler, missionary at Carmel. The Georgia Guard were pretty rough in handling these men. Dr. Butler was tied to a horse and had to follow along rapidly over terrible roads. At night, the horse stumbled, tore him to the ground, and, becoming frightened, began to gallop, dragging him over rocks and trees. He was all but killed. At the trial, all the missionaries promised to leave the Cherokee country at once save Drs. Worcester and Butler who refused, also, to take the oath, whereupon they were promptly taken to the penitentiary to await another hearing.

The Conference in Salem, meanwhile, had addressed a letter to Governor George R. Gilmer, of Georgia, asking protection for Byhan until the Postmaster General had acted upon his resignation and sent the advice of that Department as to the disposition of the Office. In case that Byhan had already been arrested—Conference was taking no chances—they asked for his release on the same ground.

The case of Worcester, et al., was tried in the Superior Court of Georgia, within a few weeks of their arrest, before Judge Clayton. He ruled that not only must Worcester be released because, as Postmaster at New Echota, he was under the jurisdiction of the United States, but he and the others must be freed because they were missionaries and the United States Government was directly interested in them, having assisted all the mission schools financially with their buildings and with their running expenses. So these missionaries were released and returned to their posts. Elias Boudinot hastened to communicate the good news to Byhan and he to Clauder and N. Byhan, at McNair's, who returned joyfully; the one to the Springplace school, the other, to Oochgelogy and his anxious wife and congregation.

Governor Gilmer's reply to the Conference was most courteous. He stated that he had ordered the officers not to molest the *Moravian missionaries*,* and that they might remove at their leisure. He wrote, too, that the Presbyterian missionaries had been released in accordance with the opinion handed down by the Georgia Superior Court.

Alas, short-lived was the new hope inspired by the decision of the Court! On May 30, came the news that Judge Clayton's ruling had been declared unconstitutional and all the other missionaries had again been arrested. The Moravians received the first blow at Oochgelogy. On May 31, as Clauder was quietly engaged in teaching school, a detachment of the Georgia Guard rode up and took him prisoner. He had time only to say farewell to his wife and left the school girls, weeping and terrified, in their seats. He was taken to the headquarters of the commanding officer stationed at Brother W. A. Hicks' house, and there questioned. Clauder stated that the instructions received from his Society were to the effect, he should remove from Cherokee country at once, if he could not pursue his missionary labors peaceably. He also quoted what had been communicated from Salem of the Governor's letter, namely, that the Moravian missionaries would not be molested. Upon this frank statement he was released and could return to his frightened family and school. Next day came the following note over which Clauder was considerably "helped up:"

"Hickses, May 31, 1831.

"Dear Sir: The character which you have sustained being so contrary to that of others, I have determined to make you a distinguished

---

* They had received instructions from Salem to take no part in political agitations or discussions whatsoever, but strictly to mind their own business. As Moravian missionaries, they would have taken exactly this course even had no instructions been received. That other missionaries *were* molested, and the Moravians were not was due to their policy of quietly going about their own (Master's) business.

object of our forbearance; you will, therefore, remain with your family in quiet and pursue your own inclination until further directed.

"Should you be in future directed to comply with the laws and leave the territory, time will be given you to comply with at least as much convenience to you as at this time.* With my best wishes for your success in the cause in which you are laboring, and be pleased to accept my personal respect and esteem,

"C. H. NELSON, Sub-Com., Ga. Ga."

This was fine; however, Nelson was, after all, only a "Sub-Com." Already on July 8, Clauder received the following:

"Dear Sir: Any protection that my note of May last may have given you is *withdrawn*.

"Very respectfully,

"C. H. NELSON, Sub-Com., Ga. Ga."

Meanwhile, Dr. Worcester and Dr. Butler at their second trial again persistently refused either to quit the country or to take the oath. Nine others were tried with them and took the same stand, whereupon, all were condemned to 4 years' imprisonment in the penitentiary at hard labor. Marched to prison, pardon was once more offered to all, before the open gates, on condition that they would not again reside in the Cherokee country. With this offer they all complied, except Drs. Worcester and Butler, who were thrust into prison. Although the United States Supreme Court decided that these missionaries should be at once set at liberty, yet they were not released until January, 1833, the State at first refusing to give them up, except at the point of the bayonet.

The notice to Clauder that protection had been withdrawn was, in effect, a warning to leave his station within ten days. It meant "go!" The Diary of Oochgelogy records that the feelings of the missionaries as they prepared to leave their beloved flock of faithful Christians were inexpressibly sad and heavy. A last, blessed Holy Communion service was held with them on July 17th. Old Christian David said: "Tell them, the friends in Salem, that one old heathen has turned to God after he had grown old in the service of sin. He has heard the good Word of God and experienced its saving power." Clauder admonished his Cherokee Brethren and Sisters to be faithful to the end and charged them

---

* Ten days' notice.

to keep on holding services among themselves, as there were several Brethren at Oochgelogy gifted along that line. During the final prayer, all were in tears. After a heartrending farewell, Clauders, with their little child, and Mrs. Anna Maria Gambold left Oochgelogy, going first to Springplace and from thence, by way of McNairs, they journeyed to Salem in August, 1831. They left behind at Oochgelogy, a congregation numbering 35 souls.

Byhan and his family felt very keenly their loneliness, after the other missionaries had departed, and were filled with grave apprehensions for the future. The Indians clung to them pathetically, realizing that, ere long, *their* missionaries would have to leave. Word came from the Helpers' Conference asking the missionaries to notify the Salem authorities at once, when they received notice to quit Springplace, and two four-horse wagons would be sent immediately to fetch them and their movable property. This was announced to the congregation and received in tears.

Harrowing days followed. Indians and whites, journeying back and forth, stopped at Springplace for food, shelter and horse-feed, and the missionaries dared not say "no" to these demands. In general, in those distracted times, it was very noticeable how the non-Christian Indians went back to excesses of all kinds, drinking, immorality, theft and the like. By contrast, the Christian Indians remained firm and true. Samuel, one of the members, remarked sadly, that when the missionaries would go they would be like sheep without a shepherd. Byhan reminded him of the Good Shepherd who never forsakes His sheep!

One day in the fall of 1831, Lieutenant Brooks arrived at Springplace with a company of men and asked Byhan, who was sorting mail at the time, if they could have pasture for the horses and shelter for themselves, which Byhan answered in the affirmative. Lieut. Brooks was very friendly and Byhan made use of the opportunity to tell him that his Society in Salem had instructed him to leave after due notice had been given. Looking over the mission premises, Brooks remarked that it was a great pity the missionaries could not make up their minds to take the oath, for they would have to lose so much which they had improved here. When he saw he made no impression with this line of argument he said, "Well, you will not be molested here, because we are convinced that you have not meddled with our political affairs like others who will have to abide by the consequences." After they had been fed and lodged as well as possible, this detachment left next morning to do some arresting in the vicinity and Brooks said, on leaving, that they would be back in a few days. The Springplace Diary adds, by way of comment, "this was not the best of news!"

Agents of the United States Government were now putting on a propaganda of persuasion with the Cherokees, trying to get their consent to remove and were enrolling the names of those who were willing to go.

The close of 1831 found 71 members on the roll at Springplace, many having been added during this, outwardly, dark year.

Byhan feeling himself give way under the strain, early in 1832 requested to be relieved of his post. The Salem Brethren, through the aid of the Congressional Representative, secured Clauder's appointment as Postmaster at Springplace and in April, Clauder and his wife and two little children and sister-in-law, the Single Sister Dorothea Ruede, left Salem and, after a journey of 17 days, arrived safely at Springplace on the 19th. On the 23rd the wagon started on its return journey to Salem with the Byhan family. "Thus," writes Clauder, "we were once more privileged to labor for the spiritual good of our dear Cherokee converts."

Miss Ruede took charge of the school and conducted it with much enthusiasm and marked success.[*] New converts were added, under the Divine blessing, several of them being particularly promising for the strengthening of any future mission. Meanwhile at Oochgelogy,[†] George Hicks and Christian David Waytee were holding good meetings each Sunday. One Sunday in each month, Clauder visited the station, preaching and administering

---

[*] After three years' intermission of the Government grants in support of the school, Congress voted $850.00 for Springplace in 1832. This action was taken largely due to the efforts of Representative Williams, a friend of the Brethren's Church.

[†] At Springplace, "Samuel" regularly leads the praying of the Litany in Cherokee.

the Sacrament of the Holy Communion to the little flock of
faithful Cherokees—a great consolation and encouragement for
them.

The Federal Government, through its agents, is working hard
for the peaceful removal of the Cherokees. More and more of
the Indians are realizing the oppression they will have to en-
dure if they remain and are listening to the proposals of the
United States which are very fair and profitable for them and
they see that if everything that is promised is carried out, the
Cherokees will have no reason to regret their move.†

---

† The United States Government made the following propositions to
the Cherokees: 1. The land west of the Mississippi shall be secured to
the Cherokees and shall be sufficiently extensive and suited for agricultural purposes. 2. The United States promises to protect the Cherokees from the invasion of other Tribes. 3. The United States will provide them with schools, teachers, Council Houses, and houses for a few
of the Chiefs. 4. The Cherokees shall have an agent residing in Washington City at the expense of the United States. 5. The Cherokees shall
have the right to make their own laws and have their own Government.
6. No white people shall be permitted to enter their country except
those having a permit from the United States Agent. 7. The United
States will provide mills, blacksmiths, iron, steel, plows, hoes, etc.
8. Each adult in the Nation shall have a gun, and each family be provided with sufficient blankets. 9. Provision is made for all Cherokee
orphans. 10. The Cherokees shall be removed at the expense of the
United States and subsisted for one year after arrival in the new
home. 11. The United States will pay them for their improvements and
stock of every kind left behind. These proposals were submitted to the
National Council of the Cherokees in August, 1832. The Council was a
very stormy one: the majority of the Chiefs fought against making a
treaty with the United States nor would they entertain the above propositions. Stubbornly they held out against removal under any conditions.
Boudinot, John Ridge and others who wished to accept the proposals of
the United States were hissed "traitors." Boudinot filed his resignation
as Editor of the "Cherokee Phoenix." It appeared at this Council that
there was a division in the Cherokee Nation: John Ross, Principal
Chief, was bitterly opposed to the removal of the Cherokees, and demanded of the United States Commissioners at least 12 months' time
in which to consider a treaty for removal. John Ridge's party wished
to accept at once, bowing to the inevitable, in order to avoid the hardships of another year of uncertainty and oppression. When the Council
adjourned, nothing had been accomplished, but much bad feeling was
aroused.

To use Clauder's words about 1832, "The year passed away in peace from without and the enjoyment of the smiles of our Divine Lord within." One hundred and thirteen souls were now in connection with the mission. It proved to be the last year at dear old Springplace!

On the very first day of January, 1833, the Cherokee lands having been previously distributed by lottery, claimants presented themselves for Springplace.* At 3 p.m., 20 people, in 5 wagons and carts appeared, and demanded possession of all the mission houses and property. Clauder declined to surrender the place and cited the laws as he knew them and the promises that had been made. Toward evening these people became more and more insistent in their demands and finally made a forcible seizure of the station. They unloaded their wagons and occupied the school-house, the scholars' house, the workshop and one half of the dwelling, permitting Clauder, for the present, to retain the other half for his family and Sister Ruede. The party had brought plenty of whiskey along and when night came Springplace, where for many years each night had resounded the Indian children's sweet song of praise and the voices of united prayer, echoed with the discordant sounds of drunkenness and revelry. They demanded from Clauder the key to the church but he finally dissuaded them from entering the sanctuary. Clauder wrote to Governor Lumpkin for deliverance from this intrusion but received no answer from him or any agent of the Georgia

* Before this date Clauder had received a visit from an agent of a Mr. James Nix, of Henry Co., Ga., who had drawn the lots on which Springplace was located. The agent had papers purporting to give him power of possession. Clauder remonstrated that he must consult with the Directors of his Society and because of the Post Office, when the agent cut him short by asking him whether he would give possession or not. "No," said Clauder. "Then the law must take its course," said the agent. Probably Clauder did not sleep much that night! A few days later he received the following note from General Hardin at Milledgeville: "The lot whereon you reside is drawn and the grant for it is issued. Mr. James H. Bryan is the purchaser from James Nix, the drawer, and I have this day purchased the place from Mr. Bryan. I ask the kindness of you to take the usual good care of the houses, fences, orchards, gates, etc., and to consider yourself at home upon these conditions." Hardin rented the premises to three families—18 persons in all—and these are they who roughly took possession.

government. Those were hard days for the missionaries. Salem
was far away and quick advice from the Brethren there could
not be obtained, but Clauder must act quickly. He says, "After
enduring untold suspense and vexation, I resolved to vacate the
place where I could no longer pursue my calling and, with the
assistance of Brother Adam Butner, of Salem, who came as an
angel from Heaven, unexpectedly, to visit us in our great tribulation, we removed to Connesauga, within the limits of the State
of Tennessee, where our well known friend, Captain David Mc-
Nair, permitted us to occupy a farm belonging to his son and
which was then vacant."

Before his departure, Clauder had given over the Post Office
to a Mr. Bishop who promised to take care of it for him. The
Indian Brethren were most helpful in getting things packed and
put in order for moving, though they were sad at heart. Again
quoting Clauder, "To abandon this time-honored spot where the
first convert from the Cherokee tribe was baptized in 1810; where
first the feet of them that brought glad tidings of great joy rested in their travel to this tribe of Indians and where so many
prayers and tears had been offered to God and so many tokens
of His goodness witnessed—this was a consideration far more
painful than any amount of unrighteousness inflicted upon us
by the miserable wretches around us. But the Lord gave us enlargement." Thus was Springplace abandoned as a mission station.

The officers of the Society appealed to their Congressman
about the property they had been obliged to relinquish and were
advised to appraise it and send the estimate with a petition for
redress to Congress, through the Secretary of War, which was
done. The property was appraised as follows: Oochgelogy,
$4676.50; Springplace, $2878.00, a total of $7554.50. This sum
was allowed the Society by Congress, through the efforts of Mr.
John Williams, Commissioner of the Federal Government. His
commission of 15% amounted to $1113.17, so that the Society
received $6441.33, which amount was held in trust for the mis-
sion among the Cherokees when it could be re-established in
Indian Territory. None of this money was ever diverted to any
other use; the Brethren regarded it as a deposit to be sacredly
kept for the Cherokees and they never broke faith with the In-

dian. Within a few years Springplace became a county-seat and the Moravian church was turned into a Court-house.

(Having followed the story of this mission to its close in Georgia, it is important we should understand how the enterprise had been financed. In the mind of the writer, this point has an important bearing on the outcome of this mission. Studying the accounts, it was found that the Cherokee mission was maintained from 1801 to 1819 at a cost of $9,000.00. While this outlay seems very small, it must be remembered that the purchasing power of the dollar was very great, compared to what it is now. In those days, even the one-half cent entered into the accounts. By far the greater part of the $9,000.00 came from the "Gemein Diakonie" of the Unity, i.e., the Unity's invested funds. The contributions from Salem were small, though probably representing real effort and sacrifice, again considering money in those days as it was earned. The accounts of the year June 1, 1830, to May 31, 1831, show a budget of $1,138.11 made up and expended for the Cherokee mission and of this amount $335.56 came from the Finaucial Board of the Unity.

(It appears that no attempt was made to invite the converts from the Cherokees, when such fruits of the mission came by the grace of God, to share in the financial requirements of the work. Once it is recorded that Brother Charles Hicks made a contribution. If there was a collection-plate at Springplace or Oochgelogy it escaped mention in the Diary which records the life of the mission down to the smallest detail. Here was *the* weak point of the mission as the writer sees it. The mission did not need the support of the Christian Indians nearly so much as those Indians needed to support the mission, and that is saying a great deal, for even the casual reader will admit the great financial straits which continually hampered the work. If it be objected that the Indians had no means to contribute, it may be stated in reply that, if heathen Cherokees could raise $3500 in bets at a ball game, Christian Indians certainly might reasonably be expected to bring an offering to the Lord who was so precious to them. And the writer is persuaded *they would have done it* had they been trained in this as well as they were in other Christian graces. The Godfrey Haga legacy which came, in 1825, to the Society for Propagating the Gospel among the Heathen, was veritable help from the Lord and made possible the widening of the mission among the Cherokees, but no part of it should ever have been used to cover any expense the Cherokee members themselves could have shouldered. When it is recalled from the story how, on Sundays, usually the entire congregation stayed for dinner, how children in school were boarded and, often, kept in clothes and the Sisters did even the mending and darning for them, these and other sidelights from the conduct of the mission show how it was possible for good Christian Indians to regard it as perfectly natural that the mission should supply not only spiritual but, also, material needs. Even the smallest contribution in money, produce, manufacture or labor on the part of an Indian member would make him a better Christian, cause him to love his mission and missionary more and lead him to feel responsibility for the work. We failed to develop that sense of responsibility in our Cherokee Christians, and this may be considered one direct cause for discontinuing *our* mission among this Nation when Baptists, Methodists and others went on. Of course, there were contributing causes for the close of our work in the Territory, but the lack of support, moral and financial, was the main reason. And the lesson which this teacheth is good doctrine for churches and their officers even unto this day.)

Though Springplace was lost to the mission, the work did not cease. The situation at Capt. McNair's was really very favorable for the carrying on of the work, for many members lived in this vicinity and were now nearer to their missionary than before. After a few repairs had been made to the house Capt. McNair had so kindly thrown open, the missionary family was in very comfortable quarters. Another little house on the premises was arranged to accommodate a school which Miss Ruede at once resumed. The Indian Brethren expressed themselves willing to build a meeting-house, but owing to unsettled conditions it was not deemed advisable to incur additional expense. Thus Clauder's labors became of an itinerary nature and the services were held in different homes, near and far. A special blessing seemed to rest on these meetings. They were largely attended and many Cherokees were seeking Salvation. Members of other denominations came and sought affiliation with the Moravians from the fact that their own missionaries were gone.

Clauder journeyed regularly to Oochgelogy, also, and found the members there steadfast. A meeting held in Brother John Jacob's house found all the members of the congregation present besides many strange Indians. It was now possible to have an Interpreter at almost every service as several Brethren were well qualified for this work. The Book of Acts in Cherokee had recently come from the press and was widely distributed and read, and Gospel tracts began a blessed ministry among the Indians. But the former mission property at Oochgelogy, once orderly, neat and inviting now presented a sad spectacle of rack and ruin. Two white families were on the place.

Springplace had become a place for drinking and carousing. Sick at heart, Clauder would ride by, thinking of the high days of blessing the Lord had given there. One of the men living on the place had received appointment as Postmaster and after Clauder had checked over the accounts with him he was free from all Government responsibility.

During the years 1833 and 1834, about 1500 Cherokees had voluntarily emigrated to the new territory.[*] The U. S. Indian Agent for the Cherokees begged Clauder to advise his congregation to remove as a whole, for the longer they remained the harder their lot would be. Clauder could not take sides, for the Nation was still bitterly divided over this question.

The Cherokee Council in 1834 was the scene of more wrangling, but no progress was made towards settlement of their problems. Many of the Chiefs were still expecting a turn for the better in their fortunes, hoping their lands would yet be secured to them. The minority, who saw that holding out against the inevitable was futile, had no power to act.

The treaty of cession of the year 1835 has been referred to. Ratified by the Senate, in 1836, heedless of the remonstrances made by the real officers of the Cherokee Nation, it became

[*] Some were coming back and their reports of the new territory were not reassuring. They did not feel at home there. Clauder wrote that they looked emaciated and pitiful as most of them had suffered with fever. Some Indian widows, after having lost their husbands through a quick death in the new home, walked back—a distance of 800 miles—and settled in Tennessee. Unfortunately, that State, too, was preparing to extend its jurisdiction over all the Indian lands within the State limits.

evident, under these circumstances, that the poor Cherokees would share the same fate their southern neighbors, the Creeks and Seminoles, had experienced, i.e., they would be removed by force of arms if they did not go voluntarily. A two-year time limit was stipulated in the treaty for the complete removal, and already a large military force was stationed within the Cherokee limits, ready to strike the blow when the circumstances would warrant it. Great confusion prevailed among the Indians. Some, of the more reckless order, advocated waging war in defense of the lands which the Great Spirit had given them, others favored less sanguinary measures, while a great number availed themselves of the inducements offered by the treaty and enrolled for emigration and among these latter were the majority of the Moravian Cherokees.

Amid so many sad occurrences of those days, the life within the mission congregation was particularly spiritual, warm and bright. An old, blind Cherokee woman, "Ziyanona," thought to be 100 years of age, was baptized in the name of Jesus after she had joyfully answered the usual questions asked of the Moravian Candidates. Over this unusual spectacle, this exceptional manifestation of the grace of God, all present at the service were moved to tears. An Indian Sister, Rachel Perry, lay upon her death-bed and on the Sunday before she died spoke these words: "My Brothers and Sisters are today gathered to sing beautiful songs and are enjoying happiness. *Their* happiness will soon be disturbed by needs and troubles from without; *I* am going to the enjoyment of eternal happiness where no storm can any more reach me."

Just at the time when the removal of the Cherokees was made certain by the Treaty of 1835, Captain McNair was obliged to ask Clauder to vacate his house and farm which he had for three years placed at the disposal of the Moravian mission, rent free. His son had been married and now came home to settle on this place. Other indications pointed to the futility of securing another temporary location for the mission. Chief John Ross returned from Washington in August of 1836 and said he had not yet given his consent for the Nation to be removed as he hoped for better terms from the Congress of 1837. But even John Ross admitted that, ere long, the Cherokees would have to move. George Hicks, returning from Council, brought word that the aforesaid agreement would be carried out regardless of John Ross and that if the Cherokees would not move peaceably they would be removed by force. Several hundred troops were already located around the Council House, "so as to be handy." Again. Clauder found himself in a situation where something must be done and he could not wait for instructions from his Board. He decided to pack their movables, to return to Salem with his family and Miss Ruede and, later, to come back alone or with some other Brother to accompany the Indian Brethren and Sisters on their long journey.

The last service was held on August 28, 1836, marked by deep sadness but, also, by calm trust in the Lord. The missionary admonished his flock to be faithful "in the things which they had learned and been assured of," and to settle as near together as possible when they arrived in Indian Territory. Then on August 31, at George Hicks' home, Clauder knelt on the ground and commended the members of the Cherokee congregation, gathered from among the heathen, in fervent prayer to God for safe keeping and guidance on their long journey and asked His blessing upon them in the new home. After selling their cattle and grain and storing their goods with Capt. McNair, the missionaries left for Salem on September 12, arriving on the 29th of the month. Lest Conference might think that Clauder had acted hastily or forsaken his post too soon, Brother George Hicks sent the following letter to Brother Theodore Schultz:

"Bradley County, Tenn., Sept. 10, 1836.

"Rev. T. Schultz: Dear Brother, Being intimately acquainted with the peculiar difficulties of our Brother Clauder, I take the liberty of addressing a few lines to you at his request.

"Under the provisions of the Newton Treaty there is but a very limited time allowed our people for removal, and as the painful experience of the last seven years has taught us that the U. S. Government is determined at all hazards to remove this Nation, I for one, and together with very many of my fellow citizens, am determined to remove to the country allotted for the Cherokees at an early date, the Government furnishing me with the means necessary for my removal.

"Our sufferings here have been indescribable, and it is a heart-sickening thought to think of lingering longer upon this our unhappy soil.

Trusting to the assistance and direction of the Lord of the universe, I am feeling inclined to take my staff into my hand and seek a home in the west.

"I am greatly comforted by hearing from Bro. Clauder, that he is ready and willing to accompany us, or to follow us, to the west, and, as he has been compelled to give up his habitation to its owner, and believing it to be altogether unadvisable for him to locate himself anew in this land, I think that this plan with which he will make you acquainted is the most practicable and reasonable one that can be adopted under existing circumstances.

"If it is the intention of your Board to renew the mission in the west and you should feel disposed to send pioneers thither on an exploring tour, I should be happy to have them in my company and would, with great pleasure, afford them all assistance in my power.

"I remain your sincere friend and brother,

"GEORGE HICKS."

The same Brother offered to receive into his own house in Bradley County, Tenn., any missionary from Salem who would visit the Cherokee flock in their distress and before their removal. Accordingly, Brother Clauder, with his family safely in Salem, left that place on March 1, 1837, for a visit to the Indian congregation. He had been instructed by Conference to do the work of an itinerant preacher and pastor, using George Hicks as Interpreter, Conference being willing to grant Hicks a small compensation for these services which took much of his time. Clauder arrived March 14 and was received by his Indian Brethren and Sisters with special joy. A very large congregation gathered at George Hicks' home on the first Sunday after his arrival, hungry for every word he spoke, and several Cherokees made profession of faith in Christ.

It developed that during the absence of the missionaries, the Indian Brother Boas had been faithfully visiting and exhorting the members. He found them scattered here and there, but true to the Faith and most of them growing in grace. Boas, also, had regularly kept services, assisted by Brother Samuel, in different homes, and the audiences had been large.

Easter Sunday found a congregation of 100 assembled. One full-blood Cherokee, "Tsu no gy,"* was admitted into the church by Baptism on that day. This was his testimony: "The sins of my former days are gone; I feel entirely different to what I did

* Meaning "squirrel."

formerly and I think of nothing but serving my Saviour." Although very old, he walked for miles from one preaching to another. Several others were received into the church during the months of Clauder's visit.

When warmer weather came and the house audiences continued to grow, the Cherokee Brethren erected "shades" here

MILES VOGLER.

and there, that is, roofs of pine boughs in the open, with logs for benches and a platform for the speaker.

On this visit Clauder found a town standing around Springplace on the fields the missionaries had cultivated for many years. The dwellings, school and church were still intact and the fruittrees planted by the missionaries, though very old, were still bearing.

At this time a young man came forward in the Friedberg, N. C., Moravian congregation with the desire to serve the Lord in the Moravian mission field. Conference at Salem had several

14

interviews with Miles Vogler* and it was decided that he could, just now, be of great service to Brother Clauder, in that he had some experience as a teacher, having taught at Friedberg, and done good work in the Sunday School. Beginning in this way, it was thought Vogler might become a future missionary among the Cherokees. He accepted the call to any work for Christ among the Cherokees which he might find at present and left Salem June 12, 1837, arriving at George Hicks' on July 2. He was well received by the congregation. Clauder and Vogler now built for themselves a small cabin in the neighborhood of George Hicks.

On July 15, Capt. McNair passed away and in him the Moravian mission lost another good and faithful friend. Brother Clauder now had the privilege of rendering him a service in recognition of the great debt of gratitude which the Church owed the good Captain for his many acts of accommodation and his last great kindness in giving the mission a home for three years,

---

* Miles Vogler was born Dec. 17, 1810, at Friedberg, N. C. Here he was reared and, with his older brother, Jesse, enjoyed the pastoral care of the Rev. Henry A. Schultz and imbibed the missionary spirit. After having been associated with Mr. Thomas Wilson in the early days of the Salem Post Office, Miles taught school in Flat Rock, near Hope, Ind. Both brothers volunteered for service among the Indians, Jesse becoming associated with the New Fairfield, Canada, Indian mission, and Miles accepting a call to the Cherokees in 1837, coming from Hope to Salem, from whence he set out for the Cherokee country. His first work among the Cherokees was done as assistant to Bro. H. G. Clauder and he proved himself very able, especially in school work among the Cherokee children. On May 2, 1838, he accepted the call to become a full missionary among the Cherokees and to follow them to Indian Territory. On March 28, 1839, Bro. Vogler was married to Sister Sophia Dorothea Ruede at Salem, and together they served among the Cherokees until October, 1844, when a call came to them to the West Indies, where they labored successively on the Islands of St. Thomas, Santa Cruz and St. Kitts: in all, eight years, when a call came to them to return to the Cherokees, which they followed gladly, for the hearts of both Brother and Sister Vogler were attached to the Indians. (The Cherokees had named Vogler, "DeKansesky.") They returned to the Territory in 1852, and it was at Mt. Zion, a station in the renewed Cherokee mission, that Bro. Vogler died, Aug. 1, 1854. His grave lies in the New Springplace graveyard with the inscription, "Miles Vogler, Missionary of the United Brethren," the dates and the Cherokee legend: "Here rests a missionary."

SOPHIA (RUEDE) VOGLER.

free of charge: Clauder prepared Capt. McNair's body for burial and then conducted his funeral service, using the Moravian ritual. McNair was a friend to Indian and white and a particular friend to messengers of the Cross from all denominations.

God's grace shines brightly in dark times and such were these days for the poor Cherokee Christians of whom Clauder wrote:

"Our entire Indian congregation was now, in consequence of National affairs, in a dispersed condition. Those formerly residing within the limits of Georgia had shared our experience of 1833, by a violent removal, and were sojourning, in poverty and suffering, within the Tennessee limits. Their condition affected my soul more than I can describe. But they had heard of the goodly inheritance laid up in heaven for God's children, they believed in and loved Jesus and held fast to their faith and were undismayed, though their earthly losses and sufferings were great."

This from Brother Clauder's personal diary. Writing to Salem, he asks special prayer for the following: 1. "A-wo-di," a Candidate for Baptism for nearly two years. She had come to Clauder with tears in her eyes and begged soon to be baptized. She said she had given herself up to the Lord and had no greater desire than to be in His Church. Her husband was "Red Bird," a brother of David S. Taucheechy. 2. Charlotte, Samuel's daughter, likewise a Candidate for Baptism, a tender young soul, formerly a promising scholar at Springplace. 3. "Tsu-no-gy," (already noted). 4. Jesse, Israel's son, a promising youth, former scholar at Springplace, truly anxious to be a follower of Jesus. Clauder requests prayer, also, for the following: Mary Jane Boas, Susanna James and Rachel Sanders, Candidates for Confirmation. Praise God for all these precious fruits in dark, trying times! Clauder notes that even some of the "veterans of the ball ground and all-night dance" are becoming concerned about spiritual things.

Herman Ruede.

Unostentatiously, Vogler tried teaching a few children in the missionaries' cabin, so that our Brethren might not come into bad repute with the Government as encouraging the Indians to remain. Then came a request from the Rev. D. S. Buttrick, Presbyterian missionary at Brainerd, Tenn., always of one heart and soul with the Moravians, for Bro. Vogler to take charge of the school there as they had lost most of their workers. David S. Taucheechy was to be his assistant. After consulting his Board in Salem, Vogler accepted this proposition in which lay several advantages. Not only could he teach some children of Moravian families who were now attending school at Brainerd, but he was, also, within easy reach of most of the members, to whom he could continue to minister and Brainerd was a good home for the winter. Subsequently, Bro. Buttrick reported to Salem the excellent work Brother Vogler was doing.

September 8, 1837, Bro. Clauder reached Salem from the Cherokee country to confer personally with Conference about the work and to visit his family. Since March 1, when he had set out, this Brother had traveled 2250 miles on horseback, which means that over 1600 miles were covered in visiting and preaching at widely scattered points. After a rest of five weeks, he set out again for the Cherokee congregation, to see how they were faring and to minister to them in Word and Sacrament.

Brother Clauder found about 20 of his Cherokee members ready to emigrate, gathered with a large company about two miles from the Indian Agency. Among them were Richard Sanders and family, Wm. Henry and family, Boas and family, John Jacob and family, Sinwakee and family—and these were the flower of the congregation. Already, they were drawing rations from the Commissary of Subsistence and, therefore, under the terms of the treaty, they would be among the first to go. (At this time the officers of Government were fearing hostilities on the part of the Ross party.) Clauder and Vogler held frequent services in this camp, with very large congregations, and the meetings were greatly blessed. In the celebration of the Lord's Supper the covenant was made, between the members now about to leave and those who remained to go with later companies, to remain true to the Lord until they should see Him face to face.

And now came a heavy cross for faithful Bro. Clauder to bear. Some of the "Ross Party" were circulating rumors that he was favorable to the last treaty and in line with the "Ridge Party," citing as evidence that he had helped to appraise the mission property, for which compensation had been received, and alleging that he had already been named as missionary for the new Territory by the Treaty party. Deeply grieved as Clauder was over this suspicion resting on him when he had labored hard from the purest motives, we can only wonder that, in the ferment of these times among the Cherokees, he had been able to remain free from mistrust and accusation for so long. The members were loyal to him, every one, but for the good of the cause in prospect for a future mission, Clauder thought best to retire from this service altogether, and to return to Salem, leaving Bro. Vogler in the field. After a most affectionate farewell service in which Clauder received expressions of appreciation and love from his Indians whom he had helped so much, he left on Dec. 19. Passing the Agency on his journey, Bro. Clauder had a conversation with General Smith about the Cherokee exodus, in which the General remarked that, among all the Indians in camp, the Moravian Cherokees distinguished themselves by exemplary conduct and there had not been a single deviation from the path of duty and virtue! This splendid testimony was excellent medicine for a faithful missionary who was suffering persecution and exile. Coming on the eve of their departure which marked a close of the mission among the Cherokees in the east, this good testimony to the work of the Moravian Church cheers our hearts even now as we read it. Clauder reached home by the end of December, 1837, having given nine years of his life to the Cherokee mission.

At the beginning of 1838, Vogler wrote that the company of which above mentioned families were a part, had gone into winter quarters about 16 miles west of Bro. George Hicks' place, as the muddy roads rendered an advance impossible. Vogler had visited the camp and preached from the words, "For ye know the grace of our Lord Jesus Christ, that though he was rich, yet for your sakes he became poor, that ye through his poverty might be rich."* This discourse, so appropriate and so comforting, moved many Cherokees to tears.

As the two-year period, stipulated in the Treaty, was nearing its close and no further concessions had been obtained from Congress, the Society in Salem deemed it necessary to take some definite steps toward the transplanting of the mission. It was decided to call Bro. Vogler to Salem to talk matters over. He arrived in April, 1838, and reported that the first company of exiles was resuming the march and that the Indian Brethren had urged him to accompany them, but he had declined for the reason that his presence among them might again be interpreted to mean that the Moravians were in sympathy with the Ridge Party. He reported also, that the Government was taking all necessary steps to carry out the terms of the Treaty during 1838.

Brother Miles Vogler at once offered to go to the Territory to serve in the mission there and, as his labors among the Cherokees had been greatly blessed, Conference had no hesitation in joyfully tendering him the call to go as a full missionary among the Cherokees. With him young Bro. Herman Ruede, aged 20, was commissioned to go to help in a future school and the outer arrangements of the mission. Bro. Ruede had been assisting the Rev. Henry A. Schultz in the school at Friedberg and had, for some time, manifested a strong desire to work among the Cherokees. Further, Conference called on the Rev. John Renatus Schmidt, former missionary at Springplace and Oochgelogy, to accompany these younger Brethren first to Brainerd, Tenn., and then to the west, to superintend the establishing of the new mission. Bro. Schmidt was well qualified for this work as he was beloved by the Indians and experienced in school and mission work among them. At this time, he was serving the Colored congregation in Salem. He gladly responded for this responsible service. These three Brethren were congenial and devoted to the Lord and His cause; a better trio to follow up the work in its uncertain state scarcely could have been selected.

After Brother Vogler had been ordained on May 2, a Deacon of the Moravian Church, preparations were made to send them at once on this mission. A stout wagon and good horses were procured, anticipating a long, hard journey. The three Brethren

* 2 Cor. 8:9.

were constituted a Mission Conference with preliminary power
to act. Schmidt was designated Chairman, and Ruede, Secretary. They were to journey at first to Brainerd and from thence
they were permitted to journey with the Cherokees or by themselves, as seemed best. In the new Territory, they were to do
all in their power to visit and gather the members of the flock.
Rigid economy was enjoined upon them. On May 4, 1838, the
congregation at Salem was called together and, in a peculiarly
solemn service, these three Brethren were commended to the
Lord, in the service of the Cherokees, wherever He might lead
them.

The three Brethren reached George Hicks' in Bradley County,
Tenn., in safety and were warmly welcomed. Brother Schmidt
received an enthusiastic welcome from those of the Brethren and
Sisters who had known him before. The three occupied the
small cabin adjoining Hicks' house, where Ruede began a small
school at once. Ruede was especially interested in learning the
Cherokee language, and applied himself to that task with all
diligence. Meetings were held at the different camps where the
Cherokees were gathered before starting on their journey.
Large numbers of the Indians who had refused to enroll for emigration were now placed under arrest and confined in barracks,
ready to be deported. Thus at Springplace, the Brethren, when
they passed through found 200 Indians under guard.

One of the first acts of the missionaries was to make a trip to
Oochgelogy to visit the grave of Bro. John Gambold. They had
brought with them from Salem a gravestone to place upon this
grave. The mound was intact and still surrounded by woods.
After shaping-up the grave and placing the stone the Brethren
built a fence around the last earthly resting place of this servant
of God.

A letter was received in Salem in July, 1838, from Dr. S. A.
Worcester, who has for several years been living at Parkhill,
Indian Territory. He stated that the company which had win-
tered around Brainerd in 1837, had arrived safely in the western
home and that the Cherokees seemed much pleased with their new
location and were building homes and looking forward to the
time when their missionaries would be with them.

Chief John Ross passed through Salem, also in July. His efforts for the modification of the treaty had failed in the main, though he had received some concessions, e.g., the Cherokee Nation received One Million Dollars more for their eastern homes, therefore, Six Millions in all; also, the time for removal was extended by several months. Chief Ross, on his part, agreed to co-operate with General Scott, U. S. A., in the removal of the remainder—i.e., the greater part—of the Nation, roughly estimated at about 13,000. They were to travel in companies of 1,000, and for each such company, the Indians themselves might select the leader, subject to the approval of General Scott.

Brother George Hicks received the appointment to lead out 1,000 of his countrymen, which he accepted. He determined to leave about Sept. 25 if his complement had been assembled by that time. Before setting out for the west, this Brother brought his two daughters, Delilah and Emma, to Salem to enter them in the Female Academy. These girls were accepted in view of the many services Hicks had rendered the mission, and soon felt quite at home in the school. The Salem Brethren were much pleased with Brother Hicks, as they found him to be a sensible and godly man, and ready and anxious to do all in his power for the re-establishment of the mission.

Last letters from the missionaries among the Cherokees, east of the Mississippi, were received in Salem, Oct. 4, 1838, and stated that they would begin their journey on Sept. 17, D. V. They had decided to travel alone, instead of accompanying members, for these were now numbered in with and scattered among companies of 1,000. George Hicks had found it necessary to delay his start by several weeks, much later than the Brethren thought they ought to go. So the three started alone in their wagon, westward bound.

It is not within the scope of this story to follow the various companies of Cherokees on their long and weary way to their destination. Months elapsed before the trans-location was completed. Meanwhile, even Chief Ross acknowledged that he had delayed the removal too long. Daily, the morals of those who remained in the east waxed worse. Many who enrolled, deserted on the slightest pretext and had to be hunted up. Of two companies of 1,000 each, which had gotten as far as the Tennessee

River, 1,000 Cherokees had returned, "murmuring against Moses and Aaron." Some were transported part of the way by boat until the water-courses became so low that boats could no longer navigate. The greater part of the many thousands made the journey by land. Measles and other epidemics broke out and death took a terrible toll among the emigrants. It is recorded that none of the Moravian Cherokees perished *en route*.

The Cherokee Nation, east,* is on the way to a new land set apart for them west of the Father of Waters. While the Cherokees continue on their march, let us follow our three pioneer missionaries on their trip to the Indians' new home and get a glimpse of this Territory.

---

* When the main body of the tribe was removed to the west, several hundred fugitives escaped to the mountains of western North Carolina, where they lived as refugees for some years until, in 1842, through the efforts of Mr. Wm. H. Thomas, an influential trader, they received permission to remain on lands set apart for their use in western North Carolina. They constituted the nucleus of the present eastern band of Cherokees in Swain and Jackson Counties, North Carolina.

CHAPTER XIX

THE MISSIONARIES' JOURNEY WESTWARD AND A BRIEF DESCRIPTION OF INDIAN TERRITORY

"Westward Ho," a small, two-horse wagon with three missionaries! Traveling over the mountains from eastern to middle Tennessee, they came through Nashville and turned north into Kentucky, passing through Hopkinsville, where they were obliged to rest, for one of the horses had been badly galled by the collar. A small boy mistook them for peddlers and inquired, "Have you any gooth to shell?" Onward they came, through Salem, Ky., and to the Ohio River, which was very low at this season of the year. The ferry was a small boat with paddle-wheels operated by a steam engine and was just large enough for two teams. Traversing some barren country in southern Illinois, they came to the Mississippi on the border of Union County, where the stream was about a mile wide and it took 15 minutes to be rowed across. Thence into Jackson, Missouri, in which section they found many German settlers who had emigrated from North Carolina years ago. Caledonia, Mo., was the next station, "where we devoured a very tough biped of the feathered tribe." At Steelville, Crawford County, the missionaries viewed some of the famous lead mines of Missouri.

After crossing the Meramec River, they came to a famous spring, which was supplying more water than the Meramec. Almost surrounded by a perpendicular bluff 50 feet high, this gigantic spring discharged into the Meramec through a basin 30 feet in diameter and supplied two forges, a sawmill, a grist-mill and a blast furnace with power. No bottom of this huge spring had yet been sounded.

In this State, also, our travelers saw the farmers breaking the virgin prairie. Yokes of oxen were hitched each to a wagon, to the rear axle of which were attached two plows. The oxen have grazed the night before on the sod they are to destroy next day. The sod is very tough and the plow is set deep enough only to cut and turn under the sod in order that it may rot. Corn is planted immediately in the wake of the plows and needs no further attention and the yield is about one-half as much as from fully cultivated land. It is called "sod corn" and is used mostly for fodder.

Big Piney River, which Brother Schmidt describes as a fine stream, was next crossed and the wagon rolled into Waynesville. The Brethren had now entered the Grand Prairie, extending to the Rockies. Springfield, they found to be a little town in the prairie. After having traveled 362 miles in the State of Missouri, they entered Arkansas, passing through Fayetteville, Washington County, and from here went on to the border of Arkansas, leaving the United States and entering Indian Territory on October 27, 1838, having been 41 days on the journey of over 860 miles.

Indian Territory, that immense reservation west of the Mississippi, came to be, first, by reason of the fact that the Indians, the largest number of whom originally inhabited the eastern coast of North America, were being continually forced westward by the settlement and expansion of the whites and, secondly, because the influence of the white man and his Government planted among the Indians the idea of tribal autonomy which was rapidly developed and tenaciously clung to, especially by the "Five Civilized Tribes." For these reasons, a separate home for the red man became necessary and was selected by the Government of the United States.

The boundaries of the Territory were, north and south, the 37th degree and the 33rd degree of latitude, and, east and west, the 94th degree and the 100th degree of longitude, west of Greenwich. These parallels included the later Territory of Oklahoma,* and the whole tract comprised an area of 54,215 square miles, bounded, on the north, by Kansas; on the east, by Arkansas; on the south, by Texas; on the west, by Texas.

---

* Oklahoma was part of the "unorganized or Indian country" set apart by Congress in 1834. The Creeks, in 1866, ceded the western part of their domain in Indian Territory for 30 cents an acre, while the Seminoles gave up their entire holdings for 15 cents an acre. Congress, in 1885, authorized the President to open negotiations with the Creek and Seminole Indians for the purpose of opening these vast, vacant lands to white settlement. This was accomplished in 1889, and a mad rush for the best lands ensued. From time to time, additional lands were opened up. The agitation for Statehood began in 1891, but was blocked until 1907, when Oklahoma and Indian Territories were admitted as one State, under the name of Oklahoma.

This territory was carved out of the immense "Louisiana Purchase," from France, in the year 1803, by which the area of the United States at that time was more than doubled.

Indian Territory is drained by the Red River, and its branches, the Canadian River, and its branches, and the Arkansas, and its branches, besides innumerable small streams. Along the rivers there were broad stretches of fertile lands, covered with natural growths of timber of various kinds. Through the western portion of the Territory, extended a belt of timber about 50 miles wide; the rest of the land, in the main, is a rolling prairie.

Outside of the area covered by Oklahoma Territory, the land included within above parallels was assigned, principally, to the "Five Civilized Nations," viz., Creeks, Seminoles, Cherokees, Choctaws and Chickasaws, of which reservations the portion for the Seminoles adjoined and was, virtually, a part of the Creek country, as the Seminoles belonged to the Creek confederacy.

The large reservation for the Cherokees lay in the northeast corner of the Territory and covered about 3800 square miles. Besides this, the Cherokees had been assigned a very large territorial extension, known as the "Cherokee Outlet," more than twice the area of the reservation. Eventually, the "Cherokee Outlet" was sold to the United States Government.

The northeastern part of the Territory, north of the Arkansas and Canadian Rivers, is a plateau, deeply scored by streams. West of this, the country is broadly undulating and the largest extent of prairie lies within the then Cherokee and Creek reservations. In these reservations, too, were found fields of bituminous coal and wells of petroleum.

Cherokee Reservation lay in a belt particularly rich for agriculture and well watered. Brother Schmidt wrote that the land is exceedingly fertile—the soil is black—and ground and climate well adapted for growing almost all kinds of grain, vegetables and many fruits. For many years the main crop was corn, because stock-raising was conducted on a large scale.

The climate is warm and, before the Territory was well settled, was very humid, hence unhealthful. Now, the climate may be said to be warm and genial, with a mean temperature of about 60° F.

On their arrival in the Indian Territory, the Cherokees reinstated their government, with Tahlequah as the capital, the United States having guaranteed them tribal authority. The government of the "Five Civilized Nations" was patterned, in general, after that of the States, in that they had an elective "Principal Chief," a National Council, with Senate and House of Representatives, Judicial Districts with a judge, marshall, sheriff and deputy sheriff and two constables for each District, and a complete system of public schools. This form of tribal self-government was quite successful for a number of years, until the increasing white population of renters, etc., who found themselves without a voice in the government, caused the United States to seek extension of Federal authority over the entire Territory, which was accomplished in recent years, and then lands were allotted in severalty and the Indian was absorbed into the white man's Government.

CHAPTER XX

THE RENEWED MISSION UP TO THE CIVIL WAR, 1861

Arrived in the Territory, the missionaries made inquiries at once about the Moravian Indian families already in the new home, and information received was most gratifying. They learned that the conduct of the Moravian Cherokees on the long journey had been above reproach and they had gotten for themselves a good name with the officers of the Government. General Arbuckle, now stationed at Fort Gibson, was their warm friend* and through his efforts about eight Moravian families had been enabled to settle together on the Barren Fork of the Illinois River, where there was a strip of land 12 to 15 miles wide. (The Barren Fork is the east branch of the Illinois, and is also called Little Illinois River.)

The three Brethren, therefore, journeyed on to the Barren Fork. One night, they stopped at a tavern kept by an Indian woman and as they were sitting around the fire, a young Cherokee Indian came in, sat down, but said nothing. Brother Schmidt asked his name, whereupon he arose and said, "My name is Thomas Waytee. You were my instructor at Springplace." There was great joy over this meeting, as may be imagined, and it seemed the direction of Providence, for Waytee could lead them to some of their Indian Brethren.

On their journey they came, first, to Parkhill, the Presbyterian mission station. Here was Dr. S. A. Worcester, whom we have seen laboring and suffering with the Cherokees in Georgia. He welcomed them royally. In Tennessee and Georgia this good man had constantly co-operated with the Moravians in the common cause, and here, in the new Territory, he was the first to receive them and give them encouragement and assurance over the prospects for future work. Elias Boudinot—our "Buck" of former days—was now with Dr. Worcester as Interpreter. These good friends constrained the three Brethren to remain for a while at Parkhill.

*General Arbuckle said, "If ever there were any Christian Indians, they are the Moravian Indians."

Greatly strengthened, our missionaries continued their journey
to the Barren Fork of the Illinois. Here they found several
Moravian families, among them Boas, James Fishinghawk and
Sister W. A. Hicks, and a plantation had been selected for George
Hicks, who had not yet arrived. Near the center of this settlement, these Moravian members had reserved an improvement
for the mission, consisting of about 10 acres of cleared land on a
knoll, with several acres sowed in wheat. There were two good
springs on the premises and two cabins, a blacksmith shop and a
corn crib had been built. This improvement was one-fourth
mile distant from the Barren Fork of the Illinois, which flows
into the Illinois about 12 miles below this settlement, 18 miles
west of the United States line, 30 miles east of Fort Gibson and
12 miles distant from Parkhill. The Moravian members lived
within a radius of 10 miles and said they wished to remain here
permanently, and more were expected to settle in this neighborhood. Having been given power to act as a Mission Conference,
and having permission from the Federal Agent to reside anywhere in the Cherokee Reservation, the Brethren bought this
improvement for $550. Soon they were fairly well settled in
their new home and began to breathe more freely. Christmas,
1838, found 20 of their former communicants around the Lord's
Table.

Chief John Ross had given these Brethren a letter of recommendation to the Chiefs already in the west, in part as follows:

"To the Chiefs and People of the Cherokees, west:

"My Friends: In great haste I write you these lines, merely to
recommend to your acquaintance, hospitality and friendship, the Rev.
John R. Smith, the Rev. Miles Vogler and Mr. Herman Ruede.* Some

---

* Herman Ruede was born near Salem, N. C., Sept. 29, 1818. The first
four years of school were spent at Bethabara, N. C., and from there he
was taken to Salem. The Rev. Henry A. Schultz, pastor at Friedberg,
N. C., took great interest in him and gave him private lessons in Latin,
French and Greek. Bro. Ruede taught school at Friedberg and there
continued his preparation for mission service.

Brother Ruede was married to Carolina Burkhart at Salem, Oct., 1847,
but his wife lived only a short time. A second marriage took place at
Bethlehem, Pa., August 4, 1853, when Brother Ruede married Miss Maria
Smith.

On his return from the Cherokee mission, Bro. Ruede taught school

of you will recognize in Mr. Smith "Sawanookee,"* the devoted missionary of Springplace and the untiring friend of the Cherokees and of the human race generally.

"These gentlemen go out as missionary agents of the Society of the United Brethren, commonly styled Moravians, with the view of resuming missionary labors among our people in the west under the patronage of their Society. I trust you will take them by the hand as friends and receive their talk with open ears and consider it with a generous and wise heart.

"I need not state the fact to you, for it will be well remembered by many of you, that the first missionary school establishment in our Nation, which had so usefully been conducted, was by the Society of Salem from whence these good friends come.

"JOHN ROSS, *alias* KROWESKOWEE."

Brother Schmidt wrote, that within a radius of several hundred miles lived Cherokees, Creeks, Seminoles, Choctaws, Osages, Shawanose, Delawares, Senecas, etc., and that among them all there had never been such a hunger for the Word of God as was now manifest. This fits in with the striking prophetic utterance made by Zeisberger shortly before his death:

"When the clouds and storms, hanging over the Indians for a long time, have passed and there is calm again; when the time of the present indifference will have passed; when Satan will have spent his force against the Indians; better times will come when the Indians have moved out of the territory of the white men and put across the Mississippi. Then there will again be work for the Brethren among them and blessed times of refreshing."

Miles Vogler returned to Salem early in 1839. Bro. Schmidt had strongly recommended to the Provincial Helpers' Conference that a married couple should now be in the field, and for this reason, Bro. Vogler had been invited to come. He was united in

___

at Bethania and did Home mission work in the mountains. Later, he taught in the Moravian Parochial School at Bethlehem. He was publisher of "The Moravian" from 1858 to 1862. He went to Kansas, settling there in 1877. He died at Kill Creek, Osborne Co., Kansas, December 29, 1888.

* The Northern Indian."

15

marriage to Sr. Sophia Dorothea Ruede,* in February of 1839, in Salem.

Several paragraphs from the story of their journey† to Indian Territory will be of interest.

"On the 11th of March, 1839, we commenced our journey, after a very sad farewell from home and friends. We traveled by stage to Wytheville, Va., where I met with some old scholars from the Academy, as also with Mrs. McComas, and other ladies with whom I had become acquainted at Salem. Leaving Wytheville, we passed on by the White Sulphur Springs, and the Salt Mines, traveling by stage to Charleston on the Kanawha, where we took a steamboat for Cincinnati. Here we spent a week in order to make purchases for the mission. On Sunday we went to church and heard Rev. Lyman Beecher. Mr. Edmund Zevely was at that time in Cincinnati and showed us some attention. Our boat was not very pleasant, as the steerage was crowded with hogs, the city being a great pork market. The river is very beautiful, but the city was smoky, owing to the many factories, and the weather rather cloudy and rainy, so that our stay was not at a very favorable time.

"After finishing our business in the city, we took passage on a very nice steamboat, with quite a number of passengers, going west. At the mouth of the river and all along some left for other quarters, and only continued with us down the Mississippi and up the Arkansas River. Sailing up the Arkansas River was rather monotonous until arriving at Fort Smith, where we found a boat-load of Seminole Indians which had come from Florida going on to some western section. They presented a most striking appearance, more savage than any I had ever seen.

---

* Sophia Dorothea Ruede was born Feb. 22, 1809, at Friedberg, N. C. At the age of 11, she entered Salem Female Academy and, at 19, returned to that institution as a teacher. Becoming interested in mission work among the Cherokee Indians through her sister and brother-in-law, Sister and Brother H. G. Clauder, of the Oochgelogy and Springplace mission stations, Sister Ruede went out with them and remained several years in the Cherokee country, up to 1834, teaching in the mission school, mainly, during the two-year sojourn of the mission with Capt. McNair in Tennessee. Thus she was well prepared for later service among the Cherokees, whom she loved dearly. After her marriage, she served with her husband with great success in the Cherokee mission up to Oct., 1844, when they were called to mission service in the West Indies. Almost eight years were spent here and then, in 1852, came a call to go back to the Cherokees. Bro. Vogler died, after two years of service, August 1, 1854, and Sister Vogler returned to Salem. She was a member and an officer of the Female Missionary Society of Salem. She died, January 8, 1889, at Salem.

† See Bibliography No. 29.

They were yelling and dancing and behaving awfully, so that my courage almost failed me to live among Indians.

"At Fort Smith, we had to hire horses to prosecute our journey, as there was no other way of traveling. Good riding horses were scarce, and so we took the best we could get. We were now entering the Indian Territory and riding horseback was very fatiguing, especially as my nag was a poor mule and hard to keep in motion.

"We traveled on under most unfavorable circumstances, until we finally reached the house of the Principal Chief, John Ross, where we were very hospitably received and entertained on the 14th of April. On the following day, we went up to Parkhill, the Presbyterian station. We met with a very cordial welcome from Mr. and Mrs. Worcester, the missionaries. After resting a few days at the urgent invitation of Mr. and Mrs. Worcester, we set out for Barren Fork, our destination. The country was now in beautiful spring verdure, and our road through prairie land beautifully green, with many flowers. One place, near Illinois River, was particularly pretty, where we rode almost without a road over beautiful beds of violets and other flowers, and overhead we were shaded with blooming locust trees and other shrubbery.

"During the afternoon we arrived at the cabin, our future home, where we were met and welcomed by my brother Herman, and Brother John R. Smith. The house was small, with a fireplace where all the cooking was done. The place looked very uninviting. In front of the house was a barren hill and a great deal of undergrowth of brush-wood. We had to bring our water at least a quarter of a mile both for cooking and washing. Help of any kind was hard to get. Bro. Herman had constructed a trough out of a tree to use for a wash-tub, for which I found abundant use, as our traveling clothes were all ready for the wash-tub.

"There was not much cooking to do as there was daily only corn bread and bacon. Of the latter we had purchased a supply at Cincinnati and meal could be gotten by going 15 miles to the nearest mill."

Brother J. R. Schmidt, who had come to the Territory only temporarily, for the purpose of helping to establish the mission on new ground, bade farewell to the Cherokee mission and missionaries within a few days after the Voglers arrived and returned to Salem, bringing with him encouraging reports of the work thus far accomplished. There were now about 14 families around the Barren Fork and the hunger for the Word of Life was most gratifying.

Brethren Vogler and Ruede spent much time visiting the families within several miles of the mission. Services were held in the little mission cabin, for which purpose some rude benches had been constructed.

During the summer there was a great deal of sickness—fever and ague—among the families of the Barren Fork settlement. At one time the three members of the mission family were down and not able to help one another. Of this experience, Mrs. Vogler wrote: "We were 14 miles from any doctor, and had no one to send. By and by, Doctor Butler, on his way home to Parkhill, called, not knowing of our being sick. He kindly left medicine and directions how we should use it, also told us not to eat beef nor use sweet milk; the latter we did not have and beef we had eaten but once, as that was a scarce article. We improved slowly, after taking medicine. Brother Herman was first convalescent, and shortly after Dr. Butler's visit, Mrs. Worcester kindly invited us to Parkhill to spend a few weeks. Mr. Vogler returned to Barren Fork, and I remained under the very kind treatment of Mrs. Worcester, who knew as well as any physician how to treat my case, and in a few weeks, I was able and anxious to go home."

It was a sad time of sickness and death with the Indians, many of whom still lived in tents, not having been able to build houses since their arrival in the Territory a year before, and were, therefore, suffering from exposure. The Indian Sister, Sarah Bithia Hicks, faithful member always, passed away on August 22, 1839. Bro. and Sr. Vogler were present at her bedside and sang hymns, and prayed with her and the Good Shepherd was very real to her as she entered the Valley. Her dying request was that Bro. and Sr. Vogler might take care of her two younger children, Sarah and Nancy. After Bro. Vogler had preached the funeral sermon, they took these little girls to the mission cabin, stowing them away as best they could.

Attendance upon the services increased when the sickness abated and Vogler and Ruede built an open shelter for a meeting-house and organized a Sunday School with 16 scholars. The first accession to membership was Jesse, the son of Israel, received by Adult Baptism after a good confession of faith. There was great rejoicing over this in the congregation and on the part of the missionaries.

The year 1839, besides sickness, witnessed, also, much discord among the Cherokees. Those who had been residing in the west for some time wished the newer immigrants to come under *their* laws, without re-electing Chiefs. The Ross party objected. A

Council was held but the opposing factions would not compromise. Hatred between many members of the "Ross Party" and the "Treaty Party"* was implacable.† Major Ridge, John Ridge‡ and Elias Boudinot,‡ all of the Treaty Party, were foully murdered by some Cherokees of the opposing party, much to the distress of Chief John Ross, who had never countenanced violence. Finally, Chief Ross proposed that an equal number of men be chosen from each side to draw up a new code of Statutes which should then become the law of the land. Both parties agreed, buried their differences, the Committee was selected and, in due time, the Constitution, as revised and amended by them was adopted and John Ross was elected Principal Chief. With a stabilized government, the Cherokees entered upon a career of ever increasing advancement and prosperity and became the leaders in wealth, culture and influence, of the Five Civilized Nations.

Returning to the mission, we find our missionaries, in 1840, ready to change their location. The Barren Fork vicinity had proved most unhealthful,§ as we have seen, and several of the Moravian families were preparing to move away. A number of the members were living in the neighborhood of Beattie's Prairie, about 40 miles north of Barren Fork, others were intending to

---

* Instigators of the Treaty of 1835, by which part of the Cherokee Nation entered into an agreement with the United States pledging the whole Nation to remove from east of the Mississippi to the Territory.

† The missionaries suffered much anxiety under these perturbed conditions in the Nation. One day an Indian came to the mission cabin and asked the way to a neighbor's house. He was intoxicated and it was readily seen that his asking for information was not the real object of his coming. He cursed all missionaries bitterly and said they were the cause of the Cherokees having been driven from their eastern lands. He pulled out a big knife and said he would kill Vogler if he did not quit the country. Mrs. Vogler ran to their neighbor, Miller, who came and had a hard time trying to persuade this Indian to leave, which he finally did only after severe threats by Miller.

‡Former Springplace, Georgia, scholars of the Moravian mission school.

§ Bro. Vogler attributed this unhealthful condition to the many creeks and ponds around Barren Fork. In summer time, a green slime settled on these and vitiated the atmosphere with a disagreeable odor.

move here and the wish was expressed that the mission might, likewise, be removed thither. Consulting with Conference in Salem, advice was received that the missionaries might settle at Beattie's Prairie, if the National Council of the Cherokees would give permission. Chief John Ross kindly brought this before the next Council, with recommendation, and Beattie's Prairie was formally designated for the Moravian mission. Now from Sister Vogler's account:

"We accordingly made the necessary arrangements, after a suitable location had been selected, and commenced our journey. Brother Herman undertook to drive a two-horse wagon with most of our trunks and what little bedding we had. Father and myself, with the two little girls had to travel on an open wagon, there being no other way. We had umbrellas and blankets in case of rain. This was in the month of March (1840), not quite a year since we arrived.

"The first day we made good headway, and got into comfortable quarters for the night. The next day it was cloudy and rained some. Brother Herman traveled ahead of us, but we overtook him in a prairie, in rather an uncomfortable plight: his nose was bleeding and he was walking aside of his wagon, being pretty heavily laden. Here I felt homesick and experienced something of a poor missionary's life. We stopped here in the prairie and bought some ginger-cakes which tasted very good, as we had seen none since coming to the country. Bro. Herman had got considerably ahead of us and we saw nothing more of him until we arrived next day at Brother George Hicks'.

"When we finally got through the prairie, one of our horses got sick, and we were in the woods with no house near. We stopped to rest the horse, but he seemed to get worse instead of better, so Father set out in the woods to see if he could find help. He finally came to a saw-mill, where he got something to give the horse, but nothing would do any good and he died soon after. Here I sat in the wagon with my little girls, while Father went back to the saw-mill to get a horse, where the rough men kindly agreed to give us their apology of a bed where the little girls and I rested for part of the night, and Father fared the best way he could with the two men. We had some provisions along, which served to appease our hunger and an old black woman made us some coffee.

"We succeeded in borrowing a horse from the mill, which helped us on to our journey's end, about six miles farther. We were very kindly received by our Brother George Hicks and his wife, at whose home we remained until we could move into a small cabin near the spot selected to commence the mission.

"The day after our arrival, Father and Brother Hicks went to Mr. Thompson's to confer about the place for a house, and found a small log cabin about one mile from Mr. Thompson's which afterwards became our house. Mr. Thompson was a white man who had married a half-breed woman, but a good looking person, and in every way, a nice person. They had a large family of children and were, therefore, anxious for a school. It was agreed upon that the cabin before mentioned should be made habitable, and we were to move in as soon as possible. Meanwhile, we obtained leave to put our boxes and trunks into a very small cabin at our Sister Lydia Chisholm's (Brother Hicks' mother). In this we had barely room for what few things we had, and used one of our goods boxes for a table, as we had nothing of the furniture kind but three borrowed chairs. The Thompsons were well-to-do people and helped us to many things we were in need of, also offered to assist with the building and other work. There were full-blooded Indians living in the neighborhood, but none quite near. There was, at that time, a great deal of drinking going on and we were often disturbed by drunken Indians.

"Brother Herman and Father soon commenced fixing up our future house, and had to go every morning several miles to the place, carrying their axes, saws and other tools with them, bringing them back in the evening, for fear of having them stolen. While they were gone, it often happened that drunken Indians came by, so that I was often much afraid. The work took about a month; the lumber that was needed had to be hauled about 20 miles, and we could get only enough to lay half the floor.

"In one corner of the house was constructed something to answer for a bedstead; in the other, our boxes were put, and in the space between, Brother Herman made up or down his bed every evening.

"During our stay in this little cabin, we were honored by a visit from John Howard Payne, the author of "Home, Sweet Home." He was traveling through the country, trying to get information from the missionaries about the Indians, being interested in the idea of their being the descendants of the 'Lost Tribes.' "

The improvements mentioned in the quotation above were bought by the Brethren for $150. With the help of the Indian Brethren, a school-house 18 x 22 feet was raised, about 100 yards from Vogler's dwelling, standing in a beautiful oak grove beside a good spring. Here, Brother Herman Ruede opened the school in September, 1840, with seven scholars, which number soon increased to 18. Ruede was a fine teacher and the school was a success from the start. The scholars at Beattie's Prairie were mostly half-breeds. By the middle of 1841, this school had become so popular in the neighborhood, that applications for admission had to be refused for want of accommodation, and then the families living around—mostly non-members—subscribed enough money for the erection of another 18 x 22 school-house.

which was built forthwith and opened for girls, while the first
building was occupied by the boys' school. A large number of
girls, half-breeds, took advantage of the school begun by Sister
Vogler, May 3, 1841. Brother Vogler supplemented the regular
curriculum with weekly Bible instruction. "Our schools gave us
pleasure and we felt as if we had indeed commenced the mission
work."

Brother Vogler was kept very busy, for he had several preaching places. Services at Beattie's Prairie, held at first in the
homes of the members, were conducted in the school-house. A
Sunday School had been organized immediately upon arrival of
the missionaries and now, with ample room, five classes were arranged[*] and Delila Hicks[†] and Martin Thompson, with the
missionaries, served as teachers. The program on Sundays at
Beattie's Prairie was as follows: Sunday School, 10 a.m. to 12
m., followed by preaching. Then Bible lesson and reciting of
Scripture verses until 3 p.m. These missionaries and Cherokee
Christians must have been in dead earnest!

Regular preaching appointments were kept at Barren Fork,
where the mission improvements had been rented when the missionaries removed. George Hicks usually accompanied the
preacher to Barren Fork and served as Interpreter. At one particularly blessed service, 20 communicants sat around the Lord's
Table. On such a visit to Barren Fork, Brother Vogler stopped
in at Brother Richard Sander's house on Spring Creek, 21 miles
distant from Beattie's Prairie, and learned of the death of his
mother, Sister Salome Elizabeth Sanders. She had been a Mother
in Israel and had lived a bright, consistent Christian life among
her own. Her son said that she had departed with joy to be with
her Lord. Also, the wife of Brother Emmanuel, of Barren Fork,
had gladly exchanged earth for heaven. Brother Vogler notes,
with a tinge of sadness, the passing of these and other sterling
converts of the old Springplace mission whose places are not being so rapidly filled.

---

* The Sunday School Union of Moravian Schools of Stokes County,
N. C., contributed $20 for Bibles, etc., to this school.

† Daughter of Brother Geo. Hicks. She had received her education in
the Moravian mission at Springplace, Georgia, and was then brought by
her father to Salem Female Academy where Miss Ruede, now Mrs.
Vogler, had been one of her teachers.

Vogler preaches statedly, likewise, in a little Indian village 1½ miles distant from the Beattie's Prairie mission. Large audiences assemble and to them Brother George Hicks interprets the preacher's message from the Word of God. Full-blood Cherokees live in this village and they do not like to come to the services at the mission, for the reason that whites assemble there, with the half-breeds, for worship.

Another call for missionaries came from Spring Creek, 21 miles south of Beattie's Prairie, where Brother Richard Sanders was located. Full-blood Cherokees lived in this neighborhood. Four other Moravian families lived near him and Brother Vogler had visited them several times, as their settlement lay in the direct route to Barren Fork. It was a healthful locality, fertile and well watered. Several of the Barren Fork families contemplated removing to this place, hence a school and a missionary were greatly desired. The Brethren Boas and Emmanuel were already holding little services at Spring Creek each Sunday and there was much interest. Consequently, the petition of these people for a preacher and teacher, was forwarded by Vogler to Salem, where it called forth praise and thanksgiving to God and the determination to send assistants into this hopeful and widening field.

At this time, the Single Brother, Gilbert Bishop,* of Bethle-

* Gilbert Bishop was the son of Charles David and Anna Maria (Schneckenburg) Bishop and was born March 20, 1817, Bethlehem, Pa. He learned the cabinet-making trade with Benjamin Eggert, of Bethlehem. Later he went to Salem, N. C., to work at his trade, and there offered for mission service among the Indians. He went to the Cherokee mission at New Springplace, Indian Territory, in 1841. On May 16, 1844, he was united in marriage to Miss Margaret Louise Morris, of New Jersey, at Bethlehem, and returned with her to the mission, where she died in 1846 and was buried at New Springplace. Bishop received a written ordination as a Deacon of the Moravian Church, July, 1845. On Sept. 14, 1847, he married Sister Clarissa Marietta Warner, and continued at New Springplace until 1862, when he was compelled to leave on account of the Civil War. He returned with his family to Bethlehem and shortly after took charge of the buckwheat and oatmeal mill there until 1874, when he moved to Hummel's mill, above Bethlehem, for several years and then returned to Bethlehem, working at cabinet-making and repairing and devoting the proceeds, in later years, to mission causes. He died Sept. 23, 1907.

hem, Pa., who had been on a visit to Salem, and had made a
favorable impression there as a good young man and a skillful
cabinet-maker and had received permission to settle in Salem to
follow his trade, expressed a desire to serve in the Indian mission
and was ready for service among the Cherokees, should his
parents consent, which they did. The Brethren of the Conference

DAVID ZEISBERGER SMITH.

in Bethlehem added their blessing and the call was extended to
Brother Bishop. Another missionary was sent into the field with
Bishop, namely, young Brother David Zeisberger Smith, who
graduated from the Theological Seminary, in 1841. He had been
born on the Cherokee mission field and was a promising young
man who could render splendid service in the mission schools in
addition to his labors as a missionary. With the full approbation of his parents, living in Salem, a call was extended to him
and he accepted.*

* David Zeisberger Smith, son of Johan Renatus and Gertraut (Spain-
hower) Schmidt, was born June 21, 1821, at Springplace, Cherokee

Bishop and Smith were called to a last interview with the Salem Helpers' Conference on Aug. 29, 1841. They were instructed to be teachers in the mission schools and helpers in the mission, both in spiritual and temporal work. They were given $1,000, part of which was to be used to defray outfits and traveling expenses and the balance was to be paid to the local missionaries. August 30, these Brethren met with the Congregation at Salem for the last time, when the members blessed them and sent them forth. They went by wagon to Charleston, W. Va., by boat on the Kanawha, Ohio, and down the Mississippi, but found the Arkansas River so low that boats were uncertain, hence they went by mail-stage to Little Rock, Ark., and on this trip had their first wonderful experience of seeing and riding over the great prairie. They arrived at Beattie's Prairie, October 4, having been obliged to pay $45 for transportation for the last 50

Nation, Ga., while his parents were missionaries there. His father gives the following reasons for the boy's name: 1. In remembrance of the great Apostle to the Indians, David Zeisberger. 2. So that he might remember that his forbears were descended from members of the Ancient Moravian Church—his great grandfather was Melchior Schmidt from Zauchtenthal in Moravia. (David Zeisberger was also a native of Zauchtenthal.) He entered the Moravian Theological Seminary as a member of the class of 1841. While at Bethlehem he organized and was the first president of the Young Men's Missionary Society, an organization that has accomplished and is still doing great good in the cause of Christ. Brother D. Z. Smith was ordained a Deacon of the Moravian Church on March 23, 1845, by Bishop W. H. Van Vleck and married, April 17, 1845, to Elizabeth Benezet Kummer, at Bethlehem, Pa. Smith served in the Cherokee mission up to May, 1849, when he came east and in 1850, was sent by the Church and by the Government on a journey of reconnaissance to the Pawnee Indians on the Platte River in Nebraska. May, 1852, he was married to Sister Emma A. Ricksecker, at Hopedale, Pa., and served the congregation there as assistant to Brother Peter Ricksecker for one year, when a call came to the mission among the Delawares near Fort Leavenworth, Kansas, where he labored until 1857, when he became pastor of the congregation at Line Creek, Mo., until 1860. He then lived in retirement at Nazareth, Pa., until 1862, when he was called to Henderson, Minn., serving there five years. Followed pastorates at Sharon, O., 1867 to 1870; Chaska, Minn., 1870-'73; Friedberg, N. C., 1873-'77; Bethabara, N. C., 1877-'89. He then lived in retirement at Laketown, Minn., but served the congregation as far as health would permit. Brother Smith died February 21, 1884, at Laketown.

miles of the journey! There was joy that night in the mission
cabin on the prairie!

Bishop and Smith found the missionaries at Beattie's Prairie
repairing the dwelling and the school-houses in preparation for
winter. Of the augmented mission family, Sister Vogler writes:
"In the course of time, Brethren Bishop and Smith were sent to
assist, the former to superintend the building of the new house,

SAMUEL STOTZ WARNER.

and the latter to take charge of the school. I was glad to give up
the school, as there was enough for me to do in my housekeeping,
since there were more in our family, and not often help at hand.
We now also bought a cow, which made work, but the milk and
butter came very good. Father had built a very neat 'spring-
house,' across a little stream at the foot of the hill, near the
spring." Brother Bishop, with his trade, must have been exceedingly useful at Beattie's Prairie. He was kept busy making
tables and other articles of furniture of which the family had
long been in great need.

The close of the year 1841 found a total of 72 souls in the care of the Moravian mission among the Cherokees at Beattie's Prairie and out-stations.

Operations at Spring Creek began in 1842. The Indian settlers here were discouraged because no National District School had been allotted them and according to the Cherokee law, no denominational school could be begun without the sanction of the Council. Representations were made to Chief Ross, through Brother George Hicks, and a petition filed asking that the decision not to allow a school under the Moravian Society be reconsidered and that Brethren Smith and Ruede be permitted to come to Spring Creek and open a Moravian school. Chief Ross replied favorably, saying that if these Brethren would begin a school, the move would have his approbation and he would work for the sanctioning of the school by the next Council. Wrote Chief Ross: "Above all, I am anxious that the Council should have an opportunity to correct its mistaken policy in regard to the best intentions of our dear friends, the Moravians, whose devotedness to the true welfare of the Cherokees has been uniform and steadfast."

This good will of the Chief encouraged the Brethren to make a beginning at Spring Creek, and in June, 1842, the erection of the school-house was begun. The Spring Creek Brethren worked loyally with Bishop, Ruede and Smith and in several weeks cabin and school were completed. Bishop's skill was especially valuable in the making of windows and doors. Chimneys were blocked up like the walls and then the flues and the outside plastered with clay until no wood was visible. The school was 20 x 15 feet, the cabin, somewhat larger. The buildings stood at the intersection of Spring Creek and the military road.

Sept. 11, 1842, the first meeting was held at Spring Creek and the school-house was consecrated for church and school purposes. A very earnest and happy congregation gathered. Brother Vogler preached from the 73d Psalm. Elliek Sanders interpreted. After a short intermission, the Lord's Supper was observed with 11 guests. Joseph Sanders was received as a communicant member. The station received the name "New Springplace," in remembrance of the old mission in Georgia. School opened on September 19, with 21 scholars. Many parents were present for the opening session of song and prayer. Bro. Bishop had made an alphabet of large letters. The scholars, some of them grown young men and women, were very much interested and eager to learn; the majority of them had never attended school before. Chief Ross, who had gone on a long journey east and come through Bethlehem, Pa., brought a trunk full of books from that congregation for the school and church at New Springplace. Another encouragement came from the Council of 1842: a permit was issued by that body for a Moravian school at New Springplace.

Brethren Ruede and Bishop were in charge of this new station. To quote from the narrative of their experiences:*

"Our school has commenced on Monday, the 19th inst, when we made the beginning of our labor with 21 Cherokee boys and girls, only two speaking English, and one or two have been in a school for a few months, but mostly entirely ignorant of English. They learn rapidly and it becomes more and more interesting to them.

"These children are not accustomed to be under any restraint, and if school does not interest them they will stay at home and parents have no authority or do not exercise it. If only we can keep up their spirit and make learning pleasant!

"Brother Ruede is a fine teacher and has had some experience. I, therefore, am very willing to be assistant only and often have need to cry for patience and a cheerful heart and mind in this work in which I surely never have engaged to gratify my own pleasure or desire, but simply to do the will of Him!

"Brother W. Henry has masoned out our fireplace with limestone, and it is very neatly done, so that we have a comfortable fireplace about four feet wide to give a cheerful blaze for the comfortable enjoyment of our *own* fireside.

"I suppose it will be satisfactory to my dear mother to hear some report from the culinary department. Biscuit and corn bread is the bread we commonly make. You will smile to hear that I have been baking and cooking, but I am rather an awkward hand. Often my biscuits will not rise properly; another time the crust got to be so hard that they called them 'death-balls!' I have, however, since retrieved my reputation by some good bakings. We bake with pearlash. Potatoes and some rice is all we have to boil, and pickled pork to fry. Coffee we put in a bag and pour boiling water over it, in this way it needs no clarifying. We get one quart of milk daily from W. Henry's and the children bring it when they come to school. Soap, we are to receive from our Cherokee Sister, Agatha Sanders, in exchange for soap-grease. She also does our washing and necessary mending as well as she can. Formerly, she lived

* See Bibliography No. 27.

in the family of David Smith's father at Oochgelogy and speaks some English.

"The mission is obliged to my mother for the towels with which she has supplied me. We are using them and, in fact, nowhere can purchase an article for that purpose. My blue cotton drilling pantaloons are living and doing service every week day; a remarkable stuff! I would also wish my dear mother to be without any anxiety respecting other clothing; I am well supplied."

In July, 1843, Brother Herman Ruede was called to the mission among the Delawares in New Westfield, Kansas, and Brother D. Zeisberger Smith came from Beattie's Prairie to be with Bishop in the work at New Springplace. Instructions had been received from Salem to proceed with the erection of a new house so that a missionary couple could be accommodated and put in charge of this promising station. Before Ruede left, the house had been raised, and now Bishop was making doors and windows and Smith, with the help of some Indian Brethren, was covering the roof.

Progress during the year was slow on the building, in the school and in the real work of the mission. This was due to persistent attacks of fever, which rendered Bishop and Smith helpless, alternately; sometimes both Brethren lay sick and at one time they were in such wretched health that Vogler came down with the wagon and took them back to Beattie's Prairie, where for a whole month they were under the care of Sister Vogler. To combat the fever the missionaries used a home-made decoction of dogwood bark, cherry bark and Cayenne in preference to some very indifferent Peruvian bark. Bishop wrote, after repeated attacks of fever, "O that the Lord would have mercy on us and grant us the precious boon of health! But His gracious will and purpose be done with us!"

October 1, Brother Peter was baptized and Brother John's wife, "Tooka," received from the Methodist Church, both of these accessions being at Beattie's Prairie.

At the close of the year a letter came to Bishop inviting him to come to Salem for a visit. If possible, he was to be married while in the east and then to return to the Cherokees to take full charge of New Springplace. Brother Bishop was a very conscientious man and eager to do the Lord's will, yet he had been trained as a cabinet-maker and not as a missionary. Often he upbraided himself because making tables, etc., gave him so much pleasure while preaching and teaching were so hard for him. Nevertheless, after a great struggle with himself—he went into the school-house, shut the door and *prayed it out*—he accepted the call, trusting in God to see him through!

Accordingly, Brother Smith was left in charge of New Springplace while Bishop took his journey early in the year 1844. Everything went well with Smith, alone at his post of duty, and he labored under God's blessing. The Passion Week was a particularly refreshing season, during which three full-blood Christian Cherokees took part in the services held each night. Wm. Henry read in Cherokee the story of the Saviour's last week, Boas followed with an exhortation and Richard Sanders closed with prayer. The congregations kept growing with each night and Easter Sunday, the culmination, was for them a day which the Lord had made. A few weeks later, Smith was taken down with such a severe attack of fever that it became necessary for Brother Vogler to come and take him in the wagon to Beattie's Prairie. Thus, for the second time, New Springplace was left without a missionary for a season, due to sickness.

Meanwhile, on May 16, 1844, the marriage of Brother Gilbert Bishop and Sr. Margaret Louise Morris had taken place at Bethlehem, Pa., and they arrived at the mission on June 28. Sr. Bishop contracted fever and ague at once and in the months that followed she was subjected to much sickness and suffering.

Brother D. Z. Smith was associated with the Bishops at New Springplace and the work in congregation and school was very encouraging. A full-blood Cherokee, U-di-ku-yee-ski, one day came to Bishop to have a yoke fixed and asked him for a copy of the Scriptures. Bishop encouraged this man to take upon him the yoke of Christ. Preparations were made to erect a new church at this station; hitherto, the log house built by Bishop in 1842 served both for church and school purposes. In these outer labors as well as the spiritual work of the mission, New Springplace was developing some fine Christian men; among them, William Henry, Israel and George Hicks gave promise of future great usefulness to the mission. Brother Smith was invited to come east at the close of 1844 to find a suitable companion for service among the Cherokees, where another couple was now needed.

Brother Miles Vogler had accepted a call to the West Indies in October, 1844. "Father's health had for some time been very poor, and he thought a change would benefit him. I was not very happy about the call, still I acquiesced, hoping it might be the Lord's will." Thus writes Sr. Vogler. Before these missionaries left, a complete round of visitation to all the Moravian members was made, involving 150 miles of travel, after which the Voglers took affectionate leave of their Indian Brethren and Sisters.

While in the east, Brother Smith aroused great interest in the Cherokee mission. The congregations north and south contributed towards the church to be built at New Springplace and the co-operation of the Young Men's Missionary Society of Bethlehem and Female Missionary Society of Salem was enlisted, the latter organization donating $30 "toward a new chapel at Springplace." Brother Smith and Sister Elizabeth Kummer* were united in marriage April, 1845, at Bethlehem, Pa., and started on their journey on May 5, arriving at Beattie's Prairie, June 21. This station, which now received the name of "Canaan," had been assigned to Brother and Sister Smith.

A conference of the missionaries to consider the whole field was held at Canaan, July 10, 1845. First of all, Brother Smith handed to Brother Bishop his written ordination, executed by Bishop Van Vleck, of Salem, as a Deacon of the Moravian Church. Next, the missionaries considered the instructions received from Salem with regard to Indian Helpers and Interpreters. Brother Boas, who had rendered such excellent services in this capacity, had been called home. Brother William Henry, of New Springplace, and Brother Alex. Sanders, of Beattie's Prairie, were to be designated for this office and set apart for the purpose, after careful instruction, by the laying on of hands. They were to be Interpreters, personal workers to win souls for Christ, and were licensed to conduct services in the absence of a missionary. The Salem Conference, also, directed the Brethren to proceed at once with the building of the New Springplace church.

The two candidates for the Helper's office were consecrated at a very blessed Communion service soon after, and the Indian Brethren were called together to be more fully informed respect-

---

* Born June 7, 1823, Bethlehem, Pa.

16

ing the intended church building. They took up the project
with enthusiasm, pledged their co-operation and appointed July
28, for timber-cutting. While they were engaged at this work,
Sr. Bishop prepared a good dinner each day for all the men.

Services at both stations were held with much blessing. Both
Helpers served acceptably, and usually followed the interpretation of the missionaries' sermons with an exhortation of their
own. Neighborhood Prayer Meetings were held by them successfully. The members at Barren Fork continued faithful and
usually all assembled for the monthly preaching service and celebration of the Lord's Supper. In the Bishop and Smith families
one or two Indian children at a time, usually orphans, were enjoying the comforts and advantages of good, Christian homes. Bishop
was privileged to perform his first baptism in 1845, when the
Indian Sister, Sarah Naomi, joyfully confessed her Saviour.
Several members were received by Right Hand of Fellowship at
both places during the year.

The Rev. D. S. Buttrick, Presbyterian missionary among the
Cherokees in Brainerd, Tenn., has been mentioned frequently in
this narrative and we have seen him always in brotherly co-
operation with the Moravian missionaries. He, too, had followed
his converts to the Territory and the Presbyterian mission had
been established at Parkhill, under Dr. Worcester, and at Mt.
Zion, six miles south of Canaan, in charge of Brother Buttrick.
That good man was now (1845) in very poor health and requested Brother Smith to take temporary charge of his flock,
which Smith consented to do and labored faithfully at Mt. Zion
church and Sunday School, the Lord owning and blessing his
efforts. Brother Buttrick sought to regain his health at one of
the mineral springs in the Territory, but all treatment was in
vain, and he was obliged to relinquish his work altogether.*

---

* David S. Taucheechy was a member of the Presbyterian mission at
Mt. Zion at the time when application was made to the Moravians for
their missionaries to take charge of this station. Taucheechy, it will be
remembered, was one of the most promising scholars at old Springplace
and later a student at Cornwall. His repeated desire to unite with the
Moravian Church had been met, each time, by a negative lot and
Taucheechy at last united with the Presbyterians. He died in 1848, before the Mt. Zion members had been received into the Moravian
Church; nevertheless, his was a Moravian funeral service.

The year 1846 brought great joy and, also, great sadness to the mission and to the whole Church. After a severe winter, we find our Cherokee congregation at New Springplace on Easter Sunday, April 12, marching to the graveyard in procession observing the Easter Morning Service for the first time. At Canaan, Eliza Moody was baptized and there were several professions of faith early in the year. The work at Mt. Zion had been reorganized and was moving along smoothly under Moravian leadership. August 1, a meeting was held by candle-light, and, after an earnest discourse, five Cherokees came forward to accept Christ: a widow, Sarah by name: her daughter-in-law, Wa-lie; Uda-yi; Anne Boas; and a young woman, Nani. The Spirit of God is working mightily!

And now, the deep shadows. Martha, faithful Christian wife of Helper William Henry, lay sick unto death early in the year. She requested her missionaries and Christian friends to pray for her, and they knelt around her bed. Expressing the sweetest confidence in her Saviour, Martha passed into His presence. Brother Bishop made her coffin and they bore her to the grave, singing hymns in Cherokee.

August 27, Thomas Henry arrived at night from Canaan, bearing the intelligence of Sr. Smith's very serious illness and the request for the Bishops to come next morning. On the 28th, while on the way, a messenger met them with a note from Brother Smith telling of Sister Smith's decease and requesting preparations to be made at once for the burial at Springplace. Brother Smith was left with a little daughter, four months old. In his grief, he was yet able to hold a Prayer Service on the night of his wife's death, with his Indian Brethren and Sisters, who had gathered in sympathy, and all were melted in tears. Next morning Smith read part of the service for the Burial of the Dead with the Indians who had assembled, and then set out for Springplace with the body in a carriage. Brother Bishop, in the meantime, had made the coffin and the Indians had dug the grave. Smith arrived at 4 p.m., and the funeral was held, a very large congregation attending. Brother Bishop made the address, Brother Smith, in tears, adding a few words. Then the faithful Cherokee Brethren carried the casket to God's Acre, the procession following with song in Cherokee and Sr. Smith's mortal body was bedded beside that of her Indian Sister Martha.

Although Sr. Bishop was far from well, she and her husband determined to accompany Brother Smith to Canaan to comfort him with the little girl in the motherless home as best they could. They returned home on Sept. 1, with a long-looked-for barrel of gifts from their dear parents at home. Five months it had been on the way. Arrived at Springplace, they opened the barrel—we can imagine their joy and pleasure—and found the things safe and uninjured. "Sept. 2—Rejoiced over, examined and arranged the things." Then, "Sept. 3—Sr. Bishop complained of fever. Fever seemed to increase, with great pain in the limbs. Bled her in the afternoon and cupped her." As quickly as possible, a physician was brought to the spot and he tried every remedy available. Tearfully, the members assembled on Sunday morning, Sept. 6. "I spoke to them a few words on the Daily Text: 'Fear not; only believe.' " When Bishop left the service and hurried to the bedside of his wife, the Cherokees held a special Prayer Meeting on her behalf. Already, she was leaning heavily on the arm of her "dear, dear Saviour," entering the Valley. Her husband asked her what would become of their little son,* and she replied: "Jesus will show him more than mother's faithfulness." Speaking of her distant relatives and friends, she said: "Write them, with my farewell greeting, that I am saved." To her Cherokee members she sent the message: "Seek ye first the Kingdom of God, and his righteousness." To her husband, the final message: "Stay with Jesus. We will soon see one another again." And so she "fell on sleep," aged 23 years, 7 months and 11 days! From Bishop's Diary: "There living no one in our neighborhood who could make a good coffin as I desired my dear wife to have for her last house, I engaged in making one myself. When my hands for grief would get heavy, the thought nerved me: 'it is the last office of love I can in this life do for her.' About 3 o'clock in the afternoon it was finished and we laid her in. Brother Smith preached the funeral sermon and afterwards I addressed our beloved flock, delivering the sainted one's last message of love to them. Dusk shed its departing light before the grave was filled."—In looking over the little Cherokee Hymnal, the writer wonders whether the procession accompanying the body of this girl missionary to its last resting

* Charles David, 8 months old.

place, did not use Hymn No. 86, as indicated, of which one stanza would be:

> "I would not live alway: no, welcome the tomb:
> Since Jesus hath lain there, I dread not its gloom;
> There, sweet be my rest, till He bid me arise
> To hail Him in triumph descending the skies."*

We will not stop to call these and all real missionaries heroes, they are more than that: they are good soldiers of Jesus Christ. Humanly speaking, we can only say, How sadly were the Cherokee mission-forces crippled and, besides, two little helpless, motherless children left with their missionary fathers!

Thus, the bodies of Sister Smith and Sister Bishop rest side by side, the eighth and ninth seed-corn, respectively, of God's holy harvest-field in the New Springplace graveyard.

The Brethren Smith and Bishop were fortunate in being able to make temporary arrangements for their homes. Each had an Indian boy who lived in the family and helped with the work. Smith engaged Lucretia Timer, sister of David S. Tancheechy, to oversee the household at Canaan and care for his little girl, while Bro. Bishop, with whom lived William Bons, secured an Indian Sister, Carolina, widow of Jesse Israel, to take care of them and the infant son.

Reinforcements came to the field May 10, 1847, namely, the Rev. Edward Jacob Mock† and wife Mary, and Sr. Mock's sister, Gertrude Spach. Mocks brought with them their two little children. These missionaries had been called to Canaan and Mt. Zion, where Brother Smith was in great need of help, and were heartily welcomed at a joint Lovefeast held at Canaan.

The work went forward encouragingly. At all three stations

---

* W. A. Muhlenberg.

† The Rev. Edward Jacob Mock was born Feb. 25, 1822, in Davidson County, N. C. He was baptized on March 15, 1822, by Rev. Ruede. He united with the Moravian Church on June 4, 1843, by Confirmation, under Rev. Huebener. On August 29, 1843, he was married to Sister Maria Spach, of Stokes Co. (Born May 27, 1821, daughter of George and Catharina (Seltz) Spach.)

He served as a missionary among the Cherokee Indians for 30 years, during which time he was not once east of the Mississippi on furlough.

He died at Friedberg, N. C., January 16, 1887.

new spiritual life among the young people was manifest in the year 1847. Several years ago, the young people had seemed careless and indifferent, now they were earnest and attentive and several were being saved. Another special meeting was conducted at New Springplace with good results, for three young men and five young women were admitted to the church by Baptism, on profession of faith. At Mt. Zion, too, there was a dis-

GILBERT BISHOP.

tinct work of grace. Here five young people came forward at the close of a baptismal service, after an exhortation had been given closing with an invitation to accept Christ.

Death was constantly claiming valuable members in 1847, especially at New Springplace, and from Brother Bishop's Diary it appears that he was often requisitioned for the melancholy task of making coffins, both for members and non-members. Brother John Jacob's daughter passed away February 17, happy in her Saviour. Sister George A. Hicks died March 7, likewise trusting in Him. May 14, Nicholas Saunders, good Christian Brother and one who was becoming valuable as an Interpreter, was called to his eternal reward.

New Springplace was badly in need of a teacher and it seemed
to be the finger of God which pointed to Brother Alanson Welfare,* of Salem. His grandfather, Jacob Wohlfarth, had been
one of the pioneers in the old Georgia mission among the Cherokees. Brother A. Welfare had had several conversations with
Bishop Van Vleck regarding service among the Cherokees, and
when he heard of the real need in the school, he offered his services for New Springplace. On August 24, 1847, he was received
as an Acolyte and began his journey next day in company with

CLARISSA (WARNER) BISHOP.

---

* Alanson Emerson Welfare was born Sept. 24, 1824, Salem, N. C.
Parents were John Thomas and Mary (Towle) Welfare. In 1847, he
went to the Cherokee country, Indian Territory, first as a teacher and
later served as missionary. On April 21, 1852, he was married to Sr.
Juliana E. Rothhaas (daughter of Jacob and Mary (Vogler) Rothhaas.
Born Oct. 16, 1827, near Salem, N. C. Died Dec. 5, 1897, Salem, N. C.)
at Salem and on April 25, of that year, was ordained a Deacon of the
Brethren's Church, by Bishop Herman. He then returned to New
Springplace and continued faithfully in the arduous duties of the mission. Some years later, autumn of 1855, ill health made it necessary for
him to give up his beloved labor, and for many years he lived in Salem,
in business at a watchmaker. He died May 4, 1883.

some men who were going to Iowa. Toward Welfare's outfit, the
Female Missionary Society of Salem had contributed $40.

A conference of the missionaries was held at Canaan, July 27,
1847, and Bishop writes: "Our Conference came to the decision
that under present circumstances, it is advisable that I proceed to
Bethlehem to get a wife. I wrote a letter to Brother Van Vleck
to this effect. Also wrote to parents with an enclosure to C. M. W.
I rode over to Maysville to put them into the office." Later developments explain "C. M. W." She was Sister Clarissa Marietta
Warner, the wife Brother Bishop was to receive when he came
east.

ALANSON WELFARE.

Little Charles Bishop was left with the Cherokee Brother,
William Henry, where Carolina Israel would look after him, and
Brother Bishop began his journey on August 10. On September
14, he was married, in Bethlehem, to Sister Warner* and they set
out on the return journey immediately.

---

* Clarissa Marietta Warner, born July 10, 1821, was the daughter of
Peter and Anna (Schneider) Kern, of Nazareth, Pa. She taught in the
Nazareth Parochial School for some time. On May 7, 1844, she was
married to the Rev. W. H. Warner, missionary at Friedensthal, St.
Croix, W. I., who died June 26, 1845. Sister Warner returned to Bethlehem, teaching in the Young Ladies' Seminary up to the time of her
marriage with Gilbert Bishop. She died June 6, 1902, at Bethlehem, Pa.

Work on the church for New Springplace was pushed with energy in 1848. February 11, some Cherokee Brethren began the hauling of stone for the foundation. For months previous, timber had been cut and prepared for the building. Shingle-blocks (for splitting into shingles) were cut February 16. March 9, Brother Bishop began mason work on the foundation, assisted by Brother W. Henry. Sills were laid on March 13 and 14, and on

EDWARD JACOB MOCK.

the 15th and 16th, with the help of about 40 neighbors, the framework was raised. All the skilled labor and real carpenter work was done by Brother Bishop, who worked at the building whenever his other duties did not occupy his time. Bricks for the chimney were hauled a great distance and laid up in lime made by Bishop in the kiln he had built at New Springplace. The close of 1847 saw the church under roof and the walls completed.

Cherokees continued to apply for Baptism, showing that the faithful preaching of the Gospel was accompanied by the blessing of God. Nine Candidates received the Sacrament of Baptism at New Springplace on Easter Sunday, 1848, and several were added to the church at Canaan and at Mt. Zion.

Brother Smith and Sister Gertrude Spach were united in marriage on April 18, 1848. Their happiness and united labors were of short duration; after a few months, Brother Smith was

CHURCH AT NEW SPRINGPLACE.

again plunged into deep bereavement, Sister Smith having been called Home, Nov. 21, 1848. Brother Smith left the mission in 1849, entering upon long years of service in the Church in other fields.

The year 1849 was one of particular blessing at all three stations. New Springplace witnessed a memorable event when, on Sunday, Oct. 14, the new church was consecrated. The building was 28 feet square, and by means of a movable partition under the gallery, the room could be divided into two parts, one of which served both for Sunday School and day school. There were two stoves so that each part of the church could be heated separately.

On Saturday before the day of consecration, two preparatory services were held by Brother Bishop with a discourse at each and a Lovefeast at "early candle light." Lovefeasts were always much enjoyed by the Indians and this particular occasion brought a record attendance. Brother and Sister Bishop had prepared coffee and buns for over one hundred, and their supplies were just sufficient to serve the congregation. Sunday dawned beautiful, and a real Lord's Day it was for the Cherokee mission! Brother Mock and family had come from Canaan for the services. At the first service, Brother Bishop gave a con-

CHAPEL AND SCHOOL AT NEW SPRINGPLACE.

densed review of Moravian missions among the Cherokees from the beginning on the Savannah River, Georgia, in 1735, and stated that thirty years ago, the meeting-house at old Springplace, Cherokee Nation, Georgia, had been consecrated. Bishop then preached on the text: "But will God in very deed dwell with men on the earth? Behold, heaven and the heaven of heavens cannot contain thee; how much less this house which I have built!"[*] Then he pronounced the words of consecration and prayer, followed by Mock, Bishop and a Cherokee Brother. The second service was held by Brother Mock, who preached the dedicatory sermon. Thereupon, two adults, husband and wife,

[*] 2 Chronicles 6:18.

were baptized. Their name was "Gotoquasky," to which, in Baptism, were prefixed "Abraham" and "Sarah." The celebration of the Holy Communion brought this blessed day to a fitting close.

The school was re-opened after completion of this building and Brother Alanson Welfare's health had been so far restored that he could again undertake his work. Ten scholars, on an average, attended the school. Several orphan children were received into the mission family, where the missionaries carefully watched over their temporal and spiritual growth and welfare. These

PARSONAGE AT NEW SPRINGPLACE.

children assisted in house and field wherever practicable, thus repaying in part, the expenses of their board and clothing.

Preaching was maintained at four places in the vicinity of New Springplace during 1849, some members living in each of these localities. The Cherokee Brethren themselves started and kept up a weekly Cottage Prayer Meeting which was productive of much good. Six adults were added to the flock during the year, making a total of 78 souls in the care of New Springplace.

At the close of the year, Brother John Jacob is suffering greatly in the acute stages of Tuberculosis, but gives this testimony: "I do not grieve over my sickness and sufferings; I trust in my Saviour alone, and I am assured He will accept me."

Canaan and Mt. Zion report, in part, as follows for 1849:

"At the beginning of the year, we experienced very cold weather. The meetings at Canaan and Mt. Zion were, nevertheless, well attended, some coming without shoes over the frozen ground and snow.

"Early in the spring, a Sunday School was opened at both places and each was numerously attended. Some of the neighbors kindly took an active part and assisted in the teaching of the same. The scholars committed many Cherokee and English hymns to memory.

"During the summer, we were enabled, besides the meetings on Sundays, to keep services on week-days at four different places and the people attended the same very well. All these meetings were held upon request of the people themselves and more requested than could be gratified.

"The day-school was very encouraging and was kept throughout the year, with some intermission, in order to be able to do some necessary labor."

Five souls were won for Christ from heathenism at these places during the year, bringing the total number in care of Canaan and Mt. Zion to 75.

The years 1850 and '51 were marked by steady growth and progress in each station and by the absence of hindering circumstances to the work of grace. An interdenominational organization, "The Spring Creek Bible Society," was formed for the dissemination of the Holy Scriptures, and 13 of our Cherokee Brethren joined in this good work.

Brother Alanson Welfare's health continued poor and even with Brother and Sister Bishop's assistance, the school work was growing too heavy for him. By permission of the authorities in Salem, he set out thither on a journey of recreation, Oct. 4, 1851, in company with the Indian Brother, Archie Henry. By spring, 1852, he had recruited strength sufficiently to warrant his return, and after his marriage and ordination, Brother Welfare and wife began their journey, reaching New Springplace, June, 1852. Both were stricken with fever almost immediately after their arrival. Sr. Welfare recovered quickly, but Brother Welfare's was a long, lingering illness. Additional help at Springplace was urgent, and Brother Samuel Warner,* of Salem, who had expressed a willingness to serve the Lord in this mission, was called to service and set out in company with Archie Henry, returning to his home from Salem.

Cherokee Brother Jesse Israel was received as a Helper in the mission on October 11, 1851. Brother Bishop delivered the charge to him and Brother Mock followed with an exhortation to the entire congregation, numerously assembled on that day.

The winter of 1851 to '52 was bitterly cold, the thermometer at times registering 10° below zero. Smallpox was prevalent and many families connected with the mission were down with this and other contagious diseases. The missionaries and their families were graciously spared amid an epidemic of several diseases which spread over the entire Cherokee Reservation. Our Brethren labored early and late visiting the sick, praying with them and giving medicine, aiding the destitute and burying the dead. Both New Springplace and Canaan were sorely tried by the deaths of Cherokee Brethren Thomas Henry and Jesse Israel. Both were yet in the prime of life and both had been extremely valuable, combining rare talents with the greatest faithfulness as Helpers

---

* Samuel Stotz Warner was the son of Benjamin and Anna (Stotz) Warner and was born in Salem, N. C., June 21, 1832. He received his education in the Boys' School of Salem. April 1, 1847, he united with the Moravian Church at Salem and in 1850, when only 20 years old, he offered himself for missionary service as teacher in the school among the Cherokees. After six years of labor here, he was appointed to mission service in the West Indies. Before going to the tropics, he was married to Miss Josephine Fenner, of Bethlehem, Pa.

His charge was first on the Danish Island of St. Thomas and here he was ordained a Deacon by Bishop Westerby. Thirty years of his life were spent in the West Indian mission, serving on St. Thomas, St. Croix, St. Jan and Antigua. In the year 1880 he became a member of the Executive Board of the Eastern Province of the West Indian field, and its Treasurer. In 1882, he was ordained a Presbyter. He served in this office until 1888, when ill health compelled him to leave the mission. Brother Warner lived in retirement at Bethlehem, Pa., at the time of his death, January 2, 1912.

Rev. Samuel Warner was a brother of the well-known musician and composer, Massah Miksch Warner, of Philadelphia, Pa.

and Interpreters. Henry† at Springplace and Israel‡ at Canaan and Mt. Zion. Their decease was greatly lamented by the missionaries, who found themselves asking, "Where can others be found to replace them?"

The new meeting-house at Canaan was finished in October, 1852. Besides members of the congregation, a number of heathen living in the neighborhood had cheerfully assisted in its erection. Mt. Zion was in encouraging condition, and, in both stations, there were now 84 souls under Brother Mock's care. This Brother's health was very much impaired, and often he had relied upon the late Brother Jesse Israel to keep a service in one or the other place. Additional missionaries were sorely needed and the Provincial Helpers' Conference, with the consent of the Unity's Elders' Conference, called Brother and Sister Miles Vogler from St. Kitts, W. I., back to the work among the Indians, and the call was accepted, although they were pleasantly situated in the West Indies. But they loved their Indians! The Voglers arrived in Salem, July, 1852, and set out for the Territory, as soon as circumstances would permit. An infant daughter was held in the mother's arms for all the weary miles of the long journey, only to find her little grave in the far west.

Brother Vogler, who took charge of Mt. Zion, lived with his family in a house 17 x 19 feet, all in one room, which served as living-room, dining-room and bedroom. The kitchen, 12 x 14, was separate, and had, originally, been Brother Buttrick's study. "It was a small house, though neat, with fine shade trees around it. The spring is in the woods quite a distance from the house."

---

† Thomas Henry was in his 30th year when called Home. As a boy, he had been a pupil at old Springplace, Ga., while Byhan and Clauder were laboring there. Later, he found his Saviour and, possessing gifts and willingness, was appointed Interpreter in 1847. He served with great devotion and success. During his last illness he was taken to Canaan, where he received medical attention, which, however, was of no avail. In confidence and joy of the Lord, he departed to be with Him.

‡ Jesse Israel was also a former scholar of the Georgia mission and was baptized in youth. He was appointed as Interpreter in 1847 and became Helper at Canaan and Mt. Zion in 1851. He was a man of great talent and great zeal for God; withal he walked in unaffected humility before his fellow men. He died trusting in God.

"Father's Interpreter was named Miller,* a good man who was often at the house. The Indians often came to visit us and had names like these—'Red-bird,' 'Mrs. Tiger,' etc. Red-bird's son, Lunie, lived with us and commenced teaching Will and myself Cherokee, but when Father found that he was, at the same time, instructing us in badness, our studies were stopped at once. I remember how sorry we were.

"At this time, Father taught during the summer season. Will and I were in the class with some little Indians by the name of Potts. I learned to read from the 'Frank Book' (by the word method) which is still in existence. I do think Father was a born teacher. We loved his stories, and he took great delight in us. When we did wrong, he was strict and stern so that we feared to disobey."†

A year of retrogression came with 1853. Among the Cherokees in the vicinity, but not connected with the mission, much liquor was being sold and circulated, although this was prohibited in the Territory. Brother Warner wrote that some of the Indians who came to services showed but little interest, walking in and out during the meeting and in the midst of the sermon. Many came who did not even enter the church. Good Interpreters could scarcely be found and there seemed no desire, on the part of such as possessed the ability to qualify for that office. It was hard to get the children to come to school as the parents seemed indifferent about the schools and cared little whether their children learned or not.

No official visitation had, up to this time, been made from Salem to the Cherokee mission since its removal to the west. The Helpers' Conference decided, in 1854, to heed the urgent calls from the missionaries for such a visit, and Bishop John G. Herman‡ was asked to carry out this arduous undertaking, which he decided to do, in spite of advancing years. In the company of

---

* Avery Miller, a former scholar of Springplace, Ga.

† See Bibliography No. 30.

‡ Bishop John Gottlieb Herman, born at Niesky, Silesia, in 1789. Became identified with the American congregations in 1817. 1836-'44, member of Helpers' Conference at Bethlehem, Pa. 1844-'49, member of Unity's Elders' Conference at Berthelsdorf, Saxony. 1849 to time of death, 1854, member of Helpers' Conference at Salem, N. C. Buried in Missouri, his body being fetched, in 1855, by Bro. Fogle to Salem, where it rests in the Moravian graveyard.

Brother Augustus Fogle, of Salem, the journey was begun. Augustus Fogle's* diary gives such a graphic account of the trip, the visit at the mission stations and the sad return journey that it is deemed wise to incorporate his narrative,† somewhat abbreviated from the original.

"A Journey from Salem, N. C., to the Cherokee Nation by way of New Salem, Illinois."

"*Apr. 20, 1854.* This morning a few minutes after seven o'clock, Bishop Herman and I started on a journey to the Cherokee Nation, via Hope, Ind., and New Salem, Ill. We were accompanied by Bro. Herman's family, Rev. Robt. and Emil de Schweinitz and Bro. Bahnson. At Mr. Sneider's we took dinner and fed our horses. When we started again the Brethren Bahnson and E. de Schweinitz returned but the rest went on with us. In the evening about 6 o'clock we arrived at Mr. Elisha Banner's, where we stopped for the night. Today we came thirty-one miles.

"*Apr. 21.* This morning Bro. R. de S. and Bro. Herman's family bade us farewell and commenced wending their homeward way and Bro. Herman and myself went on our way. We passed through Mt. Airy about 10 o'clock and took dinner at the house of Mr. Simmons. This afternoon we crossed the Blue Ridge at Fancy Gap. It was somewhat smoky, and we could not enjoy the scenery, only the fine water falls. A short time before sundown we arrived at Mr. Mitchell's, where we stopped for the night. Today we came twenty-six miles.

"*Apr. 22.* We made a late start and passed through Hillsville about 9 o'clock. About 12 o'clock we passed the splendid scenes of Poplar Camp. At 3 o'clock we crossed New River at Jackson's Ferry. In a

* Augustus G. Fogle, son of Christian and Anna (Stoehr) Fogle, was born Mar. 3, 1820, at Salem, N. C. Attended Salem Boys' School and learned cabinet-maker and carpenter trades. In 1844, he married Lucinda Snyder, of Friedberg, N. C. He was extremely fond of traveling and became very useful to the Church, making short trips with ministers and lay workers to all points within the Southern Province whenever called upon. His three long trips for the Church were to the Cherokee mission, Indian Territory, with Bishop Herman in 1854, with the body in 1855 and with Rev. G. F. Bahnson in 1858. The first two trips were made with a team of horses and a three-seated carriage. On the trip with Bro. Bahnson, the railroad could be used for several stretches which had been built since 1854. Horses and carriage were sold where the railroad began and others bought where it ended. Bro. Fogle, later in life, was elected as Sheriff of Forsyth Co., N. C., for one term. He died, Salem, N. C., April 19, 1897.

† The Diary of the return journey was written by Mrs. Miles Vogler.

17

short time we arrived at Mr. Raper's, where we stopped for the night. Came 27 miles today.

"*Apr. 24.* It being Sunday, we rested at Mr. Raper's. It was a long and lonely day.

"*Apr. 26.* This morning the roads were slippery from the rain that fell last night. Shortly after 9 o'clock we passed through Abington, the county seat of Washington Co. We stayed all night at Mr. Webb's, where I spent a night when travelling west with Miss Stauber. We are now in Sullivan County, Tenn. Today we travelled thirty miles. During the last 12 miles the lightning was all around and the wind was very high.

"*Apr. 27.* This morning it was clear again. We travelled till about 11 o'clock, when we were overtaken by a thunder-storm and we were obliged to stop. I put the horses under a shelter and we sat in the carriage. When it stopped raining we directed our course to Clinch Mountain, where they were at work on the road. They were making a road about 20 ft. below the other one. It was hard crossing. The men pulled my carriage across by hand and I led my horses. We crossed Holston River on a bridge. Passed through Estelleville, the Co. seat of Scott Co. Court was in session as we passed through. When we had travelled about six miles further we had showers and rain. There was a new turn-pike road, which was so muddy that for a time our horses were knee deep in the mud. At 7 o'clock we stopped for the night.

"*Apr. 28.* Suffered as much from cold as I did at any time last winter. Bro. Herman has taken a severe cold. During the morning it began snowing and continued for some hours. The mountain scenery is splendid, the woods are already green and the snow gives them a coating of silver, which is a wonderful scene.

"*Apr. 29.* Still cloudy and cold. Bro. Herman's cold is no better, so we have concluded to remain here for the day. I spent the day exploring Temple's Cave and the Natural Bridge.

"*Apr. 30.* The morning was cloudy and some snow fell, but we started on our way. The weather was so cold, that icicles two feet long were on the side of the mountain.

"*May 1.* This morning crossed the Cumberland Mts. When we reached the top we entered the State of Kentucky. The road was very rough and we had to stop for the purpose of repairing our carriage.

"*May 3.* Today came 38 m. Stopped for the night at Cave Springs at the house of Dr. Cartland. This is a very fine country.

"*May 7.* (Sunday.) We never travel on Sunday, but as there was so much drinking at the house have just left, we concluded to travel. Took dinner at Christiansburg, but finding ourselves again near a grog-shop, concluded to move on.

"*May 8.* Crossed the Ohio River at 3 o'clock in the steam ferry boat, and landed at Madison, Indiana.

"*May 9*. Made an early start to see whether we could reach Hope. After travelling 39 m. we arrived there at 8 o'clock. When we reached Bro. Clauder's, the gate was opened for us and we were warmly received.

"*May 16*. After spending a few delightful days at Hope, among many old friends of former days, we said farewell and again set our faces westward. Today we crossed Flat Rock and Blue River and passed through a rich farming country.

"*May 19*. Have passed through a number of towns, but none of any importance. Today we left our main road for four miles in order to visit Moravians from N. C. who have located in Hendrick Co. Before leaving we sang a hymn and Bro. Herman offered prayer.

"*May 21*. This is a very thinly settled region and we found it difficult to obtain lodging. Succeeded in getting in at a small house where we had a very scanty supper. We were then shown to a very narrow and uncomfortable bed, so I got the carriage-cushions and Mr. Herman's cloak and settled down for the night in a corner of the carriage while he took the bed.

"*May 22*. Ferried the Wabash river. It was very high but by having strong hands at the oars we landed safely in Lawrence Co., Ill.

"*May 23*. This morning made an early start that we might reach New Salem, but after going four miles I found that one of our horses was sick. We had to stop about four hours. I thought he would die but after using all possible remedies, he got better. I then borrowed a horse, and left him there. About dark we arrived at New Salem and stopped at the house of Bro. E. Senseman. We came quite unexpectedly for they did not look for us before the end of the week. They gave Bro. Herman and myself quite a nice room.

"*May 24*. Went back for my horse and found him quite well.

"*May 25*. Being Ascension day we had services. Bro. Herman preached in the morning in German, and Bro. Senseman, in the evening, in the English language. In the afternoon we went to Bro. Martin Hauser's to witness the marriage of his daughter. We remained until after supper.

"*May 26*. Today I was out in the country and planted some corn. Met many old friends during our stay at West Salem who had moved from N. C.

"*June 6*. This morning after bidding our friends at West Salem farewell, we resumed our journey. Bro. Senseman and Bro. Martin Hauser went with us as far as Olney, about fourteen miles from New Salem. Passed over fine prairie lands. Stopped for dinner at Mr. Shafer's, who went with us to Olney. Though but a small town, it is improving fast, as the O. & St. Louis R. R. passes through it. We visited the new Mora-

vian church, which though not yet completed, presents a pretty appearance. After looking around over the church, we sang a farewell
hymn and parted from Bro. Hauser and Bro. Senseman.

"*June* 7. Crossed a prairie 12 m. in extent. It was so cold that I
wore my blanket all day, and Bro. Herman his cloak.

"*June* 8. Crossed the Kaskasia River. Stopped for dinner at the
Carlisle Hotel, and have lodging for the night in quite a good house in
a prairie.

"*June* 9. Passed through the Looking-glass Prairie which is finely improved. Here I saw the finest wheat I have yet seen. Today the road
was crowded with market wagons going to St. Louis. Met thirty or
forty German emigrants. After dinner we went through the river hills
which were well timbered. Arrived at the ferry about 6 o'clock. As we
stood on the banks of the mighty Mississippi we saw many steam-boats
sailing up the river and lying at the wharf. We crossed on the steamer
St. Louis. The loading on this trip consisted of one four-horse stage,
one buggy, a one-horse wagon, two two-horse wagons, one horseman and
twenty passengers. We landed in the south part of the city then went
up North St., then west to the P. O. We passed the Planter's Hotel, a
splendid building. The streets are very narrow, and the buildings
mostly four stories high. My horses were as wild as deer, and the
streets so crowded with carriages and wagons that I could scarcely get
along. The city of St. Louis is 2½ miles wide and 7 miles long. The
population is about 160,000.

"*June* 10. The first night in Missouri there occurred one of the most
remarkable experiences of my life, when I look back upon it in connection with the events that followed. On leaving St. Louis we got on the
upper road to Jefferson City instead of the lower one which we had intended taking. It was very warm. Night came on and we could get no
place to stop. We were sent from house to house. 'No, can't stay,' was
the answer. The family had already retired for the night but I went
into the room and told the man we would sleep anywhere and that I
would find food for my horses, if we could only stay. It caused him to
smile. The man's name was Hoke. He said if we would go to bed without supper we could stay. I made the bargain. It was now 10 o'clock
and we had travelled 40 miles. He sent his son to show us our quarters.
The room was very dirty, but it was better than none. My bed was at
the head end of Mr. H's. In the morning he grew restless and suddenly
cried in a shrill trembling voice: 'Augustus! Augustus! Augustus!' I
ran to his bed and asked what was the matter. He said: 'There is
something horrid pending for me in this state!' This shocked me very
much, but he would give me no explanation. After breakfast we made
our way through the farm to the public road. Mr. Herman had but
little to say and seemed in deep thought. When we got to the public
road we stopped when Mr. H. said: 'Now do as you like; take me back

to St. Louis, or take the road to the left for the Indian Nation. I was too old to undertake the trip. But the Conference wished me to come. I spent a week in considering, and was much in prayer. My mind urged me to go. But I now see I was unfit for such a journey. On you will depend all.' This caused me great distress that I cannot describe. I said: 'From here to Salem is about 900 miles the way we came and about 400 miles to our destination. We have come nearly or quite two-thirds of the way and it would seem strange to turn back.' He said: 'Well let us go on, but on you will depend all.' Of course this conversation caused me much uneasiness, especially when, as we proceeded, he began telling me what to do if he should die on the way.

"*June 11.* Between St. Louis and St. Charles we passed through a broken country, very rich and much improved. It reminded me of Wythe Co., Va. As we had to wait an hour for the boat before crossing the Missouri, I sat on the bank of the river, viewing the town of St. Charles on the other side. With three men on a raft of timber we crossed on the steamer Teleyrop, and landed at St. Charles. Here we spent the remainder of the day and visited the Cathedral, a splendid edifice.

"*June 12.* Passed through a beautiful prairie today. Stopped for dinner at Mr. Shelton's. Mr. S. had been out hunting and had the good fortune to bring home a deer.

"*June 14.* Passed a drove of cattle from Texas. Fulton, the County seat of Calloway Co., contains some handsome buildings.

"*June 15.* Crossed the Mo. and landed at Jefferson City. The State house is quite an ornamental building.

"*June 19.* Travelled over a prairie twenty-five miles in extent. For twelve miles we did not pass a single house.

"*June 21.* Stopped at Mr. McCullah's, quite a good house. It is in Stone Co. The country is stony for the greater part of the way.

"*June 22.* Continued in the Brush prairie for some time. When we got to the timbered land there is a prairie every seven or eight miles. Here our road lay across the Ozark Mts. The grassy hills were green and beautiful.

"*June 23.* We crossed Flat Creek eighteen times. About 11 o'clock we corssed the Arkansas Line. About 5 o'clock reached Bentonville.

"*June 24.* Hurried on. At 1 o'clock got to Maysville, which stands on the west boundary line of Arkansas. On one side of the street live whites, and on the other side, Indians. We stopped at a house on the U. S. side and heard that Mr. Vogler was in town. I looked for him and found that he was gone. After I got directions we went five miles and arrived at Mr. Mock's about 4 o'clock. They were all well. They live in sight of the road leading from Maysville to Fort Gibson. There are but few full-blooded Indians here.

"*June 25.* This is Sunday. I went three miles further to Mr. Vogler's on foot. I wended my way through the woods. When I reached the house Mrs. Vogler was in the yard; at first she did not see me, but when she looked up she came running as active as a girl. After some time we went to the church a few hundred yards away. Mr. Vogler preached and Mr. Miller, one of the first converts, was the Interpreter.

"*June 26.* Bro. Herman and I went to Mr. Vogler's, where we spent the day. It is a small house, though neat, with fine shade trees around it. The spring is in the woods quite a distance from the house.

"*June 27.* A Conference held at Mr. Vogler's. The children were sent into the yard to play. All at once there was a cry and on running to the spot three wolves emerged from the copse of hazel bushes with a howl. No one was hurt.

"*June 28.* This morning we went to Springplace. Mr. Vogler met us and went with us. We passed a few Indian cabins, and after going down a very rough hill we came to Spavenaugh Creek. It is so clear that a pin could be seen at the bottom, where the water is three ft. deep. After crossing the Long Prairie we reached Mr. Hicks'. His daughter, Delilah, who was educated at Salem, keeps house for him. He is like all the Indians, and don't have much to say. I gave him the gun I had brought and he could speak of nothing else. We went about a mile along the Fort Gibson road, crossed Spring Creek, then went up a very steep, stony hill and arrived at Mr. Bishop's about 2 o'clock. After putting my horse away I went up to the church to see Mr. S. Warner, who teaches a school there. About that time Mr. Welfare and wife had come and we all ate Vesper (according to the German custom) at Mr. Bishop's. In the evening Mr. Herman went to see Mr. Welfare. He will remain there and the horse we keep at Mr. Bishop's, where I stay. I have a very comfortable room up stairs.

The church is on a hill in the woods, surrounded by locust trees. It was originally all prairie land. The graveyard is about a hundred yards from the church. I counted thirty-three graves, three of which are missionaries' wives. Mr. Welfare lives a short distance east of Mr. Bishop's house. The smith-shop is in front of the house. Behind the house is a 17-acre field. They have four horses and eight or nine cows. Between Mr. Bishop's and Mr. Welfare's, the bushes are so thick as to completely hide the houses from each other.

"*June 29.* Repaired my carriage in the blacksmith shop.

"*July 1.* Visited some Indian families with Mr. Welfare.

"*July 2.* This being Sunday, there was S. S. at 11 o'clock and preaching at 12 o'clock. Bro. Herman preached and Mr. Hicks interpreted. After the close, Mr. Wm. Henry, the father of Archie, delivered a prayer, in the Cherokee language. After the service the Indians came to shake hands. About 40 were present.

"*July* 6. This morning when I came home I found an old Indian, Israel by name, with whom I had become acquainted. He took me by the hand and led me to where he had hung two large venison hams, done up in leaves. He made me understand that I must eat some before I went away. He is the most friendly Indian I have yet seen. This evening went over to Mr. Hicks'. His daughter, Delilah, remembers from Salem School, Misses Bagge and T. Peterson and Mrs. Benzien.

"*July* 7. This morning we returned to Canaan.

"*July* 9. This being Sunday, we all went to Mt. Zion, which the Indians call the White house, because it is whitewashed. Quite a number were present. Bro. Herman preached and after a short intermission the Lord's Supper was administered. It was a solemn service.

"*July* 11. This morning at 6½ o'clock we bade adieu to our friends at the mission and started on our homeward way. The parting was a sad one. Crossed the U. S. Line at 8 o'clock.

"*July* 12. This morning travelled for 16 miles and stopped at a fine spring. In the evening stopped at Mrs. Mason's, which I must call the traveller's home.

"*July* 14. This morning Bro. Herman felt sick, but wished to go on. He went about 10 miles when I found he was getting worse, he had chills and a high fever and appeared to be wandering in his mind. He would ask for Mr. Vogler, etc. There were only small huts along the road and those were from 5 to 8 miles apart, so I went on to Mr. Smith's, where I put Mr. Herman to bed. After a nap he said he felt better and wanted to go on. Much against my will, I went on. Before long he grew worse and asked me where Mr. Kluge and Senseman were, when they had stopped and all such things. Once when I was getting water for the horses, he tried to get out of the carriage and fell. I dropped my bucket and ran to lift him up. He had not hurt himself by the fall, however, and I succeeded in getting him back into the carriage. He was not able to stand alone and I was beyond reach of help. So I hurried on to the place at which I had intended stopping, Mr. McCullah's, where we stopped on our way out (Stone Co., Mo.). The day had been very hot and dusty—and I was thankful for this resting place. I got Mr. Herman out of the carriage, put him to bed and waited on him as well as I knew how, before I unhitched. It was a lonely feeling to be in this wild, strange country with a man so sick that death seemed staring him in the face. Mr. McCullah keeps a good house and we were kindly received.

"*July* 14. Brother Herman had a better night than I expected. He was anxious to start but I objected. Sent for the Dr. who lives 20 miles. At 11 o'clock Dr. Pranty came and administered medicine.

"*July* 15. This morning, Mr. H. seems better. Dr. P. is a fine-looking, portly man. His wife is a granddaughter of Daniel Boone, of Kentucky. About 6 o'clock the fever returned. There was Methodist preaching in the porch, which caused a great deal of disturbance. Mr. H. had not much rest. About thirty stayed for dinner.

"*July 17.* Mr. H. has had a hard night and is, I fear, rather worse. I sent one man for another Dr. and another back in haste to Canaan for Mr. Mock and Mr. Vogler, who I surely hope will come, although it will be four days before they can reach this place, as it is 95 miles. About 9 o'clock Mr. McCullah and Dr. Tittington came. I was much pleased. He forthwith gave some medicine, and stayed all night with me and helped me with Mr. H.

"*July 18.* This morning Mr. H. is more quiet. The Dr. went home but said he would be back by night. About dark the fever came on again. He was quite out of his mind and I had a very hard time with him.

"*July 19.* This morning the prospect of Mr. Herman's recovery seems almost out of the question. Dr. Tittington came about 6 o'clock; he did not like the appearance of his patient at all. He has some fever and is completely out of his mind. For the most part he is with his family. Mr. McCullah stayed with me at night, and a dreadful one it was.

"*July 20.* The Dr. came this morning and said he feared that Mr. Herman would not live till night. My feelings it is impossible to describe. He sometimes appears conscious for a moment, and told me to take care of his clothing, give his spectacles to his wife, and take the pony to his daughter. At my request Mr. McCullah offered a prayer by the bed-side, and the hymn, 'Alas, and did my Saviour bleed' was sung. He lingered until 10½ o'clock at night when he quietly breathed his last. (It is a singular fact that Bro. Bernard de Schweinitz died on the same day while on a visit to his brother in Salem, N. C. Mr. Herman's remains were removed to Salem and the two sleep side by side.)

"*July 21.* This morning before day we started three men 7 miles to the green prairie to dig his grave on a Methodist graveyard. There being no one nearer than 24 miles to make the coffin, I said I would make it myself. Pine wood was all I could get. At day-light I commenced. I covered the outside with black velvet and the inside with white muslin. That was all I could get. We waited for Mr. Vogler and Mock till 12½ o'clock. As they did not come we had to start for the graveyard. About 5 o'clock we buried him. There were about thirty persons present. We sang from the Methodist hymn-book:

> 'Come let us join our friends above,
>   That have obtained the prize,
> And on the eagle wings of love
>   To joys celestial rise.
>
> 'One army of the living God
>   To his command we bow;
> Part of the host have crossed the flood
>   And part are crossing now.'

I tried to get a minister but could get none, so I attended to all to the best of my ability. I returned thanks to the kind friends who aided me during his illness, and also for digging the grave, as they charged nothing. About 12 ladies were present. It was a hard task to turn from the grave of my fellow traveller, here in the distant west. I thought of what he told me when I asked what course to pursue in case of his death. He said, 'If possible, bury me in a Protestant graveyard, if not, anywhere, for the earth is the Lord's and the body is only dust. But my funeral I should like held where my family is.' I thought of all this and of how the family must feel, could they know of all this.

"When Mr. McCullah and I got home from the funeral Mr. Vogler and Mr. Mock were there. They shared my sorrows though it was a sad evening, as I rehearsed the subject.

(In looking back over these days when sad events followed each other in quick succession we can clearly see how our own plans were defeated and overruled for good.)

"On the following morning Mr. V. said to me: 'Augustus, don't undertake this journey by yourself. It is a hot time and you will have a dreary journey. Return with me and go with my family to North Carolina in the autumn.' 'By no means, I never can do that,' I replied. After breakfast the horses were harnessed. On going out, found one of the horses was lame. 'Don't you see, dear Brother,' said Mr. Vogler, 'that you cannot go by yourself.' 'I must go,' was all I said. He with the rest, was standing by the carriage, in very low spirits. When I shook hands he said: 'If you are de'ermined to go, the Lord be with you!' I gave the horse the word to start and in doing so the pony bit one of the horses. Mr. Vogler came to my help and said a third time: 'Don't you see it will never do to start alone; do as I have requested you.' I said: 'Mr. Vogler, I am going home.' Mr. McCullah then said: 'There will be a hack down from Springfield and one of you could accompany him.' Mr. V. said: 'Mr. Mock, you get in and come back with the hack. I will remain until Mon. and we will go back together.' Again we bade farewell. Mr. Vogler was crying as I have never seen a man cry.

"Went 16 miles hard driving to reach the hack—got within 8 miles of Springfield. Mr. M. had complained of feeling ill and I hurried on and got a bed for him. There I saw the owner of the hack at the hotel. He threw up his hands and said, 'If I didn't forget you!' Then springing on a horse that was tied before the house he attempted to overtake it. But the horse was so lame he was obliged to give it up. I knew not what to do—there was but one thing left, that was to go back to the Nation with Mr. M., who was not able to sit up. I made a bed in the carriage for him by putting a plank across the seats with a buffalo robe over it and proceeded. This was Sunday. When we reached Mr. McCullah's Mr. Vogler was preaching. When we met he said: 'I give you credit for changing your mind.' 'I have not changed my mind, etc.' To get away from his importunity I strolled away among the Ozark Mts., but on my return the same subject seemed uppermost and he again begged me not to try to leave again. As Mr. M. could not ride I said I would go with them to Mrs. Mason's where we would have dinner. We did so. After dinner we again parted. Mr. Vogler crying as far as I could hear him. I heard him call in the distance. I stopped—looked back—he was calling me to come back. I went. He took my hand and said: 'Brother, I give you my hand, my heart, and my honor that I will trouble you no more if you grant me one favor.' 'What is that?' 'Go with us tonight and tomorrow you may go on.' I could not refuse this appeal. We journeyed on and spent the remainder of the afternoon talking over old times and Friedberg, which seemed to please Mr. Vogler very much.

"On the top of Pea Ridge the left fore-wheel of the carriage ran off and I had to go back half a mile to find something that had dropped from the wheel. I found it and on coming back found my fellow travellers, Mr. M. in the carriage and Mr. V. lying asleep under a tree. When he awoke I noticed his changed look and he complained of feeling very ill. Not knowing what to do, I made a rude couch by putting a plank across the corner of a rail fence and covered it with a buffalo robe. After resting here for a time we undertook to travel on. We inquired at the first house we reached if we could stay all night. At first we were refused. 'Where are you from?' asked the man of the house. 'From N. C.' 'What part of the State?' 'From Salem.' 'Do you know old John Holland?' Upon replying that I did he said, 'Come right in.' So we were fortunate enough to get a room. The two men were very sick and I had a terrible night. With great difficulty we went on next day and reached Mt. Zion.

"*July 28.* This morning I wrote a letter home, stating all my troubles and every effort I had made to get home. When the Dr. came he said I would have to go to Maysville for some articles for Mr. Vogler, whom he found no better. When I reached Canaan I found Mr. S. Warner, who had not yet heard of Mr. Herman's death.

"*July 29.* This morning Mr. Welfare went over to Mr. Vogler's before breakfast to finish a letter to Mr. de Schweinitz which occupied him several hours.

"*July 30.* Mr. Vogler seemed much better. After preaching (by Mr. Warner) he called Mrs. Vogler and asked her to prepare an old-fashioned German vesper which he said we would all enjoy once more together. Before she had prepared it, however, Mr. V. grew suddenly worse and calling his wife, told her that he was going to die, and that he would like to see Mr. Bishop once more. Accordingly, I hastened at once to go to Springplace. I rode by starlight through the long prairie. It was lined with cattle and my horse was constantly taking fright. When I left the main road it was very dark, and I arrived at Mr. Bishop's at 12 o'clock, after a lonely ride. I called and Mr. B. knew me by my voice. He was greatly surprised, as he had not yet heard of Mr. V.'s sickness, nor even Mr. Herman's death, supposing that, by this time, I was safely on my homeward way.

"*July 31.* This morning Mr. Welfare having heard of my arrival, came over. I went home with him for breakfast. Mr. Bishop hurried on to Mt. Zion to see Mr. Vogler.

"*Aug. 1.* This morning at 4 o'clock started back to Mr. Vogler's. On the road I met Mr. Warner, who told me that Mr. V. died at 3 o'clock and that he was to be buried at Springplace the next day. Also, that it was his last request that I should bring his family to Salem. I went on an Indian trail, a lonely path through the woods, but three miles nearer. When I arrived at Mt. Zion, I found them in great distress. Mr. Bishop and four or five Cherokees were there. I remained all night. It was a time of deep sorrow.

"*Aug. 2.* This morning at 4 o'clock I arose and made preparations for taking Mrs. Vogler and the children to the funeral. We arrived there at 2 o'clock. The services were brief. About thirty Cherokees were present and seemed to be deeply affected. After the address we went to the graveyard. They sang Cherokee verses on the way to the grave. Mr. Bishop prayed the usual litany in the English language. It seemed so hard to see the little children standing there, though they little knew their loss. We men all stayed to finish the grave. How little did I think when I first saw Mr. V. that I should remain to close the door of his last earthly house!

"*Aug. 3.* This morning Mr. Warner and I went to Canaan for the purpose of moving Mrs. Vogler's things from Mt. Zion.

"*Aug. 5.* When we arrived at Springplace we learned that Mrs. Vogler's youngest child had the flux.

"*Aug. 6.* Went over from Mr. Welfare's, where I have been stopping, to Mr. Bishop's. Found the child very sick. I thought it was a hopeless case. Remained until after dinner, when Mrs. Vogler asked me to go for a Doctor. I started for Talequah about 3 o'clock but the Dr. was not at home. I then went to Park Hill for Dr. Heath. This was five miles further on, twenty-five miles in all. After going about two miles I missed the road. It was on a prairie and it was a fine moonlight night. Not knowing how to proceed, I lay down and letting my horse graze, I trusted that some one might come to guide me. With my ear to the ground, I heard in the distance the tramp of horses' feet, though I knew not if it was friend or foe. On approaching, the rider proved to be an old colored man on a mule. I asked him what he would charge to put me on the road to Dr. H's. He said he did not think he could do it for less than 5c! And there was never a happier darkey than when I rewarded him for his pains by giving him a silver quarter. About 9 o'clock I got to Mr. Worcester's, where the Dr. made his home. Mr. W. is a Presbyterian minister and after learning my errand invited me in and treated me most cordially. The Dr. and I started at 11 o'clock and the moon lighted us nearly all the way to Springplace. We arrived just at day-break.

"*Aug. 7.* Went to bed early. After sleeping but a short time, Mr. Welfare roused me and told me the child was dead.

"*Aug. 8.* This morning I went over to Mr. Bishop's to make the coffin. About 3 o'clock Mr. Bishop delivered a short address, and then we went with the remains to the graveyard. We sang a Cherokee hymn.

"*Aug. 9.* While at work on my carriage I heard screams from the house of Mr. Weaver, a small house near Mr. Welfare. A heavy plank had fallen on their little child and killed it instantly.

"*Aug. 10.* This morning I made the coffin and in the afternoon attended to the burial.

"*Aug. 13.* This is Communion day here as it is in Salem. On this day I was reminded of Bro. Herman and Bro. Vogler. Today four weeks ago they communed with us here and now they have joined the church triumphant.

"*Aug. 21.* This morning Mrs. Vogler and family went to Park Hill and Tahlequah. I accompanied them. Tahlequah is the capital of the Nation. We spent the night at the house of Mrs. Nave, who was educated at Salem and was a former pupil of Mrs. Vogler's. She treated us with the greatest kindness and made many inquiries about the persons she knew while at school.

"*Aug. 23.* This morning after breakfast Mrs. Nave went with us to Tahlequah, from where we went to Park Hill to visit Mr. Worcester, now the oldest minister in the Nation. He has been laboring here for twenty-nine years, and has translated a large part of the Scripture into the Cherokee language. We were warmly received here.

"*Aug. 24.* This morning we left Park Hill. Mrs. W. gave us books of remembrance when we left. After spending some time at the Seminary, Mrs. Nave went with us to the house of her father, John Ross, the Chief of the Cherokees. He had sent us a cordial invitation to visit them and we were kindly received. Mrs. Ross is a white lady from New Jersey. She was educated at Bethlehem, Pa. They have a very pretty home and finely furnished. The house is situated on a hillside, and surrounded by fine oak trees. The grounds are adorned with flowers and summerhouses, etc. After dinner I walked out to see the farm, which is quite extensive. About forty slaves were at work. We had a very pleasant evening and Chief Ross told us about the laws of the Nation. The Council meets the first Monday in October. The Nation is divided into districts and each one elects five representatives which constitute the Council, a body that makes or revises the laws with the sanction of the Chief.

"*Aug. 25.* This morning I went to see the garden, which is very fine and large. There are a great variety of fruit trees, also an arbor of grapes, about 100 feet long. I also saw a servant bring the sheep up to salt; there were 93 in all, and very fine and large. After bidding farewell, we returned to Springplace.

"*Aug. 28.* Mr. W. and I started to Van Buren, about 80 miles from here, to procure iron necessary for repairing my carriage. Along the water courses there are some rich and fine farms. The country about Grand River is in the heart of the Nation. As for the Indians, the full-bloods live in cabins, in close neighborhoods. They have small clearings and raise not quite half of what they need. They spend most of their time playing, fishing and hunting. Passing along the road you may see from ten to fifteen playing marbles or shooting with their bows and arrows. When they see a white man coming, they run and hide in the bushes. Many of the half-breeds have fine farms, own slaves and have plenty around them. In their dress, they are very fond of red. Many of the older ones do not wear hats, but have a shawl or handkerchief tied around their heads. The women are often seen with a child strapped to their back, they will visit in this way for miles.

"*Sept. 8.* Mr. Bishop and I started at 4 o'clock for Canaan. Found nine letters from Salem. I received orders to bring Bro. Herman's things. Mr. Warner and Mrs. Vogler also returned to Canaan.

"*Sept. 10.* Mr. Bishop held services in memory of Mr. Vogler. The house was well filled as there were many friends who came to pay their last respects.

"*Sept. 14.* Mr. Welfare very ill at Springplace, and I took my carriage to Maysville to be finished. At Canaan we found Sarah Vogler also ill with flux.

"*Sept. 16.* Went for the Dr. as the child was no better.

"*Sept. 18.* These days were days of deep anxiety for we did not know whether little Sarah Vogler would live or die.

"*Sept. 21.* There seems to be a change for the better. Heard also that Mr. Welfare was better.

"*Sept. 25.* Little Sarah is improving.

"*Oct. 2.* Went to Maysville to have one of my horses shod. Passed over the ground where Fort Wayne once stood.

"*Oct. 4.* Have bought two ponies; these with Puss I hitched to the carriage, and am now packing up and making final preparations for the journey.

"*Oct. 9.* Took leave of the friends, and after so many efforts to start which all failed, there seems now to be a time when nothing comes to draw us back. Took dinner at Dr. Hayden's by invitation and spent the night at Mr. Dann's, where we found Bro. and Sr. Welfare, who had met us to go with us as far as McCullah's.

"*Oct. 10.* Left Maysville, thankful for the kindness shown us. Travelled quite briskly, but had to stop at a black-smith shop to have something done to Tom's foot as he was walking lame.

"*Oct. 11.* Had a late start from Bentonville and rough roads till 2 o'clock. Stopped at a house to make coffee for our dinner. The woman was very cross and told us she was always pestered with people calling for things. She said: 'You must fetch your water and make your coffee yourself. I have had the tooth-ache all day and a lot of work to do.' I told her I was sorry she had the tooth-ache. By and by we got on pretty good terms and she gave us milk, and made some droll inquiries and wished us a safe and happy journey.

"*Oct. 12.* Left Mrs. Mason's after breakfast and took along with us Mr. Herman's pony; he at first appeared reluctant to go but was soon taught what he had to do. Went on a few miles and met some families moving from Iowa to Texas and our Billy pony took fright and caused Puss to fall down, but by good management she was raised and we went on. Had plenty of good roads, but several sprinkles of rain. Bro. and Sr. Welfare went in their carriage but the rest of us took shelter under a tree. Passed the house where Bro. Herman was taken sick.

"*Oct. 13.* Willie had his first ride on the gray pony. Arrived at McCullah's at 11 o'clock, took dinner and went over to Bro. Herman's grave. A neat paling fence has been made. We all felt very sad as we stood around the grave of our dear Bro. Herman in this lone spot in a land of strangers. Bro. Welfare made a sketch of the grave and surroundings.

"*Oct. 14.* Left McCullah's. In the morning it was quite cool and our wraps and shawls felt very comfortable. At noon arrived at Springfield and met some missionaries on their way to the Creeks and Choctaws.

"*Oct. 15.* Went to the Methodist Church but had to leave before the services were over, as the children were restless. Spent the rest of the day rather unprofitably.

"*Oct. 16* Parted from Bro. and Sr. Welfare. Met many moving to Texas. Arrived at Hollis' about dusk and found another family here with children, so we were obliged to sleep upstairs without fire.

"*Oct. 17.* Continued onward. Quite a pleasant morning. Stopped at a poor house for the night. Shabby accommodations; the man gone to California.

"*Oct. 18.* This morning Puss' leg was very much swollen, so we turned her out and hitched up the three ponies. Here we went over rough hills and dry dusty roads, a curiosity to everybody we met.

"*Oct. 19.* Came but 22 miles to Mitchell's in sight of Waynesville. Our land-lady was sulky, and we did not feel very welcome.

"*Oct. 20.* Had an early start, but an uncommonly rough road across a ridge, barren and uninhabited. Passed but one house before we came to the place we wished to reach. We had a hard shower of rain and wished very much to get in, but were refused, so kept on two miles further where we were taken in, and felt welcome.

"*Oct. 21.* Puss' leg swollen very much so we went to poulticing. We felt rather despondent about our situation. About 10 o'clock some travellers passed on their way to Indiana, and Puss was traded away.

We regretted to see her go, but we could do no better, and we found we had made a good exchange. After the trading was over we went to washing, trying to make the best use we could of our stay. Got all our clothes washed and ironed.

"*Oct. 22.* Stopped at Houston's. Met with a friendly reception. Mr. Houston has been to Salem, four of his sisters having been educated here.

"*Oct. 23.* Spent Sunday in writing letters and making a way-bill for home.

"*Oct. 24.* Left Mr. Houston's very early. Lodged at Mr. Martin's, 32 miles from Houston's, had a very poor fare and miserable beds. Our road lay along the bottom near the creek, and it was very difficult to find after dark.

"*Oct. 25.* Passed Harmony, Caledonia and Webster. At Webster is the Smithing furnace, connected with the lead-mines. Had a very rough road, almost impassable, and at one time came near upsetting. Met numbers of people moving from Tenn. and Kentucky, bound for the new territory and for this state. One wagon had a bleeding deer suspended from the back. The women looked very genteel, but rather dejected at the prospect before them.

"*Oct. 26.* Rose early and stopped at a black-smith shop to have Rock's shoe fastened. Had muddy roads and passed poor houses, with poor prospects for the night. Met eight wagons moving families from Tennessee. Called at three houses to stay all night and received a positive refusal. After traveling some time after dark, we got in with an old German, Hauch, by name. The family consists of an old couple and two young couples. Of all the places we saw this is the most disorderly and filthy; still we were glad to get under shelter. When we got to the supper table there was a little lard lamp stuck between the logs. Mrs. Vogler sat at one end of the table and I at the other. There was some raw bacon near my end of the table, and Mrs. Vogler, taking it for cheese, asked me please to pass it. When she tasted it she found it to be raw bacon. She afterwards remarked that it was the first time she had ever seen or heard of raw bacon being put on the table. After supper I went out to the barn to tend to my horses; one of the young men went with me and it was late before I got back to the house. The young man showed me my bed, which I never could have found alone. Willie and I always sleep together and Mrs. Vogler with the little girls. Willie was already asleep when I got to bed. In Mrs. Vogler's room there were 200 bu. of wheat on the floor, through which they had to wade to their beds! (I always took the precaution to put my money between the bedding and the sheet, not under my pillow as travellers generally do.) Towards day I was awakened by my pillow being moved. I made a grab but touched nothing. Then I lay still and began to snore; presently I felt a hand slip under my pillow. I made another grab and touched a man's hand. Then I jumped up and said: 'Dead or alive. I am going to see who this is! Who is it?' 'Es ist mich.' The next morning I found out that he and his wife had made a bed at the head of my bed. The old man said he was sorry I had been disturbed, he supposed that he might have touched my pillow with his feet. I afterwards learned that the old man had been accused of robbing travellers that slept at his house.

"*Oct. 27.* Left Hauch's early, and came through a pretty part of the country. Took dinner at Mrs. Fullenvillers. She has accommodated as many as eighty men at a time who were at this place buying land. Came only 18 miles to John McLane's, a pretty good house. He was out sowing wheat. The old lady was quite alone, but received us kindly. The news here was that a new born babe had been found in one of the neighbor's yard, and as yet no clue had been found. Spent a very comfortable night.

"*Oct. 28.* Today we came on eight miles to the Mississippi. The road winds through the valley, and has some steep places. We had to wait for the boat more than an hour. When it arrived it brought three wagons and one carriage. The people were moving for Missouri. The horses pulled bravely and we soon got up the bank and proceeded. In passing some lakes or ponds we saw some swans which looked very pretty on the water. Came through Jonesboro; quite a pretty town. Came 27 miles and had to put up with very shabby accommodations at Mr. McWeaver's, a very rough family who need somebody to civilize them. Mrs. V. and the children lay down on the floor. I slept in one corner in a bed-stead, and two other men in the other corner.

"*Oct. 29.* In the morning the two men rose early and sat up by the fire entertaining those of us who were still in bed by some talk that was rather out of place. We felt sorry to start on Sunday morning, but felt that we could not spend the Sabbath here profitably, so we determined to go on, hoping to reach a better place. We stopped at a Mr. Weaver's; a very good place. This gentleman is from Pennsylvania. We were treated very kindly and charged very moderately. We heard here that several persons had died of Cholera during the past week.

"*Oct. 30.* Left early, had an interesting and very rough road, retired quite late at Scott's. The first floor of the house has but one apartment with four beds. In one corner by the fire lay the son with a bruised leg; on the opposite side sat a man making shoes. They were friendly and gave us a place by the fire. We see many sickly people in this state (Ill.). Good water is scarce; we see at every door a small wagon with a water-keg to haul water. As we stopped today to water a man directed us to a kind of slough, saying that is the kind of water many persons used for drinking. We see fields with excellent young wheat, but corn is everywhere a failure. Today we passed Vienna. It has but four good houses, the rest are very poor looking. The place is very rough looking, and does not promise to improve much. We came off with a high bill at Scott's.

"*Oct. 31.* A very bad way today; especially on the Ky. side of the Ohio. Crossed the river in a horse boat. While on the river a nice steamer came down. Arrived late at Mr. Barnett's; he has relatives in Cabarrus Co. (N. C.). He has two sons, very talkative and inquisitive. Slept well, and after a hearty breakfast proceeded on our way.

"*Nov. 1.* Came through Princeton, which contains a college rather in the suburbs. The building is pleasantly situated on a rising ground, with an enclosure of about half an acre for a pleasure ground. There is a Telegraph office in this place connected with Nashville. We had to travel late in order to reach our destined place. Had good roads and moonlight and found it without difficulty. Slept cold, as we had not cover enough.

"*Nov. 2.* Great improvement in the appearance of the country. More good buildings and better farms. Saw a drove of 300 turkeys going to water. Stopped early at Wood's to have some screws made for the carriage. A neat little place a short distance from the public road. Mr. Wood spoke of Mr. Welfare and Archie, who stopped here on their way to Salem some years ago. Had some washing done and had everything ready in good time for starting.

"*Nov. 3.* Passed Hopkinsville, quite a business place. Met several persons anxious to buy our gray pony.

"*Nov. 4.* A great change in the weather during the night, so that we were quite comfortable with the curtains down. Passed Keysburg and Barren Plains. Crossed the Red River twice, the last time at Cross Plains, a little town where we are stopping to rest on the Sabbath.

"*Nov. 5.* Walked down to the river to see some movers who wished some information and a way-bill. They seemed pleased with the attention, and on parting we wished each other a safe journey.

"*Nov. 6.* Today we passed through the finest country we have yet seen on our journey. Our road for 20 miles was turnpike. We passed Galatine, a neat and pretty town. On either side, the country is rich and fine, settled by wealthy farmers, who have fine horses and extensive farms. Came 31 miles and stopped at Mrs. Smith's. After supper Mrs. Smith played on the piano, which is the first music we have had on the journey.

"*Nov. 7.* After passing Hartsville, had diversified and sometimes mountainous scenery. Many farms have beautiful beach groves, neatly fenced. Each farm has something new and seems to vie with the surrounding ones in buildings and gardens. Before reaching Carthage, had a picturesque view of the Cumberland River, which winds its course through a gap in the Mts. At Carthage we saw some of the prettiest churches of the West. Some of the Carthagenians wanted to buy 'Pet,' the pony. Cumberland River is quite near town. We crossed on a flat. Coming up the bank, Willie and Sarah rode Pet, the latter holding fast around her brother's waist. As they saw a gentleman ap-

18

proaching on horseback, the little girl felt abashed and suggested riding behind a huge chestnut tree that stood at the roadside—which hid pony and all. The gentleman was much interested in watching the maneuver, and told us when he rode up that he had passed our advance guard. Among the peculiarities of Middle Tennessee is the mistletoe covering the naked trees so that they seem entirely green. Some of the chestnut trees grow to an enormous size. We saw some ten feet in diameter.

"Nov. 8. The familiar laurel and sour-wood trees showed themselves, and seemed to say that we were getting on towards home. Came 11 miles and stopped to feed as our Billy pony was a little sick, and did not eat any breakfast. We made coffee and ate our lunch. As we stopped to inquire the way, we were asked if we were not show people! Came 26 miles and stopped at Mr. Diddy's, where we were entertained with true Tennessee hospitality.

"Nov. 9. Journeyed on, and struck the mountain road two miles from town. The ascent for some distance was very steep, and the scenery wild. About three miles from the foot of the mountain is quite a fashionable watering-place which is said to be much frequented during the summer season. After descending about 6 miles our road became more gradual and finally quite level and sandy. Stopped for the night at Mr. Wallace's. Our room is without a table and almost without window-panes. We have put up a shawl to keep out the cold wind. Our fare was very poor. Some time after dark the wind began to blow furiously and it rained after midnight.

"Nov. 10. It is still raining. We consulted about proceeding on such an unfavorable morning; however, we concluded to start, and drove hard to reach Mr. Kimer's, 24 miles. Our accommodations are better than last night and we are glad for a shelter after such a wet ride. After supper two men from N. C. came in, who had been to the West on a speculating trip. They made very free and kept the room full of smoke. In the morning a gentleman came in to see us. He proved to be a Methodist preacher who had been among the Cherokees, and was personally acquainted with some that we knew.

"Nov. 11. We left and had prospect of a fair day, for which we were very glad. Cleared towards the middle of the day. Called at Mr. Jordan's and inquired the way to the Cascade, then hitched our horses and walked over. We at first stood on the top and looked down; this view reminded us much of the celebrated Hawk's nest at New River. We then descended by a circuitous path on stones almost like a stair-case. Above us hung a wall of rock dripping with water. When we had descended about half way we got a good view of the chasm below and the water falling 130 feet over a beautifully curved bed of rock. On the east side the rocks are about 200 ft. high, and on the opposite side where we descended, they gradually become lower and are lost among the hills. There is a mill quite near the falls. No place in

Nature can be richer in evergreens. White pine, laurel, magnolia and cedar are richly interwoven and afford much to delight a lover of Nature. The road leading along the side of the mountain from the Cascade to the fort is very good, having on the left, almost the entire length, a ledge of rock, and on the right in some places stupendous precipices, but appearing at a distance like an entire bed of evergreen. At some places there are many names carved on the rocks; we stopped to see if we could find any that were familiar, but found none. Came down the mountain safely and arrived at a village called Post Oak Flats. Had 'Rock' shod and got to Mr. Eskridge's by 5 o'clock. This is quite a large establishment with good accommodations.

"*Nov. 12.* Being Sunday, we spent the day here and it was rather gloomy. The old lady, though apparently not long for this world, is craving more riches. There are about 70 slaves belonging to the estate, and to us they seemed quite troublesome. During the night it snowed.

"*Nov. 13.* This morning it is very cold, and still continued to snow. We wrapped up as well as we could, but had a severe day. Travelled 29 miles and put up at Campbell's Station, Russel's Hotel. The house is large and comfortable. The stage came in about midnight, had broken down on the way.

"*Nov. 14.* Started on a clear, cold morning over rough, frozen ground. Passed through Knoxville. It contains some very pretty houses, but so many that are dilapidated that the beauty of the place is spoiled. Crossed the Holston River, and stopped at Smith's, 10 miles from Knoxville.

"*Nov. 15.* Passed on to Hay's Ferry, 25 miles today. Took up lodgings for the night at the house of Mrs. Hay, on the banks of the French Broad.

"*Nov. 16.* Had a rather late start, crossed the ferry. Went on three miles and had some work done on the carriage at a blacksmith shop. Had interesting scenery on the Pigeon River, which we crossed on a free bridge. The cedar and pine are particularly rich and green. Passed on some miles and reached the banks of the French Broad. Most romantic scenery along its banks, and seldom got out of sight of the river. Came in contact with at least six droves of hogs and were obliged to wait at the toll-gate to let them pass. Drove late after night to get to Mrs. Weaver's and could not enjoy the scenery so well, still we could discern the river to our right and the great mountains to our left.

"*Nov. 17.* Had an early breakfast and quite a cold morning. Passed by Chimney Rock on the banks of the French Broad. The scenery here is very grand. Passed the famous Paint Rock which is the dividing line between Tennessee and North Carolina. Stopped at Mr. McClaney's, where we were serenaded by hog drovers, nine in number.

"*Nov. 18.* Still travelled on the French Broad, leaving it sometimes for a mile or two, but not entirely, until within a few miles of Asheville, which we found a neat little village. Towards evening it grew very cold and we made all haste to reach Alexander's, our intended destination. Before arriving there we entered Swananowa Gap and commenced ascending the Blue Ridge. Had a warm reception at Alexander's and were very glad for Sunday.

"*Nov. 19.* (Sunday.) Spent most of the day by the fire. In the morning found snow on the ground.

"*Nov. 20.* Had a late start. Had five miles to the top of the mountain, the ascent is very gradual, and the road good. The descent is somewhat steep, and great care is necessary in driving. Came 20 miles and passed through Morganton. Came on briskly 11 miles to Conelly's, which is the only stopping place for some distance. Had very comfortable quarters, and were treated well though the landlord was absent and the son and daughter were preparing to start to Georgia.

"*Nov. 21.* Crossed the Catawba River at Island Ford about dusk. Could not see the opposite bank of landing but got safely across. Found the stream quite flush and rather rocky. After crossing, travelled for some time seeking lodging; called at two places but could not get in, so that we were an hour in the night before we stopped at a Mr. Douglass', rather a poor place. The man of the house had gone to a corn husking and his daughter to a quilting. The old lady got us a kind of a supper and we went to bed.

"*Nov. 22.* Went as far as Statesville, where we had some work done on the carriage and the horses shod.

"*Nov. 23.* Passed through Statesville, and rather a barren portion of our old State. Statesville is one of the poorest towns we have met with on our way, still the idea that we are only 56 miles from Salem makes it a pleasant stopping place. Stopped at Mr. Akle's towards evening. Felt very, very comfortable. Heard several items of news from Salem. Enjoyed a good supper and retired, thankful to God for his mercies.

'Each sweet Ebenezer I have in review,

Confirms His good pleasure to help me quite through.'

"*Nov. 24.* Left Mr. Akle's early. Travelled briskly, and arrived at Mr. John Hall's at 2½ o'clock. Enjoyed a fine 'vesper' here, the first since we left Canaan. Our team attracted much attention while we passed through Clemmonsville, but we did not halt as the sun bade us adieu soon after we left town. The moon shone dimly through the clouds, giving us sufficient light to see the road. Passed through Winston we think unnoticed, and arrived in Salem as the old town-clock struck eight—very thankful to God for His gracious protection over us during our long and tedious journey of more than 1400 miles."

Mt. Zion was put under Bro. Mock's care after Bro. Vogler's death, and the work at this point continued to prosper. On March 9, 1855, four adult Cherokees were baptized and three confirmed here and the church, 30 feet square, could not accommodate one-half of the Indians who came to the service.

The work at the other stations was "looking up." Cannan could report, at the end of 1856, a total of 102 souls. A real work of the Spirit of God was going on there. Notable was the conversion of Joseph Vann, grandson of James Vann, the first friend, patron and benefactor of the Springplace, Georgia, Moravian mission. Mock had visited Vann and prayed with him five years ago when Vann was seriously sick. Vann arose in one of the meetings at Canaan and said that he had tried to resist the Spirit of God ever since that time, but would do so no longer and, from henceforth, wished to live for Christ alone. Vann was a very fine, promising young man. Splendid home meetings were being held in the neighborhood of Canaan at Mr. Cochran's and Mr. MacCrarey's in which James Vann, Red Bird Tiger and half-breed James Ward, Jr., were very active. New Springplace, likewise, experienced a genuine awakening in 1856, and twelve full-blood Cherokees came forward accepting Christ and later united with the church, bringing the total membership at New Spring-place at the end of the year to eighty-three. The missionaries were adopting the method of stated series of evangelistic meetings with splendid results.

James Ward, Jr.,[*] wrote to Salem in 1857, asking to be allowed to come into the service of the Moravian Church as a teacher. He was a member of the Methodist Church and was having success as a teacher, in one of the National schools of the Cherokees. Bro. S. Warner did not hesitate to recommend him to the Board at Salem.

The object of the official visit of 1854 had been but partially attained owing to Bishop Herman's death, hence the Provincial

---

[*] James Ward, Jr., born in Georgia, November 15, 1826. Educated at Dartmouth College. Married February 9, 1854, to Miss Esther Hoyt, granddaughter of Assistant Chief George Lowry, on her mother's side, and of English descent on her father's side. She was born March 18, 1826, in the "Old Nation" of the Cherokees, east of the Mississippi, and died, January 12, 1864, at West Salem, Ill.

Elders' Conference at Salem planned another visit in 1858, which
Bro. George Frederick Bahnson,† President of the Conference,
undertook to carry out in person. The months of October and
November were spent by Bro. Bahnson on this visit in company
with Bro. Augustus Fogle. They traveled in all possible ways,
by railroad, steamboat, wagon and horseback. On horse they
went up and down the steep Indian trails covered with small,
loose stones and on horse they forded streams, yet they suffered
no ill health whatever and sustained no damage at all on the
journey covering several thousand miles. They arrived at
Canaan, October 22.

Bahnson was greatly surprised over what he found had been
accomplished by the Moravian mission; he found that the influence exerted by our missionaries in the uplift of the Nation
was really wonderful, much more good work had been done, and
was going on, than he expected to find. Some of his experiences
and impressions follow :

"Received a hearty welcome from Bro. Mock and his family at
Canaan. Many half-breeds reside around this station. They much re-
semble the whites and, like them, live mostly on larger plantations.
The banks of the smaller rivers are inhabited by full-bloods, that is,
Indians of unmixed race, who gain a subsistence from small farms,
their wants being few and simple. All the half-breeds speak English
and some of them have no acquaintance with the Cherokee language.
Not a few of them are well educated, having attended good schools in
the States.

"Bro. Mock labors among both these classes with much success. He
understands more of the Cherokee language than most of the half-
Indians. During my stay, he delivered his first address in Cherokee.
On Sunday, October 24, I preached in the new church (Canaan). This
building, which is very neat and comfortable, was erected by Bro. Mock,
assisted by the Indians, without any expense to the mission-fund. Bro.
Mock opens the church one hour before the meeting and holds the full
service even if only one Indian is present!"

While Brother Bahnson was preaching,* ten full-blood Cherokees entered, having with them three prisoners in chains.

"The Cherokees have no gaols, and those who are accused of murder
are chained and delivered into the charge of men appointed for the
purpose, until they can be tried.

---

† Member of the Conference since 1849 and President, 1856-'69. Consecrated a Bishop in 1860. Died in 1869.

* His text was 1 Timothy 2:4.

"After I had spoken, Bro. Joseph Fiddler,† full-blood, delivered an address in Cherokee. My feelings were peculiar when Joseph, in his cotton dress, stood beside me addressing his countrymen in what was, to me, an unknown tongue, and I thanked God, with tears of joy, that He had, through the instrumentality of our mission, prepared him as an instrument to the making known of His Gospel."

Accompanied by Mock and the Interpreter, Avery Miller, Bahnson made many visits in the homes of members in the Canaan neighborhood, noting especially, a call made on "Hannah," a remarkable Cherokee character. She was, probably, the oldest member ever in the Moravian Church, certainly the oldest ever baptized by Moravian missionaries, having been born in 1740, therefore, at this time, 118 years old. Bahnson writes that the house was the smallest he had ever seen, being 10 x 12 feet, with clay floor and a fireplace. Upon a bed lay Hannah, the oldest person Bahnson had ever seen. ("She was all wrinkles.") She was very weak but able, at times, to go about on a stick. At the age of 108, she had been baptized by our missionaries and had answered the baptismal questions heartily, with childlike faith and eyes full of tears. When Bro. Bahnson prayed with her—her son-in-law interpreting—she punctuated his prayer with "amens" which came straight from her heart. Of late years, she had not been able to come to the services, but comforted herself with the thought that the Lord came into her small house to be with her. Bro. Mock told Bro. Bahnson that her tiny dwelling was a real Bethel. (Hannah died in 1860 at 120 years of age.)

A new school-house was being erected at Canaan in which it was proposed to employ Joseph Vann, of whom Bro. Bahnson speaks highly, as teacher. Altogether, the official visitor felt much encouraged over the situation at Canaan and the work accomplished there.*

---

† He played a fiddle!

* The missionaries, Bahnson found, were very modest and reticent about hardships and dangers they had endured. He mentions one experience Sr. Mock had in earlier days. A party of drunken Indians, near Canaan, had murdered another, and, after they had danced around the body for some time, they entered the mission house with bloody hands. Sr. Mock was alone at the time. The Indians demanded bread. Greatly terrified, Sr. Mock gave them all she had in the house and they left, without molesting her in the least.

New Springplace was next visited. The missionary staff here consisted of Gilbert Bishop and wife, Clarissa, James Ward, Jr., teacher, and Archie Henry, Interpreter. "James Ward looks like a white man, his splendid wife can be recognized as a Cherokee. Archie Henry, several years ago, spent some time at Salem and Friedberg, at the latter place to learn English under Bro. Hagen's instruction." Lemuel Wilson was another good Interpreter serving at Springplace; also, the venerable George Hicks still served occasionally in this capacity. Bahnson was particularly delighted to make the acquaintance of the latter. A convert in the old mission in Georgia, Hicks had lived a long, consistent, useful Christian life, serving the mission as Interpreter and in many other ways. He had served his people, likewise, as a public official in many important National concerns. At the time of Bahnson's visit, Bro. Hicks was a member of the Senate of the Cherokee Nation and enjoyed wide influence which he used for Christ and the Church.

"On Sunday, October 31, we partook of the Holy Communion at New Springplace, for which occasion Bro. Mock had come from Canaan. Bro. Bishop first delivered an address on the Doctrinal Text for the day, Bro. Mock then preached on Haggai 1:5, after which I spoke on the Daily Text from the Old Testament. The people around Springplace are full-bloods, hence all had to be interpreted, which took much time as the Cherokee language has very circuitous forms of expression. After this, the Sacrament was administered. The Lord was graciously with us.

"The Indians sit quietly and reverently in a manner which could well teach whites a lesson. Only, the preacher must not forget that when a real Indian is interested he will not look at the speaker, but, resting his head on his hands, will fasten his look on the floor—apparently taking no interest whatever."

Next day, November 1, a Mission Conference was held at Springplace. Bro. Ward was received, as an Acolyte, into the service of the Church and was chosen Secretary of the Mission Conference. Ward was "a sincere and promising Brother who devotes himself to his duties with his whole soul." Bahnson felt that there was good prospect of more native Helpers serving in the Cherokee mission. The tone of feeling which he observed among the Cherokee Brethren and sisters and, particularly, their prayerful spirit, were very encouraging.

Springplace had a noteworthy character to match "Hannah" at Canaan. Father "Israel"—Indian name "Caselawi"—was seventy and lived a distance of four miles from Springplace, but never missed a service, walking to church and back with his aged wife. He had been baptized November 18, 1827, at Old Springplace by John Renatus Schmidt. He had washed his robes and made them white in the blood of the Lamb and through the years he had walked as a real child of God. Always, he was smiling and contented. Israel was one of the few remaining full-blood, typical Cherokees. In former days he was a famous hunter and kept the mission well supplied with game. As a hunter, he had a feat to his credit which could scarcely be duplicated; with gestures, he would relate how he had crept up to a wolf undiscovered and had killed the wolf with a club! He had never ridden in a wagon until the day when Bahnson and Bishop drove up to his house to take him to Tahlequah to sit for a photograph. Thinly clad, he came into the carriage, depending upon Bro. Bishop to have a woolen blanket for him. He wore real Indian shoes. A copy of Israel's picture* taken that day at Tahlequah is shown and in his features we see reflected the Christian traits mentioned by those who knew him.

Brother Bahnson spent a few pleasant and not unprofitable days at Tahlequah, the capital of the Nation. The Legislative Assembly and the Supreme Court were then in session. Bahnson met some of the leading men of the Nation and preached in the court-house to an interesting auditory. He also spent an exceedingly pleasant evening at the home of Chief John Ross, who warmly commended the work of the Moravians for his people.

Sunday, November 7, came the beautiful and solemn services of dedication of the new church at Canaan, followed, a week later, by the celebration of the Holy Communion at Mt. Zion, at which service Bro. Bahnson had the great privilege of baptizing an aged, white-haired Indian who received the name "Abraham." This blessed meeting brought Bro. Bahnson's visit to a fitting close.

---

*See Frontispiece. Photo by courtesy of the Rev. W. H. Vogler, Nazareth, Pa.

In the year 1859, the Presbyterian station at Caney Creek was turned over to the care of the Moravian Church. The Rev. John Huss, missionary there, had died and the Presbyterian Board was unable to fill the vacancy. Caney Creek came under Mock's charge, so that he now had a "four-point circuit:" Canaan, Mt. Zion, Grand River and Caney Creek. Large audiences at Caney Creek welcomed the Moravian missionary when he came to take charge. Bro. Mock writes that never has the Moravian Church stood higher in the esteem of the Cherokee Nation than at this time. There are 127 names on the roll at Canaan.

At New Springplace, 1859 was, likewise, a year of progress. A total of 13 new members came into the church. Bro. Lemuel Wilson was appointed Interpreter in place of Archie Henry, whose failing eyesight compelled him to give up his office. Bro. Abraham, living in the settlement on the Illinois River, was appointed a native assistant to aid in caring for the souls in that neighborhood. Bishop had two regular preaching places besides Springplace, namely, Bro. Abraham's settlement, just mentioned, and in the schoolhouse at Long Prairie. He preached, also, at Barren Fork whenever possible. The new schoolhouse at Springplace was completed in this year and consecrated to the purposes of Christian education in the Lovefeast on Sept. 28. Bro. Ward was very successful as a teacher, the attendance was increasing and the school enjoyed a good reputation in the community.

CHAPTER XXI

THE CIVIL WAR: ITS EFFECT UPON THE CHEROKEES AND UPON THE MORAVIAN MISSION

The years 1860 and '61 were characterized by great excitement and disturbances among the Cherokees. The bitterness of feeling between the North and South extended throughout the nation. Many of the Indians were wealthy slave owners, and vehemently opposed the dissemination of any doctrine at variance with their traditional customs. "Stand Waytee," the leader of the "Ridge Party," organized his followers under the title of "Knights of the Golden Circle," and espoused the Confederate cause, while a counter organization was formed by those loyal to the United States Government, and chiefly from among the Ross faction. These latter were the "Ki-tu-whas," better known as the "Pin" Indians. This society had been organized years before, by John Ross and the Rev. Evan Jones. The latter as a strong anti-slavery partisan, and sympathized with the Union, while the former at first rejected all overtures and determined to remain neutral during the contest. Gen. Albert Pike, in behalf of the Confederacy, endeavored to treat with Ross, but their meeting only resulted in an order from the Chief that strict neutrality should be observed by his followers. At a meeting held in Tahlequah, August, 1861, at which a large number of Cherokees were present, and loud in their clamours for alliance with the South, John Ross changed his views and determined, like the large majority, to ally himself with the Confederacy.

A strong party dissented and attached itself to the Union cause. The country swarmed with soldiers. Thousands of men camped in the neighborhood of our mission premises. The armies of the North and South alternately ravaged the Territory. The Cherokees being divided among themselves, there was safety for neither life nor property. Houses and mills were destroyed, cattle and stock were stolen and killed.

Chief Ross raised a regiment, placing at its head Colonel Drew, of the Home Guard, and in his address mentioned that they were to act in concert with the troops of the Southern Confederacy. This regiment, as well as that of Stand Waytee, fought side by side at Pea Ridge and elsewhere.

Col. Drew's men, however, were in a wretched condition at the
end of ten months' service. Half clad and ill fed, having never
received payment for their services, and finding that the Federal
troops of Col. Weir were obtaining prestige in that portion of the
Nation, the ill-treated warriors revolted *en masse*, and went over
to the enemy.

Chief Ross, finding himself abandoned by Drew's regiment,
concluded to make a virtue of necessity and become a loyal man.
Such, he said, had been the impulse of his heart, but he had been
overborne by the strength and power of the Confederate government, and felt constrained to save the material interests of his
people from total destruction. He was, therefore, escorted out
of the country by Colonel Weir's regiment, and went to Philadelphia, where he remained three years. In the meanwhile, Stand
Waytee, at the head of a small army, not exceeding eight hundred
warriors, had many engagements with Federal troops, and in the
spring of 1863, after the Government had returned the refugees
to their homes in time to plant their crops, he scoured the
country in the vicinity of Tahlequah, and drove before him the
frightened tillers of the soil, who fled for safety to Fort Gibson,
until that post sheltered no less than six thousand refugees. The
latter had brought back with them supplies and material for
agricultural pursuits, which fell into the hands of Stand Waytee
and his followers. At the termination of the war, a general
Council meeting was convened at Fort Smith, which was attended
by delegates from the tribes west of Ninety-eighth degree Longitude, as well as those of the Five Civilized Tribes. They were
met by United States commissioners who, on the part of the
Government, proposed various measures for their future. The
Commission, however, refused to recognize John Ross as a proper
representative of his people, as his record had been such as to
excite want of confidence. The meeting broke up without the
accomplishment of any business, and nothing was done until
June 13, 1865, when the United States concluded a treaty with
the Southern Cherokees, represented by E. C. Boudinot. This
party acknowledged the freedom of the negro, but refused to
adopt him into the tribe. In August, 1866, a treaty was ratified
with the "Ross Party," or loyal Cherokees, not, however, until
the Commission had agreed to recognize John Ross in his official

character of Principal Chief. The termination of the war was fraught with misery for many of the wretched followers of Stand Waytee. The loyal party, as soon as they returned to their allegiance in 1863, passed an act of Council confiscating all property (houses and stock included) belonging to the Southern refugees, who were living in the greatest destitution on the banks of the Red River. Before a reconciliation was brought about, the proposition was seriously considered of securing a home for Waytee and his followers in the Chickasaw Nation, but the death of Ross, which took place in Washington, August 1, 1866, moderated the party feeling, and they finally returned to dwell among their people.

For the Moravian mission, the confusion and turmoil of war and the Territory overrun by bands of lawless Indians brought disruption under most distressing circumstances. During 1861, the missionaries and their faithful congregations were kept in constant anxiety. In the first half of 1862, the Cherokee country seemed to grow more quiet and the missionaries wrote to Salem that the pressure of the war had relaxed somewhat and they were beginning to breathe more freely. This reassuring message came to Salem, August 11, 1862. Then, for a long time, nothing was heard from the field and the news which did eventually reach Salem told that the gravest fears of the Church for the missionaries and the mission had been realized.

Sept. 2, 1862, the blow struck New Springplace. A band of about 30 or 40 horsemen belonging to the Federal side, partly Cherokee Indians, partly white men, appeared at the station. Gilbert Bishop and wife with their children and Mrs. Ward and children were in the house at the time; Ward was missing. From a letter written by his son, D. E. Ward, to Salem, years after, follow the details:

"At about 4 o'clock p.m., Sept. 2, 1862, my father, as was his custom, saddled his horse preparatory to going after the milch cows. He stood fully a minute before mounting, as though he had a presentiment of what was to happen. I noticed him closely,* for I longed to go with him, but had been refused. Then, with a jump, he vaulted into the saddle and started toward the Creek at a brisk gait. He seemed hardly to have gotten out of sight before we heard a volley of musketry and

* D. E. Ward was seven years old at this time.

in less than five minutes, 20 Indians had surrounded the house, painted,
to disguise their features. They proceeded at once to rob the house,
led by one whose form I seemed to recognize. He seemed familiar with
every place where valuables were kept. After he had gotten what booty
he wanted, he came to the door—(we were all huddled together on the
back porch)—and in Cherokee told my mother to make ready to go
with them. I recognized his voice and told mother that it was Jesse
Henry. She then also recognized him. (Jesse Henry died in 1870 or
1871 of remorse for this very act, making a confession to J. B. Jones, a
fellow preacher, for Henry, after the war, became a minister in the
Baptist Church and was also a member of the National Council at the
time of his death.) My mother after being carried away, was released
about 20 miles from home, and was absent that night, next day, the next
night and until late in the afternoon of the day following, during which
time she had nothing to eat, was lost in the forest, and had to carry my
two brothers, who were twin babies three months old. The Indians
would not permit Lucinda (our servant girl) to accompany her."

Bro. Gilbert Bishop was made a prisoner and led away by the
party at the same time when Mrs. Ward was taken. Bishop was
taken to Fort Scott, 60 miles away. After several weeks' imprisonment, he received his freedom, through the efforts of Gen.
Blount and succeeded in rejoining his family.

Upon Mrs. Ward's return—she was all but dead—search was
instituted for Ward. Gilbert Bishop's son, Edwin, was going
through the woods when, to his horror, he found, half concealed
in the bushes, a skeleton which he knew, by the boots and the
keys lying on the ground, to be the remains of Ward, who had
been shot and his flesh devoured by hogs. Edwin Bishop* took
up the remains carefully and carried them home in a wheel-
barrow, then made a rude coffin, and, with his mother's help, dug
the grave. Mrs. Ward had fainted, but roused herself to stand
by the grave while Mrs. Bishop read the burial service.

Afraid to remain longer in danger and loneliness, the two
families, fourteen in number, gathering together a few neces-
saries, embarked in an ox-wagon for Maysville on the Arkansas
line. Passing Hildebrand's Mill, the good miller added 100 lbs.
of flour to the loaded wagon. Mrs. Bishop said: "I have no
money to pay you," but Hildebrand replied, "Gilbert Bishop
will pay me." Then they moved on to Maysville.

---

* E. P. Bishop, Bethlehem, Pa., then between 13 and 14 years of age.

Some days later, the rattle of sabres was heard, and on came the cavalry of Union troops, the baggage wagons, and, last, a settler's wagon. In this wagon was some one besides the driver, and the Bishop children cried: "O, there's father!" He had come with the army, hoping to find trace of his family.

Mrs. Ward, with her family of five children succeeded in making her way to West Salem, Ill., where they arrived in a most destitute condition, but were kindly cared for at the home of the Moravian pastor there, the Rev. Herman Tietze. The fatigues and hardships and sorrows she had undergone bore so heavily on Sr. Ward that she sank under them, in spite of the tenderest care and nursing. She died soon after her arrival at West Salem.

Gilbert Bishop obtained transportation for his family in a baggage car to some point in Missouri. From there he could communicate with friends who sent means for traveling by rail to Bethlehem, Pa., where they arrived late in November, 1862.

Meanwhile, Bro. E. J. Mock with his family had been obliged to flee from the station Canaan, October 1, 1862, and, soon after, Canaan and Mt. Zion were entirely destroyed. The Mocks made their way to Missouri and settled there temporarily. Several members at Canaan perished, the rest were scattered.

New Springplace was greatly damaged. Members were scattered far and wide, most men were in the armies of the North or the South, and the women and children were in a pitiful condition.

Once more, the Cherokee mission was wrecked. Throughout the Civil War there could be no upbuilding. The results of years of hard toil and patient endurance were dissipated. It seemed as if our work among the Cherokees had ceased forever!

CHAPTER XXII

REHABILITATION OF THE MISSION AFTER THE CIVIL WAR

The Treaty of 1866 between the United States and the Cherokee Nation brought peace to a perturbed people, regulated their distracted affairs anew and made possible for the tribe, once more, development and progress in civilization. Amnesty was declared for all criminal acts committed during the war, and the United States guaranteed to the people of the Cherokee Nation the quiet and peaceable possession of their country.

Previous to the drawing up of this treaty, a deputy from Congress, in 1865, visited the Cherokee country to obtain accurate information, and two articles of importance, sanctioning and even encouraging resumption of our mission work were thus brought forward and incorporated into the treaty:

"ARTICLE 30.

"The United States agree to pay to the proper claimants all losses of property* by missionaries or missionary societies, resulting from their

---

* "The following is a correct list of the losses sustained by the Moravian Board of Missions in the Cherokee Nation during the late rebellion:

"4 head of horses—$100	$400
"4 head of horses—$50	200
"1 wagon and harness	100
"1 carriage and harness	100
"1 set blacksmith's tools and some iron	100
"1 set of cabinet, turning lathe and shoemaker's tools	73
"Farming utensils	100
"1000 bu. corn at 50c per bu	500
"75 bushels wheat at $1 per bu	75
"3000 bundles oats at $1 per hundred	30
"Hay and fodder	75
"150 bu. Irish potatoes at 50c bu	75
"50 bu. sweet potatoes at 50c per bu	25
"20 large killing hogs at $15 each	300
"40 stock hogs at $5 each	200
"40 head of cattle at $10 each	400
"10 beds and bedsteads at $20 each	200
"Bedding, clothing and dry goods	100
"Groceries, bacon and lard	50

being ordered or driven from the country by United States agents, and from their property being taken and occupied or destroyed by United States troops, not exceeding in the aggregate Twenty Thousand Dollars, to be ascertained by the Secretary of the Interior."

"ARTICLE 14.

"The right to the use and occupancy of a quantity of land not exceeding one hundred and sixty acres, to be selected according to legal subdivisions in one body, and to include their improvements, and not including the improvements of any member of the Cherokee Nation, is hereby granted to every society or denomination which has erected, or which with the consent of the National Council may hereafter erect, buildings within the Cherokee Country for missionary or educational purposes. But no land thus granted, nor buildings which have been or may be erected thereon, shall ever be sold or otherwise disposed of except with the consent and approval of the Cherokee National Council and the Secretary of the Interior. And whenever any such lands or buildings shall be sold or disposed of, the proceeds thereof shall be applied by said society or societies for like purposes within said nation, subject to the approval of the Secretary of the Interior."

Before ever this treaty was concluded, word was received in Salem, Feb. 19, 1866, that the Unity's Mission Board, in Herrnhut, had decided that the Cherokee mission should be continued. This was a true missionary spirit for a Board to have when the material results of years of toil and expenditure in this field lay in ashes and the spiritual interests were broken and scattered!

The Salem Brethren took up the word and commissioned Bro. E. J. Mock, still living in Missouri, to make a journey of recon-

"3 cooking stoves at $25 each	75
"3 heating stoves at $20 each	60
"Table and kitchen furniture	25
"Books and stationery	100
"Damages to farm and buildings	500
"1 Melodeon	50"

Affidavit was made by Bro. Bahnson, President of the Board, as to the correctness of these items for which reparation was claimed under Article 30 of the Treaty of 1866. Through the efforts of Judge J. W. Wright, Washington, D. C., the petition for redress was granted, the Government paying to the Moravian Board about 80 cents on the dollar—the actual amount being $3279.69.

19

naissance into the Territory and to ascertain the situation with regard to the property of the Moravian mission.*

Following paragraphs are from his report:

"Leaving Springfield June 29, 1866, I traveled as far as Bentonville in Arkansas, and from thence, partly on foot, partly on horseback, reaching the borders of the Cherokee territory on July 2, and two days later, the former station of Canaan, now lying in ruins. At the sight of my old home I was deeply grieved. Church, houses and stables and even the fences and hedges had fallen a prey to the flames. Riding to the place where our dwelling had stood, the sight of the few remaining ruins recalled to my remembrance the many sighs and prayers on behalf of our Cherokees which had ascended from this spot to the Throne of Grace. I turned towards the ruins of the little church which I had built almost entirely with my own hands and quite at the expense of the Indians, who had most readily contributed what they were able— a heap of ashes was all that remained. With a heavy heart I bent my steps towards the burial ground and rested for a time among the graves of the departed.

"On July 6, after spending the night at Maysville, five miles from Canaan, I proceeded to New Springplace, about 20 miles distant. On the way thither, I found almost every house destroyed or burnt down, but at the station itself, four families were living. Men, women and children hastened to welcome me, gave me hearty hand-shakes, and I felt very happy to converse once more with my people *in the Cherokee language.*"

Mock found the mission buildings still standing, though in a very dilapidated condition. Doors and windows were broken; fences burnt; even the little woods near the schoolhouse had been

---

* On March 27, 1866, Bro. Gilbert Bishop, at Bethlehem, Pa., had written to Chief John Ross, then in Washington, D. C., with a delegation on treaty business, asking whether Bro. Mock would be permitted to return and resume mission work. The Chief replied, under date of April 10, 1866, in part as follows:

"In reply to your inquiries, permit me to say that I can see no reason why Mr. Mock should not return and occupy Springplace, or any one of your mission stations, immediately. I do not hesitate to say that the Cherokees will hail with delight the renewal of the Moravian work in their midst. Your missionary operations having been only suspended, by the war, I can see no necessity for any application being made for 'permits.'

"Members of the Delegation unite with me in the hope that your many years of devotion to our people will be greatly blessed, and that we shall yet have it in our power to reward, in some measure, your sacrifices for our good."

cut down. Everything would have been devoured by the flames but for the exertions of the few families who had remained on the spot and had worked with might and main to quench the fire. A man, Thompson, had died, soon afterwards, from over-exertion

PRINCIPAL CHIEF JOHN ROSS.
(Kroweškowée.)

in working heroically to save the station. All the cattle had been driven away and the agricultural implements were ruined.

"Went to Spavinaw next day, where I found many old friends and met with a hearty welcome. I joined with them in singing 'our Cherokee hymns.' All the natives with whom I spoke expressed a strong desire that a missionary might again be appointed to live with them and instruct them."

Bro. Mock's report sent to Salem greatly encouraged the Board there to proceed with the renewal of the mission. A call was extended to Bro. Mock to resume, as much as possible, the work at Springplace, which call he gladly followed and moved his family to the station. Mission activity among the Cherokees after the war was thus resumed, first, by the Moravians, who were, for some time, the only missionaries on the ground. The beginning was very discouraging, because so few of the members were left in this locality. George Hicks and other strong members were dead, the balance of the congregation scattered. Bro. Mock held on in spite of all difficulties and, in the meantime, another door was opening.

Chief John Ross* died in Washington, D. C., in 1867, and his remains were brought to Tahlequah to be buried among his kindred and people, whom he had governed for 40 years. Bro. E. J. Mock was invited by a committee of the National Council to preach the funeral sermon of the Hon. John Ross, which he did on June 1, 1867. On this occasion—a great honor for the Moravian Church—Bro. Mock made the acquaintance of Mrs.

---

* This remarkable man was of Scotch and Cherokee origin. His father, Daniel Ross, a native of Scotland, came down the Tennessee River with a trading expedition towards the close of the Revolutionary War, and was captured by Cherokee warriors. He owed his life to the intercession of John McDonald—at one time British agent among the Cherokees—who had married a Cherokee woman and was living in the Nation. Daniel Ross promptly fell in love with his deliverer's daughter, Mollie McDonald, and they were married. John Ross, one of the children of that union, was born Aug. 3, 1790. At the age of 19, he was special messenger for Col. R. J. Meigs, U. S. Agent for the Cherokees. In 1813, Ross was commander of a Division of Cherokees under Gen. Andrew Jackson. He was elected as Principal Chief of the Cherokee Nation in 1827 and was re-elected every four years. Up to the time of his death he served in this office, a period of 40 years. It was during his chieftaincy that the Cherokee Nation attained the distinction of becoming the most highly advanced aboriginal tribe on the North American continent. Chief Ross laid the corner-stones of the Cherokee Male and Female Seminaries at Tahlequah in 1847 and lived to see the handsome brick capitol building of the Cherokee Nation at Tahlequah. The Chief had always attended church worship and was a particular friend and patron of the Moravian missions among his tribe. He made a public profession of Religion in 1852. His second wife, a white woman, from New Jersey, was a graduate of the Moravian Seminary at Bethlehem, Pa.

Jane Nave, daughter of Chief Ross. Jane Ross Nave* earnestly entreated Bro. Mock to hold regular services in Tahlequah, which he gladly consented to do and the work began most auspiciously, new members being received in August, October and December of the same year (1867).

MRS. JANE (ROSS) NAVE.
(Daughter of John Ross.)

---

* She had been a student at the Salem Female Academy about 1835-'37 and Miss Sophia D. Ruede—later Mrs. Miles Vogler—was her favorite teacher. At Salem, Jane Ross learned to love the Moravian Church. In the Territory—now Mrs. Nave—she took a prominent part in all activities for the advancement of her people and was deeply interested in Christian missions. During the war, she fled for safety to Bethlehem, Pa., with her children, and while there was received as a member of the Moravian Church, Feb. 28, 1867, by Bro. Edmund de Schweinitz. Three of her children were baptized at the same time. The ceremony took place in the same congregation in which, 125 years ago, Sept. 16, 1742, Count Zinzendorf baptized one of the first Indian converts. After her return to the Territory she became matron of the girls' school at Tahlequah, continuing a firm friend of the missionaries. A few years later she died, and almost with her last breath sent a message of love to Salem.

Bro. Mock held his services in the dining hall of the Female Seminary, the floor of its large schoolroom having been broken down by the great weight of provisions which had been stored there for the use of the army.

During 1868 and 1869, Bro. Mock continued to labor here and the work prospered steadily, thirty-nine persons having connected themselves with the church. He was assisted by Bro. Wesley J. Spaugh,† from Friedberg, N. C., who had come, of his own accord, to be of some use in the Cherokee mission. Mrs. Jane Nave was the superintendent of a very flourishing Sunday School.

Services were kept, also, in the Parkhill vicinity—the late Presbyterian mission—and in August, 1869, eight persons united with the Moravian Church there. Besides, Mock preached at Springplace, where the work was looking up, and at Spavinaw, where there was a great awakening in 1869, several Cherokees uniting with the church in October.

In the year 1870, Bro. Theodore M. Rights* was called to the Cherokee mission, particularly to the work in the vicinity of Tahlequah. Bro. Rights and wife arrived in October and lived in two rooms of the Female Seminary. After a year's trial, the school was discontinued and in February, 1872, Bro. Rights and wife removed to the mission premises near Parkhill, renting a house formerly occupied by the Rev. S. A. Worcester, of the American Board, now owned by Rev. Worcester's daughter.

---

† Some years later murdered in the Chickasaw Nation.

* Theodore M. Rights, M.A., was born Aug. 7, 1846, Friedberg, N. C., son of Rev. C. Lewis and Elizabeth (Hughes) Rights. Received his schooling at Salem Boys' School, N. C., Nazareth Hall and Moravian College and Theological Seminary, graduating in 1867. He taught at Nazareth Hall until 1870, in which year he was ordained to the ministry by Bishop Henry A. Shultz at Nazareth, Pa. On Aug. 2, 1870, he was married to Miss Hannah W. Riegel—born at Bath, Pa., Oct. 7, 1838, daughter of Daniel and Hannah (Weaver) Riegel—and they followed the call as missionaries to the Cherokee mission in August, 1870, and served in that field until 1896. After leaving Indian Territory, Bro. and Sr. Rights served in the mission among the Delawares, New Fairfield, near Bothwell on the Thames in Ontario, Canada, until 1904. After this, lived in retirement at Nazareth, Pa., active in the local congregation there. Served Graceham, Md., 1919-'20. Bro. Rights died April 1, 1922.

An official visit to the Cherokee mission was made in the spring of 1872 by the Rev. Emil A. de Schweinitz, of the Salem Provincial Board. At New Springplace, he found Bro. Mock in charge and the mission was in a very encouraging status. The buildings, solidly constructed by Bro. Gilbert Bishop, were in good condition. Additions to the church, while not numerous, were frequent and the widely-scattered members were gradually settling nearer the station. Under the care of New Springplace were 68 communicants and a total of 146 souls. A flourishing mission school of 54 scholars was taught by Mr. Richard Wolfe, a Cherokee; Bro. Mock giving religious instruction. Preaching places served by Bro. Mock, besides Springplace, were Maysville, 25 miles distant; Barren Fork of Illinois, 22 miles distant; and Smith's, 15 miles distant. Mock's long residence of 25 years among the Cherokees had made him one of them; he was greatly attached to the people and they esteemed him very highly.*

At Parkhill, Bro. de Schweinitz found Bro. Rights preaching to our people in the Presbyterian church, by courtesy, there being 57 members in the Parkhill district. Bro. de Schweinitz was very favorably impressed. Here is the recommendation from his report:

"In order to carry on the work successfully, we must have a regular station, i.e., church building and dwelling for the missionary. The consent of Council has been obtained for the transfer of the former station, Canaan, destroyed during the war, to any part of the country we may select. Parkhill district, by unanimous consent, is the most desirable and suitable location. The establishment of a station involves the outlay of a large sum of money; if the necessary amount can be spared from the mission funds, a station should be opened here."

The Board at Salem received Bro. de Schweinitz' recommendation favorably and negotiations were begun with Mr. Rufus Ross for his improvements between Parkhill and Tahlequah. These premises, located about 45 minutes' ride from Tahlequah, con-

---

* Mock's Indian name was "The Crow" and was applied to him because he wore a black coat on his coming among them. This name spread and the Moravians were called "The Ravens," and Bro. de Schweinitz, while on his visit, was promptly called "Chief of the Ravens." The Cherokees called the Methodists, the "Loud Talkers;" the Presbyterians, the "Soft Talkers;" and the Baptists, "The Baptizers."

sisted of 35 acres of land, fenced, a four-room house with separate kitchen and a stable. Nov. 12, 1872, this improvement was bought for $1900, and Bro. Rights and wife removed thither in February, 1873. In the fall, the corner-stone of the church was laid and the building was erected at a cost of $1800, a later addition being a tower and bell, together costing $160. This church was dedicated on Sunday, June 14, Bro. Mock preaching the sermon from Luke 12:32, "Fear not, little flock; for it is your Father's good pleasure to give you the kingdom." The station was called Woodmount, as it was situated on a beautiful, wooded hill in a choice section of country, richly adorned by nature.

In March, 1876, Bro. Rights was appointed superintendent of the Female Seminary at Tahlequah.* Bro. Joseph Hillman,† a nephew of Sr. Rights, who had spent the previous summer visiting and assisting Bro. Rights, came with his mother to take charge of Woodmount. The church proved to be unfortunately situated, neither in town nor far enough away from town to secure a large audience. Still, the work was greatly blessed, the Communion seasons always being particularly refreshing.

Bro. E. J. Mock retired from service in the Cherokee mission in the year 1877, after 30 years of faithful service, during which time he had not once been east of the Mississippi. One of his last good deeds for his Indians was done in 1875, a year when crops had failed and provisions were very scarce. Mock made arrangements with some merchants to extend credit to the Cherokees for

---

* About 100 children were being educated here at the expense of the Nation. The offer to Bro. Rights to take this position showed the confidence in which Moravians and their missionaries were held among the Cherokees. The Board at Salem felt it would be of advantage to the work to have Bro. Rights in this position and authorized him to accept the superintendency.

† Born at Nazareth, Pa., son of Owen and Matilda (Riegel) Hillman. Graduated from Moravian College in 1870. Taught at Nazareth Hall and after his ordination in 1872, served several charges: Gracehill, Iowa; Harmony, Iowa; Chaska, Minn. Bro. Hillman was then called to the Cherokee mission, serving during the years 1877-1881. After having served Palmyra, N. J., and Easton, Pa., he entered the service of the Presbyterian Church. His last charge was at Lambertville, N. J. Bro. Hillman, at present, is living in retirement at Hackettstown, N. J. His wife was Miss Minnie Beers, of Phillipsburg, N. J.

a total amount of 40,000 lbs. of provisions until the next annuity would be paid, which amounted to about $10 per head. Bro. Rights was called from the Female Seminary to fill the vacancy at New Springplace caused by Bro. Mock's retiring from the work.

At Woodmount, it became increasingly evident that a change in the location of the mission was necessary. The Moravians were asked, as there was no other church building in Tahlequah, to move the Woodmount church into town. People from Tahlequah urged that the membership could be greatly increased by this change, which would, likewise, cause the Moravian Church to be better known throughout the whole Nation. The Church decided to follow the invitation and friends in Tahlequah and vicinity contributed $200, being half the expense of the removal. As there was no other church building in the town, it was occupied by the different denominations in turn.

Bro. Hillman labored faithfully in Tahlequah and Bro. Rights assisted him, all he could, from Springplace. Services were held regularly and were very well attended. A Prayer Meeting held on Thursday nights seemed to be especially appreciated. Four Communion seasons were observed each year, at which the attendance was invariably good and much blessing was experienced. In general, the work at Tahlequah seemed to teach that growth in grace among the Indians of this generation was very slow and their ideas of vital godliness, vague. One reason for their exceedingly poor apprehension of spiritual truth is to be ascribed to the fact that there was among them, as a general rule, no real home life. The absence of all respect for parents was now common; appeals to the young to regard the feelings of their parents and kindred fell upon unappreciative ears, and spiritual truths which should have been impressed on the minds of the children were entirely neglected. Adding to this the inherited desire for strong drink and the prevalent immorality in the country at this time, one can somewhat imagine the state of society, especially among the mixed bloods, and the amount of grace it required for a Cherokee convert to keep himself unspotted from the world.

On the second and fourth Sundays in each month, alternately, Bro. Hillman preached, likewise, in the two National Seminaries in Tahlequah.

One of the most faithful members in this field passed away in 1878. Sister L. J. Vann was a granddaughter of the late Chief Ross and "She was the most active, earnest and self-denying member of this church. (Tahlequah.) We miss her counsels, her words of kindness and encouragement and her prayers in our behalf; her death has left a void which it will be difficult to fill. Her's was a ripe heart; her meekness was particularly noticeable." Bro. Rights preached her funeral sermon from the words, "She hath done what she could."*

The report of Springplace for the year 1878 notes steady progress and much encouragement though no great numerical increase. The minds of the Cherokees are again unsettled for, once more, the white people are hungering after their lands. A committee from the United States Senate visited in the Nation during the year and it is feared this committee will recommend to Congress a Territorial form of government to displace Cherokee autonomy.

Further, Springplace reports for 1878 the putting of the graveyard in good repair. The Springplace graveyard marks quite an interesting spot in the Cherokee mission, for here, besides the mortal remains of many Christian Indians won as trophies for Christ, are resting the bodies of Miles Vogler, Margaret (Morris) Bishop, Elizabeth (Kummer) Smith, Gertrude (Spaugh) Smith, Eugene Bishop and Mattie E. Rights. Here, too, is the shallow grave of James Ward, assistant missionary, who had been murdered during the Civil War, and buried by Sister Bishop and her oldest boy. For the latter grave, the Female Missionary Society of Bethlehem furnished an appropriate stone and other friends in Bethlehem helped to defray the expenses of putting a neat fence around this God's Acre.

---

* Mark 14:8.

The year 1879* brought seemingly little progress in either field. Bro. Darius E. Ward, son of James Ward, Jr., and his wife were developing into valuable Sunday School workers at Springplace and outstations. No Interpreter was available for the full-blood Cherokees, but a native Methodist minister, Chenuquin, preached in Cherokee, sharing the services with Rights. Other denominations were feeling and lamenting the general apathy towards Religion which seemed to have spread over the tribe.

In 1880, Bro. Hillman returned east to take a position as a teacher in Nazareth Hall and Bro. Rights served both stations, Springplace and Tahlequah. Our work in Tahlequah did not prosper. The Baptists had built a church for themselves and the Presbyterians were anxious to build for themselves or to buy the Moravian church building. Negotiations for this were begun in 1882, and it was thought best to sell as we seemed to have no prospect of success in Tahlequah. The church was sold the same

---

* Bro. Rights gives an interesting and instructive account of a fair for the Indian Territory held at Muskogee in 1879: "The Secretary of the Interior was present and representatives of about 20 wild tribes were on hand. Of especial interest was the Sac and Fox delegation. They are not straight and tall as other Indians, but lithe and muscular. Their use of their blankets is wonderful. Although the days were warm, yet, in some shape or other, they had their blankets on their bodies continually. Lying on the ground they wrapped themselves in them; in walking, they were thrown about their shoulders and trailed down to their feet; if they wished to mount on horseback, they were folded about their waists and hips and, though they had no stirrups, yet they managed to keep their blankets about them while they made their leap and settled themselves in the saddle.

"We observed one making his toilet before entering the fair grounds, and he was particular about it as a fashionable lady. It took him over an hour to paint his face before a small looking glass, then he donned a bright, green-figured shirt, fastened around his head a strip of fur adorned with ribbons hanging down and added a necklace of clam shells and dyed feathers in his hair.

"Comparing these wild Indians in discomfort and squalor with the Cherokees, Creeks and Choctaws who had come in stout wagons and in clothes, speech and manners differed little from their white neighbors, it was plainly evident what an immense advance had been made by the tribes who had embraced the Christian religion, which was the first real civilizing agency among them.

year to the Presbyterians for $700. Monthly services were still held in it at the invitation of the Presbyterian brethren. Also at Parkhill, by request of Bro. Stephen Foreman, Rights preached once each month in the Presbyterian chapel.

Springplace went forward quietly during 1883, the Sunday School doing especially good work under the leadership of Mrs. D. E. Ward. There was now a National School near Springplace and no mission school was required, though some of the older members, remembering the "good old days," wished for their youth a school where not only head, but heart, also, would be taught.

Efforts were made to extend the work, Bro. Rights preaching in the Duckworth neighborhood and at Beck schoolhouse with good attendance at both places. There was stated preaching, also, at Barren Fork, a neighborhood now destitute of Gospel privileges. A union Sunday School was being conducted at Parkhill in which Mrs. Rights was active and Bro. Rights held

---

"There were good agricultural exhibits and a ladies' department of fancy work and canned goods that was fine. Some furniture made by Indians was equal to that of any cabinet maker.

"The Secretary of the Interior made a speech lauding their progress, but sounding a note of warning. The States surrounding them were more populously settled than their territory and, in time, the tide of immigration would flow on them. He urged the Indians to prepare for this in advance. They should divide their lands and give to each individual a title in fee simple to his portion.

"At noon, a public meeting of the Sunday School convention was held in the fair house. There were helpful addresses. The crowd gathered was one of many nations. 'Yellow Bear,' the Arapahoe Chief, stood calm, dignified and, apparently, an interested spectator. Rev. Allen Wright, of the Choctaw Nation, presided over the meeting; about him sat visiting ministers, native missionaries and preachers from the various tribes, and a large choir of Cherokee singers who sang several hymns in their native tongue. In the crowd, there were the dusky African, the blanketed wild Indian, the blue-coated soldier from the neighboring Fort, the fashionably-dressed ladies of civilized nations, mingled with the wondering white visitors from the bordering States. When the assemblage sang, 'There is a Fountain Filled with Blood,' we felt, as never before, that 'God hath made of one blood all nations of men,' and that 'many out of every kindred and tongue, and people and nation' shall stand before His throne, redeemed by the blood of the Lamb."

Prayer Meeting each Friday night at the Male Seminary in Tahlequah. While the Moravian Church could not reap a direct harvest from this and other work done, from time to time, in the Seminaries, the Church, in this way, became widely and favorably known among the intellectual and influential Cherokees.

What reads like modern history of 1922 is the story of the troublesome problem of enforcing the "dry" laws among the Cherokees in the years around 1883. The Cherokee Nation had severe laws against the introduction and sale of spirituous liquors and yet these were being constantly smuggled into the country in small kegs, on horse or concealed in wagons containing flour or other articles. The United States authorities traced and arrested such parties most diligently, and upon conviction, imposed sentences of confinement in distant penitentiaries, *but the profits were so great* that this traffic continued and wagons were frequently escorted by armed men ready to resist the officers of the law. Mrs. Emma Molloy was employed, in 1883, by the "Cherokee Temperance Union," to deliver a series of temperance lectures before the *National Council of the Cherokees!* She preached Christ as the only source of strength to the tempted and the fallen. Many not only signed the pledge but were converted to God.

The mission in 1883 again lost valuable members by death: Sister Lizzie Israel, a devoted member at Springplace, had been a "stand-by" ever since Bro. Gilbert Bishop's early ministry. Sister Lizzie Ross—educated at Bethlehem, Pa., during the Civil War—who with her mother and sisters formed the nucleus of the work around Parkhill, had been a faithful helper of the congregation, and the missionary, Bro. Stephen Foreman, of Parkhill, likewise, had passed away.

These changes in the Parkhill district rendered it no longer desirable to depend on the Presbyterians for facilities for worship, hence, in 1884, Bro. Rights began preaching and Sunday School in the mission house at Woodmount. This had not been removed to Tahlequah when the church was moved there in 1877. For two years services were held in the Woodmount parsonage, then steps were taken for the building of a church, for which Bro. Rights drew the sketch. It was 30 x 20 feet, with a pulpit recess, six windows and one door and could seat about 130 people.

Without, the church was painted white and the native pine finish of the interior was oiled to bring out the grain. The cost of the building was $500. Woodmount church was two miles south of Tahlequah and was beautifully situated. To the west, was the hill which gave the church its name and, at the foot of the hill, a never-failing spring of clear, cold water, called the "Chapel Spring." Services of dedication, largely attended, were held Oct. 17, 1886, and, in the interval between meetings, a bountiful dinner was spread for all. A protracted meeting was held in the newly-built church, at which much interest was manifested and there was a real work of the Spirit of God. Eleven persons came forward professing faith in Christ.

Having followed the development at Woodmount, we must go back, for a moment, to the year 1884, in which year Bro. J. Benjamin Lineback* arrived from Salem to serve in the Cherokee mission. He served at several preaching-stations with encouragement, living at Springplace.† The Sunday School at Springplace was encouraging with 50 names on the roll. There were several conversions in 1884 and an earnest spirit of prayer was abroad, many of the members praying in the meetings and without solicitation. Bro. Lineback preached regularly at Flynt Creek and White Oaks schoolhouses and precious souls were saved; six at White Oaks in 1885. White Oaks was 16 miles south of Tahlequah. Lineback was sadly in need of workers for the Sunday School: when he was preaching at one appointment there were none who could take charge of the Sunday School at the other.

Rights was preaching (1885) at the Court House of Illinois District, 25 miles southeast of Tahlequah, a well-populated neighborhood, and at Caney Creek, 15 miles southwest of Tahlequah, where good audiences assembled in the schoolhouse.

---

* Born at Salem, son of William and Sarah (Hauser) Lineback. Married to Sr. Alice O. Rights at Bethania, N. C., in 1870. Ordained to the ministry July 31, 1870, at Nazareth, Pa. Served congregations as follows: Friedberg, N. C., 1877-1881; Lebanon, Mo., and from there to the Cherokee mission in 1884; later lived in Siloam Springs, Ark.

† The farm at Springplace was worked by a renter.

Cheering advances were being made in Christian civilization among the Cherokees, although our own work progressed but slowly at this time. The Cherokee tribe numbered more preachers, church members and places of worship than ever before. Schools were increasing in number and the Male and Female Seminaries at Tahlequah—in the class of first grade high schools at the present time—were doing excellent work.

The weakness of the Moravian work among the Cherokees in these years may be attributed, largely, to the distance of our work from the home base and to the fact that we were operating in the field on the plan of a foreign mission while other churches were settling down to well-organized frontier home mission activity along denominational lines, and were pushing their schools. The Methodists had their Presiding Elders; the Presbyterians, their Presbyteries; the Baptists, their Associations. The Moravians had two lone missionaries, preaching here and there and working as best they could, far from any denominational help and their Board 1500 miles away, so that frequent visitations could not be undertaken on account of the great expense involved.

Bro. T. M. Rights decided to make a change in the year 1890, accepting a position as a teacher in Nazareth Hall. The people were exceedingly sorry to have him leave, for Bro. Rights had a good name everywhere. Judge Adair, Superintendent of the Female Seminary, said, "We are all sorry to have him leave, for as a preacher he stands at the head of the best in the Nation."

The Rev. C. Lewis Rights* was sent from Salem on an official visitation to the Cherokee mission in the summer of 1890. Bro. Rights visited at all the stations and preaching places and found that much more good work had been done than had ever been reported. Bro. Benjamin Lineback's wife was Rev. Rights' daughter and Bro. T. M. Rights, his son. Bro. Lewis Rights heard on every side how good the people felt toward Bro. T. M. Rights, now in Nazareth, Pa. They said he was their preacher, doctor,

---

* Bro. Lewis Rights was born June 22, 1820, at Salem, N. C. Entered the service of the Church at the age of 24, serving first in the mountains of Virginia, then at Friedland, N. C., Bethania, N. C., Kernersville, N. C., etc. He became a member of the Southern Provincial Board in 1865 and its President in 1879. He died at Tahlequah, I. T., Jan. 9, 1891

nurse and comforter!† Bro. Lewis Rights found the congregation at Woodmount like sheep without a shepherd since Bro. T. M. Rights had gone, and did not like to leave the work in this unsettled condition, hence he decided to remain, temporarily, in the mission to hold the work together until a successor could be appointed. His wife was with him and they lived at Tahlequah, well beloved by Moravian members and those of other denominations.

After five months of blessed service in the Woodmount congregation, Bro. Rights preached his last sermon in that church on Dec. 1, 1890. After the sermon, he administered the Holy Communion; his prayer was peculiarly impressive, in which he said: "We are communing far away from home; perhaps our next Communion will be in Heaven." The evening of Dec. 24 was dismal and stormy. Our dear Brother was anxious to be with his congregation in their Christmas festivities. Although he was not feeling well, he said he might never have another chance to speak to the people. He did not preach, but had a Scripture reading, and talked and prayed. On the afternoon of his death the Methodist minister, the Rev. J. J. Lovett, called to see him. Bro. Rights was sitting by the table, with his face resting on his hand. After some conversation he took the Bible and handed it to Bro. Lovett, asking him to lead in prayer, in which he joined in responsive "Amens." In about two hours he fell asleep in Jesus. Funeral services were held in Tahlequah, Jan. 10th, all the ministers of the different denominations being present, and again at Springplace, whither the remains were taken for burial on Jan. 11.* Here the services were conducted by John Ross, Sabbath School Missionary for the Presbyterian Church, in his youth a pupil at the Moravian School, Nazareth Hall, Pa.

---

† One man related that one night, at midnight, there was a knock at his door, and there stood "Parson" Rights, almost frozen. He had preached twice that day and started for home, 25 miles. He had to swim Flynt Creek, and in an hour his clothes were solid ice and he would have frozen to death if he had not found fire and shelter.

* Later brought to Kernersville, N. Carolina, and laid to rest in the Moravian graveyard there.

Bro. T. M. Rights returned to the field in the summer of 1891 and felt much encouraged over the hearty welcome he received. He worked doubly hard, endeavoring to keep the whole work together, when Bro. Lineback left Springplace in the same year. Bro. Rights divided his month as follows:

1st Sunday, Woodmount,	11 a.m.—Prayer Meeting,	7 p.m.
2nd Sunday, Braggs,	11 a.m.—Mohr's,	3 p.m.
3rd Sunday, Woodmount,	11 a.m.—Prayer Meeting,	7 p.m.
4th Sunday, Springplace,	11 a.m.—Hildebrand's Mill,	7 p.m.

A gracious spiritual awakening came to Woodmount in the same year. A Mrs. Adair and her husband, evangelists, conducted a protracted meeting, at the invitation of Bro. Rights, which was productive of much good. The church could not hold the congregations that assembled for these evangelistic services, hence the Brethren erected a "brush arbor" for services in the open air. In all, 29 persons made profession of faith in Christ and 19 of them handed their names to Bro. Rights for membership at Woodmount. Personal workers were developed among the members; Bro. Rights speaks of one-half the audience, during the evangelistic campaign, *seeking* the Way of Life and the other half endeavoring to *point out* "The Way," and lead their fellow men to Christ. The whole church was awakened and lifted to a higher spiritual plane. Bro. D. E. Ward, Sunday School Superintendent and valuable helper, felt the impulse to be, under God, of even greater service to the mission. Writing to Bishop Edward Rondthaler[*] at Salem, he thus expressed himself: "What I am, by the grace of God, is through the instrumentality of the Moravian Church. My gratitude shall no longer be confined to thoughts and words, but by actions may I be able to disseminate the principles inculcated to others, that the good seed may not be lost."

Bro. Herman Beck arrived in the field in 1892,[†] having been sent from Europe to serve in the Cherokee mission. He was ordained a Deacon of the Moravian Church, at Salem, and was stationed at Springplace, giving Bro. Rights some much-needed assistance.

---

[*] As a young man, Bro. Rondthaler had been Ward's teacher at Nazareth Hall.

[†] 1892–1895.

20

A change in the administration of the Cherokee mission is in prospect in 1892, but, before we speak of that, in the next chapter, a general survey of the whole field and its status at this time is important for the reader.

WOODMOUNT. Services well attended and audiences increasing. "As we climb the hill on which the church stands, we are often surprised and gratified to see the number of buggies, wagons and saddle horses that are standing near the church. We are especially glad to see the wagons, for they come loaded with whole families, from the venerable grandmother to the infant in its mother's arms." Sunday School under D. E. Ward has increased in numbers and interest. A blessed Passion Week and Easter season were experienced and on the 13th of August celebration there were several accessions to church membership. A day-school was maintained during the greater portion of the year, the teacher of which was paid in part by the mission at the rate of $12.50 per month and in part by the parents, who paid 75c per month for each scholar.

SPRINGPLACE. After Bro. Beck's arrival, more attention was given to this station. This is a difficult field of labor, and the prospects are not as encouraging as ten years ago. A protracted meeting was held during the year and several who had grown careless and left the church were reclaimed. The missionaries tried to revive the Sunday School, but the members were very indifferent towards it. Members have cleaned the graveyard and repaired the fence.

ULM CHAPEL. Three miles west of Springplace. A Bavarian, George Mueller, who married a Cherokee wife, had put up a log chapel at Ulm Post Office and asked the Moravians to take charge of the work in this neighborhood. The logs were unhewn oak, the windows had no glass, the seats were plank nailed to the wall on one side and to a plank on the other and without backs, yet when the congregations, that sometimes filled it, gathered in, and all joined heartily in singing some familiar hymn, it was good to be there. Some day this will be a densely populated section and there is hope to have a good church and school here.

WASHBURNE'S MILL SCHOOL. Ten miles west of Springplace on Spring Creek. This work is among full-bloods who speak nothing but Cherokee. A school here was conducted by Mr. Daniel Smith, hired by the mission for $20 per month. Progress was slow but gratifying. The need for religious work here is great. The Indians spend their Sundays in hunting and fishing and shooting corn-stalks with their bows and arrows, upon which latter game they bet money and clothing. The work cannot be carried on without an Interpreter and there is none at hand, though Bro. Rights thinks Miss Proctor, a full-blood who taught at Woodmount for some time, might qualify for this office with some training.

BRAGGS. Twenty-eight miles southwest of Tahlequah. People very indifferent here and the Sunday School has been abandoned. Regular services are maintained.

MOHR'S. Four miles east of Braggs. People are building a schoolhouse and Bro. Rights promised to aid them by getting windows and a door. A few Moravians live here who are anxious for services and the other people seem well disposed. Fertile soil and nearness to the railroad make this point a good prospect for our mission.

WHITE OAK. Sixteen miles south of Tahlequah. At one time, there were several members here, but the work has not prospered. Several came, from time to time, and expressed sorrow for the past and desired to connect themselves with the church, but when arrangements were made they drew back. "I was sent for to preach the funeral of a young lad who died with consumption. Speaking with him before his death, I found that he had put his trust in Christ. After the funeral, a young woman came to me and said, 'The next time you come down, Mr. Rights, I want to join your church.' I tried to impress upon her the necessity of breaking with evil companionship, and being faithful in prayer, and received her promise that she would try to follow my admonitions; but when I came the next time, she, too, had passed away."

CHAPTER XXIII

THE FINAL CHAPTER

A change seems again to be impending for the Cherokee Nation.
Many white people now live within its limits as renters of land,
which they may lease for only one year, have no school privileges
and no vote. The Cherokee Outlet or Strip, a large tract of land
containing over six million acres to the west of the Cherokee
Reservation, which had been leased for several years by the
Cherokees, for $200,000 per annum, to a company for use as a
cattle range, is now under consideration for a possible sale to the
United States. Many Cherokees urge this, thinking they will
get a large, per capita share of the money from the sale. There
is a growing dissatisfaction both among the Cherokees and in
Congress with the present method of holding lands in common;
some of the wealthier persons are able to cultivate immense tracts
of land, poorer Indians have a small patch of three to five acres.
Many now openly advocate the division of their lands in severalty,
each one, whether rich or poor, to own the same number of acres.
When this time comes, many Indians will sell off their individual
lands to white settlers. These will become more numerous and
demand equal rights and privileges with the Cherokees. Thus,
whereas the Cherokee Nation is now—while we are looking about,
in 1892, over the whole field of our mission—a government within
a Government, the day will probably come when the Cherokee
territory will become part of the States of the Union and the
Cherokees themselves, citizens of the United States.

Now for further light on the coming change in the administration of the Cherokee mission, negotiations for which began in the
year 1892.

"Bro. B. Romig, of the Unity's Mission Department, writes that the
Southern Provincial Elders' Conference proposes to give up the care of
the Cherokee Indian mission and inquires whether, in case this should
come to pass, we would accept the care of this mission with the others
already entrusted to our oversight. We will reply that we are surprised to learn of such a proposition from the Brethren in the south,
but that we will consent to assume this additional responsibility, if the
Unity's Mission Department cannot devise a better plan."—Minutes of
Provincial Elders' Conference, American Province North, Aug. 27, 1892.

Further:

"Bro. Romig, Unity's Mission Department, sends some letters in which the rather discouraging condition of the Cherokee mission is set forth and asks us to accept the charge of this work. We agree to do so."—Minutes Northern P. E. C., Oct. 17, 1892.

Further:

"Bro. Rondthaler, of the Southern P. E. C., writes, among other matters, that the transfer of the Cherokee mission to the Northern P. E. C. may be considered accomplished."— Minutes of Northern P. E. C., Feb. 2, 1893.

Thus, after having had charge of the work as agents for the Mission Department of the Church for nearly 100 years, the Southern Province requested to be relieved of this charge, and, at the request of the Unity's Mission Department, the Northern Province accepted the agency for this work.

The log building in the Mohr's neighborhood was completed in 1893 and this station was named "Mt. Zion," in fond recollection of the earlier church with the same name, destroyed during the Civil War. Charles Maxwell, a Cherokee and an earnest Christian, was engaged to teach a school here, partly at the expense of the people who sent children for instruction, partly supported by mission funds. Preaching services were held on the second Sunday in each month, with encouraging attendance. A real awakening took place here in April of the following year and 21 persons, composed of full-blood and half-breed Cherokees, united with the nucleus of a congregation already existing in this locality. Another step in the right direction was taken with the beginning of the custom of receiving offerings at the services. Money was very scarce and the people could not give much, but the practice developed a new grace in their Christian character.

The Cherokee Nation sold the "Cherokee Outlet" or "Strip," mentioned above, to the United States in 1893 for nearly eight million dollars. The Indians expected this large sum to be turned over in one payment and had already figured out that every man, woman and child would receive $300. When once it became known that the agreement had been ratified, merchants bought large stocks of goods and sold on credit, and very many of the Cherokees proved the truth of the adage: "Light come, light go."

They stopped working and seemed to care only to be at the stores as often as possible. The one part intent on spending the money as rapidly as possible, the other, on selling large stocks of goods to get hold of this money! A great depression followed when it became known that payment for the "Strip" was to come in five annual instalments. Merchants gave no further credit and were themselves heavily involved with eastern firms for goods bought. Those in a hurry to spend repented at leisure. One full-blood had bought a wagon and harness for $90 on credit and, after a few months, sold both for $10 in cash! Religious work was seriously hampered; the Indians were not thinking of spiritual things.

An official visitation to the Cherokee mission was undertaken, in 1895, by Bishop Benjamin Romig, of the Unity's Mission Board, accompanied by the Rev. Edmund A. Oerter, of the Provincial Elders' Conference, North. On Sunday, June 16, these Brethren participated in the services at Woodmount, at which two grandchildren of the late Chief John Ross were baptized. Forty were present at Sunday School on that day and between fifty and sixty at the preaching services. An official interview with the members after the service brought out the following points: The members knew very little about the Moravian Church and about the original work by Moravians among the Cherokees in Georgia. (Lack of books and records and the translocation of the tribe would largely account for this.) There were few Moravian Cherokee members in comparison with the membership of other denominations because the Moravians were not so aggressive and were very careful about receiving members from other denominations. The Baptists have a great advantage in possessing several full-blood ordained preachers. The mission should not be abandoned. No man in Tahlequah is more highly respected than Bro. Rights and it would be a detriment to the entire community were the Moravian mission to cease. The members were asked why, if they valued their minister and the mission so highly, they did not contribute to his support and relieve the mission fund? *The idea appeared new to them,* but was well received and Bro. D. E. Ward agreed to canvass the congregation and see what could be done.

The visiting Brethren were taken to Braggs station, where the schoolhouse was crowded with attentive auditors. The singing was especially hearty. Brethren Romig and Oerter had their first experience of spending a night in a Cherokee home—a half-breed husband and a full-blood wife. The home was neat and comfortable and the wife was intelligent and had had some education. She showed many Indian traits, especially in lighting her pipe and smoking complacently while sitting on the porch in conversation with the ministers. She was greatly interested in Sunday School and was endeavoring to organize a School at Braggs. Thanking her, next morning, for her hospitality, the Brethren received the answer: "O, no occasion. Your sort is always welcome!"

Mt. Zion was visited, where much interest was shown and the people begged for more services. Several Germans lived here who had married Cherokee women and were rearing large families of half-breed children.

New Springplace—or Oaks, as the station and neighborhood were now called—was less promising. Bro. Herman Beck and wife were in charge. Mostly full-bloods lived in this section, who understood little or no English, and our missionaries understood little or no Cherokee. The Baptists in the community, with their full-blood preacher, were making good progress. On Monday following the Sunday when the visiting Brethren came to Oaks, there was a funeral of a young Cherokee woman not fully identified with the church. A large company was present. Bishop Romig addressed the people on the words: "Prepare to meet thy God."[*] Brother Oerter led in prayer, Bro. Beck conducting the service. To the visitors, it was a weird scene: the rough-looking Cherokee men, women and children; the graveyard in the midst of the woods; the shrieks and wailing of the mourners—a sorrow without much hope. The buildings at the station, Bro. Gilbert Bishop's handiwork, had stood for many years and would stand for many more. Soon after the official visit, Bro. Beck was called to mission service in Nicaragua, Central America, the work at Oaks no longer warranting a missionary couple there. Bro. D. E. Ward was called to take charge of the station as a lay worker.

---

* Amos 4:12.

having the use of the land and dwelling he, in turn, to look after the Sunday School and perform such other services as his ability warranted. Stated preaching was to be supplied by Bro. Rights from Woodmount.

All the while, the political situation of the Cherokee Nation had been growing more unsettled. The Five Civilized Tribes, viz., Cherokee, Choctaw, Chickasaw, Creek and Seminole, numbered at this time, with all their half-breeds and tribal adherents , about 71,000 souls, while the non-citizen element in Indian Territory numbered at least 200,000, consisting of renters, business men, whites living in the Territory by consent of the Indian governments on official or other legitimate business, but the great majority being illegal "squatters" or unrecognized claimants to Indian rights, against whose presence the Indians never ceased to protest. The Five Civilized Tribes as well as the United States Government realized that there must come a change in the status of the Indian and his Territory: the demands of the whites for schools and equal privileges were becoming more and more insistent; the administration of justice between Indian and white, which always involved action in the United States Courts for every case, was very costly; unscrupulous white persons were increasingly taking advantage of full-blood Cherokees. The sentiment for the abolition of the Indian governments and allotment of land to the Indians in fee simple and the Territorial form of government gained such force that by Act of Congress, March 3, 1893, the President was authorized to appoint a Commission of three—known later as the Dawes Commission, from its distinguished Chairman, Senator Henry L. Dawes, of Massachusetts —to negotiate with the Five Civilized Tribes for "the extinguishment of tribal titles to any lands within that territory, now held by any and all of such Nations and tribes, either by cession of the same or some part thereof to the United States, or by the allotment and division of the same in severalty among the Indians of such Nations and tribes respectively as may be entitled to the same, or by such other method as may be agreed upon........to enable the ultimate creation of a State or States of the Union, which shall embrace the land within the said Indian Territory." In 1895, the Commission was increased to five members, with enlarged powers and the survey of Indian Territory was ordered and begun. The meaning of such survey was too plain to be disregarded and it was justly considered as the initial step, solemn and authoritative, toward the overthrow of the Indians' communal holdings.

The general prosperity and advancement of the Cherokee Nation at this time may be judged from the report of the Cherokee National Board of Education to the United States Agent. He reports 4,800 children attending two Seminaries, Male and Female, two high schools, and one hundred primary schools, teachers being paid from $35 to $100 per month for nine months in the year. Fourteen primary schools were for the use of the negro citizens of the Nation, besides which they had a fine high school, kept up, like all the others, at the expense of the Cherokee government. Besides the National schools there were 12 mission schools helping to do splendid work for children of both citizens and non-citizens. The orphan asylum ranked as a high school in which 150 orphans were boarded and educated, with graduates every year. The Male Seminary, accommodating 200 pupils, and the Female Seminary, accommodating 225 pupils, were large brick structures 240 x 150 feet, three stories in height. Three members, all Cherokees by blood, constituted a Board of Education. The Secretary adds, that the Cherokees are proud of their schools and educational institutions, and that no country under the sun is so blessed with educational advantages.

In March, 1896, Bro. Rights was called to mission service in New Fairfield, Canada, the only remaining work of the Moravian Church among the Delawares. He remained in the field until a successor could be appointed, reporting increased interest at Mt. Zion at this season, several Cherokees being brought to a saving knowledge of Christ and uniting with Mt. Zion chapel. Mr. Charles Maxwell, Cherokee teacher, was employed at $25 per month to supply the Mt. Zion school, in addition, he was asked to do missionary work, visiting and holding services according to his ability and standing, at Mt. Zion and Braggs. An appropriation was made by the Society for Propagating the Gospel among the Heathen for school books and desks at Mt. Zion.

A report from Bro. Rights in August, 1896, gives particulars of the gracious awakening at Mt. Zion, already mentioned. Thirty-six persons had been added to the church and now needed careful attention. Bro. Rights was requested by P. E. C. to move from Woodmount to Mt. Zion, temporarily, to assist these people in becoming established in their faith and organized into a Home Mission congregation.

A call to become Superintendent of the Cherokee Mission was tendered the Rev. T. W. Shields*, Aug. 11, 1896, the Board deeming him eminently qualified to test the possibilities of the enterprise. Provincial Elders' Conference felt assured that his experience in evangelistic and mission work, his interest in the development of the Third District of the American Moravian Church, North, to which the Cherokee mission would be assigned and his general fitness for the needs of the situation pointed Bro. Shields out as the right man for the place. He was informed that the work among the Cherokees was in a state of transition from a Foreign to a Home mission of the Church and that the Board depended upon the results of Bro. Shields' good judgment and consecrated labors to determine whether the mission could be carried forward or must be abandoned. Bro. Shields arrived in his new field in September of the year and was warmly welcomed. Bro. Rights left in October, following his call to Canada. The members were urgent in asking Bro. Shields to reside at Braggs, for here and at Mt. Zion, nearby, the work was most promising and needed careful attention. Indians continued coming to Christ under Bro. Shields' ministry and there were frequent accessions to membership. Woodmount and Springplace were served once each month.

The Unity's Mission Board turned over the entire mission in Indian Territory to the northern P. E. C. in November, 1896. Plans were at once made to have the Cherokee mission assume the status of several Home mission congregations of the Northern

---

* Bro. Thomas W. Shields was born Oct. 2, 1850, near Kernersville, N. C. Educated in Drew Seminary, New Jersey. Married to Miss Charlotte Reinke in 1883. Served in Tobago, Barbadoes and St. Thomas, W. I., 10 years. Had been pastor at West Salem, Ill., for nearly three years when called to Indian Territory. Bro. Shields died in November, 1913.

Province with Mt. Zion as the center. S. P. G. agreed financially to sponsor the work for a limited time, the same to be carried on under the direction of the Board of Church Extension. The idea of advancing self support was to be continually held up before the Cherokee congregation and the annual appropriation for the work was to be steadily diminished, thus placing more responsibility for the work upon the members. After they would have assented to and signed the "Brotherly Agreement" of the Moravian Church and contributed to Synodal expenses at the rate of 15 cents per member per annum, the Cherokee congregations would be entitled to representation at District Synods by an elected delegate.

Gradually the work assumed a more encouraging aspect. Six new members were received at Springplace in November. A certain Bro. W. N. Thomas, a local preacher of the M. E. Church who had been active in the Braggs neighborhood, desired admission into the Moravian Church. This was granted by P. E. C. and Bro. Shields was authorized to use Bro. Thomas as an assistant wherever possible, for he was a good man and influential. Brother Shields was much pleased, also, with the work of the Cherokee Bro. Charles Maxwell, employed by the Church as teacher at Mt. Zion and Superintendent of the Sunday School there and of a Union Sunday School at Braggs. He took an active part, also, in the Prayer Meeting. Bro. Thomas was received into the church at Mt. Zion and the Board at Bethlehem agreed to give him a compensation of $100 per year for rendering special services to Bro. Shields as an assistant.

The "Brotherly Agreement" was signed by the Woodmount members on March 7, 1897, and a Committee of three Sisters was elected to have local charge of the work. Bro. Shields wrote that the Woodmount Brethren were not sufficiently interested to hold office! Mt. Zion followed, on March 14, with the signing of the "Brotherly Agreement," and two Brethren and three Sisters were elected a Committee. To these Congregations, as they were now constituted, the Provincial Elders' Conference addressed a cordial letter, welcoming them into the ranks as Home mission churches, assuring them of the earnest desire of the Board to witness their constant growth in grace and usefulness and exhorting all to steadfastness and zeal in the Christian life; the letter closing with a word of special advice and encouragement for the Committees elected. At Springplace, where there were more full-blood Cherokees, the matter of the "Brotherly Agreement" and the suggested effort towards self-support aroused considerable opposition, the Indians claiming that the grant of 160 acres of land according to the Treaty of 1866, when the Springplace mission was resumed after the war, meant that the work was to be carried on as a (Foreign) mission with no intention that the members should contribute anything.

In these trying and unsettled times an official visitation was urgent and Provincial Elders' Conference commissioned one of its members, the Rev. M. W. Leibert, to undertake this journey in the early months of 1898. He arrived at Braggs, I. T., on March 9th and that same evening preached at Mt. Zion to an audience of about 100. After the service an official interview was held with the members in which the following points were brought out :

MT. ZION has been a preaching place for twelve years, but the congregation has been organized only three years, and there are now 53 communicant members. The field is favorable, well-settled and not occupied by any other church. The people are poor, but devoted and earnestly desire the mission to be continued. Bro. Leibert advocated self-support, which plan Bro. Shields has been endeavoring to introduce. It is a new idea and will require some time to gain ground.

As to other points visited :

BRAGGS showed little appreciation of Bro. Rights' and Bro. Shields' labors among them. No one out of this neighborhood but Bro. W. N. Thomas had joined the Moravian Church.

WOODMOUNT, about two miles out from Tahlequah. Large audience present for Bro. Leibert's sermon, but the congregation numbers only 28 communicants. Of these, the majority were really devoted members. This station has but little prospect for growth owing to the proximity of the Presbyterian mission at Parkhill in the country and the various churches in the town of Tahlequah. The mission tract of 160 acres is but partially cultivated, though it contains much good land which might be made productive. Bro. W. N. Thomas is residing in the mission house.

SPRINGPLACE. There are 28 communicant members here and the service at which Bro. Leibert preached was well attended. The people here are better able, financially, to support the work than those living around Woodmount and Mt. Zion, but show less disposition to do anything along this line. Nevertheless, Springplace is a good field and should be more intensively worked.

Bro. Leibert's report showed clearly that the work should be pushed forward. Over 200 souls were in our Church's care, most of whom were loyal and could and would support the work in kind if not in cash. The report, further, suggested the placing of a married missionary at Springplace, with a competent renter on the farm, and the calling of a young Brother, single or recently married, to Woodmount to live with Bro. W. N. Thomas. These Brethren could serve Woodmount, White Oak, Braggs and Mt. Zion.

Provincial Elders' Conference took action on the report by calling Bro. S. C. Albright* to be Pastor and Superintendent of the entire work, Bro. W. N. Thomas continuing as assistant, and P. E. C. contemplated placing additional missionaries in the field as soon as more settled conditions should warrant such action. (Owing to Sr. Shields' poor health, Bro. Shields had requested to be relieved of his work in Indian Territory.) Bro. Albright accepted his call and, after having been ordained and married, arrived at Braggs, Aug. 4, 1898. Encouraging introductory services were held at each station.

The Society for Propagating the Gospel took the following action with regard to the Cherokee mission on Dec. 13, 1898:

"WHEREAS, The Unity's Mission Department seems unable to entertain the idea of temporarily reassuming the work in Indian Territory, and,

"WHEREAS, The S. P. G. recognizes the desirability of continuing the enterprise experimentally, and,

"WHEREAS, It is apprehended by some that technical difficulties exist in the support by the S. P. G. of a charge under control of another body; therefore,

"*Be It Resolved*, That the S. P. G. suggests to the Provincial Elders' Conference the transfer both of the management and maintenance of said field from the latter to the former Board for a period not exceeding

---

* Pastor, Trinity Moravian Church, Utica, N. Y., 1922.

five years, during which time its interests shall be advanced on the lines recently inaugurated by the P. E. C., with a view to securing self-sustenance. Upon expiration of which term, if not before, it shall revert, with such recommendations as the S. P. G. may be in a position to offer, to the P. E. C. either for acceptance among Home Mission congregations or for final abandonment."

From this action of the S. P. G. and the fact that the Provincial Board was in correspondence with the Dawes Commission—explained earlier in this chapter—stating our claims to the farms at New Springplace and Woodmount, it may be gathered that the Moravian Church was resolved to push the Cherokee mission with renewed vigor and wisdom.

Political agitation regarding the Indian and his lands came to a head in the Curtis Act, a comprehensive legislative provision of Congress "for the protection of the People of the Indian Territory." It consisted of 29 sections, chief of which was the ratification of the Treaty between the Five Civilized Tribes and the U. S. Government. It became an Act of Congress, June 28, 1898, and was finally ratified by the Cherokee Nation, Feb. 1, 1899. It provided that all lands belonging to the Five Civilized Tribes be equally allotted, with due regard to value and fertility. The Dawes Commission was charged with the effective execution of this law. The entire control of tribal revenues was taken from the Five Civilized Tribes and vested with a resident supervising inspector, the tribal courts were abolished, allotments were made compulsory, and authority was given to incorporate white men's towns among the Indian tribes. By this Act the Five Civilized Tribes were reduced to the condition of ordinary reservation tribes, under Government Agents, with white communities planted in their midst.

The distribution of all tribal territory by allotment proceeded with the granting of sixty acres of land to each and every individual, resident or otherwise, who could claim blood connection with one or another of the Five Civilized Tribes. The allotment of those selecting town sites was to be on an equal appraisement basis. A reasonable amount of land was to be reserved for all public buildings. Each of the tribal educational institutions received forty acres of land. The M. E. Church, South, was privileged, by special legislation, to pay $10 per acre for sixty acres of land then in the possession of the Willie Haskell College. This same privilege was granted to other higher schools of learning, claiming possession of lands, tribal institutes excepted. Churches were allotted four acres each for church and parsonage.

To make this Government distribution of Indian land constitutional, and to make possible these allotments to the Five Civilized Nations, the Secretary of the Interior was authorized to bring suit, or file claim against these Nations for the possession of all territory claimed by them, on the ground that it never really belonged to them, but to the U. S. Government. It was on the basis of this ruling that the Moravian Church forfeited its right to the 160 acres at Oaks, (Springplace,) and the other 160 acres at Woodmount, the latter purchased directly from the Indians, as has been narrated.

Efforts made by P. E. C., coresponding with the Secretary of the Interior and Congressman Kirkpatrick, to secure from the Government either a larger allotment of land or some rebate for the loss of Moravian Church property, were unavailing. With both 160 acre farms gone—the four acres granted churches in the case of Springplace not even taking in the mission buildings—it was deemed impossible to continue the work without large and long-continued outside support. Bro. Thomas at Springplace tested the Cherokees as to their willingness to buy in the land for the church, which they had the right to do, but they declined to do anything! How the glory had departed from Israel! O! for a Charles Hicks or some of the kindred spirits of the old Springplace, Ga., Moravian mission, at this time of emergency! As it was, it seemed to the P. E. C. that members and others who had been deriving benefits from the Church for years and were not willing to rally to it in the moment of need, were not worthy of its services. It must be remembered, however, as pointed out earlier in this narrative, that up to within three years of the close of the mission, the Moravians had made practically no effort to teach their Cherokee converts the responsibility of giving. True, even now they had not much to give, but a ready spirit to contribute what they were able would have encouraged further sacrifice of men and money by the Church to continue the mission.

Anticipating adverse decision in regard to the Cherokee mission lands, the Provincial Synod of the Moravian Church, convening at Lititz, Pa., Sept., 1898, had authorized a discontinuance of this work if it became plain to the Board that efforts in that field should cease. Accordingly, the missionaries Albright and assistant Thomas were authorized to receive bids looking to disposal of the improvements at Oaks and Woodmount as advantageously as possible. Very small sums were eventually received, hardly enough to pay the traveling expenses of the missionaries to new fields. Bro. Albright accepted a call to serve the Moravian congregation at Oakland, Mo.; Bro. Thomas, while not received into the ranks of the Moravian ministry, received permission to serve the Moravian congregation at Macedonia, Mo. Before leaving Oaks, (New Springplace,) Bro. Thomas had committed to a Mr. Miller the care of the Moravian graveyard, that hallowed spot where reposed side by side the mortal remains of Moravian missionaries and their Cherokee Christian converts awaiting the Resurrection morn; "for the Lord himself shall descend from Heaven with a shout, with the voice of the archangel, and with the trump of God: and the dead in Christ shall rise first." (I Thess. 4:16.)

CONCLUSION

It remains briefly to record a work that has been carried on for the past thirty years among the Cherokees by a man who though himself belonging to another Christian denomination, deserves notice in these pages along with the Moravian missionaries among the southern Indian tribes. The Rev. N. L. Nielsen,* a Danish

* Writes the Rev. N. L. Nielsen of himself: "As a young man of 24 I left Denmark in 1888, for the purpose of finding an Indian tribe somewhere in the United States to be a missionary to them and preach Jesus Christ and Him crucified, if possible to win some of them for the kingdom of God. I went to the Danish Lutheran Theological Seminary, Blair, Nebr., to study for work as a missionary. Just a year before I graduated I came in touch with a Dane who was married to a Cherokee woman, and through them I found an open door in the Indian Territory near Tahlequah, the capital of the Cherokee Nation." The Rev. Nielsen began his labors among the Cherokees in the year 1892, at Moodys, about 10 miles north of Tahlequah. He was, therefore, about 12 miles north of Woodmount, where Bro. T. M. Rights was stationed at that time, and 15 miles south of New Springplace, (Oaks,) where Bro. Herman Reck was stationed. Speaking of these Brethren, Nielsen says, "It seemed like I had found some of my own people and Church."

Lutheran missionary, entered largely into the labors of the Moravian Church in the Cherokee field and his faithful efforts through three decades, continuing up to the present time, have been signally owned and blessed of God.

Stationed at first at Moodys, ten miles north of Tahlequah, Nielsen formed a true brotherly acquaintance with the Moravian Brethren laboring in the field. After the Moravian missionaries left the Territory, he went to Oaks occasionally to collect some money for Bro. Herman Beck due the latter from some of the Indians around that station. Nielsen saw these people as sheep having no shepherd and, at their earnest request, preached for them occasionally. He found them more interested in spiritual concerns than the Cherokees in other localities, hence he made Oaks one of his regular appointments, preaching twice each month.

"I saw it was a good field of labor, really better than the one at Moodys. Here was already a good foundation laid; here were more Cherokees by blood than at Moodys, where the whites were crowding them out. After I had taken up the work in this way, I was surprised one day to hear from the Rev. Paul de Schweinitz,* Bethlehem, Pa., asking me to look after some of the Moravian members and, if possible, be of some spiritual help to them, as the Moravian Church did not expect to work any more amongst the Cherokees. So I took it as from the Lord and suggested to the Lutheran Board that we make our headquarters at Oaks, and it was decided to do so. Thus it came that we moved to Oaks in 1902."

A mission school was begun at once with about 60-70 children and young people, mostly Cherokees. Nielsen organized his congregation in the fall of 1902 with about twenty members from the Moravian Church. In addition, he baptized some adults and some children of Christian parents, ranging from infants to twelve years of age. In some cases, whole families united with the church. The congregation grew from year to year and numbers at present (1922) 200 members and about an equal number have died during the past twenty years. There are still living a few of the old Moravians who are under the care of this Danish Lutheran mission, but who wish to remain Moravians to the end of their days. The old church has been torn down and the other

---

* Secretary of Missions, American Moravian Church.

21

buildings and mission property are in the possession of the Miller family, descendants of Moravians but belonging to the Rev. Nielsen's church. The cemetery at Oaks (Springplace) is kept up in good order.

"We have a nice church here which will hold about 300 persons and a two-story school building with four rooms; capacity 130 pupils. Three teachers are instructing the children and young people and many of them have graduated and are teaching school in the Counties round about. We are building a boarding-school and hope it will prove to be a help in the mission work.

"Our work here has been blessed from above, but we might not have had so good a success had it not been for the good and faithful Moravian missionaries who had been here before us, and God led us into their work. The Moravians have laid a good foundation, and their work has not been in vain: it will shine to the end of days. So we thank God for the Moravian Church today. We wish you had some more men and women you could send out to the Indians in North and South America."

After fifteen years of negotiation, the Cherokee Commission reached an agreement with the Five Civilized Nations by which the government of the Cherokee Nation, with the others, came to an end, March 3, 1906, and the Cherokee Indians, native and adopted, became citizens of the United States.

* * *

The final chapter is nearly written: the story, but for some helpful truths and present-day inspiraton it would give us, is finished.

Some points of weakness in the work have been noticed, others will suggest themselves and there is no doubt but that, managed in just the right way, this mission could have "carried on" successfully through the years. May this phase of the work which is not so bright be passed over in the conviction, which the writer would like to share with the reader, that it would be hard to find, in the glorious history of Christian missions, a work of similar scope in which our Saviour has been more abundantly glorified by the success attending the preaching of His blessed Gospel than in this venerable mission.

May it have been borne in upon the reader that, in His matchless love and grace, God would have all men to be saved and has, in His Son, met the needs of all for Salvation and all things. The mission among the Cherokees was undertaken by those who believed this and obeyed God, "the Lord working with them."

These pages have portrayed a labor of *love* among those whom some might consider to be among "the least of His brethren." The love of Christ has ever constrained the Moravian Church to cultivate for Christ the hard fields of the earth. Such, among many others, was the Cherokee field.

The Cherokee mission of the Moravian Church is a demonstration of *faith*. Here was a band of Brethren who could not make a great beginning and their lone missionaries in the Indian country did not even know the Cherokee language, yet they ventured for God, counting on God, and He used "the things that are not as though they were." Faith was the victory: the Cherokee field ripening in glorious harvest.

Again, the mission was, very particularly, a work of *hope* and *patience*, and these have been characteristics of other missions of the Moravians. Three years of self-sacrificing witness for Christ passed before the first convert from among the slaves on the island of St. Thomas came forward; six years elapsed in Greenland before the gathering of the first-fruits; ten years among the Cherokees before the baptism of Margaret Ann; fifteen years of toil in the almost untillable Himalayan field before two souls responded.

Finally, the Cherokee mission is an example of *thoroughness* in the Lord's work. Perhaps our Church at that time was too indifferent to appearances and numbers; at any rate, our missionaries among the Cherokees were in no hurry to report converts as in our day "accessions" are counted. The missionaries were conscientious as well as thorough and, possessing spiritual insight, they were not afraid to deny admission to such as lacked real conversion. Their endeavor was to bring the convert into a personal relation with Christ rather than to enter his name on the church books.

Consequently, this story records the *smallest possible lapse of converts* into heathenism—and this, too, is a characteristic of Moravian missions. Under persecution, ostracism and blandishments of the world, Moravian converts have stood the test.

So substantial and admirable was the work done among the Indians by the Moravians that one wonders what the result would have been if the first mission among the Cherokees, in Georgia, and missions among other tribes could have grown and developed undisturbed. There is no reasonable doubt but that, in peace and quiet, the Cherokee and other Indian tribes would have been evangelized, highly civilized and made a power for God and righteousness in our country.

That there are precious souls of Cherokee Indians in our Father's House as the result of this mission will be glory for Him and for us and should incite us to heartfelt gratitude and praise and, above all, provide an additional stimulus to press forward in the one really important work for Christ's followers: ''Go ye into all the world and preach the gospel to every creature,''[*] and ''make disciples of all the nations,''[†] until He come!

> "Oh, what praise in highest strain,
> By the ransomed host in heaven
> Will be given
> To him who brought us to God
> By his blood.
> When of every tongue and nation
> There will be with exultation
> But one flock and shepherd known.

> "Amen, Jesus' words are true;
> Surely he his gracious promise
> Will accomplish:
> Ye, his servants, ready stand
> In each land,
> Yea, in the most distant places,
> Till he comes, to sound his praises,
> And make known his saving name."[‡]

---

[*] Mark 16:15.

[†] Matth. 28:19, A. R. V.

[‡] Christian Gregor. Hymn No. 724 in "The Liturgy and Hymns of the American Province of the Unitas Fratrum or The Moravian Church." Bethlehem, Pa., 1876.

THE END

INDEX.